P9-DUK-077

Also available from Routledge

On the History of Economic Thought
British and American Essays
Volume I
A.W. Coats

The Sociology and Professionalization of Economics
British and American Economic Essays
Volume II
A.W. Coats

The History and Philosophy of Social Science
Scott Gordon

New Directions in Economic Methodology
Edited by Roger E. Backhouse

The Meaning of Market Process
Essays in the Development of Modern Austrian Economics
Israel M. Kirzner

The Philosophy of the Austrian School
Raimondo Cubeddu

THE USES AND ABUSES
OF ECONOMICS

BY THE SAME AUTHOR:

THE USES AND ABUSES
OF ECONOMICS

Contentious essays on history and method

Terence Hutchison

London and New York

First published 1994
by Routledge
11 New Fetter Lane, London EC4P 4EE

Simultaneously published in the USA and Canada
by Routledge
29 West 35th Street, New York, NY 10001

Typeset in Baskerville by
Pat and Anne Murphy, Highcliffe-on-Sea, Dorset
Printed and bound in Great Britain by
T.J. Press (Padstow) Ltd, Padstow, Cornwall

British Library Cataloguing in Publication Data
A catalogue record for this book is available from
the British Library.

Library of Congress Cataloging in Publication Data
Hutchison, T. W. (Terence Wilmot)
The uses and abuses of economics: contentious essays on
history and method/Terence Hutchison.
p. cm.
Includes bibliographical references and index.
1. Economics – History. 2. Economics – Methodology.
I. Title.
HB75.H793   1995   330'.09–dc20
94-2482 CIP

ISBN 0–415–09404–6

To my great-grandchildren:
in the hope that the maintenance and
growth of useful economic knowledge
may help to make the twenty-first
century rather less unpleasantly
unstable than, at the moment,
it looks like becoming.

CONTENTS

FOREWORD

I

Of the papers in this volume the earliest published, in very nearly its present form, is No. 2 on Jeremy Bentham as an Economist, which first appeared in 1956. At least one paper, however, incorporates material from earlier essays or reviews, notably No. 3 on James Mill and Ricardo, which draws on writings from 1952 and 1953. Quite a large proportion of the volume, however, has originated since 1991, that is, No. 5 on Ricardian Politics, No. 9 on Subjectivism, No. 12 on Jacob Viner, and No. 13 on The Uses and Abuses of Academic Economics; while much of No. 10 on Hayek and Mises has been written since 1990. Brief 'Addenda (1993)' have been appended to Nos. 1, 2, 3, 6 and 11. No. 9 on Subjectivism has not been published before, nor have most of Nos. 10, 12 and 13. Fuller details of the origins and previous history of all papers are given in the first Note to each item. I would add that though I have sought to eliminate superfluous repetitions, I have not assumed that all readers will read all the papers; so I have occasionally repeated points or quotations from one paper in another paper (or papers) where these may also be highly relevant.

II

Two items in this volume (Nos. 3 and 7) have appeared before, not as articles in journals, or conference papers, but as chapters of books. This may seem rather unusual. The reprinting of journal articles, however, has now become a major industry. Vast compendia of articles on the major economists, or on particular branches or 'schools' of economics, have been produced, which may well be useful to students and researchers. In concentrating so exclusively on journal articles, however, these mammoth collections may be encouraging the neglect of *books*, which still contain, and will continue to contain, an important part of the literature of many, or most subjects.

I must declare an interest at this point, as one who has published several fairly large books, which have been comprised mainly of separable chapters, or articles, some of which had previously been published in journals, and some of which had not; because it seemed to me that the more previously unpublished work a new book contained, the less uninteresting it might, perhaps, be. These chapters which have not appeared in journals will never appear in most of the vast collections of 'articles', though the main respect in which they differ from journal articles may be that they seek to arouse interest in a broader context, or longer historical perspective than isolated studies of individual economists, or more narrowly conceived subject-areas, may usually manage to cover.

Admittedly these two chapters included here have not undergone the scrutiny of a journal editor. Nevertheless, with the systematic reprinting of journal articles now proceeding on the scale it does – not to mention the multiplication of sometimes marginally different new editions of the more successful textbooks – it seems to me that it may be quite justifiable to make available, in some new context, previously published chapters of books, *if*, of course, they make therein a relevant and useful contribution.

III

When I was collecting these pieces together two larger themes, or groups of issues, seemed to emerge, to one or other of which each item contributed something, from one angle or another. The first such theme, covering the eight essays in Part I, was that of progress and regress in the development of political economy and economics, in particular regarding that major transition, turning-point, or even, perhaps, 'revolution', widely recognized as having begun around 1776 or the following decade or so, and associated with Adam Smith's *The Wealth of Nations* and the emergence of English 'Classical' Political Economy. No dogmatic generalizations, however, regarding any kind of overall progress or regress in the subject are offered, which would obviously have to be based on the particular intellectual values, or index numbers, which were brought to bear in assessing 'progress' or 'regress' or on what were regarded as the most important aims of the subject at different junctures.

The rest of Part I is devoted almost entirely to Ricardo and Jevons, the two most brilliant innovators among British economists of the nineteenth century, who both died tragically prematurely, when they might both have developed their ideas in surprising directions, had they been granted more time. One's view of the subsequent history of economics, in the nineteenth century and beyond, depends very largely on one's views and interpretations of Ricardo and Jevons, and on how far one accepts – as I do – the latter's verdict on the former.

Many historians of economic thought would probably hold that benefits, or gains, exceeded costs, or losses in knowledge, more or less emphatically, with regard to all three of the major transitions, turning-points or 'revolutions' of the last quarter of a millenium: that is, the 'Classical', or Smithian turning-point, of around 1776 or 1790; the Neoclassical turning-point around 1870; and the 'Keynesian', or Macroeconomic turning-point of the 1930s. I would, however, guess that both the Neoclassical and the Keynesian turning-points might, by a certain non-negligible minority, be regarded as showing at least heavy losses or costs, which by some might even be held to exceed the gains or benefits. I would guess, furthermore, that the English Classical–Smithian turning-point, or new 'paradigm' – to use a now old-fashioned term – would be regarded, most widely, and unquestionably, as resulting in the most certain and unqualified gains and benefits, or cost–benefit ratio. While not prepared to argue for a dogmatic denial of this pre-eminently favourable cost–benefit ratio for the Classical–Smithian 'revolution', I do, in the essays of Part I, try to insist on some serious questioning of this English Classical pre-eminence and, in particular, of the Ricardian contribution to that pre-eminence.

IV

The second group of themes which are discussed in the five papers in Part II, those of 'Subjectivism, Methods and Aims', are examined with an emphasis on the links between these concepts. First, there are links with, or implications for method of a 'subjectivist' approach to economic theorizing. The axiomatic, a priorist, or preponderantly deductivist method, from Senior to Mises and on to the mathematical refinement of general equilibrium analysis, is well suited to analysing the simplified case, so ubiquitously examined from Ricardo onwards, of what Carl Menger called '*Allwissenheit*', or full knowledge and freedom from uncertainty. The axiomatic and deductive method, however, as has long been apparent, is much less serviceable for dealing with problems where real-world ignorance and uncertainty – and, therefore, subjectivity in decision-making – are more inevitably and consequentially involved, such as fluctuations and cycles, investment and money. Such problems must require, preponderantly, a more empirical, inductivist and institutionalist method, if much is to emerge which transcends the trivial, the vacuous and the tauto-logical, and is productive of significant contributions to predictive capacity.

Second, in Part II, the obvious link between methods and aims is empha-sized. The overriding aim of nearly all economists, of nearly all schools, has, for centuries, until comparatively very recently, been that of contributing towards less unsuccessful, real-world policy-making, by governments and private enterprise. This overriding aim suggested, or imposed, certain long-standing methodological guidelines and distinctions, such as the normative-positive distinction, and the desirability of the empirical testing of theories on which policy measures might be based. With the formation, since about the middle of this century, in most leading countries, of a vastly larger-scale academic profession, concerns and links with real-world policy problems have, at important points, been weakened, and the position of real-world policy-relevance has lost something of its dominance as an overriding aim of the subject. At the same time, traditional disciplines and distinctions – not illogically by those accepting or supporting the shift in the aims of the subject – have been widely rejected as outmoded and irrelevant 'positivist' restrictions. Naturally enough, if pure mathematical 'rigour' and aesthetics have acquired the highest prestige, or if much of economic theorizing has come to be regarded as 'a good game', or as part of an intriguing, academic, ongoing 'discourse' or 'new conversation', then the longstanding aim of policy-relevance and its accompanying methodological disciplines and distinctions can be – and should be – dispensed with.

In the sub-title, I have described these essays, or some of them, as 'contentious'. It might be asked whether the history and method of economics raise issues or questions which it is appropriate or justifiable to treat contentiously or combatively. Certainly, if the main objective of economics is the pursuit of pure, mathematical elegance, or abstract 'rigor'; or if the kind of economic theorizing to be aimed at should consist of empirically vacuous taxonomy or non-predictive, but otherwise unspecified 'understanding', then, certainly, contentiousness or combativeness, in discussing the issues of the history and method of economics, should indeed be regarded as overheated and inappropriate. The long and widely-held view, however, for centuries taken implicitly for granted by nearly all economists, was that the aim – and the quite practicable aim – of the subject was to help to promote less unsuccessful policy-making, private and public; and that the success or failure of policies may, in turn, be seriously promoted or jeopardized by the state of economic knowledge or ignorance. For those who still hold to this traditional view, economics is to be regarded as a profoundly and practically serious subject, so that vital issues whether of policy or theory, or of history or method, may well arise in the discussion of which contentiousness and combativeness may be thoroughly appropriate.

For the history and method of the subject cannot be regarded as separate, irrelevant, 'outside' intellectual areas or interests, detached from the main battlegrounds. The opposing schools, tendencies, parties, sects and groups, into which economists throughout the modern history of the subject have divided themselves, have been engaged in constructing their versions of the history of the subject so as to point to an impressive intellectual pedigree for their characteristic doctrines and ideas, as an important weapon of persuasion. The English Classicals, the Marxists, the Historical School, the Keynesians, the Austrians, the Marxo-Sraffians, now the pure Mathematical Formalists, or Abstractionists, have all attempted, or are attempting, to build up the prestige and influence of their ideas by putting forward their own mainly self-serving accounts or versions of the history of the subject, or of the relevant sections thereof.

Similarly, though to a lesser extent, particular methodological doctrines have been used to promote the ideas and doctrines of the various leading theoretical schools; or of the historical school, the mathematical school, or the praxeological school. From the physiocrats to the Chicago school and to the Austrian followers of Mises, particular methodological doctrines have been used in attempts to validate the particular theoretical and policy conclusions of the school.

So those specially concerned with the history and method of the subject have often been, and should have been, as involved in the practical seriousness of the subject as profoundly as those concerned with theory and policy; and this kind of practical seriousness may not merely justify, but call for, 'contentious' argument.

It has been said of George Orwell that:

> he believed that human kind benefited from the unrestrained use of strong and vivid language, and he would have regarded the lexical pussyfooting of much American academic discourse as political cowardice.
>
> (Samuel Hynes, *New York Times*, Book Review Section,
> 3 November 1991, p. 3)

It is, of course, by no means only American academic 'discourse' against some of which such a charge can be made. Anyhow, as the Princeton professor added:

> Orwell knew that he would offend people; he also knew that offensiveness is a necessary consequence of opinions strongly held and openly expressed. . . . An idea that offends no one is not worth entertaining.

So if one still holds to the long-assumed view that economic discourse, whether concerned with 'theory' or policy, or with the method and history of the subject, is significantly involved with profoundly serious real-world problems, no apologies may be necessary for attempting to follow, where appropriate – and undoubtedly here very feebly, clumsily and at an incomparably remote distance – the views of George Orwell regarding 'contentiousness'.

Part I

PROGRESS AND REGRESS IN POLITICAL ECONOMY: SMITH–RICARDO–JEVONS

1

FROM WILLIAM PETTY TO ADAM SMITH AND THE ENGLISH CLASSICALS[1]

I

Adam Smith's *The Wealth of Nations* (1776) provided the main foundations for the doctrines of the English Classical school, which constituted the dominant orthodoxy in England for about a century down to 1871, the first powerful and lasting theoretical orthodoxy in the history of political economy. In its own day and on its home ground English classical political economy achieved a kind of influence and prestige unsurpassed in the subject before or since. The English classical economists – or some of them – put forward their own version of the history of the subject, which has long remained powerfully influential. This classical version of the history of political economy to a large extent eliminated the predecessors of the English classicals from serious consideration, proclaiming that before *The Wealth of Nations*, or before the appearance of the classicals' own works, all, or almost all, had been darkness and error. Smith himself had provided the seeds of this revolutionary classical version in his somewhat ungenerous treatment of his predecessors, and by rather indiscriminately attributing to them, or to many of them, the errors of what he called 'the mercantile system'.[2]

This classical version of the history of the subject was built up most notably by the two Mills and McCulloch. J. B. Say even went so far as to proclaim that before Smith 'there was no political economy' (1841, 29), a view which long remained influential and which is still heard today, as when it was recently stated in Oxford that 'economics in the modern sense was as good as invented in one country (Scotland) only 200 years ago' (Bliss, 1986, 368).

I reject this classical version of the history of the subject as I reject the subsequent self-glorifying aspects of the Marxian and Keynesian versions. There was, however, one particular *aperçu* regarding the history of political economy which seems of fundamental importance and which provides a vital corrective of the English classical version: Karl Marx, undeniably a great pioneer scholar of the history of economic thought, stated that it was not Adam Smith but William Petty who was the 'founder of political economy' (1951, 15).

Today, however, it may not seem very helpful or accurate to nominate any one individual – Aristotle, Petty, or Smith – as *the* founder of the subject of political economy or economics. Nor need one find acceptable Marx's definition of 'classical' political economy as running right through from Petty, in the second half of the seventeenth century, until about 1830, the date which Marx regarded as signifying the close of one period and the opening of a new period (marked, of course, by Marx's own first publications very shortly after). It seems, on the other hand, that the division and dating of periods, widely followed today, is more convenient according to which the appearance of Smith's *The Wealth of Nations* in 1776 marked the opening of the English classical era, and was followed, after 1871, by the neoclassical period. We would suggest that the English classical phase may be regarded as having been preceded, from 1662 to 1776, by the Pre-Classical Period, opened by the work of Sir William Petty.[3] For, as Marx observed, Petty's writings marked a significant turning-point, or starting-point, in the emergence of modern political economy as a serious, more-or-less disciplined, independent subject, and introduced a profoundly creative period in its development, a period which may be said to have begun with Petty's first and most important work on political economy, his *Treatise of Taxes and Contributions*, of 1662. Moreover, Petty's work inspired a great boom or blossoming of the subject in England in the closing decade of the seventeenth century.

II

Like his 'mercantilist' predecessors, Petty was primarily concerned with putting forward and advocating practical policies. In his *Treatise of Taxes and Contributions* (1662) he reviewed the principles of public finance for the new regime of the recently restored monarchy of Charles II, examining the main heads of public expenditure and the kinds of taxes with which the expenditures should be financed. What is significantly new and important in Petty's work was the extent to which he sought to base his policy arguments on more explicit theories, and on the application of quantitative methods, which in turn were supported by what he claimed were the principles of scientific method. Thus, though primarily concerned with policy, Petty's work stimulated a new and profound concern with theory and method, in order to provide a more reliable basis for policy.

Petty's policies were 'mercantilist' in that they required governments to take responsibility internally for maintaining a high level of employment by fiscal, monetary and public works policies, so as to help relieve poverty. This concern with poverty and unemployment constituted by far the greatest single difference between Petty's treatment, in his *Treatise*, and that of Adam Smith in *The Wealth of Nations*, 114 years later, of the internal economic policies of governments. Externally, Petty held that government must be responsible for maintaining the balance of trade, as far as was necessary, by encouraging exports and restraining imports – though he held that the exclusion of imports

4

was unnecessary and undesirable 'until they much exceeded our exportations' (1662, 60). Certainly Petty entertained no notion of any self-adjusting mechanisms working sufficiently effectively, painlessly and expeditiously, with regard to the level of employment or the balance of trade. He showed himself, however, to be well aware of the 'naturally' beneficent possibilities of economic freedom, maintaining that it was better

> . . . to take away burdensome, frivolous and antiquated impositions and offices. I conceive even this were better than to persuade water to rise of itself above its natural spring. We must consider in general, that as wiser physicians tamper not excessively with their patients, rather observing and complying with the motions of nature, than contradicting it with vehement administrations of their own, so in politics and economics the same must be used.
>
> (p. 60)

Petty's theoretical ideas were expounded very much *ad hoc*. His ideas about value, and about rent as a surplus, were put forward as methods for the assessment of properties for tax purposes. On value, he departed fundamentally from the traditional ideas of the natural law analysis (which were never as influential in England as they were elsewhere, and were to be, briefly, in Scotland). Petty's approach to the question of value, in terms of the quantity of labour and land, that is, from the cost side rather than from that of utility, demand and scarcity, was, during the classical period in England, to achieve much importance, though Petty's treatment amounts to little more than *obiter dicta*.

Both Petty's policy arguments and his theoretical ideas were based on an explicit methodological programme. As a founder member of the Royal Society, Petty held that the methods being applied so successfully by his colleagues to the natural world, could and should be applied with similar success to the political and social world. In particular, Petty stressed parallells between medical and politico-economic studies, or

> . . . between the Body Natural, and Body Politic, and between the arts of preserving both in health and strength; and it is as reasonable, that as anatomy is the best foundation of one, so also of the other; and that to practice upon the politic without knowing the symmetry, fabric and proportion of it, is as casual as the practice of old women and empirics.
>
> (p. 129)

It was above all useful knowledge which, following Francis Bacon, Petty and his friends in the Royal Society sought after, and politico-economic knowledge could hardly be of much use for policy guidance without quantitative estimates. As Petty stated his methodological creed:

The method I take to be this, is not very usual; for instead of using only comparative and superlative words, and intellectual arguments, I have taken the course (as a specimen of the political arithmetic I have long aimed at) to express myself in terms of number, weight, or measure; to use only arguments of sense, and to consider only such causes, as have visible foundations in nature; leaving those that depend upon the mutable minds, opinions, appetites and passions of particular men, to the consideration of others.

(p. 244)

Petty may well have been overconfident regarding the possibilities of useful quantitative economics, or of what he called 'political arithmetic' (of which Adam Smith was to proclaim: 'I have no great faith'). What, however, was vitally new and important about Petty's methodological contribution was not simply his attempt to introduce quantification, but the fundamental challenge he laid down – which was answered in deeply conflicting ways in the course of the pre-classical period, and subsequently.

It is this pioneering attempt at methodological standards which marks off Petty's work as moving onto a higher intellectual level than had been attained by the brilliant pamphlets, written some four decades earlier, by the leading English mercantilist, Thomas Mun. Moreover, Petty's work so wide-ranging and richly packed with new ideas, gave a powerful stimulus and impetus to the great advance in the subject in England which reached its climax in the closing decade of the seventeenth century. Locke, Barbon, North, Martyn and others contributed to this advance, together with Graunt, Halley, Gregory King and Davenant in Petty's own field of 'Political Arithmetic'. This was a phase in the history of political economy in which, perhaps more than in any other, English writers were leading the world. But from the beginning of the eighteenth century English pre-eminence in the emerging subject of 'trade' (or political economy) declined much more rapidly even than it had been achieved. Throughout the eighteenth century, until the first works of Malthus appeared right at its end, the strictly English contribution was very modest indeed compared with the works of Italian, French and Scottish writers. Nevertheless, most of the great pre-classical writers of the eighteenth century, such as notably, Cantillon, Galiani and Quesnay, were indebted to the pioneering English works of the previous century, which provided an essential platform for the great international advance in the subject which began in the late 1740s.

III

Adam Smith's *The Wealth of Nations* was, regarding two or three very fundamental theoretical questions, 'revolutionary' in that it broke sharply and profoundly with the ideas of a considerable majority, or even, at some important

6

points, with almost all, of his predecessors. On the other hand, with regard to one or two fundamental ideas, Smith's work may be viewed as the culminating expression of a long evolutionary development which had been in progress through the century or more of the pre-classical period, and which may be traceable even before that period opened. We have just noticed an early suggestion of such an idea in Petty's treatment of the role of government in economic policy, when he referred to 'naturally' beneficent economic forces, which should not, and often practically could not, be overridden by government. As the seventeenth century proceeded, the grand idea was gradually emerging of a free market economy based on the three principles of, first, a far-reaching harmony, or potential harmony, between individual self-interest and the public interest; of, second, the equilibrating tendencies of the forces of supply and demand in free markets; and of, third, the higher productivity yielded by specialization and the division of labour, as far as free markets provided the scope for this division to extend itself.

Following Petty, a number of writers towards the end of the seventeenth century proclaimed the benefits of economic freedom, though in an *ad hoc*, selective manner, regarding particular cases or markets, rather than as a systematic doctrine based on an analysis of human nature. In England, Barbon, North, Davenant and Martyn all argued for economic freedom in this or that direction. The foundations, however, of a more systematic *laissez-faire* philosophy had already been laid by French moralists, and especially by Pierre Nicole (1625–95) in his *Moral Essays*, first published in 1671. Nicole's contribution, though noted by the omniscient Jacob Viner, has not been as widely recognized by English writers as it deserves to be. Nicole was an austere Jansenist, who strongly emphasized the Fall of Man and the sinfulness of human nature. He saw the human situation as one where people were greedy and rapacious for material wealth, while Providence had ordained that isolated individuals were unable adequately to satisfy their needs and wants, and so had to come together and cooperate in societies, or economies, to survive. Nicole regarded human beings very much as had Thomas Hobbes, who held that only an all-powerful, autocratic government would be able to restrain individual aggressiveness and preserve some kind of order. Nicole, however, though politically a conservative authoritarian, perceived how, in the economic life around him, the pursuit of self-interest, which, if completely unrestrained, would shrink from no kind of ruthlessness or rapaciousness, could be, and in fact, was being, tamed and canalized, in free markets, into more or less beneficent, or at least comparatively harmless, channels. There are passages in Nicole's *Essays* which precisely anticipate Adam Smith, a century later: in particular Smith's celebrated remark, early in *The Wealth of Nations*, that 'it is not from the benevolence of the butcher, the brewer, or the baker, that we expect our dinner, but from their regard to their own interest' (1776, 27). Nicole described how a traveller, seeking accommodation for the night, could find an inn, where he would be welcomed and accommodated, not because of the Christian charity of the inn-keeper, on which it would be impossible to rely, but on his host's being motivated by the powerful incentive of self-interest. It was the capacity of markets for guiding the ferocious forces of individual greed and self-interest into beneficent, or non-maleficent, channels that had raised mankind from the depths of anarchy and savagery.

It was the great contribution of Bernard de Mandeville, the Dutch doctor who settled in London, to combine the ideas of Nicole, and other French moralists, with those of English writers on 'trade', and to have passed on to Adam Smith this fundamental idea of the harmony (or harmonizability) of private and public interests, in his *Fable of the Bees* (1714) with its motto, 'Private Vices, Public Benefits'.

The idea of the harmony of interests was combined with that of the beneficent equilibrating tendencies of supply and demand, put forward most powerfully at this time by Pierre de Boisguilbert (1646–1714), the Rouen magistrate and fierce critic of the nationalistic economic *dirigisme* of Colbert and his master, Louis XIV. According to Boisguilbert (to whom Marx assigned a pioneering role in French political economy, similar to that of Petty in England) a competitive balance should be sought between the two sides of the market. To bring about this 'equilibrium, the unique conserver of general opulence', it is necessary 'always to maintain an equal balance between sales and purchases. . . . It is with the aid of this equilibrium, or balance, that the seller and buyer alike are equally forced to listen to reason and to submit to it' (1707, 992–3).[4]

The third interlocking idea, that of the heightened productivity brought about by specialization and the division of labour, received increasing attention in the pre-classical period, notably from Petty, Martyn, Mandeville, and especially and very fully from the much-neglected German Cameralist, Ernst Ludwig Carl (1682–1743). Apart from using the example of pinmaking, Carl emphasized the different endowments and talents of individuals and countries as grounds for the division of labour (or 'separation of functions') a point neglected by Adam Smith. (See Carl, 1722–3, II, 132–3.) What was remarkable about Carl's work was that though he was the outstanding early expositor of the advantages of the division of labour, and although he based on this great idea an opposition to export restrictions, he nevertheless held fast to the cameralist doctrines in favour of extensive governmental regulation and supervision of the economy.

The perception of the harmony of interests, and of more-or-less beneficent self-equilibrating tendencies in free markets, together with the recognition of the greatly increased productivity forthcoming from more intensive specialization and the division of labour facilitated by more extensive markets, were, of course, often accompanied by policy recommendations in favour of freedom from government intervention in the economy. But not always, or to an extreme extent. These free market forces and tendencies, though recognized as operating to an important degree, were often regarded as not working out sufficiently effectively, rapidly and reliably, to preclude the need for government intervention. Nevertheless, gradually, in one sector after another, state regulations and restrictions came to be increasingly rejected. One of the earliest cases was that of interest rates, attempts to regulate which were opposed by Locke and other writers in the 1690s (though some usury laws were still supported in *The Wealth of Nations*). Then free labour markets were recommended by Mandeville, while soon after came the very important case for freedom of international trade, supported by the discernment of self-adjusting forces at work in balancing exports and imports. The credit for having first advanced the case for freedom of trade, based on the self-adjusting flows of the precious metals, is usually ascribed to David Hume (who was followed by Adam Smith in his *Lectures*, but not in *The Wealth of Nations*). There were, however, one or two predecessors of Hume, notably Isaac Gervaise (1720), Jacob Vanderlint (1734) and Richard Cantillon (17??). Cantillon described the workings of a self-equilibrating mechanism in international trade, but did not draw free-trade policy conclusions.

A number of major writers in the pre-classical period who were comparatively early in discerning certain self-adjusting tendencies in free markets (e.g. Mandeville, Cantillon, Tucker) were not prepared, as were subsequently their classical successors, to rely in such almost unqualified terms on free-market mechanisms, without some considerable measures of government intervention. Some of these important writers have even been described (or denounced) as 'mercantilists', as Mandeville and Tucker were by Jacob Viner. This denunciation may seem to approach a *reductio ad absurdum* in the use of that unsatisfactory term of abuse. (Presumably the complete *reductio ad absurdum* would be to call Adam Smith a 'mercantilist' because of his support for retaliatory import duties, and for other major governmental regulation with regard to shipping and interest rates.)

IV

So much for the main evolutionary component of *The Wealth of Nations*, in so far as a central theme of his work represented a culminating re-statement of an idea, or a line of thought, which had been gradually developing in the preceding, pre-classical period. The revolutionary component of *The Wealth of Nations*, and subsequently of the orthodox classical body of doctrines, was more profoundly theoretical, and eventually methodological. It was, of course, the classicals themselves who insisted both on how comprehensively their own doctrines broke with the errors of their predecessors, and on the firmly established orthodoxy of their new doctrines.[5] In fact, most of the main classical theories had only few, or brief anticipations in the pre-classical phase. As regards the classical population theory, there were one or two important anticipators such as Botero, Cantillon and Wallace. Other classical theories, such as that of the accumulation of capital, had only a brief, but

9

important, prehistory, confined mainly to the writings of Quesnay and Turgot.

It could probably be shown that, of the theories and lines of thought which are alive and receiving wide support today, the number that were developed coherently before 1776 is considerably larger than the number which first emerged in England between 1776 and 1870. The pre-classical theories, however, were mostly excluded, rejected, neglected or diminished by the main representatives of classical orthodoxy, who made it perfectly clear that they had very little use for the ideas of their predecessors. Several of the leading pre-classical ideas and theories have, in the century or more since the demise of English classical orthodoxy around 1870, fought their way back to widespread acceptance, and, in some cases, have probably won majority support, as a result of the various protests, rebellions or revolutions against classical orthodoxy which have occupied so much of the last hundred years of the history of economic thought. The seventeenth- and eighteenth-century writers did not, of course, employ the same terminological or mathematical precision by which twentieth-century academics have set such great store, but the pre-classical writers did clearly formulate these main ideas, theoretical and methodological. Let us now focus on four of these fundamental theories or lines of thought.

(1) First, there were the theories of money, employment and what is today called 'macroeconomics' developed in various directions by, among others, Petty, Boisguilbert, Hume and Quesnay, and especially fully by Sir James Steuart. These writers, like most other writers of this pre-classical period, treated involuntary unemployment, hoarding, deflation and the money supply as presenting serious problems or dangers. The pre-classical ideas and lines of thought in this field, were, however, swept away and driven into the 'underground', as Keynes put it, by classical orthodoxy. (Sir James Steuart's massive treatment of these subjects (1767) was, of course, not even mentioned in *The Wealth of Nations*.)

(2) Second, alongside the Smithian–classical 'macroeconomic' revolution, there was a profoundly important 'microeconomic' shift of emphasis with regard to the fundamental concepts of value and utility. The treatment of value and utility was not so sweepingly exclusivist, nor did it possess the same direct policy impact, as the Smithian macroeconomic doctrines, but was of far-reaching theoretical and doctrinal significance. The approach to the central, fundamental questions of utility, value and price, developed by the writers of the natural-law tradition, such as Pufendorf, Burlamaqui and Hutcheson, and, in Italy and France by Galiani and Turgot, was neglected, diminished or excluded, for about a century in England, by the exponents of Smithian–classical orthodoxy on the subject of value.

(3) The fundamental recognition of, and emphasis on, the role of ignorance, uncertainty and erroneous expectations, which played such a central and vital part in the work of Boisguilbert, Cantillon and, especially, Condillac, was, to

a dangerous and highly misleading extent diminished or excluded from the main orthodox, English classical theories or models.

(4) The historical–institutional method, developed by the Scottish historical school, was first significantly, if briefly, applied to political economy by David Hume, and then more extensively by Sir James Steuart. In *The Wealth of Nations*, of course, the historical method played a massive role, so that Adam Smith was obviously in no way responsible for the subsequent exclusion and neglect of history by English classical orthodoxy, which provoked the protests of the German historical school and of subsequent historical and institutional critics. In fact, of these four fundamentally important rejections, or exclusions, of English classical orthodoxy Adam Smith must be assigned almost total responsibility for the first; an important initial (though far from total) responsibility for the second; a minor degree of responsibility for the third; and no responsibility at all for the fourth.

V

(1) The Smithian–classical doctrines of money, saving, investment and employment could be regarded as simply a major extension of the idea, or model of beneficent self-adjustment which had been developing gradually in the pre-classical period. Smithian macroeconomics, however, went so decisively further in its theoretical and policy implications than had previous expositions of self-adjusting mechanisms, and represented and proclaimed itself as such a profound and comprehensive break with preceding (so-called 'mercantilist') doctrines, that *The Wealth of Nations* may validly be regarded as introducing a revolution in theory and policy in this major branch of the subject. Moreover, classical macroeconomic orthodoxy succeeded in maintaining, in Britain, a dominant position, as regards theory and policy, for something like a century and a half.

Before *The Wealth of Nations* there had been little more than incidental hints of the classical macroeconomic doctrines, in the writings of Josiah Tucker, Hutcheson and one or two others, with the most important such anticipation consisting of a paragraph in Turgot's *Réflexions* (1769) on saving and investment. Most of the writers of the pre-classical period had been persistently and profoundly concerned with the adequacy or stability of the money supply; with the possible damage from hoarding, or excessive frugality; and with the serious dangers of involuntary unemployment. Following *The Wealth of Nations* these problems eventually ceased to be regarded as serious by representatives of classical orthodoxy. It should be noted also that classical orthodoxy broke not only with the so-called 'mercantilists', but with Hume and Quesnay with regard to money, saving, luxury and public spending. Smith's followers added very little that was fundamental to the doctrines he proclaimed in *The Wealth of Nations*, which went on to achieve such an exclusive domination and prestige, especially in Britain, as both Keynes and Schumpeter emphatically and justifiably complained. Sir John Hicks has explained the revolutionary success and long domination of classical macroeconomics in terms of the intellectual fascination of the simple, self-adjusting model (or 'system'):

> How is it to be explained? It is not simply the reaction against Mercantilism. . . . I believe that it is to be explained – that the whole change is to be explained – if we attribute it to the power of a model. . . . It was because the model paid no attention to plans and expectations that it neglected uncertainty and liquidity; so that the bridge between real theory and monetary theory, of the possibility of which Hume had some inkling, remained unbuilt. The only monetary theory which could match the static real theory was one which concentrated upon the more mechanical aspects of the monetary system; this is just what the 'classical' Quantity Theory was. The responsibility for all this goes back to Adam Smith; it is the reverse side of his great achievement.
>
> (1965, 41)

Indeed – as Sir John insists – Adam Smith was almost entirely responsible for the rise to dogmatic orthodoxy of the classical, macroeconomic model. Certainly it may be agreed that it was well worth setting out the kind of self-adjusting model of saving and investment, which Smith and Turgot elaborated, and from which Smith proceeded to draw such vitally important consequences for government policy. But before such important conclusions for policy were drawn, it would surely have been desirable that the necessary assumptions, the real-world conditions regarding knowledge, on the one hand, and money and banking institutions, on the other, had been more clearly envisaged and stated. It is one thing to assert that government intervention is, in practice, unlikely to reduce economic instability and unemployment; and it is quite another thing to belittle or deny the practical possibility of serious economic instabilities in real-world market economies.

Recently, however, during and since the occurrence of the Keynesian revolution, in the 1930s and 1940s, stark conflicts of view have been evident, the main outlines of which were fairly clearly prefigured in the contrasts between the two great Inquiries by Steuart and Smith, in the closing decade of our period. The Smithian–classical doctrines, however, not only proceeded to deny the seriousness of involuntary unemployment, which had so profoundly concerned many of the leading writers of the seventeenth and eighteenth centuries, but also dismissed the dangers of hoarding, or of interruptions in the circulation of payments, which had been regarded so seriously by Boisguilbert, Quesnay and others. Indeed the suggestion seemed to be conveyed, at some points, that 'money didn't matter'. According to Smithian–classical orthodoxy, the business cycles of the nineteenth century – like the unemployment and depression which caused Petty and Boisguilbert so much concern – were to be regarded as frictions. J. S. Mill tended to dismiss the problem of cyclical unemployment as 'unimportant', maintaining that 'the normal state

12

of affairs was a state of full employment' (Link, 1959, 168, 177–9; and Hutchison, 1978, 154n).

The study of business cycles, therefore, one of the main sources out of which twentieth-century macroeconomics developed, was, with one or two exceptions, initiated and advanced, until well into the twentieth century, mainly by economists outside the dominant English classical orthodoxy, and also outside the main neoclassical schools of thought. As Wesley Mitchell put it:

> It was not the orthodox economists . . . who gave the problem of crises and depressions its place in economics, but sceptics who had profited by and then reacted against their teachings. From Adam Smith to Mill, and even to Alfred Marshall, the classical masters have paid but incidental attention to the rhythmic oscillations of trade in their systematic treatises.
>
> (1927, 3; quoted in Hutchison, 1953, 374)

If, on the other hand, the ideas of Petty, Boisguilbert, Steuart and others had not been so summarily and comprehensively swept aside, the problems of instability and unemployment might have received more attention, and the eventual Keynesian protest would have been, in large measure, unnecessary. We would emphasize here that we do not wish to take sides, at this point, for or against classical, or mercantilist–Keynesian, macroeconomic theories and models, but simply to register a protest against a premature, dogmatic exclusivism.

VI

(2) Not only regarding the fundamentals of 'macroeconomics', but also as regards the basic approach to the theory of value, and 'microeconomics', Adam Smith in *The Wealth of Nations*, and still more Smith's leading classical followers, rejected or neglected one of the most important lines of thought developed in the pre-classical period: that concerning the analysis of utility and value.

The vital turning-point came at the end of chapter 4, Book I, of *The Wealth of Nations*, at the very outset of Smith's treatment of the central problems of value and price, when he proceeded to sever the connection between 'value-in-use' (or utility) and 'value-in-exchange', by denying that a good must possess utility if it is to possess value-in-exchange. Here Smith made a fundamental break with the subjective concept of utility, developed by a long series of predecessors, which had included many of the scholastics, especially the important Salamancan School, as well as the natural-law philosophers, Pufendorf, Hutcheson and Burlamaqui, who emphasized that a good possessed utility if someone believed that it did, even if this belief turned out to be foolish or erroneous. This subjective concept of utility was inherited by Adam Smith from Hutcheson. Smith proceeded, however, to change to a realist, objective concept of 'value-in-use', rarely to be found in economic literature before or since. As Alfred Marshall put it regarding Smith's concept of value-in-use:

> Adam Smith makes himself the judge of what is useful to other people and introduces unnecessary confusion.

> (1975, 125)[6]

Moreover, Smith's objective concept of utility possessed obvious authoritarian implications diametrically contrary to his great libertarian message.[7]

The subjective utility approach to the problems of value and price was advanced very significantly in the pre-classical period in Italy and France, and especially by Galiani (in his *Della Moneta*, 1750), and by Turgot (in his paper 'Value and Money' of 1769, where he acknowledged the influence of Galiani). In these works are to be found the basic concepts and ideas of the neoclassical theory of utility, value and exchange, as developed by Carl Menger and Léon Walras. As the Russian pioneer of mathematical economics, V. K. Dmitriev, observed:

> We find all the information needed for the construction of a finished theory of marginal utility in the work of such an 'old' economist as Galiani.

> (1902, [1974], 182)

Adam Smith, on the other hand, in *The Wealth of Nations* (not in his earlier *Lectures*) led the treatment of the theory of value in the direction of labour and cost-of-production. He did not himself put forward a labour theory of value except for the extreme case of a primitive hunting economy, but his leading classical successor, Ricardo, went decisively further in developing a labour theory.[8]

In the 1870s, in fact, came the most important, and, in the long run, the most widely accepted of the various protests, 'rebellions' or 'revolutions', against English classical doctrines: that concerned with the fundamentals of utility, value and price. Whether or not the neoclassical protesters against English classical value theory were fully aware of their pre-classical fore-runners, they were, in fact, calling for a return to the kind of analysis of utility, scarcity and value developed by the natural-law writers, and, especially, as regards the emphasis on utility by Galiani and Turgot – not to mention Daniel Bernoulli.

Considerable, though not total, responsibility for the switch of emphasis towards a labour and cost-of-production analysis of value and price, as well as for the comparatively minor role assigned to value-in-use, or utility, must rest with *The Wealth of Nations* and its author, and with the 'tiresome', 'awkward' and 'unhappy' alteration which he introduced regarding the concept of value-in-use.[9]

A historian of value theory before Adam Smith, writing when the neo-classical theories of Jevons and Marshall, Menger and Walras, were at the

14

peak of their influence, justifiably claimed of the writers on value of the seventeenth and eighteenth centuries: 'So much was done that there is scarcely any proposition of importance in the modern discussion of value [i.e. *c.* 1900] which was not either stated or suggested by the writers of this first period of economic science, and which had not been discussed before Adam Smith' (Sewall, 1901, 124).[10]

There would have been little or no need or scope for any 'Jevonian revolution' – as Maurice Dobb once called it – or even for the measure of evolutionary reform undertaken by Marshall, if the ideas on value and price of Galiani and Turgot, and of the natural-law philosophers, had been given their due weight in the dominant English classical orthodoxy of 1776–1871; or even if such contemporary English utility theorists as W. F. Lloyd had received some recognition from the authoritative classical spokesmen who were instead proclaiming that they had brought the theory of value to a state of complete perfection.

Auguste Walras (1831) had complained that the admirably balanced value analysis of Pufendorf, Hutcheson and Burlamaqui, had remained 'buried in a treatise of natural law'; and had pointedly enquired regarding the natural-law theory: 'Why has it not already passed into the writings of economists?' The English classicals must surely bear most of the responsibility for this burial, while the role of first – though not sole – gravedigger must surely be assigned to the author of *The Wealth of Nations*. Adam Smith and Léon Walras received an almost identical inheritance regarding value theory, the natural-law analysis descending to Smith through Pufendorf, Carmichael and Hutcheson; and to Léon Walras, through Pufendorf, Burlamaqui and Auguste Walras. It is of interest to contrast what Adam Smith, and subsequently Léon Walras, made of the same natural-law inheritance.

It may be added, in conclusion, that it is not necessary here to take sides, very dogmatically, for or against a labour and cost-of-production explanation of value and price, as against theories based on utility and scarcity. What is to be criticized is the dogmatic, overconfident rejection or exclusion of a vital and valuable line of thought, which has, in fact, subsequently become an essential component of the modern theory of value.

VII

(3) Next, in the 1930s, at about the time the Keynesian 'revolution' was getting under way against Smithian–classical macroeconomics, another parallel, but perhaps even more fundamental protest was being heard from several writers, including Hayek and some members of the Swedish school, and, most forthrightly, from Keynes himself. This fundamental criticism had been launched by a number of isolated protestors from the 1870s onwards, notably by the historical economist Cliffe Leslie in 1879 in his remarkable paper 'The Known and the Unknown in the Economic World'. Keynes's formulation of

this protest probably remains the best known: 'I accuse the classical economic theory of being itself one of those pretty, polite techniques which tries to deal with the present by abstracting from the fact that we know very little about the future' (1937, 192). More recently this accusation has been expressed in the penetrating critical *aperçus* of Professor George Shackle and his neo-Austrian followers. This fundamental objection focuses on the limitations of the – often tacit – classical assumption of full knowledge, and on the exclusion from so many classical and neoclassical models of any serious role for uncertainty, ignorance and erroneous expectations.

Some, though certainly not all or most, of the responsibility (or credit?) for this vast simplification must be laid at the door of Adam Smith and *The Wealth of Nations*. As already noted, Sir John Hicks has observed that Smith, in his treatment of saving, investment, money and hoarding, 'neglected uncertainty and liquidity' (1965, 41). Adam Smith, however, did not go nearly so far in excluding uncertainty and ignorance as did his successors, notably Ricardo, who incorporated much more comprehensively, and, at points, explicitly, the assumption of certainty and full knowledge into the main body of orthodox economic theory – in so much of which it has so long enjoyed a vital position, with only intermittent protests regarding its inadequacy (see Hutchison, 1978, chapter 7).

The pseudo-objectivity of the classical cost-of-production approach to value may have encouraged this profound simplification. Viewed superficially, costs seem to be objective, knowable and often fairly accurately known. Certainly, also, the full-knowledge model was well worth developing. There have always been some real-world conditions to which it has represented a reasonable approximation. The assumption, however, that the supply of correct knowledge was usually ample and costless was often introduced inexplicitly, and was likely to be seriously confusing in the analysis of economic fluctuations and instability.

It was mostly French writers, of our period, who had first recognized the vital role of uncertainty and erroneous expectations in real-world problems, particularly with regard to the extreme and dangerous fluctuations in the supplies and prices of grain, or the staple foodstuff of the people. Boisguilbert was the first economist to give ignorance and uncertainty their due role in economic processes. Cantillon also recognized the uncertainties facing the entrepreneur in his pivotal role in a market economy. It was, however, Condillac, in the opening chapters of his *Commerce and Government*, who launched his analysis of suppliers and demanders in the market with an explicit recognition of the ignorance, uncertainty and erroneous expectations with which decisions would necessarily have to be taken. As Condillac explained at the outset of his analysis of value and price:

> The utility being the same, the value would be greater or less depending only on the degree of scarcity and abundance, if this degree was known with precision . . .

16

But this degree will not ever be known. It is, therefore, principally an opinion that the greater or less value [of goods] is founded.

(1776, 10)[11]

Erroneous expectations, and the vital subjective element in market decisions, rooted in ubiquitous uncertainty and human ignorance, were largely excluded from orthodox classical analysis. The role of uncertainty and erroneous expectations came to be recognized only in the study of business fluctuations which was long pursued mainly by outsiders and rebels against classical orthodoxy. If the ideas of Boisguilbert, Cantillon and, especially, of Condillac, had not been so totally disregarded in the orthodox English classical system of theory, and if this orthodoxy had not concentrated, as far and as long as it did, on the simplification of full knowledge and correct expectations, then the subsequent protests of Cliffe Leslie, Keynes, Shackle and others would have been unnecessary, and economic theory might have been much better equipped to face the fluctuations and instabilities of the twentieth century.

VIII

(4) Most of the main methodological doctrines and approaches maintained and debated in the twentieth century were first expounded and developed in the pre-classical period. The empirical and quantitative approach of William Petty has already been discussed. At another extreme, the deductive, geometric, Cartesian method, later so influentially advocated by Senior, Cairnes and Mises, was briefly supported and brilliantly employed by Dudley North. Especially notable was the masterly use of abstraction by Richard Cantillon, who demonstrated its role so much more explicitly and clearly than Ricardo (usually mis-described as its founder or discoverer).[12] The major methodological development on which we would focus here is that of the historical approach pioneered by the Scottish historical school (though the brilliant institutional–relativist criticism by Galiani, in his *Dialogues* (1770) was certainly outstanding).

David Hume, in his own day more famous as a historian than as a philosopher, stated: 'I believe this is the historical age and this the historical nation' (*Letters*, ed. Greig, 1932, vol. II, p. 230). Certainly, in the middle decades of the eighteenth century, in much of Western Europe, a remarkable surge of interest in history and historical inquiry took place. Vico and Montesquieu were the inspiring pioneers, with Montesquieu's work much the better known. The *Esprit des Lois* was translated into English in 1750 and had probably its most powerful effect in Scotland. Earlier, the natural-law system of moral philosophy, as developed in Glasgow by Carmichael and Hutcheson, had not provided much scope for the historical method, though Adam Smith, from an early stage of his work, had shown an interest in an historical approach (see Skinner, 1965, 3). In the second half of the century Hume's claim that

17

Scotland was 'the historical nation' acquired much justification, and it was pre-eminently Hume himself who led the way by providing the philosophical foundations, and by demonstrating the possibilities in moral philosophy, or in the moral or social sciences, of the historical method, a method and approach closely linked with his empirical principles. Indeed, Albert Schatz went so far as to claim that Wilhelm Roscher's manifesto of the German Historical school, in 1843, had been fully anticipated in Scotland, a century previously: 'David Hume, already in 1741, had done more than formulate it, he had applied it' (1902, 61). Certainly, as regards political economy, one of the first and most important, if small-scale, applications of an historical method and approach is to be found in Hume's economic and political essays. The full-scale application, however, of history to political economy, came with the two great, contrasting Scottish *Inquiries*, that of Sir James Steuart into the principles of political economy, and that of Adam Smith into the nature and causes of the wealth of nations. This approach was, however, to a large extent discarded, or seriously neglected, when the deductive, abstract method of Ricardo and Senior came to dominate English classical orthodoxy.[13] Obviously Adam Smith had no responsibility for this rejection. The Scottish historical movement had, however, rather faded away in the earlier decades of the nineteenth century, when David Hume's title of 'the historical nation' passed from Scotland to Germany. The protests of the German historical school, as expressed by Wilhelm Roscher in 1843, revived the case for an historical approach in political economy, and were followed in England, in the 1860s and 1870s, by Cliffe Leslie and others – and, later on, by institutionalist critics.

There would, of course, have been little scope for the German historical critique, or for various subsequent historical and institutionalist protests, in England and elsewhere, if the Scottish historical method of Hume, Steuart and Smith had continued to have as important a role in political economy, as it had in *The Wealth of Nations*; or if Adam Smith's work had continued to provide the methodological model for the dominant corpus of economic doctrine. Moreover, the intellectual balance, maturity, caution and healthy scepticism of such early exponents of the historical approach as Galiani and Hume would have provided an essential, if unpopular, antidote to the pretentious claims of the physiocrats and the classicals.

IX

The historical–institutional method and critique, the neoclassical–Jevonian revolt, the Keynesian 'revolution', the expectational Keynesian–neo-Austrian protest, make up a considerable part of the history of political economy and economics over the last 100 years or so, since the decline and fall of English classical orthodoxy around 1870. All of these four ideas, theories, or lines of thought, had been initiated, or significantly developed, before 1776, and had been largely excluded from or diminished in the English classical corpus of doctrines. One has, therefore, to go back to the seventeenth and eighteenth centuries, before English classical orthodoxy came to dominate, if one wishes to follow the history of several of the most significant theories, ideas and issues, which have been debated and developed in the twentieth century.[14]

We conclude, therefore, with a total rejection of the long-influential view that political economy was founded or created in 1776. In fact, Adam Smith was not the founder of political economy, but the founder of English classical political economy – which some classicals considered was the same thing – because they maintained that no one had thought or written seriously about the subject before them. Political economy, however, was not created by one person in one country, but by many people in several countries of Western Europe. Whether or not it was fully adequate and proper for Adam Smith to make no mention whatsoever in *The Wealth of Nations* of such predecessors as, for example, Petty, Carl, Tucker, Galiani, Verri, Turgot, Condillac and Steuart – and to refer only once to Cantillon – such treatment of the economists of the seventeenth and eighteenth centuries is completely inadequate and misleading for serious twentieth-century students of the history of political economy.

Apart from the brief and local regime of the physiocrats in France (whom some English classicals followed, methodologically or philosophically, much too closely), the first attempt to establish a kind of revolutionary orthodoxy was that of the English classicals, who swept away as erroneous, or outmoded, so many of the immediately preceding ideas, theories or lines of thought. This classical *coup* was uniquely successful (much more so than subsequent rather similar attempts by Marxians and Keynesians).

Writing of Smith's achievement in *The Wealth of Nations,* Jacob Viner maintained that he

> gave to economics for the first time a definite trend towards a logically consistent synthesis of economic relationships.
>
> (1928, 116)

Such processes of logically consistent synthesizing, together with their accompanying processes of selecting, simplifying and systematizing, sometimes also combined with changes in interest and emphasis, may bring impressive gains in the form of enhanced analytical or persuasive power. As a part, however, of such processes, serious exclusions or omissions are very likely to occur. There was a certain shift of emphasis from trade to growth, as the central focus of interest – though this should not be exaggerated. *The Wealth of Nations* remained much concerned with trade and exchange. Questions and alternatives were, however, dropped or ignored, complications got left out, possibilities were not followed up – e.g. in the Smithian–classical synthesis, questions regarding the relation between utility and value, and regarding the effects

19

of hoarding money, or of changes in liquidity preference, or of uncertainty and erroneous expectations.

The gains and losses of such turning-points or revolutions tend to be much exaggerated both by their supporters and by their opponents, who tend to represent the 'revolution' in question as being either all gains, or all losses. We are not, of course, attempting here any cost–benefit assessment of the Smithian–classical revolution – from which the benefits were certainly very considerable. Such benefits are not relevant so far as our pre-classical period is concerned. It is the losses which are relevant, for they represent a large part of the achievements of the pre-classical period. These losses, moreover, have been largely ignored, or at least very insufficiently appreciated, because of the tenacity of the classical version of the history of the subject, according to which few or no such losses could have existed, since political economy, in any intellectually serious form, hardly existed before the appearance of *The Wealth of Nations* and the establishment of the English classical orthodoxy.

A further point is concerned with the role of orthodoxies in the history of political economy and economics. Orthodoxies are sought or established for the influence and prestige which they bring to the subject, or to those practitioners of the subject who proclaim the orthodoxy. The first successfully established orthodoxy, that of the English classicals, was followed – after a brief confused interregnum in England in the 1870s – by the neoclassical academic orthodoxy led by Marshall; this was, in due course, followed by the Keynesian orthodoxy, or the Keynesian–neoclassical synthesis which, in major respects, dissolved some time around 1970.

Since about 1970, for the first time in about a century and a half or more, that is, since the establishment of the English classical orthodoxy, there has been, over a major area of the subject, fundamental divisions with no prevailing orthodoxy anything like as dominant as any of the three or four major orthodoxies of the previous century and a half. Certainly, regarding microeconomic doctrine, a considerable consensus prevails, in which, incidentally, ideas or lines of thought which originally emerged in the pre-classical period play a fundamental part. This consensus, however, seems overshadowed by the division in macroeconomics, regarding both theory and policies, which was prefigured by the basic contrast between the doctrines proclaimed in the great *Inquiries* of Sir James Steuart, on the one hand, and of Adam Smith, on the other (1767 and 1776).

Of course, a relevant orthodoxy, based on a reasonably well-tested consensus should be the prime objective of a disciplined subject, but not a premature orthodoxy, to a serious extent ideologically based and biased, sought for the sake of the influence and public prestige which an established, widely accepted body of doctrine can command. Since the dissolution of the consensus based on the Keynesian–neoclassical synthesis, around 1970, the decline in the influence of the subject has been deplored, and calls have sometimes been heard for a new synthesis. Such calls should be treated with some reserve. The establishment of a new orthodoxy might be based on excessive losses and exclusions.

The outstanding qualities of *The Wealth of Nations* have always provided much justification for regarding 1776 as perhaps the most important single date in the history of political economy. What, however, needs much more critical examination is the narrowness of the basis on which Smith's classical followers successfully established their claims to orthodoxy. Also requiring much more critical examination is the version of the history of political economy propagated by the classicals in support of their claims. For classical orthodoxy, while building on much too little of the work of its predecessors, consigned to oblivion much too much. Much too much, moreover, of the influence and durability of the classical version of the history of the subject seems to have depended on its convenient, labour-saving, Anglo-centric, Anglo-linguistic bias. A less inadequate and inaccurate view of the achievements of the pre-classical period is necessary, both for its own sake, and for achieving a fuller and more balanced appreciation of the subsequent development of the subject, including the work of the classical, historical, neoclassical and Keynesian schools. A more accurate view, and more adequate perspective, of the history of political economy and economics is also required for a clearer understanding of what kinds of growth, or progress, in economic knowledge have been achieved and of what kinds might reasonably be expected in the future, which might serve as a basis for less unsuccessful policy-making.

ADDENDUM (1993)

I would like to comment briefly on two works, covering, in very different ways, much of the same ground, which appeared almost at the same time as *Before Adam Smith* (1988).

(1) A very scholarly and extremely concise overview of the history of economic thought by Professor Murray Rothbard, who acknowledges a debt to Schumpeter, appeared in 1987 ('Adam Smith Reconsidered'). Rothbard commends highly and deservedly the progressive and enlightening view on value of the late Scholastics, especially those of the school of Salamanca, and of Italian and French writers who were pioneers of a utility approach to value in the seventeenth and eighteenth centuries. Rothbard, however, while scathingly critical of Smith, barely mentions Ricardo. Though this view of the history of economic thought might be described as 'Schumpeterian', it may more suitably be characterized as 'Jevonian' and as deriving from Jevons's brilliant, trenchant Preface to the second edition of his *Theory of Political Economy* (1879), one of the finest pioneer essays on the history of economic thought ever penned.

(2) Professor David McNally, in his very interesting work, *Political Economy and the Rise of Capitalism* (1988), interprets some of the leading writers on

political economy from Petty to Smith as concerned with the problems of agrarian capitalism, rather than acting as apologists for the emerging industrial capitalism. McNally provides much justification for his interpretation and criticism, in which he employs what is called 'the surplus approach', linked with a labour theory of value. Such an approach may well have a certain explanatory value with regard to some important contributors to the emergence of political economy in the seventeenth and eighteenth centuries.

In *Before Adam Smith* I was only secondarily concerned with interpreting the writers of the seventeenth and eighteenth centuries in terms of the economic history of the period. Primarily, I was concerned with interpreting the writers from Petty to Smith in terms of their contributions to what have been identified as theories serviceable in explaining and predicting the more important real-world economic processes of the twentieth century. Certainly the earlier theorists may be interpreted as trying to explain contemporary processes and problems. But they usually claimed much more for their conclusions than merely an historically-relative relevance. Especially, for example, the Physiocrats made sweeping claims to universalist certainties. In terms of relevance to real-world processes and policies in the twentieth century the 'surplus approach' and labour theories of value seem to have little significance or usefulness.

Interest in the applicability of earlier economic theories to twentieth-century processes and policies seems to have declined among historians of economic thought today. But it remains a legitimate interest. Naturally Marxians, having suffered catastrophic losses in present and future relevance, will be clinging desperately to whatever bits and pieces of the past they can lay their hands on. Those more interested in the applicability and usefulness of economic theories to present processes and policies are entitled to study the history of economic thought from that viewpoint, rather than devote their energies to defunct ideas of well-confirmed empirical invalidity and practical uselessness.

NOTES

1 This paper is a revised version of the Bateman Lecture delivered at the University of Western Australia on 20 July 1987. Much of it is incorporated in the 'Postscript' (Chapter 21) of my book, *Before Adam Smith: the Emergence of Political Economy, 1662–1776*, published by Blackwell in 1988. I would like to take this opportunity of expressing my warm thanks to the Head and members of the Economics Department for their friendly hospitality.

2 As Wilhelm Roscher long ago stated:

> Our widespread custom of categorizing the entire period of the development of economic theory, before the physiocrats, under the name of mercantile system, is highly unsatisfactory. The well-known picture in the traditional textbooks, of a mercantilist, corresponds with some of the more insignificant writers of the

seventeenth and eighteenth centuries; but the most significant are by no means described by the term.

(1851, 122)

3 The term 'pre-classical' was introduced by Professor Douglas Vickers in his *Studies in the Theory of Money, 1690–1776* (1959).
4 The passage from Boisguilbert's 'Dissertation de la nature des richesses' is quoted by Professor Gilbert Faccarello in 1983. I am much indebted to Professor Faccarello's writings on Boisguilbert and for his advice and criticism.
5 According to J. S. Mill, writing of economists before Adam Smith:

> Before the appearance of those great writers whose discoveries have given to political economy its present comparatively scientific character, the ideas universally entertained both by theorists and by practical men, on the causes of national wealth, were grounded upon certain general views, which almost all who have given any considerable attention to the subject now justly hold to be completely erroneous.
>
> (1844, 47)

Regarding the new Ricardian science of political economy James Mill maintained:

> Among those who have so much knowledge on the subject as to entitle their opinions to any weight, there is wonderful agreement, greater than on any other moral or political subject. . . . There is no branch of human knowledge more entitled to respect.
>
> (1836, 382)

The claims of J. R. McCulloch could hardly have been higher:

> The errors with which the Political Economy was formerly infected have now nearly disappeared, and a very few observations will suffice to show that it really admits of as much certainty in its conclusions as any science founded on fact and experiment can possibly do.
>
> (1824, 9)

6 As Nassau Senior remarked:

> Aristotle's description of value as depending on demand . . . approaches much more nearly to perfect accuracy than Smith's who, by adopting labour as a measure of value, and talking of labour as never varying in its own value, has involved himself and his followers in inextricable confusion.
>
> (1928, vol. II, 45)

Though they make their point in rather categorical black-and-white terms, there are strong reasons for the conclusion of De Roover and Schumpeter. According to Schumpeter, Smith was 'far below' Galiani on the subject of value and price (1954, 188), while De Roover, the distinguished authority on scholastic economics, concluded:

> The Doctors, especially the members of the school of Salamanca, made one of their main contributions in developing a theory of value based on utility and scarcity, which is more in line with modern thinking than that of Adam Smith.
>
> (1955, 186)

7 On the contradiction between Smith's libertarian message and his peculiar, objective concept of utility, see Hutchison, 1978, 14–15.
8 Ronald Meek seemed to go too far in maintaining that:

It cannot be too strongly emphasized that any approach to the problem of the determination of value from the side of utility and demand (as opposed to that of cost and supply) would have been regarded by him [Smith] as quite alien to the general outlook of *The Wealth of Nations*.

(1973, 73)

From a non-Marxian viewpoint, however, M. L. Myers justifiably claims that Smith 'will never let go of a labour theory of value' (1983, 117).

9 The adjectives 'tiresome' and 'exceedingly awkward' are applied to Smith's treatment of utility and value by Professor Marian Bowley (1973, 110 ff), and 'unhappy' is applied by Professor S. Hollander (1973, 136). Professors Bowley and Hollander, who seem to go well beyond the call of duty in their defence, are extremely steadfast supporters of Smith's theories. Their use of these adjectives regarding Smith's treatment of this central and fundamental concept of value theory, seems to say a great deal.

10 As a French writer maintained regarding the contribution to value theory of Galiani, Turgot and Condillac:

The radiant glory of Adam Smith and his pleiad of disciples rejected their advances, consigning them to the shadows of oblivion, although their own notion of value constituted not progress but regress. Today it is abandoned and the doctrine currently triumphant is the psychological theory put forward by Galiani, Turgot and Condillac.

(Dubois, 1897, 864)

11 Regarding Condillac's insistence on the subjectivity of *scarcity* (as well as utility) Isabel Knight explains:

. . . a governing principle of Condillac's entire economic theory is that it is opinion, not fact, which determines everything. . . . Thus everything important in economics – including, as we shall see, productivity, labour, money – rests on value, defined as a subjective opinion, which varies relative to the same object not only according to general circumstances but according to the person who has the opinion.

(1968, 236 and 248)

12 Cantillon's moderation and explicit clarity in the use of abstraction may be sharply contrasted with the opaque excesses and ambiguities of Ricardo, which have made his writings a permanently inconclusive battleground of contradictory, ideological misinterpretations (though these excesses have, of course, greatly enhanced Ricardo's reputation for profundity).

13 As Roy Pascal noted in his seminal article: 'It is very remarkable how this whole historical school becomes lost in the nineteenth century' (1938, 177). According to Professor D. C. Coleman, most of the blame for the distortion and 'bowdlerization' of the role of history in political economy should be ascribed to 'the two southbound Scots', James Mill and McCulloch (1987, 20). Regarding the historical deficiencies of Mill and McCulloch, Professor Coleman continues:

Such an absence of interest in the economic past dovetailed exactly with the structure of Ricardo's own thought. . . . So, by the mid-nineteenth century, the combined efforts of Mill, Ricardo, and McCulloch had gone far to remove these historical elements from the formulation of economic theory.

(1987, 27–8)

14 One very well-known school of economic thought of which there were only few and

24

minor anticipations before Adam Smith was that of Marxian economic theory (though the materialist interpretation of history was suggested by John Millar of the Scottish school (Adam Smith's most distinguished pupil) and *may* have descended from Millar to Marx *via* Thomas Hodgskin). Marxian economics was not so much a revolt against classical political economy as an offshoot of it, with its roots in the Manchester of the 1840s. Searching for some kind of pedigree for the labour theory of value before *The Wealth of Nations* Marxian historians have not been able to find very much. The labour theory of value was mainly a product of the English classical period (which was historically incongruous, because this was just the period when anything like a simple labour theory was, more rapidly than ever before, becoming positively useless).

REFERENCES

Bliss, C. (1986). 'Progress and Anti-Progress in Economic Science', in *Foundations of Economics*, eds M. Baranzini and R. Scazzieri, pp. 363 ff.

Boisguilbert, P. de (1707). 'Dissertation de la nature des richesses', in *Boisguilbert ou la naissance de l'économie politique*, eds J. Hecht and A. Sauvy, 2 vols, 1966.

Bowley, M. (1973). *Studies in the History of Economic Theory before 1870.*

Bryson, G. (1945). *Man and Society, the Scottish Inquiry of the Eighteenth Century.*

Carl, E. L. (1722–3). *Traité de la richesse des princes et de leur états*, 3 vols.

Coleman, D. C. (1987). *History and the Economic Past.*

Condillac, E. B. de (1776). *Le commerce et le gouvernement considerés relativement l'un a l'autre*, in *Oeuvres de Condillac*, 21 vols, 1821–2, vol. 4.

De Roover, R. (1955). 'Scholastic Economics: Survival and Lasting Influence', *Quarterly Journal of Economics*, 60, pp. 161ff.

Dmitriev, V. K. (1902). *Economic Essays on Value, Competition and Utility*, translated by D. Fry, 1974.

Faccarello, G. (1983). *Information, anticipations, et équilibre macroeconomie chez P. de Boisguilbert.*

Faccarello, G. (1986). *Aux origines de l'économie politique liberale.*

Galiani, F. (1751). *Della moneta*, introduction by A. Caracciolo, 1963.

Galiani, F. (1770). *Dialogues sur le commerce des blés*, ed. F. Nicolini, 1958.

Hicks, Sir John (1965). *Capital and Growth.*

Hollander, S. (1973). *The Economics of Adam Smith.*

Hume, D. (1932). *Letters*, ed. J. Y. T. Greig, 2 vols.

Hutchison, T. W. (1953). *A Review of Economic Doctrines, 1870–1939.*

Hutchison, T. W. (1978). *On Revolutions and Progress in Economic Knowledge.*

Hutchison, T. W. (1985). 'On the Interpretations and Misinterpretation of Economists', in *Gli economisti e la politica economia*, ed. P. Roggi, pp. 323ff.

Hutchison, T. W. (1988). *Before Adam Smith: the Emergence of Political Economy, 1662–1776.*

Knight, I. F. (1968). *The Geometric Spirit: the Abbé de Condillac and the French Enlightenment.*

Leslie, C. (1879). 'The Known and the Unknown in the Economic World', in *Essays in Political and Moral Philosophy*, n.d.

Link, R. G. (1959). *English Theories of Economic Fluctuations, 1815–1848.*

McCulloch, J. R. (1824). *A Discourse on the Rise, Progress, Peculiar Objects and Importance of Political Economy.*

McNally, D. (1988). *Political Economy and the Rise of Capitalism.*

Mandeville, B. de (1714). *The Fable of the Bees*, ed. P. Harth, 1970.

Marshall, A. (1975). *The Early Writings*, ed. J. K. Whitaker.

Meek, R. L. (1973). *Studies in the Labour Theory of Value*, 2nd ed.

Mill, J. (1836). 'Whether Political Economy is Useful', in *Selected Writings*, ed. D. Winch, 1966, pp. 371ff.

Mill, J. S. (1844). *Essays on Some Unsettled Questions of Political Economy*.

Mill, J. S. (1848). *Principles of Political Economy*, ed. W. J. Ashley, 1909.

Mitchell, W. C. (1927). *Business Cycles*.

Myers, M. L. (1983). *The Soul of Modern Economic Man*.

Nicole, P. (1671). *Essais morales*, 1715 ed.

Pascal, R. (1938). 'Property and Society: the Scottish Historical School of the 18th Century', *Modern Quarterly*, 3, pp. 167ff.

Peach, T. (1986). 'David Ricardo's Treatment of Wages', in *Ideas in Economics*, ed. R. D. C. Black, pp. 104ff.

Petty, W. (1662 et sequ). *Economic Writings*, ed. C. H. Hull, 2 vols, 1899.

Roscher, W. (1851). *Zur Geschichte des englischen Volkswirtschalftslehre im sechzehnten und Siezehnten Jahrhundert*.

Rothbard, M. (1987). 'Adam Smith Reconsidered'. Reprinted in *Austrian Economics*, ed. S. Littlechild, vol. I, pp. 5ff., 1990.

Say, J. B. (1841). *Traité d'économie politique*, 6th ed.

Schatz, A. (1902). *L'Oeuvre économique de David Hume*.

Schumpeter, J. A. (1954). *History of Economic Analysis*.

Senior, N. W. (1928). *Industrial Efficiency and Social Economy*, ed. S. L. Levy, 2 vols.

Sewall, H. (1901). *Theories of Value before Adam Smith*.

Skinner, A. (1965). 'Economics and History', *Scottish Journal of Political Economy*, 12, pp. 1ff.

Smith, A. (1776). *The Wealth of Nations*, eds R. H. Campbell, A. S. Skinner and W. B. Todd, 2 vols, 1976.

Steuart, Sir J. (1767). *Principles of Political Economy*, 3 vols.

Turgot, A. R. J. (1769). *Réflexions sur la formation et la distribution des richesses*, ed. and trans. W. J. Ashley, 1898.

Vickers, D. (1959). *Studies in the Theory of Money, 1690–1776*.

Viner, J. (1928). 'Adam Smith and Laissez-faire', in *Adam Smith 1776–1926*, ed. J. H. Hollander, pp. 116ff.

Walras, A. (1831). *De la nature de la richesse et de l'origine de la valeur*.

2

JEREMY BENTHAM AS AN ECONOMIST[1]

I

In the perilous spring of 1941, at the original suggestion of J. M. Keynes, the Royal Economic Society commissioned Dr Stark to prepare a comprehensive edition of Bentham's economic writings. Dr Stark's task did not include the tracking down of long-vanished documents as had that of Ricardo's editor, but rather lay primarily in deciphering, sorting, selecting from and piecing together the masses of manuscript material at University College, the British Museum and Geneva. These vast heaps of papers were only legible with great difficulty, and were shuffled about in a state of complete confusion, which such pagination as Bentham had provided only aggravated rather than alleviated. Everyone interested in the history of economic thought, and in Bentham in particular, is very deeply indebted to Dr Stark for the devotion and skill with which he has produced these three volumes and for the great interest and illumination they afford.

Dr Stark's problems have inevitably, in the nature of the case, been those of continual selection and arrangement. The more or less insoluble problems of selection were on two fronts: that of selecting 'economic' from 'non-economic' writings – necessitated by modern specialism – and that of selecting those worth including from the masses of notes and fragments. Since, almost by definition, a 'scholar' is one who never trusts, if he can possibly help it, any other selection or arrangement than his own, one might run the risk of appearing 'unscholarly' unless, at least formally, certain reservations were expressed. (Not that we wish to press such reservations, because Dr Stark had the obvious and valid reply that if one does not like *his* selection and arrangement, then one can go and bury oneself in the Bentham manuscripts for ten years, as he did, and produce one's own.)

Dr Stark informs us that before the publication of this edition only 'at best the tenth part' of Bentham's economic writings had been available in print (I, p. 11). It is difficult to estimate the percentages of new and previously published material in these three volumes, since some of the texts have been re-arranged or expanded as compared with the versions already available. But it does not seem that very much more than a half, or two-thirds at the most, can be new, and therefore very large quantities of Bentham's economic writings must still remain in manuscript, being presumably too repetitive, fragmentary or incoherent to do anything with.

The great services which these volumes afford might be briefly described as follows. First, they enable us to consider for the first time Bentham's contribution to political economy, which though it certainly does not take the form of a carefully finished, well-rounded achievement, easy to weigh up, is nevertheless chock-full of powerful, fertile and independent ideas on some of the perennial and fundamental problems of economic analysis and policy. At least some of the misconceptions about Bentham's standing as a political economist ought now to be removed (at any rate, for example, the statement Keynes once made that Bentham 'was not an economist at all' (1926, p. 21). More particularly, these volumes put before us in all their profusion and variety Bentham's ideas on the theory of money, investment and employment,[2] and they tell a deeply interesting story of the development and the fundamental changes in his ideas on this subject. Bentham devoted about eighteen years to political economy (c. 1786–1804), and in that time moved from a thorough-going acceptance of the 'classical' Smithian doctrines on saving and investing and their implications for policy, to what amounts to a thorough-going rejection. After 1804 he never actively returned to the subject or showed much interest in the great new developments of the Ricardo era, except for a very minor pamphlet in 1821. This story provides us with another of those ironies in the history of economic thought – all the more ironical in this case in view of the tremendous fame and influence of our author – where good original ideas, fundamentally acceptable to most economists of a subsequent period, were left buried and suppressed while the stage was dominated by doctrines now mainly and fundamentally rejected.

These volumes add little or nothing to the analysis of utility and diminishing utility available in Bentham's already published writings. It has often been pointed out, obviously with much truth, that Bentham's development of, and emphasis on, the two concepts of maximization and utility make him above all the ancestor of neoclassical economic theorizing, and especially of Jevons and Edgeworth. But these ideas were developed in Bentham's political, legal and philosophical writings. As an *economist*, as today defined, Bentham made no attempt to develop an economic calculus or a theory of relative values and prices. His economic theorizing, in fact, is of an exactly opposite pattern to that typical of the neoclassicals. It is *not* mainly abstract, deductive and 'microeconomic', tightly organized around the assumption of a maximizing individual; but on the contrary, is rather practical, 'macroeconomic', concerned with aggregate monetary problems, and if not statistical, at any rate concerned to exploit such crude statistics as were available, while being ready for and calling for more.[3]

Finally, these volumes make it possible to reassess, as seems rather badly needed, Bentham's theory of economic policy, or his views on the role of the state in economic life. Our next three sections will refer briefly to some comments of Bentham on utility and value, will go on to tell in more detail of the development of some of his ideas on money, investment and employment, and will then discuss his doctrines on the role of the state.

II

As we have said, these volumes add very little that is new on the felicific calculus or the analysis of utility, to which Bentham had made such original contributions, mainly in his already published non-economic writings. Nor does Bentham attempt a systematic analysis of value and price. The most important new passage on this subject in these volumes takes the form of an interesting criticism of Adam Smith's treatment of utility. This comes in *The True Alarm* (1801), the opening sections of which are the nearest we get in Bentham's writing to a systematic account of economic principles. After emphasizing that 'all value is founded on utility . . . where there is no use, there cannot be any value' (III, p. 83), Bentham goes on to Smith's distinction between value in use and value in exchange, complaining that Smith 'has not attached to it clear conceptions'. Bentham is referring, of course, to the famous fatal sentences in *The Wealth of Nations*, almost the only ones throughout the book where value in use or utility gets any explicit mention, where Smith says, quite definitely, that value in use is in no way necessary for value in exchange, and vice versa, and that the two are in fact 'frequently' quite separate. Bentham criticizes Smith not for the distinction itself but for the way in which he formulates it, and for illustrating it by the paradox of water and diamonds. Bentham himself resolves this paradox on lines which clearly point in the direction of the marginal utility theory, that is, by invoking the plenty or scarcity of the supply, though he does not, of course, actually introduce the marginal concept:

> *Water* is the example he has chosen of that sort of article which has great value with a view to use but none with a view to exchange. In order to realize how erroneous the latter assertion is, he would only have had to consult in London the New River Board, and to remember that at Paris he had seen it sold retail by those who carry it into the houses.
>
> He gives *diamonds* as an example of that sort of article which has great value with a view to exchange and none with a view to use. This example is as ill chosen as the other. . . . The value of diamonds is . . . a value in use. . . .
>
> The reason why water is found not to have any value with a view to exchange is that it is equally devoid of value with a view to use. If the whole quantity required is available, the surplus has no kind of value. It would be the same in the case of wine, grain, and everything else.

Water, furnished as it is by nature without any human exertion, is more likely to be found in that abundance which renders it superfluous: but there are many circumstances in which it has a value in exchange superior to that of wine.

(III, pp. 87–8)

It is clear that if Bentham had ever got down to formulating precisely a general theory of value his approach would have differed fundamentally from the 'classical' analysis of Smith and Ricardo. He would have continued in the tradition of Galiani, Pufendorf and the Schoolmen.[4]

III

Bentham's economic writings deal mainly with macroeconomic questions arising, in several cases, out of topical issues of war finance and inflation, or 'how to pay for the war', and his theoretical analysis is centred around questions of capital, saving, investment, money and employment. His starting-point was that of a thorough-going, but even then by no means uncritical, disciple of Adam Smith.[5] He accepted, to start with, the Turgot–Smith analysis of saving and investment (the cornerstone of 'classical' economics in the Keynesian sense) and, what went logically with it, the unqualified approval of 'parsimony' and saving, and what came to be the Ricardo–Treasury view of the uselessness and waste of public works and public investment. On the other hand, in his later economic writings we find Bentham completely and fundamentally rejecting this self-same set of ideas, putting his finger very precisely on the limitations in its assumptions and applicability, and advocating in consequence completely different policies and a very different attitude to the role of the state in economic life. The trend of Bentham's thinking on these subjects is perfectly clear, though in writings that are often unfinished and dashed off in a completely unrevised note form, there are numerous deviations and inconsistencies around the trend.[6] If he had devoted a certain amount of time and patience to the task of working his ideas up into a finished, balanced treatise, or if he had found some understanding disciple to help him in this task – instead of Dumont, Mill and Ricardo – it is clear that Bentham could have produced a work as outstanding as Thornton's *Paper Credit*.

Bentham's first economic work, the well-known *Defence of Usury*, is primarily a policy pamphlet containing little in the way of theoretical analysis. Though devoted to criticizing Smith from a more-Smithian-than-Smith point of view, it is entirely under the influence of Smith. We have now a hitherto unpublished postscript to the *Defence* which shows how his theoretical interests were developing. Here Bentham gives us a restatement of the Turgot–Smith theory of saving and investing and draws from it the logical implication that voluntary 'parsimony' or saving always must result in, and is unconditionally necessary for, capital accumulation. He writes: 'Whoever saves money, as the phrase is, adds proportionately to the general mass of capital. . . . The world can augment its capital only in one way: viz. by parsimony' (I, pp. 196–8), and 'parsimony' here means voluntary private individual saving. This leads on, as Bentham puts it, to 'the development of the Principle "No more trade than capital" or "capital limits trade" '(I, p. 201). In the *Manual* Bentham actually complains that Smith had not been explicit enough in proclaiming this principle, though he adds, with more justification, that Smith 'conforms to it in every recommendation he gives, and writes almost throughout as if it were constantly uppermost in his thoughts' (I, p. 233).[7]

The principle, Bentham tells us, 'that the trade of every nation is limited by the quantity of capital, is so plainly and obviously true as to challenge a place among self-evident propositions' (I, p. 212). As we know, propositions in economics laid down as plainly and obviously true and self-evident very often, when one begins to dig into them, fold up into definitions, tautologies or, at best, trivialities. So rather than argue over what Bentham 'really meant', in the abstract, by this principle, it may be more fruitful to consider what in practice it implied for him by observing the lively political rabbits which he conjures out of this collapsible opera-hat. The first political rabbit to emerge from this proposition 'No more trade than capital' has '*laissez-faire*' written all over it. It is the same animal (or at any rate one of a very similar species) as the Ricardo–Treasury view. As Bentham puts it:

> Therefore no regulations nor any efforts whatsoever, either on the part of subjects or governors, can raise the quantity of wealth produced during a given period to an amount beyond what the productive powers of the quantity of capital in hand at the commencement of that period are capable of producing.
>
> (I, p. 201)

Hence government action can only *divert* investment resources from one line to another, not raise the level of investment.

The *second* important political rabbit – perhaps a rather surprising one – which Bentham conjures from his principle of 'No more trade than capital' is that it would pay Great Britain to give up her colonies – or at any rate that there are no economic advantages, in the form of the investment opportunities they provide, to outweigh the burdens and expenses of their upkeep.

The chain of argument is that there is only a fixed fund of capital; there are always just as profitable outlets for this at home, which do not require the extra military and administrative expenses that colonial investment necessitates. This assumption, that there are always just as profitable investment outlets at home – which incidentally seems possibly to conflict with Bentham's often-repeated generalizations about the falling rate of profit – is based on a sort of Say's market analysis applied to agriculture, to the effect that the supply of savings–investment will always create its own profitable

31

demand – which is really implicit in the Turgot–Smith analysis.[8]

After *The Defence of Usury* and a brief essay on *Colonies and Navy* (1790), Bentham's next main economic work is the *Manual of Political Economy* (1793–95), from which we have already inserted some quotations.[9] In this treatise on the principles of economic policy Bentham is still to be found emphasizing most strongly the *laissez-faire* conclusion which he takes to follow from his doctrine of 'No more trade than capital': government can only *divert* investment funds, not raise the total level of investment.

> Whatever is given to any one branch, is so much taken from the rest. . . .
> If the government money had not taken that direction, private money would if the government would have given it leave. . . . Every statesman who thinks by regulation to increase the sum of trade, is the child whose eye is bigger than his belly.

(I, pp. 234, 241 and 252)

However, though continually repeating such sweeping categorical assertions, Bentham does for the first time introduce a qualification, which was to grow later into an extensive body of monetary analysis. This qualification comes in a note at the end of the *Manual* headed 'Connection of the Paper Money Question with the Rest of the *Manual*'. Though 'forced accumulation' by means of taxation is first referred to in the main part of this work, the proper concept of 'forced saving' (though not, of course, the *term*), appears first in this addition on paper money.

Bentham writes, Government 'can't increase wealth because they can't increase capital. Is there anything it can and ought to do to increase capital? Does paper money, for instance, increase capital?' (I, pp. 269–70). Bentham's answer in equally brief note form is:

> If all were fully employed it [the issue of paper money] could not increase industry. If any were unemployed, or not fully employed, it might increase industry *pro tanto*. . . . It actually is productive of an addition to the mass of national wealth, in as far as it gets extra hands, or sets them to work at extra hours.

(I, pp. 270–1)

However, at this point, in contrast with his later views, Bentham simply mentions this possibility as an abstract theoretical *curiosum*, and considers that in practice attempts by governments to act on it would be dangerous.

This is the last that we have from Bentham on the subject for several years. But it was a turning-point. For when he returns to the subject Bentham advances straight through the cleft he had thus opened in the Turgot–Smith savings–investment analysis and in the Principle based on it, of 'No more trade than capital'. In fact, he completely abandons that Principle and the particular assumptions on which it rests, as well as the policy conclusions he drew from it.

His lengthy work on *Circulating Annuities* (1800) – unfinished like so many of the others – is concerned with his scheme for interest-bearing government notes which would serve both as paper money and small savings certificates. Here Bentham strenuously analyses the effects of changes in the quantity of money on the level of economic activity. An increase in the quantity of money may, Bentham repeatedly tells us, either or both raise prices or raise output – if initially there is unemployed or misemployed labour available. He observes:

> In political economy as in chemistry, results are scarce ever obtained pure: while part of the new influx [of money] is employing in producing the beneficial result of an increase of real wealth through the medium of profitable labour, other part will be employing itself in the raising of prices of labour here and there, and thence of this and that class of goods: and, indeed, it is scarce possible that a new mass of dormant labour should be called forth into act without making some addition to the recompence given to the mass already in employment.
>
> (II, p. 313)

Above all, Bentham notes, monetary inflation may be a serviceable policy in '*war time* – a time in which money having to be raised in large quantities for the service of government, must for a time be diverted from other channels' (II, p. 315).

The effects of monetary expansion depend on how or where the new money initially enters the system and on the propensity to consume or save of those who initially receive it. It is not too anachronistic to use the modern terms, for Bentham quite clearly understands something of the significance of the consumption function, and even attempted a very rough calculation of its order of magnitude. For example he notes: 'It cannot be supposed that upon the mass of income from labour – most of it . . . being the labour of the poorest classes, – the ratio of savings to income can amount to anything like what it does in the case of income from profit of stock: to anything like $\frac{10}{15} = \frac{2}{3}$ of the amount of income: one should scarcely expect to find it amount to $\frac{2}{30}$' (II, p. 324 n). Bentham also notes that a higher percentage of the new money paid out to highly-salaried officers will be saved than of that paid out to the lower-salaried (II, p. 322).

At one point Bentham rejects the possibility of deflationary cures for unemployment and is led into some most 'mercantilistic'-sounding statements, in direct contradiction to his earlier principle of the fixed relation between voluntary saving and capital formation:

> No addition is ever made to the quantity of labour in any place, but by an addition made to the quantity of money in that place. . . . In this point of view, then, money, it should seem, is the cause, and the cause *sine qua non*, of labour and general wealth.
>
> (II, p. 326)

He adds: 'This and a great deal more that might be added, is not in Adam Smith – but it belongs not the less to the science so well taught by Adam Smith' (II, p. 330).

In fact, in a remarkable footnote Bentham proceeds to criticize Smith for at least one of the main themes of his attack on mercantilism:

> Though 2 millions' worth of gold and silver is not worth a farthing more than 2 millions' worth of anything else, there is not on that account any absurdity in the exultation testified by public men at observing how [great] a degree what is called the balance of trade is in favour of this country. . . . Seduced by the pride of discovery, Adam Smith, by taking his words from the kitchen, has attempted to throw an ill-grounded ridicule on the preference given to gold and silver.
>
> (II, p. 337n)

In fact, Bentham claims that he has indicated the way in which 'an answer may be found to a question for which I have in vain endeavoured to find an answer in Adam Smith and other books' (II, p. 339) – that question is by what process and with what chain of causation new money enters the economic system. He complains that 'for my own part, I must confess, I never was able to obtain what to me appeared a clear insight into this part of the subject from the instructions of Adam Smith. Metaphors taken from wheels and water seemed to take the place too often of definition and exemplification' (II, p. 342n).

In his different works Bentham alternates, superficially somewhat confusingly, between warnings against the damage done by *de*flation and forebodings as to the injustices of *in*flation – long and short term (as in *The True Alarm*). But whether he is concerned with the one or the other Bentham constantly emphasizes the crucial importance of whether the initial situation is one of full employment or one where there are unemployed resources, that is, there is no question for Bentham of full employment, or something near it, constituting some sort of realistic norm or equilibrium towards which the system actually 'tends'. Bentham fully appreciated the distinctions implied between *in*flation and *re*flation, and *de*flation and *disin*flation. For example, at the end of his pamphlet *Paper Mischief Exposed* (1800–1) Bentham examines the effects of what he calls 'the money-hoarding system', or 'the system of laying up hoards of money on the part of government, in reserve for casual exigencies' by some kind of budget surplus (II, p. 453). (Incidentally the 'Paper-Mischief' is not that of paper money as such, which Bentham approves, but that of the unregulated issue of paper-money by numerous private banks.) In a period of full employment, or over-full employment, with prices rising, such 'government hoarding' will not lower output but will damp down the rise of prices. But on the other hand, 'let us suppose that there exists in the country a quantity of unemployed capacity for labour. . . . In this case the defalcation from the mass of money is really productive of a correspondent, though not equal, defalcation from the mass of wealth. The money hoarded by government, and hence defalcated from the stock of money in circulation, is parcel of the money raised by taxes: the taxes are imposts laid, for the most part at least, if not exclusively, on expenditure' (II, p. 454).

Bentham's next work is called *The True Alarm* (1801), its subject being the long-term and short-term dangers and injustices of inflation (especially with an unregulated private note-issuing system). Bentham wavered between writing a formal treatise and a polemical pamphlet and in the end – as usual – abandons the work unfinished. However, he turned the manuscript over to his editor Dumont, who ten years later (in 1811) consulted J. Mill and Ricardo about preparing it for publication, and we have the Notes on this work which Ricardo then made (*v*. Vol. III of Sraffa's edition p. 259).

Here Bentham attacks the Turgot–Smith savings–investment analysis at its roots, by setting out the different ways in which the individual can use his money income. Bentham explicitly includes what he calls 'laying it up' – a possibility omitted in Smith's analysis of saving and investing. He also very precisely puts his finger on the two vulnerable points in that analysis – which nevertheless, as Schumpeter has shown, remained so extremely influential right through the nineteenth and into the twentieth century. These two vulnerable points are, first, analysis in real terms applied with no (or no adequate) qualification to a monetary economy; and, second, exclusion of the possibility of what Bentham calls 'laying up' or the possibility of 'hoarding'.

Later on Bentham examines the effects of an increase in frugality or decrease in consumption (III, p. 120). The first effect of a decrease in consumption, if it is not offset, is a fall in prices and then of production. But, of course, the fall in consumption may be offset by an increase in investment either on the part of the savers themselves or of others who have borrowed from the savers, directly or through a banker, either to invest or consume. In this case only frictional adjustments will be necessary. But if the income saved 'instead of being put into circulation, is for an indefinite time put into a chest and kept there' then the 'case is the opposite of the preceding one'. The fall in consumption is followed by a fall in prices, production, profits and investment. Thus frugality is now, for Bentham, by no means unconditionally beneficial as it had been in his earlier writings and in Smith. In fact, Bentham goes on to extol the benefits of luxury expenditure in the manner of Mandeville:

> Let the rich and those in power spend all their revenue, as far as is possible, on superfluities, they cannot deprive the merchant of his profit on their expenditure: and as for the merchant, . . . he will not be able to rid himself of that disposition to accumulate which, to a greater or less degree, seems to be inseparable from his mode of life. Hence, whatever the manner of expenditure . . . the merchant will not fail to levy a tax on

35

prodigality for the encouragement and the increase of industry and wealth.

(III, p. 124)

Bentham also takes up in *The True Alarm* his doctrine that an expansive monetary policy can raise the level of economic activity without voluntary saving. The effects of such a policy will, of course, turn on whether or not there are unemployed resources. Here Bentham emphasizes how very difficult it is to define or perceive in practice when this exact point of 'full employment' has been reached. As to this Bentham makes a statistical estimate that would seem to require some upward revision for the period since 1800:

> A thousand politicians have ventured predictions, and a thousand politicians have been wrong. Everybody wishes to decide the question in order to declaim about the actual state of affairs and to say with emphasis that we have reached the highest possible degree of prosperity and that that prosperity is no more than a dream which is going to vanish. To me it seems that something is gained if the difficulty of pronouncing on this point is shown. It amounts to a refutation of all the positive assertions of the two parties, to giving both of them a lesson in moderation and toleration. In the eyes of impassioned ignorance there exists no difficult question.

(III, p. 148)

It is interesting to turn to Ricardo's notes on *The True Alarm* and find him expressing his complete *dis*agreement with Bentham's doctrine as to the possible beneficial effects of an increase in the money supply – he does so as repetitiously as Bentham states his doctrine.

We find Ricardo asking: 'Why should the mere increase of money have any other effect than to lower its value? How would it cause any increase in the production of commodities. . . . Money cannot call forth goods – but goods can call forth money' (reminiscent of a passage in Smith). In fact, Bentham's doctrine is for Ricardo 'a stumbling block . . . that money is the cause of riches has been supported throughout the work and has in my view completely spoiled it'.[10]

Ricardo, in fact, could see nothing at all in Bentham's doctrine, just as he could see nothing at all in Malthus's ideas on effective demand, and J. B. Say's ideas on utility and value. He was, of course, holding with the strictest logic to the Turgot–Smith theory of saving and investing – to what he called 'Mr. Mill's Principle', or the Say–Mill analysis of markets.

There is just one more point to add by way of illustrating the development of Bentham's ideas, and this is from his next work *The Defence of a Maximum* (1801) (i.e., a maximum price for bread). Bentham here referred back to his arguments in the *Defence of Usury*, fourteen years before, where he had *attacked* a *minimum* legal rate of interest. He is at pains, in defending a maximum price

36

of bread, to point out that he did not attribute to the market rate of interest any automatic self-adjusting equilibrating tendencies – a view which supporters of his attack on the control of the rate of interest had ascribed to him. This passage is of considerable general interest from the point of view of Bentham's attitude to the principles of economic policy, and his scepticism as to the methodology of equilibrium theorizing and the economic harmonies. His particular point is that the rate of interest does not adjust (or optimally adjust) saving and investment:

> Gentlemen, when they have done me the honour to join with me, as it seemed to them, in opinion on this subject, have sometimes, whether for shortness or for ornament, referred in this way to a law of hydrostatics as the ground for it. Money, according to my opinion, I mean according to their edition of it, was a sort of thing that would find its own level, or that ought to be left to find [it]. Between what does naturally take place, and what ought to take place, there is indeed some difference: but it is a difference which moralists are apt enough to overlook, which they constantly overlook as often as they talk of the law of nature. . . . Neither on that nor any other occasion have I ever given, or shall I ever give, serpents for fish, sentiment or metaphor for argument. I have not, I never had, nor ever shall have, any horror, sentimental or anarchical, of the hand of government. I leave it to Adam Smith, and the champions of the rights of man (for confusion of ideas will jumble together the best subjects and the worst citizens upon the same ground) to talk of invasions of natural liberty, and to give as a special argument against this or that law, an argument the effect of which would be to put a negative upon all laws. The interference of government, as often as in my humble view of the matter the smallest balance on the side of advantage is the result, is an event I witness with altogether as much satisfaction as I should its forbearance, and with much more than I should its negligence. Neither in that book [The Defence] nor in any other book of mine will any expression be found by which any such association is attempted to be made between the idea of money and that of a level, i.e., between rates of interest and levels. I choose rather to remain unread than feed the reader with such arguments. The particles of a mass of fluid, the particles of a mass of water, have a propensity, when left to themselves, to range themselves upon the same level: human creatures have on their part a propensity to save their own lives: and when water in the search after a level is making its way too fast into a ship, pumps are employed by men to prevail on it to get the better of that propensity, and betake itself to a higher level, and this may serve as an argument in favour of a maximum to any gentleman who finds himself disposed to consider it as such.

(III, pp. 257–8)

In comparatively a very few years Bentham had moved a very long way from his earlier wholehearted acceptance of the Turgot–Smith analysis of saving and investment and his dictum that 'every statesman who thinks by regulation to increase the sum of trade, is the child whose eye is bigger than his belly'.

IV

Our last quotation brings us to Bentham's views on the respective roles of state regulation and the free price mechanism, or his theory of economic policy – a subject which is now one on which widely diverging and even diametrically opposite views are authoritatively advanced. For a long time the consensus of opinion held that Bentham was a representative of thorough-going *laissez-faire* doctrines or, at least – which *may* be rather different – was typical of 'classical' nineteenth-century economic liberalism. Dicey and Leslie Stephen must have had much to do with establishing this view of Bentham. Dicey used 'Bentham-ism' and 'Individualism' as alternative terms, and held that 'faith in *laissez-faire* . . . is the very essence of legislative Benthamism'.[11] Keynes claimed that in Bentham 'we discover the rule of *laissez-faire*, in the shape in which our grandfathers knew it'.[12] Alternatively, Bentham and Adam Smith are linked together as the two great joint patriarchs of economic liberalism.[13] Dr Starks's editorial comments are, with some qualifications, in tune with this conception. He writes of Bentham's 'fundamental liberalism' (III, p. 32), noting that he was 'a liberal of the socially progressive variety, not a doctrinaire who would have sacrificed everything on the altar of the dead and deadening principles of *laissez-faire*' (III, p. 52). However, Dr Stark also tells us that Bentham was 'a typical 19th-century liberal in economic matters', and 'in his heart of hearts a confirmed votary of *laissez-faire*' (II, p. 8). Presumably there is no direct contradiction here, but the category of 'a confirmed votary' who nevertheless 'would not have sacrificed everything on the altar' seems to introduce an extremely difficult theological subtlety.

However, in contrast with this view of Bentham as a representative of *laissez-faire* or, alternatively, as a leading fellow-'classical' alongside Smith, Ricardo and Senior, a diametrically opposite view has been gaining ground in recent years. For example, in his centenary lecture C. K. Ogden, the *doyen* of Bentham-*forschung*, referred to him as 'the greatest social engineer in history bristling with Five-Year Plans'.[14] Sir G. M. Trevelyan 'concludes generally that Benthamism was "in many respects the exact opposite of *laissez-faire*" '.[15] Professor J. B. Brebner goes so far as to argue (criticizing Dicey) that 'in using Bentham as the archetype of British individualism he [Dicey] was conveying the exact opposite of the truth. Jeremy Bentham was the archetype of British collectivism . . . Bentham and Smith were fundamentally contra-dictory of each other in their ideas of how to secure the general good'.[16] Finally, a very recent study has concluded that 'thanks to the efforts of many current scholars it is at last becoming clear that Bentham may with more truth be called the patriarch of British collectivism than the father of individualism''.[17]

We are prepared to take the risk of opining that at least these more recent views are considerably less misleading than the opposite picture of Bentham as a representative of *laissez-faire* or, alternatively, as a classical liberal. But the one moral which clearly emerges from this rather confusing intellectual situation is that any attempt to pigeon-hole or classify (or 'classicalize') Bentham is bound to be particularly misleading, and any attempt at a precise and concise generalization about his views on the role of the State especially hazardous.[18] In the first place, much important evidence has not been available, and even now we may not have all that is relevant. Secondly, the writings themselves were often dashed off unrevised, with the author never attempting to reconcile inevitable contrasts, or strike an explicit and clear balance of emphasis. Thirdly, Bentham's own views were constantly changing, sometimes according to a steady long-term trend, while sometimes simply fluctuating around the trend or according to no discernible trend. Any attempt at a concise generalization would at least have to distinguish between Bentham's earlier and later positions.

With these volumes before us it can now be much more safely said that whatever *laissez-faire* maxims Bentham may have emitted from time to time – more frequently in the earlier phases of his economic work (*c.* 1786–95) – as the years went on, he is to be found suggesting more and more economic functions for the State, some of them very fundamental and pervasive. His injunction to the State to 'Be Quiet' ('without some special reason'), cannot signify much when one finds him going on to find enough 'special reasons' for 'noise' to satisfy a whole series of Fabian Summer Schools. But although it seems much less misleading to regard Bentham rather as a prophet of the Welfare State than of the Gladstonian Budget, we do not want to try here to categorize or classify him. We simply wish to contrast his views on the role of the State with those of Smith, Ricardo and Senior and to suggest that he cannot be regarded as one of the 'classicals', if this term is to preserve any doctrinal significance.

The contrast between what Bentham had to say on the role of the State in the economic field and the views of any economist reasonably describable as a classical liberal may be summarized under five heads:

(1) We have just seen how Bentham came to reject the Turgot–Smith theory of saving and investing and the idea of the rate of interest as a beneficial automatic regulator of saving and investment. His change of view on this subject obviously has quite fundamental implications for his view of the role of the State in the economic field. None of those regarded as typical 'classical' economists argued in the manner of Bentham that the State either could or should beneficently act on the aggregate level of investment and employment, or be responsible for maintaining these at a high level. Even Malthus is hardly a genuine and complete exception.

(2) No 'classical' economist sets out with such explicitness and detail so many and varied economic functions for the State: the Bank of England should be nationalized and the issue of paper money should be a monopoly of the Government; there should be governmental licensing and participation in all banking and some government control of speculation; there should be government activity in everything connected with the propagation of knowledge – universities, schools, agricultural and scientific research and the collection of statistics; the Government should also be responsible for hospitals, health services, transport and means of communication. A newly-published paper (*Plan for Augmentation of the Revenue*, 1794–95) suggests that the superior security and longevity of the State, as compared with private enterprise, suits it for the taking over of insurance business on a large scale, in particular life annuities, life insurance, lotteries and the various activities of friendly societies.

(3) Bentham approaches the problem of the agenda of the State by laying down four overriding ends of economic policy, subject only to – (or which are in fact the constituents of) – the supreme end of maximum happiness. The four ends are, in order of importance: subsistence, security, opulence and equality. The fulfilment of these four ends justifies any amount of State action, and three of them in their very nature – subsistence for all, security and equality – are bound to call for far-reaching intervention. This prior specification of overriding ends surely amounts to an approach to the problems of economic policy from a direction diametrically opposite to that of Smith and Ricardo. Smith, at any rate, rather starts from the fundamental beneficence of the free-market mechanism and then traces around this the framework of State activity necessary to maintain, and at exceptional points correct or supplement, this mechanism.[19]

What was really implied for Bentham in his four different ends of policy is brought out in a remarkable outline draft (or '*brouillon*') dated 22 October 1800, and headed 'National Prospects or a Picture of Futurity' (Vol. III, pp. 481–3). 'Opulence' includes 'maximum opulence of the lower classes. . . . The higher the wages of labour, the better consistent with national security'. Nevertheless, Bentham does not believe that government can raise wages above 'what is sufficient for bare subsistence to a family of average size'. But he *does* believe that government could and should be 'giving security to that measure of subsistence'. Bentham goes on to note the 'Insufficiency of the general propensity to accumulation to ensure a sufficiency of the principal subsistence for man, i.e. corn. Necessity of the interference of government for that purpose'. Furthermore government could and should promote opulence 'so far as concerns the increase of capital: by forcing *savings* from pleasurable expenditure and applying the amount in the shape of capital'.

(4)Though repeatedly urging that the individual is the best judge of his own interests, Bentham explicitly rejects the general principle that the hidden hand can be relied upon to work adequately towards the end or ends he lays down:

'That the uncoerced and unenlightened propensities and powers of individuals are not adequate to the end without the control and guidance of the legislator is a matter of fact of which the evidence of history, the nature of man, and the exstistence of political society are so many proofs' (III, p. 311).

In particular, the primary end of subsistence for all (or for as many as possible) required, according to Bentham, a policy of 'magazining', or of the wholesale storage by the state of food supplies, and the fixing of maximum prices: 'Insurance against scarcity cannot be left with safety to individual exertion'. On the subject of price-fixing he writes: 'As I have all along suspected, the horror in which it has been held by the best opinions, has nothing but prejudice, and a too indiscriminate attachment to general principles for its foundation' (III, p. 262). It is not simply that Smith, James Mill, Ricardo or Senior did not happen to put forward such far-reaching proposals, it is rather that one cannot conceivably imagine them doing anything but oppose schemes like Bentham's to the uttermost, as did Burke.[20]

(5) Bentham's explicit mention of equality as an end of policy (although he puts it last), along with the analysis of diminishing utility on which he based it, has no important parallel in the writings of other classical liberals. Certainly at other points Bentham emphasizes, in direct contrast with his egalitarianism, the importance of preserving established expectations. But this also runs counter to the principle of leaving distribution to the free market, or to Ricardo's dictum, for example, that 'like all other contracts, wages should be left to the fair and free competition of the market and should never be controlled by the interference of the legislator'.[21] Professor Stigler has emphasized 'the relative unimportance of the distribution of income to the classical economists' – a justifiable generalization so long as Bentham is not included.[22] Bentham's recognition of the egalitarian argument which might be deducible from the principle of diminishing utility, and his multifarious taxation proposals, especially that for limiting inheritance, foreshadow the whole recent trend of British tax policy. At what stage, if any, on the road to our present position Bentham would have wanted to get off the bus, it is impossible to say. But Bentham was unquestionably one of the major influences in getting the bus started on its present route, and this distinguishes him essentially – for better or for worse – from 'classical' liberals like Smith, Ricardo and Senior.

V

The greater part of this account of Bentham's economic ideas rests on material published for the first time in these volumes. Thus, as an economic theorist this most celebrated and influential of Englishmen is something of a Cournot or a Gossen, that is, one whose work as an economist was largely unknown and of virtually no influence in his own day. In contrast with his political and legislative ideas, his writings on monetary theory found no disciples to follow them up, while what *was* published of his economic writings somehow gave

41

rise to most misleading and confusing accounts of his position on the principles of economic policy.

We have already noted that when Dumont consulted Ricardo and James Mill on preparing for publication *The True Alarm* – perhaps the most important work in these volumes – they were in complete disagreement with its central theories and did not consider it worth proceeding with, or its ideas worth exploring further – in spite of the almost superhuman prestige which Bentham is supposed to have had in their eyes. Nor, for his part, did Bentham ever seem to have shown any interest in or agreement with Ricardo's *Principles*, his sole recorded comments thereon being: 'In Ricardo's book on Rent there is a want of logic. . . . He confounded cost with value'. As regards economic ideas, therefore, there seems to be no more misleading claim than Bentham's to the effect that Ricardo was (through James Mill) 'my spiritual grandson'.[23] This could only apply to some of Ricardo's political and parliamentary activities. Bentham's economic ideas, both as regards theory and policy, run on fundamentally different lines from those of Ricardo. There are no grounds for supposing that a single sentence of Ricardo's *Principles* would have been different if Bentham had never existed. The questions Ricardo formulated, the assumptions he reasoned from and the method he used are sharply distinguishable from those of Bentham. In Bentham's economic writings there are no long chains of deductive reasoning. His approach is far more empirical and statistical, and he would have rejected the idea of political economy as a mainly deductive science based on a very few fundamental and more or less self-evident assumptions – as classically described, for example, by Senior. Though J. S. Mill's general approach to economic policy diverges less from Bentham's than does his father's or Ricardo's, the theoretical differences remain fundamental; and there is no sign of the younger Mill ever having read, much less marked and digested, Bentham's unpublished economic writings.

On the two central questions of economic theory, that of the determination of relative values and that of the determination of the main economic aggregates, Bentham in his later and more definitive writings differed from the classical approach of Smith and Ricardo, all along the line. So although, like Ricardo, Bentham started from the *Wealth of Nations*, and even in *The True Alarm* writes that the work of Smith 'still is and deserves to be the textbook of political economy', this cannot bridge the quite fundamental differences in approach which Bentham had opened up. Bentham himself could not realise or foresee how important and fundamental the differences between his ideas and those of Smith and Ricardo were to become, when the lop-sided classical emphasis on labour and cost of production in value, and on the rate of interest as a smooth and beneficent regulator of saving, investing and aggregate employment were to harden into dominant and largely unquestioned orthodoxies. On the one hand, Bentham's ideas, both on value and on savings–investment and employment, follow the lines of pre-Smithian 'mercantilist' writers such as John Law, Berkeley and Sir James Steuart. On the other hand, they point forward to Jevons, Edgeworth and Marshall in one direction, and to Keynes in another. Only as a rather mild and elastic type of Malthusian does Bentham share in any of the main 'classical' doctrines. If Bentham is still to be described as a 'classical' economist, along with Smith and Ricardo, then this much-controverted adjective is virtually emptied of any doctrinal significance.

ADDENDUM (1993)

This paper on Bentham's Economic Writings, together with the next three papers on Ricardo, might be described as 'The Tale of Two Editions' (both of which I reviewed on their first appearance in the early 1950s). Both had been commissioned by the Council of the Royal Economic Society, apparently on the suggestion of Keynes, the Ricardo edition in 1925 under the editorship of Sraffa, the Bentham edition in 1941 under the editorship of Stark.

In several striking respects, however, the contrasts between the two editions could hardly have been more extreme. First, regarding their physical appearance, the ten volumes of the Ricardo edition were as spacious and sumptuous as could be desired; while the three Bentham volumes, when they appeared shortly after, were characterized – as I noted at the time – by the wartime 'austerity' of the paper and the cramped and narrow layout. Even more extreme was the contrast in the kind of reception which the two editions received. The Ricardo edition was hailed by a number of leading authorities (including, for example, Jacob Viner and George Stigler) as a masterpiece of editorial scholarship, in a considerable number of gushing reviews and review articles. The Bentham edition, on the other hand, was mostly very briefly reviewed and very little discussed. As far as I am aware, my own review article was the only one of some length devoted to Stark's edition of Bentham, which in the forty years since its appearance has had extremely little notice taken of it. This edition, for example, is not mentioned in *The International Encyclopedia of the Social Sciences* (1968), though it is a pleasant surprise to find at least *some* mention – hardly generous or extensive – in *The New Palgrave Dictionary* (1987). Such leading authorities on Bentham as Viner and Robbins do not seem to have made any public comment. Today one can only conjecture that doubts may have been entertained regarding certain qualities, or characteristics, of Stark's editing, in spite of the fact that his edition had been commissioned by the Council of the Royal Economic Society. Presumably, such doubts or suspicions were based on valid scholarly scruples, though today it seems just possible that they may, inadvertently, have been somewhat unfair.

In any case, not long after the appearance of Stark's edition, plans began to be formed for a comprehensive and definitive new 'London' edition of all Bentham's writings, which, it may reasonably have been supposed, would sooner or later include something significantly superior to preceding editions with regard to Bentham's economic works. As to the considerable neglect, or even 'sending to Coventry', of the profoundly interesting new writings in Stark's edition, I would only suggest the further possibility that this edition may have emphasized certain rather Fabian and Keynesian aspects of Bentham, which, though highly agreeable as far as Keynes was concerned, would have been most unattractive to devotees of classical liberalism, and, of course, anathema to Marxists.

Forty years or more have now passed since the publication of Stark's edition, and whether a new and superior edition of Bentham's economic writings will appear in this century seems unlikely. It might well be that no such edition will appear before the middle of the next century or even some way beyond. In fact, to one who once, very briefly, glanced into one or two boxes of Bentham manuscripts at University College, the possibility seems conceivable that no further edition of his economic writings, much more extensive and valuable than Stark's, may be attempted. The task of piecing together fragments and jottings, only decipherable with great difficulty, may seem too daunting.

Meanwhile, Bentham remains one of the giants of English political and social thought, who was an early critical and great admirer of *The Wealth of Nations*, and who went on to write with originality and profundity on important problems of macroeconomics and economic policy; while the Stark edition remains easily the most valuable edition we have of his contributions to political economy.

In the context of these essays, in Part I of this volume, I am concerned with Bentham as a major writer on political economy between Smith and Ricardo, one of many very able writers, who were critical of some important doctrines of Smith, and who disagreed fundamentally with Ricardo's doctrines on value, or on money and macroeconomics (or in Bentham's case on both). Among those regularly included as central members of the classical school there were Malthus and Senior. There were, also, Thornton, Lauderdale and Bentham, and, later on, Bailey, Lloyd and Longfield. Bentham is, in some ways, the most interesting. What is probably his most important work was not only fundamentally contradictory of the views of James Mill and Ricardo, it was suppressed by them, and the original English copy lost (*v.* Stark, vol. III, 1954, p. 17n).

Bentham's economic writings, including particularly those first published in the Stark edition, might, if widely available, together with those of the writers just mentioned, have assisted, with widespread and very salutory effects, in preventing 'the car of Economic Science' (as Jevons called it) 'being shunted on to a wrong line' – the line laid down by 'the mazy and preposterous assumptions of the Ricardian School' (Jevons, 1931, pp. xliv and li).

NOTES

1 This paper was written as a review article of *Jeremy Bentham's Economic Writings. Critical edition based on his printed works and unpublished manuscripts*, edited by W. Stark, 3 vols, 1952–4. The article appeared in the *Economic Journal* in 1956, vol. 76, pp. 337ff.

2 The importance of Bentham as a monetary theorist has been suggested by Hayek (1932, pp. 123–33). See also Viner, 1937, p. 188.

3 M. P. Mack in a recent study refers to Bentham 'spending at least ten years of futile effort trying to ferret out correct statistics for the gross national income, tax revenues, agricultural production, etc.' See 'The Fabians and Utilitarianism', *Journal of the History of Ideas*, January 1955, p. 82. Bentham showed much interest in and reliance on the contemporary attempts at Political Arithmetic of Dr Henry Beeke, who, in his *Observations on the Produce of the Income Tax* (1800), attempted to estimate the national income. Bentham also refers to the pioneer attempt at a price index-number of Sir George Evelyn Shuckburgh (1798). One may guess that Bentham was far more interested in this practical statistical attempt to measure changes in the value of money than in some of the near-metaphysical arguments over labour as a measure of value.

4 On the subject of the water-and-diamonds paradox, which had, of course, been satisfactorily resolved by a number of writers before Smith (e.g. Davanzati, Law and Galiani), Schumpeter writes of 'the astounding fact that Smith and Ricardo thought that this alleged paradox barred the way to a theory of value based on value in use' and refers to Smith 'thereby barring for the next two or three generations, the door so auspiciously opened by his French and Italian predecessors' (*History of Economic Analysis*, 1954, pp. 300 and 309). Bentham's remarks, if they had had any influence, might have helped to re-open this door. Ricardo, however, when he read this criticism of Smith by Bentham, noted emphatically in favour of Smith (cf. his comments in *Works*, ed. Sraffa, vol. III, p. 284).

    Incidentally, Schumpeter's 'astounding fact' becomes all the more astounding when one recalls that Smith's main general statement in the *Wealth of Nations* on utility and value, at any rate at some points, directly contradicts his own statements as reported in the Lecture Notes of 1763 on the relations of 'use', demand and value, and also the indications given in the Lecture Notes of the way in which the water-and-diamonds paradox is to be resolved in terms of scarcities (*v. Lectures*, ed. Cannan, pp. 157 and 176–7). Smith's famous statement in the *Wealth of Nations* also contrasts at some critical points with the treatments of utility, scarcity and value by his predecessors at Glasgow, Hutcheson and Carmichael (who has a very acute note on the subject).

5 On the Turgot–Smith analysis of saving and investment, and the sharp break it marks with preceding doctrines and on its dominating influence right down into the twentieth century, see Schumpeter, 1954, pp. 191–3 and 282–8.

6 We must regard as outside the trend of Bentham's thought, as set out in Stark's three volumes, such passages as are to be found in his early letters expounding the desirability of public works for the relief of unemployment (1776), and suggesting that with a suitable monetary and investment policy 'those commercial distresses which beget distrust and produce ruin to many respectable individuals, while they disrupt the beneficial intercourse of commerce *could* rarely happen' (1779, Bentham's italics; *v. Works*, ed. Bowring, vol. X, pp. 85 and 338–9). Those ideas could be regarded as a significant foretaste of Bentham's later position, but they come a decade before he began to devote himself regularly to political economy.

7 Bentham's 'Principle' is suggested, as follows, by Smith: 'No regulation of commerce can increase the quantity of industry in any society beyond what its

capital can maintain. It can only divert a part of it into a direction into which it might not otherwise have gone' (1976, I, p. 454). The principle of 'No more trade than capital' is, of course, highly reminiscent, or rather anticipatory of the Wages Fund doctrine. Indeed, Bentham is described as the originator of that doctrine by Marx: 'The classical economists have always been fond of considering social capital as a fixed magnitude possessing a fixed degree of efficiency. But this prejudice does not harden into a dogma until we come to the arch-philistine, Jeremy Bentham, the insipid, pedantic leather-tongued oracle of the commonplace bourgeois intelligence of the 19th century. . . . I should call Mr. Jeremy a genius in the way of bourgeois stupidity' . . . etc., etc. (1930, vol. II, p. 671).

8 Bentham's hypothesis of unlimited investment opportunities in agriculture at home is based on the assumption that the British labouring class provides an ever-expanding market for beer: 'In England, the lowest wages of labour will always find a man more bread than he can eat: therefore considerably more wheat than is produced at present, would, if not exported, not find purchasers. But the lowest wages of labour, nor wages much above the lowest, will not find a man as much strong beer as he can drink, nor even as he can drink without hurting himself. Therefore, even independently of exportation, there is no danger of the nation's being overstocked with such of the productions of agriculture as are fit for making beer. . . . Agriculture then will always find a sufficient market for itself: it is impossible it should ever fail to do so' (I, p. 206).

It would be most interesting to follow Bentham's views on the economics of colonial development. Like those of other economists of the classical period, they tie in very closely with his analysis of saving, investment-opportunities and the falling rate of profit. By and large there seems to be a considerable change in Bentham's attitude to colonial development very broadly – though far from precisely – in tune with the change we are describing in his economic ideas. But the divergences in Bentham's views on colonies seem very wide and erratic: contrast the vision with which the *Defence of a Maximum* (1801) ends and the preceding argument: 'Men spreading in distant climes, through distant ages, from the best stock, the earth covered with British population, rich with British wealth, tranquil with British security, the fruit of British law' (III, p. 302), with Bentham's argument that if the two sides had acted rationally in 1776 the Americans would have sought to remain in the British Empire, and the British would have sought to get rid of the Americans (III, p. 357). The concluding paragraphs of *The Defence* cast some doubt on E. G. Wakefield's claim to have converted Bentham in his last years (1829–31) from his earlier view that colonization was a waste of capital, to Wakefield's own strongly favourable views. Bentham had at least half-converted himself thirty years before. See R. C. Mills, *The Colonization of Australia*, 1915, pp. 94 and 152. For the latter reference I am indebted to Professor L. C. Robbins. As a further example of Bentham's vagaries one may cite his attack on the Navigation Laws at one point, and his justification of them at another (Contrast I, p. 211, and III, p. 340). Similarly with the infant industries argument for protection.

9 What appears as *The Manual of Political Economy* in Bowring's edition is, according to Dr Stark, concocted from a mixture of manuscripts of two very different dates. Dr Stark has sorted out the two works. Much of what appears as *The Manual* in this edition is published for the first time and dates from 1793–95, while much of what Bowring published as *The Manual* is now to be found in a work now called *The Institute*, dated 1801–4 – the last important work in this edition.

10 See Ricardo, 1951–2, vol. III, pp. 298, 301, 317–18 and 333. See also Ricardo's extensive comments in his first letter to James Mill in 1811 (vol. VI, p. 14). In 1822, when Ricardo visited Geneva, he further discussed Bentham's economic

ideas with Dumont: 'There were few of his [Bentham's] doctrines to which Ricardo did not object' (see Sraffa's note, vol. III, p. 261n).

11 See A. V. Dicey, *Law and Opinion in England*, 2nd ed., p. 44. Apparently Dicey had some doubts later about his equation of Benthamism and individualism. In the preface to the 2nd edition he writes: 'It is a curious question how far Bentham's own beliefs were logically opposed to the doctrine of sane collectivism' (p. xxx). On Bentham and the rule of *laissez-faire* Leslie Stephen wrote: 'In purely economical questions scarcely an exception was admitted to the rule' (*The English Utilitarians*, vol. I, p. 310). See also J. Bonar, *Philosophy and Political Economy*, 3rd ed., 1922, 1900 and 1950, p. 189, and R. F. Harrod, *Economic Journal*, 1946, p. 438, who writes: 'We cannot really have a definition of individualism that excludes Bentham'.

12 1926, p. 21.

13 See H. Simons, *Economic Policy for a Free Society*, 1948, pp. 104–5: writes of 'Adam Smith and Jeremy Bentham and the tradition of thought identified with them'. W. H. Hutt actually describes Bentham as 'holding even more unwaveringly the *laissez-faire* doctrine [than Smith], *Economists and the Public*, p. 137.

14 Cf. *Jeremy Bentham*, p. 14.

15 See the quotation by D. H. Macgregor, *Economic Thought and Policy*, p. 68.

16 See J. B. Brebner, *'Laissez-faire* and State Intervention in Nineteenth-century Britain', *Journal of Economic History*, Supplement VIII, 1948, pp. 59ff. Brebner refers to the Constitutional Code of Bentham as 'that forbidding detailed blueprint for a collectivist state'. Professor L. Robbins, on the other hand, refers to the Code as 'this great project for a practical Utopia' or 'the good society' (*The Theory of Economic Policy in English Classical Political Economy*, 1952, p. 42). We are not concerned here with whether the society Bentham was trying to outline was 'forbidding' or 'good', but simply that it is extremely different from that argued for by Smith, Ricardo, Senior and other 'classical' liberals.

17 Cf. M. P. Mack, *op. cit.*, p. 88.

18 Of the leading authorities on Bentham's view of the role of the state, Professor J. Viner seems alone to be beyond all criticism. He reminds us of the very wide range of state activities supported by Bentham without trying to categorize, classify or 'classicalize' him. See *American Economic Review*, March 1949, 'Bentham and J. S. Mill: the Utilitarian Background'.

19 Friedrich Hayek in his essay 'Individualism: True and False' classifies Bentham as a 'false' individualist, that is as a rationalistic, in a sense *a priori* individualist – who is really a precursor of totalitarian dictatorship – rather than as a 'true', cautious, empirical one. There certainly are some strains of 'false individualism' to be found in Bentham's writings, and the laying down of comparatively precise overriding 'ends' of policy is the most dangerous of them. Because the laying down of overriding ends suggests the justification of *any* means; but there are also still more pervasive strains of 'true' (i.e. empirical) individualism and 'true' collectivism (if on Hayek's definition collectivism can be 'true' and, if it cannot, such arbitrariness would perhaps be an example of 'false' individualism; *v.* Hayek, 1949, pp. 4ff.).

20 Contrast with Bentham's statement, Burke's: 'To provide for us in our necessities is not in the power of government. It would be a vain presumption in statesmen to think they can do it' (*Thoughts on Scarcity, Works*, vol. VI, World's Classics, p. 3). James Mill, though not exactly deficient in 'presumption', and supposed to be a disciple of Bentham rather than Burke, in fact was explicitly on Burke's side on this issue. In discussing a somewhat similar scheme for 'buffer stocks', put forward by Sir James Steuart, to counter extreme price fluctuations, Mill writes: 'The author, it is evident, had never reflected with any accuracy, upon the operation of free

trade, and therefore sees not the equalizing results which it is calculated to produce. He proposes, accordingly to do that very imperfectly, by a great number of very troublesome regulations, which perfect freedom of trade would do completely of its own accord. Nothing more is wanting than to leave the farmer at perfect liberty to sell his corn wherever he can get the best price for it, and the consumer to buy it wherever he can get it cheapest, without any restriction, without either burthen or encouragement. The necessary effects of this are to secure to the farmer and to the people at all times those exact prices which are best adapted to their mutual interests. To depart from this course is only to disturb the laws of nature, to gratify the freaks or the interests of particular men' (*Literary Journal*, 1806, p. 234). One cannot tell how Professor Hayek would classify this passage by Mill, but it *may* seem a clear case of 'false' rationalistic individualism, with the 'true' empiricism on the side of Steuart and Bentham. Certainly Bentham would have exploded at this appeal to 'the laws of nature' if it had come to his notice. It is also reasonable to guess that Smith, Ricardo and Senior would have been on the side of Burke and James Mill, and not on that of Steuart and Bentham. (The above quotation from Mill may be contrasted with Bentham's discussion of the rate of interest quoted at length at the end of Section III above.)

21 *Principles*, Sraffa ed., p. 105. Or compare Ricardo's statement to Trower (*Letters*, Sraffa edition, vol. VIII, 1952, p. 133): 'Political Economy, when the simple principles of it are once understood, is only useful, if it draws governments to right measures in taxation. We very soon arrive at the knowledge that Agriculture, Commerce, and Manufactures flourish best when left without interference on the part of Government, but the necessity which the state has for money to defray the expenses of its functions, imposes on it the obligation to raise taxes, and thus interference becomes absolutely necessary'.

22 See *Five Lectures on Economic problems*, pp. 1–2. Professor Stigler himself notes differences between Bentham and 'Classical' economists on this subject. Moreover, though he refers to it rather distastefully, Bentham recognizes what might be called 'dog-in-the-manger egalitarianism' as a force which policy-makers must take into account from the point of view of social peace and cohesion (and which so many over-simplified theories of economic policy of classical descent do *not* take into account). That is, Bentham did not hold to the facile and far-reaching assumption that the satisfaction an individual gets from his income is a function simply of *its* size alone, while the size of his neighbours' incomes is entirely irrelevant: 'If on any occasion the interest of the public and the interest of the individual happened to be so combined and tied together, that on condition of seeing an individual reap a profit to the amount of a hundred thousand, the public might reap a profit to the amount of a million, the plan would be turned aside from or rejected. Whatever satisfaction might be excited by the idea of the million gained by everybody and nobody, would be sowered and turned to regret by a glance of the hundred thousand pound gathered into a store of which the owner was in view' (1954, vol. III, p. 297).

23 See Bowring's edition of the *Works*, vol, X, p. 498. We have noted above a practical issue – that of price control of basic foodstuffs – where Bentham and J. Mill were on diametrically opposite sides. The example, surely, has some significance in terms of general principles. J. S. Mill noted the wide difference in cast of mind between his father and Bentham: 'His mind and Bentham's were essentially of different construction' (1924, p. 172). On the other hand, there is certainly a very close intellectual affinity between Mill and Ricardo (*v.* Hutchison, 1953).

REFERENCES

Beeke, H. (1800). *Observations on the Produce of the Income Tax.*

Bentham, J. (1838–43). *The Works of Jeremy Bentham*, ed. J. Bowring, 11 vols.

Bentham, J. (1952–4). *The Economic Writings*, ed. W. Stark, 3 vols.

Bonar, J. (1922). *Philosophy and Political Economy*, 3rd ed.

Brebner, J. B. (1948). *Laissez-faire* and State Intervention in Nineteenth-century Britain', *Journal of Economic History*, Supplement VIII, pp. 59ff.

Burke, E. (1920). *Works*, 6 vols, World's Classics.

Dicey, A. V. (1905 and 1962). *Lectures on the Relation between Law and Opinion in England during the Nineteenth Century.*

Harrod, R. F. (1946). 'Professor Hayek on Individualism', *Economic Journal*, 56, 223, pp. 435ff.

Hayek, F. A; (1932). 'Note on the Development of the Doctrine of Forced Saving', *Quarterly Journal of Economics*, pp. 123ff.

Hayek, F. A. (1949). *Individualism and Economic Order.*

Hutchison, T. W. (1953). 'James Mill and the Political Education of Ricardo', *Cambridge Journal*, VII, 2, pp. 81ff.

Hutt, W. H. (1936). *Economists and the Public.*

Keynes, J. M. (1926). *The End of Laissez-faire.*

MacGregor, D. H. (1949). *Economic Thought and Policy.*

Mack, M. P. (1955). 'The Fabians and Utilitarianism', *Journal of the History of Ideas*, p. 82.

Marx, K. (1950). *Capital*, 2 vols. Everyman edition.

Mill, J. S. (1924). *Autobiography*, World's Classics.

Mills, R. C. (1915). *The Colonization of Australia.*

Ogden, C. K. (1932). *Jeremy Bentham.*

Ricardo, D. (1951–2). *Works*, ed. P. Sraffa, vols I–IX.

Schumpeter, J. A. (1954). *History of Economic Analysis.*

Simons, H. (1948). *Economic Policy for a Free Society.*

Smith, A. (1776 and 1976). *The Wealth of of Nations*, eds. R. H. Campbell, A. Skinner and W. B. Todd, 2 vols.

Stephen, Sir L. (1900 and 1950). *The English Utilitarians*, 3 vols.

Stigler, G. J. (1950). *Five Lectures on Economic Problems.*

Taylor, W. L. (1965). *Francis Hutcheson and David Hume as Predecessors of Adam Smith.*

Viner, J. (1957). *Studies in the Theory of International Trade.*

Viner, J. (1949). 'Bentham and J. S. Mill: the Utilitarian Background', *American Economic Review*, 39, pp. 360ff.

3

JAMES MILL AND RICARDIAN ECONOMICS[1]

I

It hardly seems useful to start by discussing whether there was or was not – or whether one can properly write of – 'a Ricardian revolution'. Sir John Hicks and Professor H. G. Johnson have expressed themselves in favour of this concept which at least seems *prima facie* to be well worthy of serious consideration.[2] But in any case, if the changes brought about by Ricardo's work, and the influence which it exercised, may validly be regarded as 'revolutionary', this must surely be primarily, or largely, because of the novelty, and subsequent importance for the subject, of its *methodological* contribution. Certainly Ricardo's pronouncement that 'the principal problem in Political Economy' was 'to determine the laws which regulate this distribution' – that is, distribution between aggregate rent, profits and wages – signified a certain shift in interests or priorities, although this problem had already been broached in *The Wealth of Nations*. But it can be argued that of *much* more fundamental and lasting significance than the shift of interest or priorities regarding the subject of distribution, was the *methodological* claim that problems in political economy are problems of '*determining laws*'. Moreover, of equally fundamental and lasting significance was the *method* of extreme abstraction (or 'strong cases') by which, in his *Principles* Ricardo sought to 'determine' the 'laws' of political economy, which he claimed his new Science was establishing. The transformation in method and epistemology as between *The Wealth of Nations* and Ricardo's *Principles* is profoundly significant because it altered the mood in which the 'problems' of political economy were treated and in which 'theories', and policy-recommendations, were put forward. In fact, Walter Bagehot opened his essay on Ricardo by stressing his most important contribution: 'The true founder of abstract Political Economy is David Ricardo' (1895, p. 197).

It has long been known that James Mill played a considerable part in the intellectual development and political career of Ricardo. But the full extent of Mill's influence, and just how vital and substantial it was for Ricardian political economy, in a crucial, perhaps 'revolutionary' phase of the subject,

50

and for the subsequent development and methodology of political economy and economics, does not seem to have been fully recognized.

II

The nature of the relationship between James Mill and Ricardo was first clearly revealed, at least with regard to an important phase after 1815, in Mr Sraffa's edition of Ricardo's Correspondence (1951). We can follow there in detail the story – the rough outline of which had long been known – of the triumphantly successful twofold plan which James Mill brought off for and through Ricardo: of how he got the modest, unlettered paterfamilias and wealthy retired-stockbroker-turned-country-gentleman, first to publish to the world a treatise on the *Principles of Political Economy and Taxation*, and then, following up the written with the spoken message, how Mill pushed the still reluctant Ricardo into Parliament to proclaim the new politico-economic doctrine from the stage of the House of Commons. For the first part of the project Mill acts as an impatient professorial supervisor, admonishing, encouraging, cajoling and bullying his gifted but inarticulate pupil through the labours of large-scale literary composition. Then, as a preparation for his parliamentary career, Mill puts Ricardo through a rapid and wonderfully confident correspondence course in what he describes as 'the science of legislation' – an *exact* science as Mill presents it.

Whatever may be thought of the directions in which Mill influenced Ricardo and his career, and of the political and philosophical principles which he sought so vigorously to instil in his much less sophisticated friend, it is impossible not to respect the warmth and affection they had for one another. Ricardo drew out the least forbidding side of Mill, and they seem to have been much closer to one another personally as well as intellectually than were Ricardo and Malthus. Partly it was a case of the attraction of opposites. As a writer Ricardo always felt himself something of an amateur, at any rate outside the narrower field of monetary and banking problems, and he admired the strenuous professional intellectual, or 'hackneyed stager' as Mill called himself, who wielded such a fluent and incisive pen on any subject from India to Education.[3] Mill, on the other hand, respected the practical, successful, financial acumen and expertise of Ricardo. But it was not contrasts, but close intellectual affinities, which made possible their partnership, and which made Ricardo such a 'natural' for Mill's great project or promotion. (See E. Halévy, 1928, p. 266.)

According to Mr Sraffa, Mill and Ricardo first met 'as a result of the publication of Mill's early pamphlet *Commerce Defended* in 1808'. Bain states that Mill's acquaintance with Ricardo began in 1811.[4] In any case, the earliest extant letters show that they were on terms of close, man-to-man friendship by December or January of 1810–11. Down to the middle of 1814, while both were constantly in London, apparently they walked and talked together almost

51

daily, and there are very few letters. In view of the later commanding role which we can now see Mill exercising in his letters of 1815–18, the question obviously arises as to the part which Mill had earlier played in Ricardo's intellectual development down to 1815, in particular in the decisive broadening out of Ricardo's economic theorizing from the narrower monetary problems of his early pamphlets, a field in which he had great first-hand knowledge and expertise, and in which he made significant use of statistics, to his far more general and overwhelmingly deductive analysis of 'the laws of distribution', as presented in his *Essay on Profits* (1815), the embryo of his *Principles*. Halévy has said that when they were in London together (1811–14), 'Mill during the long walks which he loved to take with Ricardo, was chiefly concerned to give him lessons in method.'[5]

However, further significant, if indirect, evidence regarding this remarkable relationship between Mill and Ricardo, perhaps very crucial in the history of political economy, appeared with Professor Winch's valuable editions of *James Mill's Selected Economic Writings* (1966). In particular, this volume made easily available the previously not unknown, but relatively disregarded and inaccessible, early essay of Mill, *An Essay of the Impolicy of a Bounty on the Exportation of Grain* (1804),[6] as well as a similarly little known, and remarkably significant, later article on methodology entitled 'Whether Political Economy is Useful' (1836). It appears that one of these works was the first, and the other the last, of all Mill's publications.

III

In considering the possible intellectual influence of Mill on Ricardo in the seven years or so before the opening of the correspondence of 1815 and after, it seems especially worth emphasizing that although, *in 1815*, Mill is proclaiming himself as having been out of touch 'for a good many years' with the subject of political economy, *when he and Ricardo first met*, some time after 1808, it was Mill who was the senior economist, or contributor to political economy, with two trenchant publications to his name and a number of reviews, while Ricardo may not yet have published a line. Doubtless Ricardo had a first-hand knowledge and expertise in finance and banking, but Mill had expounded and developed the central, general theories of economics, which had the most decisive policy significance regarding population and natural wages, and aggregate demand and supply.

So in the early years of the Mill–Ricardo friendship, before Ricardo broadened his interests in, and grasp of, political economy, Mill may not only have been Ricardo's educator in philosophy, method, literary composition and political presentation, but may also, in his masterful way, have decisively shaped the substance of Ricardo's general economic assumptions and theorizing, in accordance with Mill's own already well-articulated doctrines regarding the central theories of political economy. Anyhow, two of the main

Ricardian doctrines of political economy, and the two with the most immediate and weighty implications for policy, had been developed by Mill in his works of 1804 and 1808, though the extent of Ricardo's debts to, or indoctrination by, Mill, is impossible to estimate precisely.

In these two works, *The Impolicy of a Bounty on the Exportation of Grain* (1804) and *Commerce Defended* (1808), Mill closely follows Adam Smith, at times almost reproducing Smith's arguments word for word. But, as he does so, Mill drastically and decisively sharpens and hardens Smith's theories, putting them in a much starker and more unqualified form, imbuing them with his own particular confident dogmatism, and giving them a much more definite cutting-edge in terms of policy applications, to the extent of making them new and different doctrines. This is more especially the case with regard to his earlier work on the grain bounty than it is in *Commerce Defended*, where Smith's original doctrine, including the policy applications, was already pretty clear-cut and unqualified.

This essay on the grain bounty has not attracted much attention, but it is closely relevant to what became Ricardo's central question, or 'model', of macro-distribution and 'progress'. Following very closely Smith's treatment of grain bounties, Mill opens his essay with the idea of the uniqueness of 'corn',[7] which is 'the only necessary article' and 'a peculiar commodity':

the very elements of society are interwoven with the laws which regulate the production of this primary article . . .

If it be said that wool is the material of one of our most important manufactures; corn is the most important material of all our manufactures. If it be of importance that the raw material of any of our manufactures should be got cheap, surely it is of importance that what is the great material of them all should be got cheap.

(1966, pp. 55 and 67)

Mill proceeds to elaborate on the crucial significance of this 'basic' commodity:

No proposition is established more thoroughly to the conviction of those who have studied the scientific principles of political economy than this; that the money price of corn regulates the money price of everything else. The wages of the common labourer may in general be reckoned his maintenance. He must earn a sufficient quantity of corn to feed himself, otherwise he cannot exist. If he is paid in money, the sum of money he daily receives must always be equivalent to the quantity of corn he must use. If the price of corn is high he must receive the greater sum of money, as his day's wages, to buy with. *This is so obviously necessary, that we need spend no more time in proving it. The money price of labour therefore is entirely regulated by the money price of corn.*

(1966, p. 63, italics added)

The idea of the uniqueness of 'corn' is then combined by Mill with an extremely hard-line version of the natural-wage doctrine and with the 'great

53

law of society' regarding the relation between wage rates and population changes – a far more drastic, unqualified and immedate version of the doctrine than that in *The Wealth of Nations*, or, at many points, in the writings of Malthus himself. In fact Mill's natural-wage doctrine amounts to a very different proposition from that of Smith, with far more definite and immediate policy implications:

> The multiplication of the human species is *always* in proportion to the means of subsistence. *No proposition too is more incontrovertible than this*, that the tendency of the human species to multiply is much greater than the rapidity with which it seems possible to increase the produce of the earth for their maintenance.
>
> . . . *No one however will hesitate to allow all that is necessary for our argument*, that the tendency of the species to multiply is *much* greater than the rapidity with which there *is* any chance that the fruits of the earth will be multiplied in Britain, or any other country in Europe. What is the consequence of *this great law of society*, but that the production of corn creates the market for corn? Raise corn as fast as you please, mouths are producing still faster to eat it. Population is *invariably* pressing close upon the heels of subsistence; and in *whatever quantity* food be produced, a demand will always be produced greater than the supply.
>
> (p. 55, italics added)

Mill then draws the conclusion that, except in quite extraordinary circumstances, the voluntary export of corn will never take place except possibly in the very short-run or after a bumper harvest: 'The nature of *this elementary principle of society*, of which we never ought to lose sight, is such that *a sufficient market is always provided at home, for all the corn which the land, with the utmost exertions of the farmer, can ever be made to produce.*'[8]

Having dealt with the proposal for a bounty on export, Mill goes on to advocate the free importation of corn arguing that 'at *all* times when the trade in corn is free, the interests of the traders in corn, and those of the people at large, are *exactly*, the same'.

It is clear that several of the key concepts, assumptions and building blocks of the Ricardian models and 'theories' are presented, trimmed, polished and ready for use, in this essay of 1804 by James Mill: notably (1) the simplified concept of 'corn' as a short-hand for workers' subsistence, a unique commodity in that it is a raw material for all production; (2) an extremely drastic, hard-line version of the Malthusian proposition regarding the relations between population changes and wages; and (3) the idea that adjustments take place so rapidly and completely that lags, or 'disequilibria', can be left out of the argument. Therefore, it seems that Mr Sraffa's statement regarding the influence of Mill on Ricardo's *Principles* may be highly questionable that: 'On the theory there is little doubt that his influence was negligible' (1951, p. xxi).[9]

We do not propose to discuss at length the second, and much better-known, of Mill's early works, which, also, he had produced before his meeting with Ricardo, that is, *Commerce Defended*. Here the 'classical' doctrine of the impossibility of general over-production is elaborated – as Mill acknowledges – from Smith's seminal and epoch-making analysis of saving and investing. Mill simply adds a mixture of dogmatism and ambiguity:

> *No proposition however in political economy seems to be more certain than this* which I am going to announce, however paradoxical soever it may at first sight appear; and if it be true, *none undoubtedly can be deemed of more importance.* The production of commodities creates, and is the one and universal cause which creates a market for the commodities produced . . .
>
> The demand of a nation is always equal to the produce of a nation . . .
>
> . . . *Every individual in the nation uniformly makes purchases, or does what is equivalent to making purchases, with every farthing's worth which accrues to him.* [10]

These doctrines, and the policy implications that followed, already had behind them the considerable prestige and authority of Smith. But they were by no means, in 1808, as dominant as they were later, thanks to Mill and Ricardo, to become. They were fundamentally challenged, not only by Spence, Mill's immediate opponent in *Commerce Defended*, but by Lauderdale and Bentham – and of course, later, in a rather confused way by Malthus. Lauderdale's arguments are equated by Mill with those of Spence, who is told that his questioning of Smith's analysis is 'pretty much as if a follower of the Ptolemaic astronomy should accuse the reasonings of Sir Isaac Newton of vagueness and confusion'. [11]

It may be said that the Smith–Mill–Say doctrine of saving, investment and the impossibility of general over-production is not closely related to the main Ricardian problem of macro-distribution. But it was pretty completely, consistently and unswervingly accepted and upheld by Ricardo. Moreover Ricardo expounded the massive, *laissez-faire* policy implications of the doctrine in Parliament, in opposing public works in the depressed year of 1819. What subsequently came to be called 'The Treasury View' is really '*The Ricardo View*'.

Between the publication of *Commerce Defended* and the crucial correspondence which began in 1815 two episodes in the Mill–Ricardo relationship may be briefly mentioned.

The *first* episode, as recorded in the earliest Mill–Ricardo letters extant (1811), relates to Bentham's essay on inflation, *The True Alarm*, which rejected the Turgot–Smith saving-is-investing doctrine, and its consequences, which had been so stoutly maintained in *Commerce Defended*. In correspondence of 1811 Mill and Ricardo agreed to advise Dumont, who had sent them Bentham's manuscript, that no attempt was worth making to prepare it for publication. Against Bentham's argument Ricardo maintained: 'The increase of money in my opinion can have no other effect than raising the prices of commodities.' [12]

The *second* episode, or example, where traces of Mill's influence may perhaps be discerned, relates to the most celebrated of Ricardo's early monetary writings, his *Reply to Bosanquet*, also of 1811. Here Ricardo deploys a kind of trenchant, even aggressive, methodological criticism which is most emphatically on Millian lines. A favourite section of Mill's Commonplace Book was devoted to 'Theory or Speculation versus Practice', in which he brings a mass of authorities to check the overweening presumption of the practical man.[13] This is precisely Ricardo's line in his *Reply to Bosanquet*. Ricardo's denunciations of the man 'who is all for fact and nothing for theory', as having 'no standard of reference', and as providing a 'melancholy proof of the power of prejudice over very enlightened minds', might, as regards substance and language, have been penned by the master himself.[14] In fact it would not be at all surprising if Mill had some direct responsibility for these controversial gambits, which can hardly be paralleled elsewhere in Ricardo's writings.

It is difficult to suppress the conjecture that those Millian 'lessons in method', mentioned by Halévy, may already have been influencing his pupil as early as 1810. Exactly how far Ricardo, from the earliest stages of his career as a political economist, was fashioned by Mill as the intellectual partner, or instrument, for Mill's projects, is bound to remain doubtful. But there does seem to be considerable evidence for such conclusions of Halévy as that Mill exercised 'a profound influence on Ricardo's intellectual destiny'; and that he 'intended to make of Ricardo the Quesnay of nineteenth-century England'.

Halévy maintains that Mill did not so much give Ricardo a doctrine, 'as develop in him the doctrinal leaning and make him a doctrinaire'.

We may agree on the latter point, but would observe that in his two early economic writings Mill may in fact have 'given' Ricardo two or three of his *central economic theories or doctrines*, or essential components of them.[15] We may suggest also that what Halévy writes of the relation between Mill and Bentham may be applied also to that between Mill and Ricardo: 'In Bentham [sc. Ricardo] he had found a great man, *his* great man, and he set it before himself to give Bentham [sc. Ricardo] an influence in his own time and in his own country' (1928, pp. 282 and 307; and Hutchison, 1953b, p. 84).

But from 1815 onwards there is no need to rely so much on conjecture or speculation. We can follow out precisely Mill's influence and methods of persuasion in his letters.

IV

The opening letter of Mill's campaign, and the first between him and Ricardo for nearly a year, was that written on 23 August 1815.[16] Before that there had been only a few miscellaneous exchanges in 1810–11, and four letters, all from Mill, in 1814. There is no suggestion that Mill is taking up a subject they had previously discussed together face to face. Mill expresses the hope that now Ricardo has 'made quite as much money for all your family, as will be conducive to their happiness', he will have leisure for 'other pursuits' and first of all for the science of political economy. For Mill explains that he is satisfied

> that you can improve so important a science far more than any other man who is devoting his attention to it, or likely to do so for Lord knows how many years.
>
> I have other projects upon you, however, besides. You now can have no excuse for not going into Parliament, and doing what you can to improve the most imperfect instrument of government.

Ricardo will find the problems of politics extremely simple, once he turns his mind to them: 'There is not much difficulty in finding out the principles on which alone good government *must of necessity depend*; and when all this is as clearly in that head of yours, as that head knows how to put it, the utility in Parliament, of even you, in spite of all your modesty, would be very great' (italics added).

However, for the time being, Mill drops the subject of Parliament; for his first main task is to urge Ricardo on with his treatise on the science of political economy. In his next letter (9 November 1815) Mill writes:

> As I am accustomed to wield the authority of a school master, I there-fore, in the genuine exercise of this honourable capacity, lay upon you my commands to begin to the first of the three heads of your proposed work, rent, profit, wages – viz. rent, without an hour's delay. If you entrust the inspection of it to me, depend upon it I shall compel you to make it all right before you have done with it.

Soon Mill is explaining to Ricardo how a treatise on the principles of political economy should be set out, that is, like a textbook of geometry, an analogy which Mill had suggested in previous writings:

> Never set down any material proposition without its immediate proof, or a reference to the very page where the proof is given. . . . On this subject (improvements in cultivation), I ordain you to perform an exercise. . . . My meaning is that you should successively answer the question, what comes first? First of all is the improvement. What comes next? Ans. The increase of produce. What comes next? Ans. A fall in the price of corn. What comes next? – and so on.
>
> (22 December 1815)

Mill breaks off at the difficult point of the analysis, but his suggestions are methodologically typical, and Ricardian economic 'theorizing' (or analysis) is in the main conceived after this pattern and based on a highly simplistic and mechanical conception of economic behaviour and processes which are to be accounted for in terms of 'proofs'.

At length, after some further robust encouragement from Mill, Ricardo sends him the draft of a large part of the *Principles* (October 1816). Mill's impression of the work is absolutely clear-cut: 'I think you have made out all your points. There is not a single proposition the proof of which I think is not irresistible' (18 November 1816). A month later, having examined some further chapters by Ricardo, Mill writes: 'Your doctrines are original and profound. I have no hesitation whatsoever in saying that they are fully and completely made out. I embrace every one of them; and am ready to defend them against all the world' (16 December 1816). Mill hardly raises one single point of doubt or difficulty.

It might indeed be said that whatever else can be claimed for Ricardo's *Principles*, certainly they possess 'originality and profundity' (though there is nothing *necessarily* virtuous in either of these qualities). But Ricardo's *Principles* certainly represented a big new departure from previous conceptions of the scope and method of Political Economy, as represented in the writings of British economists. But only a year before, Mill had confessed that 'not withstanding my passion for the science of Political Economy, it has so happened that for a good many years I have not been able to think of it [except through Ricardo's writings or conversation]'. Of course, Mill wanted to encourage the diffident Ricardo. But his immediate and complete adoption of Ricardo's new doctrines, in the exposition of which subsequent economists, even the most enthusiastic, have found serious difficulties, was almost certainly perfectly sincere. It can only be explained by the fact that Mill saw Ricardo to be applying *not only exactly the same method but also the same important assumptions* on which Mill himself had based his conclusions 7–10 years previously, and this guaranteed the soundness, and fully justified (for Mill) his unquestioning acceptance of Ricardo's new doctrines.

Soon, however, Mill is looking forward to further advancing Ricardo's political education by means of his forthcoming book, *The History of British India*:

> The subject afforded an opportunity of *laying open the principles and laws of the social order in almost all its more remarkable states, from the most rude to the most perfect with which we are yet acquainted*; and if I have been capable of explaining them, will be of some help to you, in exploring what I wish to see you thoroughly acquainted with, the course which human affairs, upon the great scale, have hitherto taken, the causes of their taking these different courses, the degree in which these courses have severally departed from the best course, and by what means they can best be made to approximate to that course. That is the field of application; and none of the pretexts you set up will avail you. *There is nothing in this knowledge mysterious, or hard – there is nothing but what anybody, who has common application, a common share of judgement, and is free from prejudice, and sinister interest, may arrive at.*
>
> (19 October 1817, italics added)

In fact, in Mill's eyes, Ricardo at this point seems to begin to bear some significant resemblance to Martin Luther: 'All great changes in society, are easily affected when the time is come. Was it not an individual, without fortune, without name, and in fact without talents, who produced the Reformation? Before I have done with you you will reason less timidly on this subject because you will know more certainly'.[17]

Ricardo in reply (9 November 1817) expresses an eager interest at the prospect of Mill's great work on the laws and progress of society: 'I am eager for information on the causes which are constantly obstructing man in the rational pursuit of his own happiness. Legislation would be comparatively an easy science if it were not so much influenced by the characters and dispositions of the people for whom it is to be undertaken.'

Perhaps we can detect in this wistful remark Ricardo's hankering after a simplified political 'model', or one of those 'strong cases', by means of which he could deal with the political world and enunciate impressively sweeping pronouncements 'in the nature of mathematical truths', by the method he had applied in political economy.

Mill, however (3 December 1817), is perfectly confident of his ability to deal with Ricardo's doubts and difficulties:

> I have no doubt about removing all your difficulties; and showing you that instead of being a science, the practical results of which must always be uncertain, rendering it always prudent to try to remain in the state we are in, rather than venture the unknown effects of a change, *legislation is essentially a science the effects of which may be computed with an extraordinary degree of certainty*; and the friends of human nature cannot proceed with too much energy in beating down every obstacle which opposes the progress of human welfare [italics added].

At last, Ricardo gets his copy of the *History* (18 December 1817): 'The long-desired book has at length arrived.' For Ricardo, it comes as a revelation:

> *If I before had had doubts of what legislation might do, to improve society, I should have none after reading what I have read of your book.* . . . My plea for caution and timidity was ignorance. . . . Legislation may not be as difficult as I imagine – I wish it may not be, for I am anxiously disposed to understand it. One of the great difficulties of the science appears to me that . . . of the government and laws of one state of society being often very ill adapted for another state of society [italics added].

We must linger for a moment over Mill's *History of India* if only to deplore the very small attention paid to this remarkable work in studies of philosophic radicalism and of the politics of classical political economy.[18] Leslie Stephen gives us no idea of it, while Halévy's hints, though penetrating and important, are all too brief. But John Stuart Mill described his father's great work as:

> one of the most instructive histories every written, and one of the books from which most benefit may be derived by a mind in the course of

making up its opinions. The Preface, among the most characteristic of my father's writings, as well as the richest in materials of thought, gives a picture which may be entirely depended on, of the sentiments and expectations with which he wrote the History.

(1924, p. 21)

The vast labours of research devoted by Mill to the historical narrative, which makes up a large part of the *History*, made it for many decades an indispensable authority.[19] But Book II of the work is concerned, as Mill had informed Ricardo, with determining 'laws of society', 'laws of human nature', 'stages of social progress', 'steps' in 'the progress of civilization', and in particular with the place of the Hindus in the 'scale of civilization', that is, with an appallingly hubristic, imperialist historicism. Mill had, of course, never been further East than, let us say, perhaps Southend, and hardly knew a word of any Oriental language. However, as he explains in his Preface, such merely empirical equipment may well be highly misleading for the historian, and is of far less importance than a grasp of 'the laws of society' and what Mill calls 'a masterly use of evidence'. Anyhow, Mill has no hesitation in pronouncing the most severe, definite and detailed condemnation of every aspect of Hindu civilization (except perhaps cloth-making) including manners, mathematics, sculpture, laws, painting, science, architecture and religion, and he concludes that the Hindus are at almost the lowest possible level in 'the scale of civilization'.

Ricardo is especially pleased with Mill's treatment of Hindu civilization. He writes off to Say (18 December 1817) and to Trower (26 January 1818):

His views on the subjects of Government, Law, Religion, Manners are profound; and his application of these views to the actual, and past state of Hinduism . . . cannot, I think, be refuted. . . . *He endeavours to refute the prevailing opinion that the Hindus are now, or ever have been, a highly civilized people. . . . I am exceedingly pleased with the work* [italics added].

Meanwhile, Mill is reassuring Ricardo as to his difficulties about the fitting of legislation to the particular state of society, or position on 'the scale of civilization', to which it is to apply (27 December 1817):

On the subject of legislation I have no doubt that we shall now understand one another. Doubtless, the laws which are adapted to an improved state of society, would not be adapted to a state of society much behind. But *it will not be difficult when we have a standard of excellence, to determine what is to be done, in all cases. The ends are there, in the first place, known – they are clear and definite.* What you have after that to determine is the choice of the means, and under glorious helps for directing the judgement [italics added].

However, Ricardo's healthy doubts are not completely flattened by Mill's steamroller, and with much native insight he cautiously directs attention to a fundamental difficulty in Mill's 'science of legislation' as applied to the government of India. May not the great criterion of utility, or the greatest happiness of the greatest number, be used to justify or even demand, the wholesale imperialistic conquest of the sub-Continent? (except in so far as the House of Commons at home might find the operation rather expensive):

> Are we to fix our eyes steadily on the end, the happiness of the governed, and pursue it at the expense of those principles which all men are agreed in calling virtuous? If so, might not Lord Wellesley, or any other ruler, disregard all the engagements of his predecessors, and by force of arms compel the submission of all the native powers of India if he could show that there was a great probability of adding to the happiness of the people by the introduction of better instruments of government. If he accomplished this end at the expense of much treasure to England, I do not think the plea would be admitted by a British House of Commons, however freely chosen. The difficulty of the doctrine of expediency or utility is to know how to balance one object of utility against another – there being no standard in nature, it must vary with the tastes, the passions and the habits of mankind. This is one of the subjects on which I require to be enlightened.
>
> (6 January 1818)

Unfortunately, there is no record in these letters showing that the enlightenment which Ricardo requested from Mill was forthcoming.[20] However, Mill continued to reassure his pupil as to 'the plain rule of utility, which will always guide you right, and in which there is no mystery' (23 September 1818). We would, however, point out that on another problem of internal policy Mill had previously suggested to Ricardo that though the principle of utility was consistent with obligations between individuals being held sacred, where *states* were concerned it was justifiable to overturn contractual obligations which clashed with the one great overriding principle: 'There is utility in making bargains between individuals strict, unless where fraud appears to have intervened. There would be utility in holding all bargains between the public and individuals null, in which the interests of the public are sacrificed' (22 December 1815).[21]

V

Before we leave this remarkable correspondence there is one further exchange between Mill and Ricardo from the year 1821 which raises the question of class antagonism, and clashes of interest. Mill remarks (23 August 1821): 'It is very curious that almost every body you meet with – whig and tory – agree in declaring their opinion of one thing that a great struggle, between the two orders, the rich and poor, is in this country commenced.'

Ricardo replies (28 August 1821) with a less pessimistic view and expresses confidence in the political wisdom of the English governing class:

> The only prospect we have of putting aside the struggle which they say has commenced between the rich and the other classes, is for the rich to yield what is justly due to the other classes, but this is the last measure which they are willing to have recourse to. I cannot help flattering myself that justice will prevail at last, without a recurrence to actual violence.

We may note, first, that this discernment of class antagonisms by Mill and Ricardo dates from 1821 when, according to Marx, 'the class struggle was still undeveloped', that is, before his cut-off date of 1830, at a period which 'was notable in England for scientific activity in the domain of political economy',[22] most notably by Ricardo. But, in fact, James Mill denounced in the most ferocious terms those who advocated the pursuit of class conflict, while Ricardo expounded doctrines of the harmony of class interests, between labourers and capitalists, in more extreme terms than any subsequent, important bourgeois 'apologist'. Ricardo argued not merely that this harmony of class interests was a fact, but that it was so 'self-evident' a conclusion of the science of political economy (as expounded by him) that 'even the lowest' would accept the point. Even Bastiat hardly went as far as this.

Regarding Mill, it must be emphasized that he was a middle-class radical, not a champion of the working class. Professor Donald Winch has very clearly pointed out how sternly Mill denounced the advocacy of labour's right to the whole product (including, for example, 'the mad nonsense of our friend Hodgskin', later so highly esteemed by Marx and Marxists and sometimes grossly misdescribed as a 'Ricardian Socialist'). According to Mill:

> These opinions, if they were to spread, would be the subversion of civilised society; worse than the overwhelming deluge of Huns and Tartars. This makes me astonished at the madness of people of another description who recommend the invasion of one species of property, so thoroughly knavish, and unprincipled, that it can never be executed without extinguishing respect for the rights of property in the whole body of the nation, and can never be spoken of with approbation, without encouraging the propagation of those other doctrines which directly strike at the root of all property.[23]

Mill continues:

> I should have little fear of the propagation of any doctrines hostile to property, because I have seldom met with a labouring man (and I have tried the experiment upon many of them) whom I could not make see that *the existence of property was not only good for the labouring man but of infinitely more importance to the labourers as a class, than to any other.*[24]

Ricardo certainly agreed with Mill's 'middle-class' view that respect for property is good for 'the workers' too. He said so himself.

In Marxist versions of the history of political economy a very important role is attributed to Ricardo as a propagator of 'the antagonism of class interests'. It is, therefore, necessary to emphasize that Ricardo believed preponderantly in the overriding harmony of class interests much more than in the kind of antagonism which Marx and Marxists ('vulgar' or otherwise) have subsequently ascribed to him, and which is a prime article of their own faith. It might be suggested that Ricardo emphasized the clash of interests between landlords and the rest of the community. But Ricardo himself *indignantly rejected*, as the most serious misrepresentation, the suggestion that he was lending any countenance to ideas of class antagonism:

> *Perhaps in no part of his book has Mr. Malthus so much mistaken me as on this subject* – he represents me as supporting the doctrine that the interests of landlords are constantly opposed to those of every other class of the community, and one would suppose from his language that I consider them as enemies of the state.
>
> *Mr. Malthus is not justified by anything I have said in pointing me out as the enemy of landlords*, or as holding any less favourable opinion of them, than of any class of the community.[25]

Otherwise Ricardo hardly went further than, first, a qualified suggestion that technical progress *might* (not necessarily would) damage the interests of labourers; and, secondly, the logically impeccable proposition that if something is divided into three relative or percentage shares, and the first of these is held constant, then an increase in the second relative or percentage share must mean a decrease in the third. Whatever partial clashes Ricardo envisaged, he regarded as decisively overridden by the broad, fundamental harmony of interests which he held to inhere in the competitive market economy, based essentially on full private property rights. Ricardo's glowing ideas about the economic harmonies are expounded as regards both the international economy, and internally, as follows:

> Under a system of perfectly free commerce, each country naturally devotes its capital and labour to such employments as are most beneficial to each. This pursuit of individual advantage is admirably connected with the universal good of the whole. By stimulating industry, by rewarding ingenuity, and by using most efficaciously the peculiar powers bestowed by nature, it distributes labour most effectively and most economically; while, by increasing the general mass of productions, it diffuses general benefit, and binds together by one common tie of interest and intercourse, the universal society of nations throughout the civilized world.
>
> (vol. I, 1951, p. 134)

What Ricardo thought about the harmony of class interests is also indicated in the following passage about the franchise, *in which not only are the interests of 'the poor labourer' and the 'rich capitalist' held to be in harmony, but it is claimed that this harmony has been so conclusively demonstrated and understood (presumably thanks to the new Science of Political Economy, as embodied in Ricardo's own teachings) that the franchise can suitably be conferred even on 'the very lowest'*:

> So essential does it appear to me, to the cause of good government, that the rights of property should be held sacred, that I would agree to deprive those of the elective franchise against whom it could justly be alleged that they considered it their interest to invade them. But in fact it can be only amongst the most needy in the community that such an opinion can be entertained. *The man of a small income must be aware how little his share would be if all the large fortunes in the kingdom were equally divided among the people. He must know that the little he would obtain by such a division could be no adequate compensation for the over-turning of a principle which renders the produce of his industry secure.* Whatever might be his gains after such a principle had been admitted would be held by a very insecure tenure, and the chance of his making any future gains would be greatly diminished; for the quantity of employment in the country must depend, not only on the quantity of capital, but upon its advantageous distribution, and, above all, on the conviction of each capitalist that he will be allowed to enjoy unmolested the fruits of his capital, his skill, and his enterprise. *To take from him this conviction is at once to annihilate half the productive industry of the country, and would be more fatal to the poor labourer than to the rich capitalist himself. This is so self-evident that men very little advanced beyond the very lowest stations in the country cannot be ignorant of it,* and it may be doubted whether any large number even of the lowest would, if they could, promote a division of property.

(1952, vol. V, p. 501, italics added)[26]

One can certainly agree with Marx regarding a certain 'naïveté' in Ricardo and also, possibly, regarding 'the scientific impartiality and love of truth characteristic of him' with which Ricardo is writing here. But though a passage similar to the above, regarding the harmony of interests between 'the poor labourer' and 'the rich capitalist', might possibly be found in the writings of Mrs Marcet – which Ricardo so warmly recommended for his daughter[27] – it seems improbable that any other major British economist in the nineteenth century would ever have penned such an extremely optimistic statement regarding politico-economic harmonies.

A certain economic pessimism is sometimes ascribed to Ricardo in respect of his forebodings about diminishing returns and the falling rate of profit. But, it seems very doubtful whether, in his view of the politico-economic prospects for the then existing system, Ricardo was basically pessimistic.[28] Certainly *politically*, Ricardo expressed a buoyant, even naive, optimism. But, in any case, economic pessimism cannot be equated with a belief in class-antagonism. Moreover, the very moderate extent to which Ricardo recognized certain clashes of class-interest did not move him one inch from upholding a strict regard for the *laissez-faire* principle in distribution. If the existence of 'conflicts' implied that there must be losers – whether these losers were labourers or landlords – *nothing must be done by government, according to Ricardo, to compensate the losers, or intervene in the free market processes which caused their losses.* In 1819 Ricardo was reported as proclaiming in Parliament:

> It could not be denied, on the whole view of the subject, that machinery did not lessen the demand for labour. . . . It might also be misapplied by occasioning the production of too much cotton, or too much cloth, *but the moment those articles ceased in consequence to pay the manufacturer, he would devote his time and capital to some other purpose.*
>
> (16 December 1819; 1952, vol. V, p. 30, italics added)

However, four years later 'the Oracle' was instructing honourable members on quite opposite lines: 'It was evident, that the extensive use of machinery, by throwing a large portion of labour into the market, while, on the other hand, there might not be a corresponding increase of demand for it, would, in some degree operate prejudicially to the working classes' (*op. cit.*, p. 305). But however fascinating may be the analytical subtleties behind Ricardo's well-known change of view about machinery, his steadfast policy-conclusion remains as an essential implication of his philosophy of political economy. In spite of the possible damage to the working classes:

> He would not tolerate any law to prevent the use of machinery. The question was, – if they gave up a system which enabled them to undersell in the foreign market, would other nations refrain from pursuing it? Certainly not. They were therefore bound, for their own interest, to continue it. Gentlemen ought, however, to inculcate this truth on the minds of the working classes – that *the value of labour, like the value of other things, depended on the relative proportion of supply and demand. If the supply of labour were greater than could be employed then the people must be miserable.* But the people had the remedy in their own hands. A little forethought, a little prudence . . .
>
> (op. cit., p. 303, italics added; speech of 30 May 1823)

Professor George Stigler has remarked that 'Ricardo is as much to be censured for his preoccupation with maximum output as certain modern economists for their preoccupation with equality' (1950, p. 10).

Perhaps this excessive preoccupation is illustrated by Ricardo's attitude to policies aimed at relieving the distress of hand-loom cotton weavers in 1820. It had been proposed that power looms should be taxed and public money applied to provide lands for those who could find no employment at their hand-looms. Ricardo's opposition to such proposals was indignant and total:

'If government interfered, they would do mischief and no good. They had already interfered, and done mischief by the poor laws. The principles of the hon. mover *would likewise violate the sacredness of property, which constituted the great security of society*' (1952, vol. V, p. 68, italics added).

VI

Perhaps to a greater extent even than with most economic theorizing the, or a, main meaning and intention of the Millian–Ricardian theories and methods can be found in the nature of the policy conclusions derived from them. Ricardo's policy conclusions, which he went into Parliament to proclaim with all the authority of the new science behind him, followed from, and depended on, with great exactness and rigidity, his 'strongly' simplified assumptions or theories. The Millian–Ricardian abstract, deductive method started from starkly unqualified assumptions (or 'strong cases') based on no systematic observation of the behaviour and knowledge of buyers and sellers, savers and spenders, parents and wage-earners. They led immediately and inevitably to sharply *laissez-faire* policy doctrines. There was little or no room for judgements of probabilities or qualifications, or for weighing up, or striking a balance between, contrasting tendencies, or for broadly political considerations, all of which belong essentially among the problems of responsible, real-world policy-making. Moreover, *Ricardo was overwhelmingly interested in policy conclusions. Abolishing the Poor Laws, cutting down the Corn Laws, stopping Public Works to relieve unemployment during depressions: this is what Ricardo was centrally concerned with, however extreme the abstractions he indulged in and however remote from the real world his models may seem to us (but not to him) to have been.* Ricardo did not buy a seat in Parliament simply to expound blackboard exercises or to read out articles for *Econometrica*. As Cannan, in terms of Ricardo's intentions, quite rightly insisted: 'Among all the delusions which prevail as to the history of English political economy there is none greater than the belief that the economics of the Ricardo school and period were of an almost wholly abstract and unpractical character' (1917, p. 302).

It may be quite legitimate, if the logical or mathematical niceties of extremely abstract 'models' are what one is primarily interested in, to concentrate one's account of Ricardo's work simply on this aspect of it. But it involves a complete misinterpretation of Ricardo's own interests and purposes to appraise his works and his purposes simply in terms of highly abstract 'model'-building for its own sake.

In fact, Ricardo's economics were of the most dangerous type: on the one hand extremely abstract, based on highly restrictive assumptions used largely for deductive facility, but also, on the other hand, intended to supply, *and regarded as supplying*, direct and trenchant implications, of immediate policy relevance, for the real world. *Laissez-faire* followed immediately and directly with inescapable logic: (1) in aggregate, macroeconomic management and policy;

66

(2) in a very stark form with regard to distribution, the labour market and the relief of poverty; and (3) with regard to the operation of markets generally, in view of their assumed, extremely rapidly self-equilibrating properties.

Taking (1) Ricardo's views on macroeconomic management and policy: *Laissez-faire* conclusions, against government action, followed logically from his (and Smith's) model. Professor Hollander has pointed out with what inexorable logic Ricardo followed out the implications of his assumptions: 'Even in the depth of economic depression Ricardo consistently insisted on the impossibility of a general deficiency of aggregate demand. The fact of unused capacity did not in any way shake his conviction that an increase in aggregate demand could not expand output' (1974, p. 23).

It must certainly be acknowledged, however, that Ricardo went much further than Adam Smith with regard to specifying a monetary framework for *laissez-faire*, which he did in his *Proposals for an Economical and Secure Currency* (1816) and his *Plan for the Establishment of a National Bank* (1824). This was a major contribution *in an area where he could claim real experience and expertise*, but a subject quite separate from his main general–theoretical interests in 'the laws of Political Economy'. Moreover, his proposals regarding the monetary framework can hardly be said to represent major qualifications or diminutions of *laissez-faire* (unless this doctrine is interpreted as equivalent to anarchism) but rather amount to proposals for the rules within which *laissez-faire* can effectively operate. The same can also be said, though considerably more questionably, regarding Ricardo's proposals for a capital levy, to reduce or remove the national debt incurred under war conditions in order to establish a peace-time normality in public finance (and which may probably have been directed primarily at the landlords).

(2) But it is with regard to distribution, wages and the relief of poverty, that Ricardo emerges as a much more drastic and thorough-going champion of *laissez-faire* than any other leading English economist. Again, his policy conclusions followed inexorably from his very clear-cut postulates, which in turn followed those of James Mill regarding the relationship between wages, subsistence and population. The Mill–Ricardo postulates, or 'model', were so much more sharply and more rigidly applied than in the corresponding much looser Smithian doctrine of the natural wage, that they should be considered as amounting to a different proposition or theory. In the *Principles* Ricardo lays it down: 'Like all other contracts, wages should be left to the fair and free competition of the market, and should never be controlled by the interference of the legislature' (1951, vol. I, p. 105).

But it was to Poor Law policy that Ricardo applied the full logic of his natural wage theory. In his maiden speech in Parliament he argued: 'If parents felt assured that an asylum would be provided for their children, in which they would be treated with humanity and tenderness, then there would be no check to that increase of population which was so apt to take place among the labouring classes' (1952, vol. V, p. 1).

To his friend, the magistrate Trower, Ricardo urged (27 January 1817): 'The population can only be repressed by diminishing the encouragement to its *excessive* increase – by leaving contracts between the poor and their employers perfectly free.'

Otherwise the prospect seemed to Ricardo to be alarming: 'The population and the rates would go on increasing in a regular progression till the rich were reduced to poverty, and till there would no longer be any distinction of ranks.'

As Ricardo put it, the aim must be to cut poor relief to the limit: 'Is not this to be done by refusing all relief in the first instance to any but those whose necessities absolutely require it – to administer it to them in the most sparing manner and lastly *to abolish the poor laws altogether?*' (1952, vol. VII, p. 125, italics added).

Again Ricardo insisted: 'Great evils . . . result from the idea which the Poor Laws inculcate that the poor have a *right* to relief' (op. cit., p. 248).

It is almost totally irrelevant to protest that Ricardo, as a generous, warm-hearted man, would, of course, have rejoiced to see a rise in the living-standards of the labouring class, or that he believed that such a rise might *possibly*, or eventually, come about. A rather vague, humane hope cannot be said to become an objective of economic policy unless some means are specified for approaching the objective. A belief in, or the promotion of, the progress of the British economy did not, of itself, imply the lifting of 'the great Malthusian difficulty' (as Cairnes was to call it half a century later); nor would simply the removal of what Ricardo regarded as the abuses of the Poor Laws. If the account is correct that J. S. Mill was detained at a police station for distributing pamphlets about contraception, at least he can be said to have envisaged and propagated *some kind* of means via which the natural wage might eventually and permanently be raised. But as an admirably respectable family man of his time such a topic was publicly unmentionable for Ricardo.

Anyhow, he certainly went considerably further with regard to the natural wage than simply making the 'assumption for certain theoretical purposes of wages at subsistence level due to pressure of population'; or merely engaging in 'grown-up talk about the implications of certain assumptions' (Robbins, 1952, pp. 84 and 215).

(3) Ricardo's 'model' of self-adjusting markets moving smoothly and rapidly to a beneficent equilibrium, depended crucially on his assumption of perfect (or adequate) knowledge. He employed this absolutely vital basic postulate more drastically and consequentially than any economist before him. As with other methods and models, James Mill and Ricardo rigorously pressed this postulate to extremes, or to the 'strong case'. In fact, to Ricardo must be ascribed the responsibility for placing the perfect knowledge postulate firmly in position at the foundations of equilibrium economics, with uncertainty – or most of the problems of the real world – 'rigorously' excluded. For example, in his *Principles* Ricardo assumes: 'Whilst every man is free to employ his capital where he pleases, he will naturally seek for it that employment which is most

advantageous; he will naturally be dissatisfied with a profit of 10 per cent, if by removing his capital he can obtain a profit of 15 per cent.'

In a letter to Malthus (1811) on international payments Ricardo acknowledged the perfect knowledge postulate *as basic to his method*:

> The first point to be considered is, what is the interest of countries in the case supposed? the second what is their practice? Now it is obvious that I need not be greatly solicitous about this latter point; it can clearly demonstrate that the interest of the public is as I have stated it. It would be no answer to me to say that men were ignorant of the best and cheapest mode of conducting their business and paying their debts, because that is a question of fact and not of science, and might be urged against almost every proposition in Political Economy.[29]

Keynes wrote: 'I accuse the classical economic theory of being itself one of those pretty polite techniques which tries to deal with the present by abstracting from the fact that we know very little about the future' (1937, p. 186).

It is Ricardo and Ricardian economics against whom this accusation should pre-eminently be directed.[30]

Ricardo's assumptions regarding the rapidity and smoothness with which markets moved to a beneficent equilibrium emerged logically from this basic postulate of perfect knowledge. His treatment of agricultural protection illustrates his conceptions as to the smoothness and rapidity of economic adjustments, as well as his occasional doubts. It is true that in his pamphlet *On Protection to Agriculture* (1822) Ricardo conceded that such protection should be withdrawn gradually, 'with as little delay as possible, consistently with a due regard to temporary interests' (1952, vol. VI, p. 266).

But in Parliament he had expressed extraordinary optimism about the speed of the adjustment process so far as labour was concerned. With regard to allowing free imports of corn: 'He would endeavour to show what would be the real effect. The prices of corn would be reduced immediately, and agriculture might be distressed more than at present. *But the labour of this country would be immediately applied to the production of other and more profitable commodities, which might be exchanged for cheap foreign corn*' (1952, vol. V, p. 82, italics added; speech of 7 March 1821).

The idea that masses of agricultural workers and farmers, with their traditional way of life – even if they had the resources to do so – *know whither* to move off '*immediately*' to the 'production of other and more profitable commodities', seems to suggest a failure to distinguish between a hyper-abstract model and the real world, which points to something having gone seriously astray with regard to the vitally important and delicate relationship between analysis and policy.[31]

Like some economists subsequently, Ricardo promised tremendous Utopian gains, if only just one or two of his favourite measures were adopted, thus bringing the British economy up to the full individualist, market ideal:

This would be the happiest country in the world, *and its progress in prosperity would be beyond the power of imagination to conceive, if we got rid of two great evils* – the national debt and the corn laws. . . . If this evil were removed, *the course of trade and the prices of articles would become natural and right*; and if corn were exported or imported, as in other countries, without restraint, this country, possessing the greatest skill, the greatest industry, the best machinery, and every other advantage in the highest degree, *its prosperity and happiness would be incomparably, and almost inconceivably great.*

(1952, vol. V, p. 55, italics added)[32]

Certainly political preconceptions played some part in reinforcing Ricardian policy conclusions. As Professor Fetter has observed:

Ricardo's belief that self-interest was the well-spring of economic development also went beyond Smith in Ricardo's almost pathological feeling that the government did everything badly. *The difference between Smith and Ricardo on the role of government was a subtle but nevertheless important one, and one that I believe most economists have neglected or underplayed. The Wealth of Nations* has far more examples than the *Principles of Political Economy* of appropriate fields for government action. But this was not the whole difference . . . Ricardo gives the impression of the universal ineptness of government.

(1969, p. 73, italics added)

Of course governments seem especially inept in so far as one is tacitly assuming that individuals are omniscient. This political preconception against government activity had also been expressed by James Mill who maintained, regarding government generally that: 'Every farthing which is spent upon it, beyond the expense necessary for maintaining law and order, is so much dead loss to the nation, contributes so far to keep down the annual produce, and to diminish the happiness of the people' (1966, p. 157).

These sturdy sentiments were echoed by his pupil: 'The country had a right to insist, and I hope will insist, on the most rigid economy in every branch of the public expenditure' (Ricardo, 1952, vol. VII, p. 90).

Moreover: 'We very soon arrive at the knowledge that agriculture, commerce, and manufactures flourish best when left without interferences' (1952, vol. VIII, p. 133).

Millian–Ricardian political economy was much more incisively *laissez-faire* in its policy implications than *The Wealth of Nations* partly because of political preconceptions, but partly, or mainly, *because Ricardo had so sharpened and hardened the assumptions and hypotheses of The Wealth of Nations, especially in relation, (1) to natural wages and the vast policy implications which this assumption contained; and (2) with regard to the perfect knowledge postulate with its implication of smooth and immediate equilibration.*

In his eloquent defence of the classical economists against the charge of advocating any crude or harsh *laissez-faire* doctrines, Lord Robbins can be considered well-justified with regard to Adam Smith, Malthus, Senior, J. S. Mill and others: *but not with regard to Ricardo*, who is not merely the *only*, but outstandingly the *most*, thoroughgoing advocate of *laissez-faire* among the major British economists. Of course political preconceptions do, as they must, play some part in such an attitude, but such preconceptions were powerfully aided and abetted by the Millian–Ricardian abstract method and the particular positive economic assumptions which Ricardo took over from Mill.

VII

Shortly before his own death, and thirteen years after Ricardo's, James Mill made a further remarkable contribution to Millian–Ricardian political economy in his essay 'Whether Political Economy is Useful' (1836). This is another work, previously rather inaccessible and little known, which has been made conveniently available by Professor Winch's edition (1966). It is reasonable to assume that this work presents a view of economic knowledge which Mill had long held and which he had pressed upon his pupil Ricardo. The argument is developed by means of a dialogue between A and B, B being Mill himself and A a pupil (perhaps originally Ricardo). Mill brings out very clearly the extent and nature of the authority, and 'the extraordinary degree of certainty', as Mill put it, which was claimed by him, and also more widely and generally, for political economy. This had been indicated by Mill's references to Newton, and Ricardo's to Euclid, and by means of their comparisons with mathematics.[33] The significance of this final essay by Mill justifies lengthy quotation. Mill is concerned to establish and explain the basis for the scientific authority of political economy:

> *J.M.:* Political Economy, therefore, possesses one of the qualities which you represented as essential to a science, that it should explain the whole of the subject to which it relates.
> *Pupil:* It is so.
> *J.M.:* The next of your essentials was, that the doctrines should be true. What, then is the test to which we shall apply the doctrines of political economy, in order to know whether they are true?
> *Pupil:* The disagreement about them, of political economists themselves, is a sufficient proof of the uncertainty, at least, of all their conclusions.
> . . .
> *J.M.:* Is it, then, your opinion, that truth is never disputed; never after it is proved? You would, in that case, reduce the number of established truths to a short catalogue. It is even denied that the establishment of property is useful, or the institution of government.
> *Pupil:* I do not consider it a presumption against an opinion, that it is

71

disputed by a few wrong-headed people. . . . The opinion of people who are capable of understanding the subject, and who have used the due means of understanding it, are the only people whose opinions afford a presumption either for or against any proposition or propositions regarding it.

. . .

J.M.: Now all political economists, in whatever else they disagree, are all united in this opinion, that the science is one of great importance. There is, therefore, according to you, the strongest presumption of its importance.

Pupil: I do not dispute the importance it might be of, were a set of propositions embracing the whole subject actually established. But I am justified in holding it of no importance, so long as nothing important is established.

. . .

J.M.: But what proof have you that the generality of those who study and know political economy, are not agreed about its doctrines?

Pupil: See what contradiction there is, on almost all the leading points, among the writers on the subject.

J.M.: I believe you are here led into an error, by a superficial appearance. . . . *You take the proportion of the writers who oppose the standard doctrines, for the proportion of the well-instructed people who oppose them; but the fact is very different. The writers are some half-dozen individuals, or less. And who are the people who write in such a case? Why, any creature who takes it into his head that he sees something in a subject which nobody else has seen.* On the other hand, they who, after studying the subject, see the truth of the doctrines generally taught, acquiesce in them, hold to them, act upon them, and do not write. Every creature who objects, writes: those who believe, do not write.

(1966, pp. 378ff., italics added)

The Pupil's last words are simply: 'I cannot but agree with you.'

James Mill presents here the standard self-sealing mechanism: anyone who seriously criticizes 'the standard doctrines' automatically disqualifies himself. Thus the authority of the new science of political economy, and its great 'laws of society', is based on the authority of 'the well-instructed people' who include a number of recognized writers together with an allegedly dominant silent majority, who do not write but 'believe' in the 'standard doctrines' – such as that, for example: 'Every individual in the nation uniformly makes purchases, or does what is equivalent to making purchases, with every farthing's worth which accrues to him' (1966, p. 136).

Or, as announced by Ricardo to the House of Commons in a time of serious unemployment: 'When he heard honourable members talk of employing capital in the formation of roads and canals, they appeared to overlook the fact that the capital thus employed must be withdrawn from some other quarter' (1952, vol. V, p. 32).

On the basic principles Ricardo had claimed epistemological parity with Newton's achievements in physics for his extremely abstract proposition about economic progress, the rise in rents and fall in profits: 'It appears to me that the progress of wealth, whilst it encourages accumulation, has a natural tendency to produce this effect and *is as certain as the principle of gravitation*' (1952, vol. VI, p. 204, italics added).

Meanwhile, as we have seen, according to his mentor, James Mill: 'No proposition is better established than this, that the multiplication of the human species is always in proportion to the means of subsistence' (1966, p. 157).

Indeed such 'standard doctrines' as these, faithfully 'believed' by an alleged silent majority, are always of the kind, in the Mill–Ricardo language, of which 'none but the prejudiced are ignorant'.

Or they are: 'a truth which admits not a doubt'.

Or such that 'no proposition is more incontrovertible', or 'seems to be more certain'.[34]

It has been held that Ricardo's great contribution, overriding that of any particular one of the various propositions and theories which are associated with his name, was that of method, or 'the technique of analysis': 'The classical economists, and *Ricardo in particular*, discovered something more important than any single generalisation; they discovered *the technique of economic analysis itself*.'[35]

Of course it is possible to take a different view of the method developed by Ricardo – as Schumpeter, in fact, did:

The comprehensive vision of the universal inter-dependence of all elements in the economic system that haunted Thünen probably never cost Ricardo as much as an hour's sleep. His interest was in the clear-cut results of direct, practical significance. In order to get this he cut that general system to pieces, bundled up as large parts of it as possible in cold storage – so that as many things as possible should be frozen and 'given'. He then piled one simplifying assumption upon another until, having really settled everything by these assumptions, he was left with only a few aggregative variables between which, given these assumptions, he set up simple one-way relations so that, in the end, the desired results emerged almost as tautologies. For example, a famous Ricardian theory is that profits 'depend upon' the price of wheat. And upon his implicit assumptions and in the particular sense in which terms of the proposition are to be understood, that is not only true, but undeniably, in fact trivially, so. Profits could not possibly depend upon anything else, since everything else is 'given', that is, frozen. It is an excellent theory that can never be refuted and lacks nothing save sense. The habit

73

of applying results of this character to the solution of practical problems we shall call the Ricardian Vice.

(1954, p. 472)

The Millian–Ricardian contribution to method, of which Mill's share was certainly a very large one, has had, and still has, a vast influence on the subject a century and a half later, and has persisted longer and more consequentially even than the role or influence of most of Ricardo's particular propositions or theories. Far from being confined to recent 'neo-Ricardian' fashions, the Mill–Ricardo method can be seen at work in neoclassical and in some branches of 'Keynesian' theorizing and in the treatment of the principles of economic policy (1954, p. 472).[36]

The contrast in method with *The Wealth of Nations* seems sufficiently profound, extreme and consequential, as to justify the adjective 'revolutionary'. The integration of history with analysis and theory so superbly, and uniquely, achieved in Adam Smith's work was shattered, hardly ever after to be fully recovered in a major treatise (except, perhaps, in its own historicist way, in Karl Marx's *Capital*). Economic history was left largely to rebels and outsiders. As an economic historian has described the consequences of the methodological revolution of Ricardo (and James Mill):

The historical aspects of the subject during a period of enormous structural change in the economy were left, by and large, to a handful of non-academic Victorian worthies. Why was the genesis of economic history so long delayed in a country and in a period which presents so much of crucial importance to the economic historian today? The simple answer is that economics as understood by the classical economists *of the nineteenth century* was an a-historical subject, not to say an anti-historical one, while history was not conceived as being concerned with things economic. The method adopted by what became known as 'the dismal science' was that of logic and deduction from abstract principles rather than that of empirical investigation and historical inquiry. The ample historical digressions employed by Smith in *The Wealth of Nations* (1776) conspicuously did not relieve the pages of David Ricardo's *Principles of Political Economy* (1817), and it was the approach laid down by Ricardo which dominated classical political economy in England. John Stuart Mill's *Principles of Political Economy* (1848), though concerned to some extent with what he called 'applications' as well as with the 'principles' themselves, followed Ricardo in treating economics in a basically non-historical manner. Economic thought in England in the generations dominated by Ricardo, Mill and the Benthamite distaste for the study of the past is to be contrasted with the line of development taking place at the same time in Germany. While Mill's system of economic principles became entrenched in English thought, the approach to economics in

74

Germany was radically altered during the 1840s and after by the so-called 'historical school' of economists.

(Harte, 1971, p. xiii)[37]

In the second edition of his *Essay on Population* (1803) and again in the Introduction to his *Principles of Political Economy* (1820), Malthus did *something* to uphold the empirical–historical method of Adam Smith. But the methodological protests of Malthus, like his fundamental theoretical protests regarding effective demand, had little effect compared with the orthodoxies so triumphantly established by Ricardo and the Mills (in spite of the various criticisms and alternatives which emerged for a time in the 1830s and 1840s).

Malthus implicitly contrasted his own views on method with those of Mill and Ricardo when he wrote: 'The science of political economy bears a nearer resemblance to the science of morals and politics than to that of mathematics.'

A similar reference was implied when Malthus was denouncing the avoidance of empirical testing and oversimplified monocausal 'models' and theories: 'These writers . . . do not sufficiently try their theories by a reference to that enlarged and comprehensive experience. . . . In political economy the desire to simplify has occasioned an unwillingness to acknowledge the operation of more causes than one' (1836, pp. 4–5).[38]

Referring simply to their doctrines on 'macroeconomics', Keynes, rather controversially, exclaimed: 'If only Malthus, instead of Ricardo, had been the parent stem from which nineteenth-century economics proceeded, what a much wiser and richer place the world would be to-day' (1933, p. 144).

Whether or not one is prepared to conclude, on the basis of Keynes's speculative historical hypothesis, that the world would have been a much *richer* place had Malthus's views had more influence, it may well be reasonable to claim that the world would have been a *wiser* place, if Malthus's later modest caution regarding the dangers of abstraction, and the limits of economic knowledge, had prevailed over the excessive pretensions and overconfidence of the Millian–Ricardian philosophy and method of political economy.

The Millian–Ricardian philosophy, or methodology, was supported by a newly elaborated version of the history of the subject in the construction of which J. R. McCulloch and J. S. Mill – as well as James Mill – played notable parts. According to this version, political economy was relatively a very new subject, born in 1776 with *The Wealth of Nations*; but it was one which had made triumphantly rapid progress in the next half or three-quarters of a century. Scientific laws of production, distribution, exchange and consumption, had been discovered, regarding the 'certainty' of which there was as much perfect and valid concurrence, *among those entitled to hold an opinion*, as existed in the science of physics, for example. In fact, regarding some vital, central theories, the subject had reached perfection with nothing for future generations to clear up.

VIII

The tendency to generalize about the English 'classical' economists has fostered the erasing of vital distinctions, notably, for example, of this important methodological contrast between *The Wealth of Nations* and Ricardo's *Principles*. The fruitful combination of history and empirically significant theory in *The Wealth of Nations* was broken. History was largely extruded from the orthodox conception of the subject for decades to come. The legacy of the Mill–Ricardo methodological revolution was one of insufficiently controlled abstraction and over-simplification on the one hand, and of over-confident pretensions on the other hand. Traces of this legacy were still discernible in economics a century and a half after Ricardo's death. In other words, in respect of the Ricardian methodological revolution there were very serious intellectual losses. Again, the consensus or majority view, as in the case of the Smithian revolution, would be that the gains far outweighed the losses (if these were admitted as significant). For Ricardo is the intellectual hero both of Marxists ('vulgar' and otherwise) and of the more dogmatic, non-Smithian kind of classical liberal. Especially, he is the patron saint of the devotees of – an often misleading and largely irrelevant – 'rigour', and of those who like to assume an air of intense intellectual strenuousness and 'profundity'. To mention fundamental doubts regarding his contribution will seem to be bad form, or even unprofessional. Nevertheless, though we were happy to subscribe to the consensus view regarding the Smithian revolution, we are *not* regarding the methodological transformation brought about by James Mill and Ricardo. In fact, we would conclude, as Walter Bagehot concluded:

> It must be remembered that Ricardo . . . had no large notion of what science was. . . . To the end of his days, indeed, he never comprehended what he was doing. He dealt with abstractions without knowing that they were such; he thoroughly believed that he was dealing with real things. He thought that he was considering actual human nature in its actual circumstances, when he was really considering a fictitious nature in fictitious circumstances. And James Mill, his instructor on general subjects, had on this point as little true knowledge as he had himself. James Mill, above all men, believed that you could work out the concrete world of human polity and wealth from a few first truths.
>
> (1895, p. 205)

Bagehot then goes on to maintain that the kind of abstractions worked out by Mill and Ricardo might constitute useful 'preliminary work', before the real-world problems, or 'life and practice', were reached. But neither Bagehot nor subsequent economists recognized the extent to which the Ricardian abstractions and the descendants thereof, depended on the perfect knowledge postulate, nor the magnitude of the simplification, or over-simplification, which this postulate represents, the postulate which plays such a vital role in abstract, deductive economics.

76

ADDENDUM (1993)

George Stigler once remarked regarding the state and development of political economy in the first two decades of the nineteenth century:

> English economics was in a state of ferment at the beginning of the nineteenth century; Adam Smith had founded no cult. The period teemed with able economists; yet David Ricardo, within a decade of his debut, was the acknowledged leader of the young science of economics. Within this decade, indeed, his chief work was done; and it was sufficient to make him the most influential economist of the century. This was an extraordinary achievement of an extraordinary man.
>
> (1965, p. 156)

Certainly this Mill–Ricardo *coup* was an extraordinary achievement, the intellectual beneficence of which has never been questioned, as seriously as it should have been, by most historians of economic thought. Among the many 'able economists' whose works and ideas suffered in influence were such outstandingly important writers as Thornton, Malthus, Lauderdale and Bentham.

Today, one is surely entitled to question whether the leadership provided by Ricardo regarding either the theory of value, or 'macroeconomic' and monetary analysis, or method, represented anything like the best available outcome for the 'science'. On such central theoretical issues as labour, utility and value, on the one hand, or money, saving and investing – or saving-is-investing – on the other hand, Ricardo's dogmatic leadership was wrongheaded. In particular, the effects of Ricardian leadership, regarding methodology, notably the tendency to extreme empirically undisciplined abstraction (in spite of appealing so strongly to many late twentieth-century academics, both neoclassical and Marxist), have, in one form or another, been deplorable right down to the present day, not least in the exaggerated and pretentious over-confidence in its own achievements.

NOTES

1 This piece appeared, virtually unaltered, as chapter 2 (pp. 26ff.) of Hutchison, 1978. Section IV and some other paragraphs appeared originally in 'James Mill and the Political Education of Ricardo', in *The Cambridge Journal*, November 1953, pp. 81ff.

2 See Sir John Hicks, 1975, p. 322, and 1976, pp. 207ff.; and H. G. Johnson, 1975, pp. 23ff.

3 As late as 18 September 1820 Ricardo writes to Mill: 'It is impossible that I should be offended by any offer of a fee which Mr. Napier might make me – nor does my pride stand in the way of my accepting it, if it is usual for persons who are amateurs, and not worth to be called authors, to be paid for their articles.'

4 See D. Ricardo, 1952, vol. VI, p. xv, and A. Bain, 1882, p. 74.

5 E. Halévy, 1928, p. 272. As Walter Bagehot emphasized regarding 'the doctrines

of James Mill: 'If Ricardo had never seen James Mill he would probably have written many special pamphlets of great value on passing economic problems, but he would probably not have written *On the Principles of Political Economy and Taxation*, and thus founded an abstract Science' (1895, p. 204).

6 Professor George Stigler refers to this Essay of 1804 as 'a first, very poor pamphlet on foreign trade' (1965, p. 306). We are not concerned here with the quality of the pamphlet but with its influence on Ricardo.

7 See A. Smith, 1937, p. 482.

8 *Op. cit.*, p. 56 (italics added). Over half a century later J. S. Mill was still upholding the same argument just when the importation of grain into this country, exported from America and other overseas countries, was expanding massively. See J. S. Mill, 1909, I.xiii.3, and IV.iv.7.

9 On the other hand, Professor Ingrid Rima has convincingly argued that the Ricardian problem of distributive shares comes from Mill's essay of 1804 and that 'analytically speaking, the behaviour of the distributive shares was Mill's chief concern' in this essay. Professor Rima goes on to emphasize how Mill's work 'paved the way *attitudinally* for the Ricardian model', and contributed to the development of the conceptual framework within which Ricardo's positive economics took shape' (1975, pp. 115 and 118; I am grateful to Professor W. Thweatt of Vanderbilt University for this reference).

10 1966, pp. 135–6 (italics added). Mill's strong anti-landlord opinions are expressed in this essay of 1808: 'The fact is that land in this country bears infinitely less than its due proportion of taxes, while commerce is loaded with them' (p. 96).

11 *Op. cit.*, pp. 133n and 144.

12 See Ricardo, vol. VI, 1952, p. 16. See also my article: 'Bentham as an Economist', 1956.

13 See A. Bain, 1882, p. 465. Professor R. S. Sayers has pointed out that the sweeping triumph of Ricardo in this controversy was by no means an unqualified gain for nineteenth-century monetary theory, as the sound points in Bosanquet's argument tended to be overlooked. Professor Sayers maintains that many of Ricardo's monetary doctrines were permeated and vitiated by the assumption 'of instantaneous adjustment to a long-run equilibrium' and concludes that Ricardo's influence 'was a major disaster'. (See 1971, p. 37 et *passim*.)

14 It is typical that Ricardo starts by castigating Bosanquet for 'availing himself of the vulgar charge, which has lately been so often countenanced, and in places too high, against theorists. He cautions the public against listening to their speculations before they have submitted them to the test of fact' (see Ricardo, 1951, vol. III, pp. 160 and 181). Mill and Ricardo obviously resisted and rejected suggestions of empirical testing – like many of their 'model'-building successors.

15 Professor W. O. Thweatt has concluded that we owe the early development of the doctrine of comparative advantage to James Mill rather than to Ricardo or Torrens. Regarding Mill's influence on Ricardo, Professor Thweatt emphasizes the use of 'Mill's words' by Ricardo in his *Economical and Secure Currency* and endorses Patten's view, approvingly cited by Sraffa, that 'Mill wrote or at least inspired the first three paragraphs of the Preface' to the *Principles*. He holds that Mill's hand may also be noted in the translations from J. B. Say and in the – according to Sraffa – 'unmistakably characteristic' phrases in the conclusion on the poor laws of the chapter 'On Wages'. (See 1976, pp. 222 and 232.)

I must, moreover, agree that Thweatt is largely justified in maintaining that George Stigler and myself were wrong in suggesting that Mill was inactive on economic matters around 1814–15. Thweatt rightly stresses the importance of Mill's article of 1814 on the Corn Laws and its influence on Ricardo. Though

peculiarly painful to do so, I must even concede that William Thweatt may be justified in observing that an abbreviation of mine of a quotation of a letter from Mill
(of 9 November 1815) was 'not quite cricket'. (See Thweatt, 1976, p. 214.)

16 References to letters to and from Ricardo are given by the dates by which they are
ordered in *The Works*, ed. P. Sraffa, vols. VI–IX inclusive, 1952.

17 Mill had made a considerable study of Luther when he translated and edited with
copious notes, *An Essay on the Spirit and Influence of the Reformation of Luther*, by C.
Villers, 1805. Among Mill's 'copious notes' is one lending the most enthusiastic
support to the doctrine of Perfectibility: 'That impulse which every individual
experiences to better his condition, and which is the inexhaustible source of
improvement in the individual, is an equally necessary and inexhaustible source of
improvement to the species' (p. 25).

18 See the valuable article by Duncan Forbes (1951): 'James Mill and India'. Mr
Forbes described Mill's *History* as 'a good and perennially useful example of the
influence on the minds of administrators and politicians of half-baked "philosophical" history'. Mr Forbes further points out that 'it is clear that Mill's method
in the *History of India* was really deductive, as in the *Essay of Government in which the
"experience test" is purposely rejected, as also in the abstract political economy of Ricardo*'
(italics added).

19 Mill's *History* was edited and continued by H. H. Wilson, FRS, Professor of
Sanskrit at Oxford (and it is his edition, published in 1858, a year after the Mutiny,
that we have used). Wilson worked on Mill's *History* because he regarded it as 'the
most valuable work upon the subject which has yet been published', but he nevertheless considered it necessary to criticize Mill's judgements on Hindu civilization
in extraordinarily severe terms: 'He has elaborated a portrait of the Hindus which
has no resemblance to the original and which almost outrages humanity. . . . *The
History of British India* is open to censure for its obvious unfairness and injustice, but
in the effects which it is likely to exercise upon the connection between the people of
England and the people of India, it is chargeable with more than literary demerit:
its tendency is evil; it is calculated to destroy all sympathy between the rulers and
the ruled; to preoccupy the minds of those who issue annually from Great Britain,
to monopolize the posts of honour and power in Hindustan, with an unfounded
aversion towards those over whom they exercise that power, and from whom they
enforce that honour; and to substitute for those generous and benevolent feelings,
which the situation of the younger servants of the Company in India naturally
suggests, sentiments of disdain, suspicion, and dislike, uncongenial to their age and
character, and wholly incompatible with the full and faithful discharge of their
obligations to Government and to the people. There is reason to fear that these
consequences are not imaginary, and that a harsh and illiberal spirit has of late
years prevailed in the conduct and councils of the rising service in India, which
owes its origin to impressions imbibed in early life from the *History* of Mr. Mill'
(p. xiii).

20 It should be noticed that Mill does give a partial answer to Ricardo's question,
further on in the *History* (vol. VI, p. 286): 'Even where the disparity of civilization
and knowledge were very great; and where it was beyond dispute that a civilized
country was about to bestow upon a barbarous one the greatest of all possible
benefits, a good and beneficent government; even here, it would require the strongest circumstances to justify the employment of violence or force.' But what are 'the
strongest circumstances', and who is the judge of them? Obviously Mill does not clear
up the question of principle as to the implications of the magic formula of utility
'which will always guide you right, and in which there is no mystery'. The formula
becomes no plainer when it appears as the criterion of civilization as well as of all

action: 'Exactly in proportion as *Utility* is the object of every pursuit may we regard a nation as civilized. Exactly in proportion as its ingenuity is wasted on contemptible and mischievous objects, though it may be, in itself, an ingenuity of no ordinary kind, the nation may safely be denounced as barbarous' (vol. II, p. 105).

21 James Mill and his pupil Ricardo may be seen as propagators of the 'false individualism' which leads towards absolute state power. See F. A. Hayek on 'Individualism: True and False' (1949, pp. 1–32).

22 See the 'Nachwort' to the second edition (1873) of *Das Kapital*.

23 Letter to Brougham, 3 September 1832, quoted in A. Bain, 1882, p. 364, and by D. Winch, 1966, p. 202. Professor Winch emphasizes that 'Mill wished to substitute middle-class rule for aristocratic domination. He was quite unable to understand the nature of the working-class movement.' Positively, Mill held quite a different view of the class struggle from that of Marx.

24 See A. Bain, 1882, p. 365 (italics added).

25 *Works*, 1951, vol. II, pp. 117–19 (italics added). Again, in a letter to Trower (21 July 1820), Ricardo insists: 'I do not consider landlords as enemies to the public good.' Here is a contemporary, Marxistically-inclined interpretation (unsupported by any actual quotations or texts) which Ricardo himself would have repudiated with the same indignation as he did Malthus's misinterpretation: 'His account of the landowner's interests, and his assertion of the need to import cheap food to England, amounted to a declaration of war on the established authorities, and pointed to a serious class conflict at the heart of the new system. In addition, Ricardo's theory implied that capitalism was subject to a process of internal degeneration' (G. Duncan, 1973, p. 51). Professor Duncan also writes (p. 114) of how Marx 'approved of Ricardo's clear-eyed cynicism'. It surely involves a total misreading of Ricardo's character and writings to discover in them the slightest drop of cynicism.

26 B. Inglis (1972, p. 205) points out how the premise was constantly appearing in Ricardo's writings: 'that the legislature must not be allowed to infringe the rights of property'. Dr Gunnar Myrdal has explained Ricardo's 'labour' theory of value in terms of Locke's doctrines regarding property. He asks: 'Is there any other way of accounting for Ricardo's labour theory of value? *It is no more than an unsupported hypothesis which leads to insuperable difficulties without being of any analytical use*' (1953, p. 73, italics added). Of course the labour theory is of great *ideological* use in extruding notions of subjective utility and hence of individual choice, and so justifying authoritarian, or even Stalinist, regimes.

27 Ricardo believed enthusiastically in the popularization of political economy. He writes to Mill (January 1818): 'You are correct in an opinion I have heard you give that the most intricate parts of Political Economy might be made familiar to the people's understanding . . . and a subject which appears at first view so difficult is within the grasp of a moderate share of talents'. On Mrs Marcet, see his letter to Mill of 10 December 1821, in which, regarding Mill's own elementary textbook, Ricardo regrets 'that you used the word "procreation" so often in a book you call a school book'. Presumably Ricardo, no more than Malthus, would have discussed publicly the subject, or methods, of birth control.

28 See Professor Samuel Hollander (1974), who produces a great deal of evidence for attributing to Ricardo a high degree of economic *optimism* regarding the British economy of his day, suggesting a quite Malthus-like ambiguity, on Ricardo's part, regarding the 'tendencies' set out in his 'model'. This model certainly lends itself, perhaps very misleadingly, to highly pessimistic interpretations – which have, of course, been seized upon and magnified for the purposes of political propaganda. Professor Hollander emphasizes (p. 45) 'Ricardo's confidence in future prospects',

and quotes Professor G. S. L. Tucker's 'careful' observation: 'Ricardo's principal conclusion, immanent throughout his work, was that profits and the rate of new capital accumulation were lower in Britain than they must otherwise have been under a more enlightened economic policy. . . . But even if the Corn Laws were not repealed, Englishmen could still look forward to a long period of economic progress' (1960, p. 162).

29 See 1951, vol. I, p. 88, and 1952, vol. VI, p. 64. The earlier comments of mine (1937) on these two passages seem reasonable: 'With Ricardo there is no uncertainty as to the relative advantages of different lines of investment. The assumption is tacitly made that it is perfectly foreseen that one will yield 10% and the other 15%, and people "naturally" select 15%'. And regarding the second passage: 'The only possible interpretation of this passage . . . seems to be that economists are not to concern themselves with what actually happens in the economic world, as this is a question of fact not of science. The "scientist" assumes that people are fully equipped with certain knowledge' (1937, p. 637).

30 Ricardo apparently regarded as quite valid the assumption that 'the wants of society were well known'. For he used this proposition in criticizing the treatment by Malthus of demand in relation to value. Ricardo wrote: 'When the wants of society are well known, when there are hundreds of competitors who are willing to satisfy those wants, on the condition only that they shall have the known and usual profits, there can be no such rule for regulating the value of commodities' (i.e. any dependence on 'the wants of mankind'). See 1951, vol. II, p. 24. This passage was pointed out to me by Dr M. Harvey-Phillips.

31 See Hutchison, 1953a, pp. 269–71. Certainly Ricardo at times entertained doubts. There is a very interesting letter written during the depressed year 1819 in which he writes: 'We all have to lament the present distressed situation of the labouring-classes in this country, but the remedy is not very apparent to me. The correcting of our errors in legislation with regard to trade would ultimately be of considerable service to all classes of the community, but it would afford no immediate relief: on the contrary I should expect that it would plunge us into additional difficulties. If all the prohibitions were removed from the importation of corn and many other articles, which could not fail to follow, this would ruin most of the farmers, and many of the manufacturers, and although others would be benefited, the derangement which such measures would occasion in the actual employments of capital, and the changes which become necessary, would rather aggravate than relieve the distress under which we are now labouring' (13 October 1819). Certainly there is wisdom here in the realization of ignorance and the scepticism regarding conclusions deduced from long-run, rapidly self-equilibrating models. It amounts to an extreme contrast with the more typical kinds of Millian–Ricardian policy analysis.

32 Brougham commented, not unfairly, on this speech as follows: 'His hon friend, the member for Portarlington, had argued as if he had dropped from another planet; as if this were a land of most perfect liberty of trade – as if there were no taxes – no drawbacks – no bounties – no searchers – on any branch of trade but agriculture; as if, in this Utopian world, of his hon friend's creation, the first measure of restriction ever thought on was that on the importation of corn; as if all classes of the community were alike – as if all the trades were on an equal footing; and that, in this new state, we were called upon to decide the abstract question, whether or not there should be a protecting price for corn? But we were not in this condition – we were in a state of society in which we had manufactures of almost every description, protected in every way' (vol. V, p. 56). Brougham might well have added perfect knowledge to the Utopian assumptions of Ricardo.

33 See 1951, vol. V, p. 38, and vol. VIII, p. 331.

34 A contemporary observer, J. L. Mallet, noted this contrast in Ricardo: 'It is impossible to be in company with Ricardo and not to admire his placid temper, the candour of his disposition, his patience and attention, and the clearness of his mind; but he is as the French would express it 'herissé de principes', he meets you upon every subject that he has studied with a mind made up, and opinions in the nature of mathematical truths. . . . His entire disregard of experience and practice . . . makes me doubtful of his opinions on political economy' (quoted in P. Sraffa, 1952, vol. VIII, p. 152). Could this contrast be one between Ricardo's own innate nature and the results of Mill's influence? Alfred Marshall's religious or racial explanation does not seem very convincing: 'The faults and virtues of Ricardo's mind are traceable to his Semitic origin; no English economist had a mind similar to his' (Pigou, 1925, p. 153).

35 *The Economist*, 1 September 1951, p. 502, italics added, quoted in T. W. Hutchison, 1952, p. 427.

36 Professor Thomas Sowell had explained the significance of the Millian–Ricardian methodological 'revolution' as follows (1974, p. 113): 'With Ricardo economics took a major step toward abstract models, rigid and *artificial* definitions, syllogistic reasoning – and the direct application of the results to policy. The historical, the institutional, and the *empirical* faded into the background, and *explicit* social philosophy shrank to a few passing remarks. Comparative statics became the dominant – though usually implicit – approach: Ricardo declared: "I put those immediate and temporary effects quite aside, and fixed my whole attention on the permanent state of things which will result from them" ' (italics added).

37 Mr. Harte's conclusions are rather unfair regarding J. S. Mill in about the last five years of his life, when, under the influence of Cliffe Leslie and the Irish Land problem, he was moving towards a historical and inductive approach. See G. Koot, 1975, pp. 320–2.

38 As Ricardo complained to Mill in a letter of 1 January 1821, regarding the errors of Malthus: 'Another of his great mistakes is, I think, this: Political Economy, he says, is not a strict science like mathematics.' Malthus had, of course, matured, methodologically, as contrasted with the dogmatic, *a priori* deductivism of his first *Essay*, which was on somewhat Millian–Ricardian lines.

REFERENCES

Bagehot, W. (1895). 'Ricardo', in *Economic Studies*, ed. R. H. Hutton, pp. 197ff.

Bain, A. (1882). *James Mill, a Biography*.

Cannan, E. (1917). *History of the Theories of Production and Distribution, 1776–1848*, 3rd ed.

Duncan, G. (1973). *Marx and Mill*.

Fetter, F. W. (1969). 'The Rise and Decline of Ricardian Economics', *History of Political Economy*, vol. I, pp. 67ff.

Forbes, D. (1951) (October). 'James Mill and India', *Cambridge Journal*, pp. 19ff.

Halévy, E. (1928). *The Growth of Philosophic Radicalism*, translated by M. Morris.

Harte, N. B. (ed.) (1971). *The Study of Economic History*.

Hayek, F. A. (1949). 'Individualism: True and False', in *Individualism and Economic Order*, pp. 1ff.

Hicks, Sir John (1975). 'The Scope and Status of Welfare Economics', *Oxford Economic Papers*, vol. 27, pp. 307ff.

Hicks, Sir John (1976). ' "Revolutions" in Economics', in *Method and Appraisal in Economics*, ed. S. Latsis, pp. 207ff.

Hollander, S. (1974). 'Ricardo and the Corn Laws: A Revision', a paper for the 6th International Congress on Economic History.

Hutchison, T. W. (1937). 'Expectation and Rational Conduct', *Zeitschrift für National-ökonomie*, VIII, 3, pp. 636ff.

Hutchison, T. W. (1952). 'Some Questions about Ricardo', *Economica*, vol. 19 (N.S.), pp. 415ff.

Hutchison, T. W. (1953a). 'Ricardo's Correspondence', *Economica*, vol. 20 (N.S.), pp. 263ff.

Hutchison, T. W. (1953b). 'James Mill and the Political Education of Ricardo', *Cambridge Journal*, VII, 2, pp. 81ff.

Hutchison, T. W. (1956). 'Bentham as an Economist', *Economic Journal*, vol. 66, pp. 288ff.

Inglis, B. (1972). *Poverty and the Industrial Revolution*, Paperback ed.

Johnson, H. G. (1975). 'The Keynesian Revolution and the Monetarist Counter-revolution', in *On Economics and Society*, pp. 91ff.

Keynes, J. M. (1933). *Essays in Biography*.

Keynes, J. M. (1937). 'The General Theory of Employment', *Quarterly Journal of Economics*, vol. 51, pp. 209ff.

Koot, G. (1975). 'Cliffe Leslie and the Historical School', *History of Political Economy*, vol. 7.

Malthus, T. R. (1836). *Principles of Political Economy*, 2nd ed.

Marx, K. (1961). *Capital*, English translation, Moscow.

Mill, J. (translated 1805: C. Villers). *An Essay on the Spirit and Influence of the Reformation of Luther*.

Mill, J. (1858). *History of India*, ed. H. H. Wilson.

Mill, J. (1966). *Selected Economic Writings*, ed. D. Winch.

Mill, J. S. (1909). *Principles of Political Economy*, ed. W. J. Ashley.

Mill, J. S. (1924). *Autobiography*, World's Classics.

Myrdal, G. (1953). *The Political Element in the Development of Economic Theory*.

Pigou, A. C. (ed.) (1925). *Memorials of Alfred Marshall*.

Ricardo, D. (1951 and 1952). *Works of D. Ricardo*, ed. P. Sraffa, vols. I–IV, and vols. V–IX.

Rima, I. (1975). 'James Mill and Classical Economics: a Reappraisal', *Eastern Economic Journal*, vol. 2, pp. 113ff.

Robbins, L. C. (1952). *The Theory of Economic Policy in English Classical Political Economy*.

Sayers, R. S. (1971). 'Ricardo's Views on Monetary Questions', in A. W. Coats, ed., *The Classical Economists and Economic Policy*, pp. 33ff.

Schumpeter, J. A. (1954). *History of Economic Analysis*.

Smith, A. (1937). *The Wealth of Nations*, Modern Library edition.

Sowell, T. (1974). *Classical Economics Reconsidered*.

Sraffa, P. (ed.) (1951 and 1952). *Works of D. Ricardo*, vols. I–IV (1951), vols. V–IX (1952).

Stigler, G. J. (1950). *Five Lectures on Economic Problems*.

Stigler, G. J. (1965). *Essays in the History of Economics*.

Thweatt, W. O. (1976). 'James Mill and the Early Development of Comparative Advantage', *History of Political Economy*, vol. 8, pp. 207ff.

Tucker, G. S. L. (1960). *Progress and Profits in British Economic Thought*.

Wilson, H. H. (ed.) (1858). James Mill: *History of India*.

Winch, D. (ed.) (1966). James Mill: *Selected Economic Writings*.

4

ON THE INTERPRETATION AND MISINTERPRETATION OF ECONOMIC LITERATURE: THE PREPOSTEROUS CASE OF DAVID RICARDO[1]

> One can build a strong case that the modern economist need not be acquainted with Ricardo's work, but there is no case for his being acquainted with an impostor.
>
> (George Stigler, 1965, p. 342)

> If, as I believe, Ricardo's impostors continue to lurk in the pages of learned journals, monographs, dictionaries of economics and textbooks, they must be exposed as such, regardless of the irritation, or inconvenience, that his may bring.
>
> (Terry Peach, 1993, p. xi)

I

Interpreting, misinterpreting and reinterpreting are a, or the, main activity of historians of economic thought or of economic literature, who, having spent much or most of their time and energy trying to interpret the major texts of political economy, go on to interpret interpretations, reinterpret reinterpretations and misinterpret misinterpretations.

'Interpret' is a portmanteau term which includes a mixed package of processes comprising exposition and explanation of what economists have written, plus explanation of why it was written, together with elucidation of meaning, and frequently, though not inevitably, critical assessment or evaluation. 'Interpretation' obviously involves, or includes, emphasizing and deemphasizing, selecting and rejecting, as well as appraising and judging. It is, therefore, almost (but perhaps not quite) inevitably, value-loaded. But the positive and normative elements can, in the interests of clarity, to a large extent, be distinguished. Editing the writings of an economist, or presenting the texts and adding some biographical dates and facts, could, not entirely of course, but up to a point, be a relatively value-free enterprise. (We shall

84

enquire briefly later just how far, for example, the probably most celebrated editorial achievement in economic literature – the Sraffa–Dobb edition of Ricardo – was a relatively detached work of value-free scholarship, and just how far it was a heavily committed and value-loaded political operation.)

II

One may distinguish between the interpretation of individual economists and their works, and the interpretation of the history of economic literature or thought as a whole, or of a large part or phase of it. Obviously this distinction might be described in terms of 'micro'-interpretation and 'macro'-interpretation. As a dichotomy, this is not nearly as exhaustive in terms of the history of economic literature, as it is, or is assumed to be, in terms of economic theories. There are histories and interpretations of schools, or of periods, or of 'revolutions', or of particular topics or subsections of the subject, which lie between the micro-study of individual economists, or of particular works, and the comprehensive macro-interpretation of the whole history of the subject or of major components. But there remains much work at, or near, the two extremes of 'micro' and 'macro'.

The subject of macro-interpretation will not be discussed much further in this paper, which is concerned primarily with the micro-interpretations of a particular economist and his writings. But micro-interpretations are often built up in order to support a macro-interpretation, or 'version', of the history of the subject.[2] In fact, the main concepts or components of macro-interpretations – 'Mercantilists', 'Classicals', 'Neoclassicals', 'Marxians', 'Keynesians' or 'Austrians' have often been more or less tendentiously shaped, stretched, compressed or stereotyped, in order to support one or other 'version' or macro-interpretation. Such 'versions' are more concerned with emphasizing, favourably or unfavourably, a particular major development, or 'revolution' in the subject, Classical, Marxian or Keynesian, while a 'macro-interpretation' is more concerned to give a general explanation of the motivating forces behind economic literature.

Turning to micro-interpretation, two levels, though often merging together, may be distinguished: (1) how an individual came to write what he did; and (2) the significance of what he wrote. As regards the first level of interpretation, how an economist came to write what he did, the role of biography is obviously vital but often neglected. The second level, that of explaining the significance of what an economist wrote, is widely and lengthily represented by all those conflicting accounts of what Malthus or Ricardo, or Mill, Marx, Marshall or Keynes, 'really meant'.

At both levels there will be frequent scope for minor differences of emphasis, especially when biographical information is not available. *But that vast, persistent clashes continue, over what major economists have 'really meant' by what they wrote, does seem to require more analysis and explanation, and notably as to how far these persistent clashes are the fault of the economists and how far of their would-be interpreters; and also as to what justification there is for such apparently major, persistent ambiguities and clashes.*

A minor source of ambiguity, or of clashing interpretations, might be the inaccessibility, or unavailability, of important texts for long periods, which then eventually come to light (like Marx's *Grundrisse*). But this should hardly prove a lasting source of clashes of interpretation. A much more important and major source of such clashes is that, over a long career, an economist may well change, or appear to change, his views. Perhaps some long-term trend may be traced, such as the common political trend from youthful radicalism towards a more mature conservatism in old age; or an intellectual trend from the advocacy of a trenchant, though perhaps highly simplified theory, towards the protective admission of increasing exceptions and qualifications, which may eventually leave little or no content in the original theory, or model. Some such trend *may* be discernible in Malthus's presentation of his population theory over three decades. Sometimes the changes in an economist's views may be in response to historical and institutional changes, sometimes in response to criticism, and sometimes more or less intellectually autonomous.

Often it is difficult to discern any major trend in an economist's changes of view, as, on the whole, in Marshall. Professor Giacomo Beccatini has referred to Marshall's sixty years of intellectual activity as his '*percorso interiore tormentato e zigzagante*'. Obviously countless problems and differences may arise in seeking to interpret sixty years of tormented zigzags. Anyhow, the inescapable fact must be recognized that, consistently or inconsistently, economists do change their views (though they may be reluctant to admit this, even with regard to others, partly because of the difficulties in dealing, in conventional theory, with changes in tastes). So the temptation is often strong and unresisted to construct inhuman, monolithic, super-consistent 'Mills', 'Marxs', 'Ricardos' or 'Marshalls'. This may be done, up to a point excusably, for purposes of elementary textbook abbreviation or simplification. Much more dangerously and tendentiously such dehumanized monoliths may be constructed and maintained for polemical or ideological purposes, either for elevating some heroic, perhaps 'revolutionary' leader; or for the exposure of some kind of bogey, or Aunt Sally, 'mercantilist', 'classical' or 'neo-classical'. Then, in order to support a particular 'version', or macro-interpretation, of the history of the subject, an over-simplified, super-consistent micro-interpretation is imposed on some key figure at an important phase of the story.

In fact, not only was Marshall's career as an economist '*molto tormentato e zig-zagante*', so was that of other leading figures, such as J. S. Mill; while the intellectual careers of such equally problematic, though more confident, and even supposedly charismatic figures as Ricardo, Marx and Keynes, though (unfortunately perhaps) not so '*tormentato*' were certainly not free of 'zigzags'. But while differences in emphasis and interpretation may well persist on many minor points with regard to the writings of Marshall and J. S. Mill, such differences are liable to become irreconcilable and fundamental in respect of the works of those who are set up as major charismatic leaders of schools or 'revolutions'. Nevertheless, those who are prepared to treat even the greatest economists as human beings should surely not find much justification for persistent, comprehensive and fundamental clashes and contradictions in the interpretation of economists' writings.

Still more dubious and dangerous clashes of interpretation may arise when it is argued, or suggested, that if some economist – say Ricardo or Keynes – were alive today, he would be supporting a particular type of economic theorizing, or of policy measures: that is, the attempt is made to establish an interpretation of such figures not simply in terms of what they meant in relation to their own time and world, but in relation to some profoundly changed time and world. As has been explained (with regard to what George Orwell might have been arguing for in *1984*):

> 'If X were alive today, he would say Y'. If someone – Z for example – makes a statement of that order, he usually means that Y is what he thinks himself, and that he wishes to invest his own opinion with the authority of X. It is wrong for Z to carry on in this way, since the authority of X is not Z's to dispose of, and since Z does not really know what X would say if X were alive, for the very good reason that X is no longer alive, and is not saying anything.
>
> (C. C. O'Brien, *The Observer*, 5 September, 1982, p. 7)

One can recall how, for decades after Keynes's death, the public was told, by those claiming his authority for their own opinions, in conditions profoundly different from those he wrote about, just what policies he would have been supporting. With regard to the interpretation of Marx's works, for generations after he was writing, it has been a matter, literally of life and death, in many parts of the world, to interpret 'correctly' what Marx meant in terms of profoundly changed historical conditions.

III

There is however, undoubtedly, one supreme and overwhelming example of an economist of the very highest prestige, who has been interpreted in the most outright contradictory terms, not merely on particular details, or regarding political or normative issues, but as to the significance of his broad, general corpus of theory, or 'Principles'. Generations of dedicated scholars have devoted decades of their refined *expertise* to the interpretation of Ricardo's central theories of distribution and value. But though all these experts would unhesitatingly place him probably among the top two or three economists of all time, they would, according to their profoundly contrasting viewpoints, insist on the most widely diverging, and even contradictory, interpretations of what he wrote. Interpretations of Ricardo show countless minor variations. But three broad categories may be distinguished regarding the meaning of his writings, and his role in the history of political economy. First, there is Ricardo as the major classical 'liberal' alongside Smith. Secondly, there is Ricardo as a proto-Marxian exponent of the labour theory of value and of fundamental class conflict. Thirdly, there is an interpretation developed by Professor S. Hollander, in his 700-page volume, of Ricardo as a comprehensively consistent, taxonomic analyst (of a type which has become much more common in the second half of the twentieth century) who anticipated 'precisely' the profoundly sceptical, even nihilistic, methodological views of Professor G. L. S. Shackle (v. Hollander, 1979, p. 640).[3]

When it is borne in mind that Ricardo, both in his own day, by his closest friends and supporters, like James Mill, and subsequently by generations of economists, has been held to have played a, or even the, major part in establishing the scientific basis and method of political economy, or to have contributed what Professor Joan Robinson described as the 'precious heritage – Ricardo's habit of thought', then, these extraordinary and extreme divergences in the interpretations of his writings (almost as though they consisted of some kind of surrealist poetry) might seem to amount to a highly peculiar, and, in fact, quite scandalous intellectual phenomenon. Perhaps it indicates something regarding the scientific pretensions of political economy and economists. Also noteworthy is that these massive ambiguities, far from damaging Ricardo's scientific prestige may seem to have done much to enhance his extremely high reputation for intellectual profundity. Nor can the smallest part in this phenomenon be assigned, as may occasionally have been the case with less fortunate writers, to any inaccessibility or incompleteness in the editions of his works. For some three decades a complete and sumptuous edition has been widely available, most expertly annotated and fully indexed.

At this point it might be asked *why* multiple interpretations are objectionable? Why not the more interpretations the better? Surely they would be that more stimulating for academic discussion and controversy. The answer depends, of course, on what sort of criteria economic literature, or 'discourse', should satisfy. No one, for example, need consider that it detracts from Shakespeare's achievement as a poetic dramatist that the hero of his 'Hamlet' can be, and has been, interpreted in many and various ways, as, for example, an 'emotional predator', a 'panic-stricken melancholiac', a 'thoughtful abrasive aristocrat', a 'scabrous neurotic', and 'indignant young troublemaker' or a 'brooding, self-possessed prince' – or as some mixture of these.[4] If, however, one holds firmly that the criteria appropriate for a poetic drama like 'Hamlet' are not the same as those for a work entitled *The Principles of Political Economy and Taxation*, one may also hold that a work such as the latter should not manifestly be open to important and profound contradictions, and has been very badly written if it is.[5]

IV

Now it must at once be insisted that there is quite a significant amount of evidence in support of *all* the main interpretations, or types of interpretation, of Ricardo's writings. Each interpretation has been built up by devoted and expert scholars, and has been subjected to searching criticism from other devoted scholars. None of these interpretations could have been persisted with, unless, in Ricardo's writings, a considerable body of evidence on behalf of each or most of them could be discovered.

The reason for the persistence and recurrence, decade after decade, of these wide and profound clashes of interpretation among expert scholars, must be the intensely felt need to establish a single, monolithic, super-consistent 'Ricardo', which in turn requires a steadfast refusal to admit the possibility of any *serious* waverings or inconsistencies. For a monolithic, super-consistent 'Ricardo' has a vital role in establishing this or that 'version', or macro-interpretation, of the history of economic thought, for which an inconsistent waverer would be useless.

Again, it is impossible to set out all the key points where ambiguities in Ricardo's writings have given rise to, or encouraged, profoundly diverging interpretations. But a summary list may be suggested, which includes many or most of the really crucial issues in Ricardo's theorizing.

(1) First, there are Ricardo's waverings on the theory of value, which, as is well known, were sometimes quite profound – as in the letter to McCulloch of 13 June 1820 – in which he stated that he sometimes thought that he would fundamentally alter his theory of value if he were to rewrite chapter 1 of *The Principles*. There has always been quite a lot to be said for the kind of interpretation of Ricardo's value theory, proposed as long ago as 1904 by J. H. Hollander, though obviously the case it represents is very far from conclusive. Moreover, it seems, on the other hand, rather misleading, and possibly tendentious, to describe Ricardo's waverings – as Dr Sraffa does – simply as 'weakening', or as arising merely from 'a passing mood', or 'a moment of discouragement', implying that on the theory of value Ricardo *must* be regarded as holding, with overriding consistency, to the particular theory which Dr Sraffa himself wishes to impute to him.

(2) Probably the most consequential and fundamental of all Ricardo's waverings and ambiguities hangs over his treatment of 'the natural wage'. There is certainly plenty of evidence, at a number of points, of his taking a decidedly hard line on the subject of the natural wage-rate and the elasticity of supply of labour. But again there are waverings on this crucial issue, not only in letters or speeches, but in the middle of *The Principles*. What Ricardo 'really meant' about the natural wage is, of course, of absolutely vital importance for his policy doctrines, and for the question as to whether any refutable predictions can be derived from his theory of distribution, or whether, simply, its implication is that virtually anything, not contradictory in terms, can, or may,

happen. Moreover, how this question is answered makes all the difference between optimistic or highly pessimistic views about the future of capitalism, as well as about appropriate policies.[6]

(3) Vital waverings can also be found in Ricardo's views about the speed and smoothness of adjustments to long-run equilibrium. Again this is an issue which is absolutely crucial for Ricardo's policy doctrines. There is certainly much evidence for Professor Mark Blaug's view that: 'The true Ricardian vice is, surely, that of treating the short run as merely postponing the long run', or that of 'appealing to the long-run consequences of economic changes, while neglecting the short-run effects' (1981, p. 2). But there are also important waverings to be found about this simplification, as, notably, in a letter in the distressed year of 1819, when he seems to recognize that policies aimed at long-run improvement may, in the short run promote additional, or possibly cumulative, disequilibrating difficulties.[7]

Other important shifts, or waverings, could be cited (e.g. on machinery) but one might generalize by observing that though, on the whole, Ricardo worked out the logic of his 'strong cases' trenchantly and consistently, he seems frequently and persistently to have been unclear in his own mind as to their applicability or relevance to the real world, and as to the significance of the qualifications and exceptions which might have to be admitted – even to the extent of the qualifications becoming more important than the original 'strong case' itself. Certainly, in his writings, Ricardo often seems to be reflecting the personality traits attributed to him by J. L. Mallet, who described how he was

> herissé de principes, he meets you upon every subject he has studied with a mind made up, and opinions in the nature of mathematical truths.
>
> (v, Ricardo, 1951, vol. VII, p. 152)

But then, quite frequently, at crucial points, the picture of incisive trenchancy is clouded over, vast qualifications are suggested, which make it uncertain whether the upshot is no more than that anything can, or may, happen, except of course, a contradiction in terms. As Professor Samuel Hollander has insisted regarding Ricardo's important qualifications to his theory of value: 'These qualifications were always present in Ricardo's mind' (1979, p. 218). On other crucial issues also, notably that of the natural wage, vital qualifications seem to have been 'always present in Ricardo's mind', *and they were qualifications which made all the difference in the real world regarding implications for policy, and indeed could fairly be held to constitute contradictions or reversals as much as qualifications.*

V

Biography has played almost no part either in the support or the criticism of any of the conflicting, or even contradictory, interpretations of Ricardo's writings. In, for example, all of Professor S. Hollander's 700 pages there is but one brief paragraph of 'Biographical Data', plus a list of works and dates. Certainly many crucial biographical facts about Ricardo are missing. But, oddly enough, attempts are even made, in the interests of a charismatic or ideological interpretation of his writings, to deny, or diminish, one of the plain facts for which there is abundant evidence, that James Mill exercised a very important and pervasive influence on Ricardo's career as an economist. Here we simply wish to underline two other very well-known features of Ricardo's biography, and to observe that certain obvious conclusions are suggested by these facts.

Our first biographical fact is that Ricardo had easily the shortest career as an economist of any major figure, of comparable prestige, in the history of the subject. The length of Ricardo's career as an economist can be measured in various ways, but it was certainly astonishingly brief, especially in relation to the weight which his name and writings have subsequently carried – and still carry – among economists of most schools of thought. His interest is said to have first been aroused when in an idle interlude at Bath in 1799 he perused *The Wealth of Nations*. But it could hardly be claimed that a reading of even this supreme work *ipso facto* at once turns one into 'an economist', or even necessarily into a very serious student of the subject. In fact, his brother added that 'it was not till some years after that he appeared to have fixed upon it much of his attention' (Ricardo, 1951–5, vol. X, pp. 7 and 35). Later, writing presumably about his activities in the middle years of the century's first decade, Ricardo reminisced to Trower about their interest in the articles on political economy in *The Edinburgh Review*, and how these

> afforded us often an agreeable subject for half-an-hour's chat, when business did not engage us.
>
> (VII, p. 246)

This hardly sounds like a very strenuous course of graduate studies – or 'apprenticeship', as Professor S. Hollander calls it (1978, p. 19) – even when Ricardo adds elsewhere that James Mill accompanied them on walks in Kensington Gardens (VII, pp. 268 and 275). Anyhow, an 'apprentice' necessarily has a master, and there is only one serious candidate for that position in the case of Ricardo.

In the first four years of his publications Ricardo confined himself to questions of money and the foreign exchanges in which he had great practical knowledge and expertise. As Dr Sraffa says:

> Up to march 1813 both his letters and his published writings show Ricardo to have been concerned only with currency questions.
>
> (IV, p. 3)

Thus it can hardly have been the case that, before 1813, Ricardo had thought and worked seriously on the theory of distribution and value but had not completed any publications. So it was only at the age of 41 that Ricardo began to broach the vast complex questions of the general theory of distribution and value – and he died ten years later. So his ten-year career as a writer on general economic theory, for four of which he was an MP, is a very small fraction of those of Smith, Malthus, J. S. Mill, Marx or Marshall. It was not, therefore, *entirely* fanciful modesty that led Ricardo to describe himself, three years before his death, as one of the 'amateurs' (VII, p. 242).

These facts make clear that none of his writings can be interpreted as belonging to a 'youthful' or 'mature' period, because, as a theoretical economist, Ricardo never had either youth or maturity. Nor does it seem possible, within the confines of a single decade, to establish an interpretation in terms of a trend in his intellectual development, say from confidence in the applicability of only slightly qualified 'strong cases', towards insistence on increasingly extensive qualifications and exceptions, with ever-decreasing empirical and predictive content.

Thus it *might* have been possible, that if Ricardo had had another twenty to thirty years of theorizing about distribution and value, a trend might have become apparent towards increasing qualifications, which might have evolved even into a thorough-going nullification and reversal of the implications of the 'strong cases' from which he had started. But this can obviously amount to no more than speculation. Meanwhile, however, the shifts in Ricardo's views, which, as we have seen, were, on some central, crucial issues, of quite fundamental significance, and make all the difference in terms of the broad interpretation of his policy stance, cannot be explained or interpreted in terms of any trend, but must be set down simply as waverings and zigzags. In fact, it seems undeniable that Ricardo never made up his mind as to the real-world relevance of his 'strong cases':

> The overriding fact surely is that Ricardo came, with tragic discontinuity, to the end of his own personal 'long-run', in no state of even relatively stable or neutral intellectual equilibrium. Moreover, the 'dynamic' process of development was crammed into so comparatively few years that no decisive trends in his thinking get much chance of emerging definitively.
>
> (Hutchison, 1953a, p. 265)[8]

VI

The second well-known biographical fact about Ricardo is his entry into parliament in February 1819 (*aet.* 46). For the interpretation of Ricardo's methodological views this is a fact which it would be dangerous to overlook, and it certainly seems to render very dubious some recent suggestions regarding Ricardo's intellectual motivation and objectives.

It was James Mill, of course, who forcefully broached the idea that Ricardo should become an MP:

You can have no excuse for not going into parliament, and doing what you can to improve that most imperfect instrument of government. On all subjects of political economy, you will have no match; and you express yourself on those subjects so correctly, and so clearly, that in a short time you would be a very instructive, and a very impressive speaker. . . . There is not much difficulty in finding out the principles on which alone good government must of necessity depend.

(VI, 252; 23.VIII.1815)

Ricardo at once shies away, almost in horror:

Your parliamentary scheme is above all others unfit for me – my inclination does not in the least point that way – Speak indeed! I could not, I am sure, utter three sentences coherently . . .

(op. cit., p. 263)[9]

It must be emphasized that Ricardo's reluctance to enter parliament sprang solely from what he regarded as his personal incapacity as a speaker, and not in the least from any lack of confidence, or ardour, as a supporter of reform, or from any doubts about the immediate and direct relevance of his economic theories to current policy-making. On these points Ricardo was firmly at one with, and thoroughly convinced by, his mentor, James Mill. Indeed, it is surely incredible that James Mill would have been so eager and insistent to get him into parliament had he not been absolutely and justifiably convinced that Ricardo would faithfully represent *his* (Mill's) view. Unfortunately, however, the intellectual reputation of the austere and energetic James Mill, has, not undeservedly, come under searching criticism, so that those attempting to build up a heroic role for Ricardo are anxious to distance him as far as possible from his mentor – even if this requires the disregarding of many well-established facts.

Needless to say, of course, Ricardo in spite of his intense, initial personal doubts, was very soon persuaded by Mill's arguments, and though some delays ensued, at a vast expense in money and time, he duly paid for, and from February 1819 proceeded to occupy, the seat fixed for him by Mill and Brougham (V, pp. xiiiff.).

So in spite of not being able to 'utter three sentences coherently', Ricardo found himself delivering, in some four-and-a-half years, over a hundred parliamentary speeches. Nor were his pronouncements confined to the 'currency' questions on which his successful city career had given him such expert qualifications. Considerably less than half of his speeches were devoted to such issues. But presumably, according to Professor S. Hollander, on questions to which he applied his politico-economic theories, Ricardo sought mainly to regale his fellow members with taxonomic or classificatory exercises, setting out a range of purely hypothetical models, without committing himself to any particular model as applicable to the real world, or as yielding predictions about it.[10]

Anyhow, there are few or no signs that Ricardo's waverings regarding the extent of the qualifications which should be applied to his 'strong cases', affected in the least his general confidence as to the broad relevance of his economic theories to policy issues, and so to the substantial guidance which they could provide. However, according to Professor S. Hollander, Ricardo adhered 'precisely' to the highly sceptical, even nihilistic, methodological position of Professor George Shackle. It really does not seem credible that anyone holding such sceptical views would ever have spent the time, effort and money involved in sitting in parliament for four-and-a-half years, and making over one hundred speeches there, or that James Mill would have been so persistently eager to get him a seat, if all that he was concerned to deliver were taxonomic exercises of a classificatory nature, putting situations in this box or that.[11]

Professor S. Hollander's interpretation of Ricardo does not make him either the confident, trenchant exponent of classical liberal policies, or the proto-Marxian pioneer of a full labour theory of value, of class conflict, and of general pessimism about the future of profits and capitalism. In Professor S. Hollander's interpretation, Ricardo emerges as a kind of academic, classificatory taxonomist, who rejected prediction as a major aim for the economist. But certainly Professor Hollander's massive volume performs the great service of collecting and setting out the considerable extent, and crucial nature, of Ricardo's waverings. The reason for setting out these waverings so extensively is, of course, to *protect* Ricardo's theories from the serious criticism, and refutation, to which his 'strong cases' would be exposed, if left only slightly qualified. Indeed, Professor Hollander seeks to present Ricardo's waverings, not, of course, as waverings, but as a classificatory review of cases, which puts them, 'in this box or that', within a broad general, empirically irrefutable taxonomy.

Professor George Stigler, on the other hand, interpeting Ricardo as a kind of Proto-Chicagoan, and presumably strongly rejecting the methodological views of Shackle, attributed to Ricardo by Hollander, would support the interpretation of Ricardo as a confident, trenchant classical liberal, who was boldly prepared to derive predictions from his theories, and indeed would have regarded that as a prime task for an economist (especially for one venturing onto the parliamentary stage).

As Professor Stigler sharply complains:

> The real objection to Hollander, however, is that in his zeal to defend Ricardo he has done him grave injury. . . .

Professor Stigler agrees that Hollander has shown up crucial waverings, or 'inconsistencies', but rejects his attempts to use these in Ricardo's defence:

> Hollander invokes these inconsistent views to defend Ricardo against various attacks, and this is a serious disservice to Ricardo. By exaggerating the slack and inconsistency in Ricardo, Hollander makes him an

unimportant fuzzy theorist – not readily convicted of any error, perhaps, but not capable of presenting a consistent theory.

(1981, pp. 101–2)

Though we do not agree that Professor Hollander has exaggerated, at all seriously, Ricardo's inconsistency, Professor Stigler is undoubtedly and unerringly accurate in his conclusion regarding the true implications of Professor Hollander's vast study. But Professor Stigler then attempts to restore some consistency to Ricardo by the method of diminishing, dismissing, or ruling out of order, the evidence in his writings which would refute the interpretation of Ricardo as a heroically consistent, monolithic figure. Certainly, the reports of Ricardo's speeches should not weigh nearly as heavily as his writings. But the grounds for generally dismissing or devaluing the correspondence, as indicative of Ricardo's state of mind, or state of thinking, are much more objectionable. It is not as though his letters, or any of his economic writings, were spread over a really long period of time, over which changes of view might be explained as other than waverings or zigzags. Moreover, in any case, Ricardo's most crucial wavering, or inconsistency, over the natural wage, is fully set out in successive editions of *The Principles*.

Finding Humpty Dumpty up on his wall of 'strong cases', extremely exposed to critical missiles, Professor Hollander has tried to get him down into an elaborately constructed position, providing comprehensive, all-round protection, which turns him into a modern academic exponent of the methodology of Professor Shackle. But Professor Hollander's protégé is very fragile, and has failed to survive intact his rescuer's attempt to get him to safety. No doubt all the king's horses and all the king's men, whether supporters of a Marxian or classical liberal interpretation, will try to put the pieces together again, by the time-honoured method of diminishing, or ruling out of order, all the writings inconsistent with the image of a heroic, super-consistent figure, of one colour or another, which they so urgently need for the particular version of the history of political economy and economics which is so important to them. But after Professor Hollander's massive efforts, one doubts whether Ricardo can ever again figure as the consistent patron saint of any of the (of course thoroughly contradictory) types of politico-economic theory, and versions of the history of economic thought, on behalf of which his prestige has been so long and ingeniously built up.

VII

For about forty years after its first volumes began to appear in the early 1950s, the Sraffa–Dobb edition of Ricardo's *Works and Correspondence*, has, in various ways, shaped and set the agenda for Ricardian studies. The heavy influence of this edition came about not only because of the important new writings it contained, nor because of its quantity of careful editorial information – the rather belated *Index* alone has been described as 'a masterpiece by itself' (Bharadwaj, 1988, p. 70). There was also the editorial Introduction to Volume I (*The Principles*) drafted mainly by Dobb.

Never, probably, has any such editorial achievement been greeted with such gushing torrents of enthusiasm by leaders of opinion at the time. In his lifetime 'Ricardo was a fortunate man', began George Stigler; 'and now 130 years after his death, he is as fortunate as ever: he has been befriended by Sraffa – who has been befriended by Dobb' (1965, p. 302). Stigler even confessed to feeling 'uncomfortable' at the extent of his own 'undiluted praise' (p. 304). Jacob Viner's reactions seem even more remarkable. After noting that there was nothing to match the new edition, in scale or in craftsmanship, Viner complained how 'grossly and systematically misinterpreted' Ricardo had been, notably by Karl Marx:

> Marx did borrow heavily from Ricardo to demonstrate inherent contradictions in capitalism which could be resolved only by socialist revolution – yet he was able to use his borrowings for this purpose only by misinterpreting them or converting them into radically different matter.
> . . .
>
> Sraffa has already made it more difficult to adhere to the standard misinterpretations of Ricardo. To those who are willing to take reasonable pains to understand him, what Ricardo meant to his time and what he still means to us today will be clear when the whole edition is available.
>
> (1951 and 1958, pp. 435–6)

Now these extreme encomia, certainly, in important respects, were highly justified, though it remains strange that neither Viner's, nor Stigler's, review article discussed at all significantly the editors' Introduction to Volume I. It is surely of key interest today – and probably should have been even in 1951 – to raise a question or two about the intentions of the editors, and just what it was they thought they had achieved. Anyhow, we now have had revealed a highly interesting and forthright statement, from the junior, but more decisive, editor, as to what he regarded as the main achievement of the Introduction to Volume I and of the edition as a whole. Writing, shortly before publication, to a Marxist comrade in Vienna, Dobb explained his and Sraffa's achievement (and it is fair to assume their intention) as follows:

> In particular I think we conclusively establish (in opposition to the traditional Hollander–Marshall–Cannan view) that there was no 'weakening' of Ricardo's enunciation of the labour theory as time went on: that in fact he reached at the end of his life a position rather close to that of Marx, so that the true line of descent is certainly from Ricardo to Marx, and not from Ricardo to cost-of-production theory au Mill to Marshall as the bourgeois tradition has it.
>
> (Pollitt, 1988, p. 63; quoted by Peach, 1993, p. 24)[12]

Needless to say, in the actual edition itself, no such blunt forthright claims, or statements of intent, were forthcoming from the editors.

An important kind of clarification might, in fact, have been achieved if such a statement had been provided at the time.[13] It certainly has a certain piquancy to put these blunt claims (and intentions) – entertained by at least one of the editors – alongside Viner's extremely optimistic notions regarding how Sraffa had 'already made it more difficult to adhere to the standard misinterpretations of Ricardo', including, most importantly, of course, the Marxian misinterpretation; and that Ricardo's full meaning 'will be clear when the whole edition becomes available' (while demonstrating, presumably, that, in the words of Dobb, Ricardo ended up in 'a position close to that of Marx').

What has in fact happened to Ricardian studies in the forty years following the publication of the Sraffa–Dobb edition is, of course, that they have come to be dominated by flatly contradictory interpretations, which purport to show Ricardo as a major, charismatic exponent and originator of almost exactly the ideas upheld by his leading, flatly contradictory, interpreters. The whole exercise has had an obviously self-indulgent aspect. If, in fact, one was ever to come across an enthusiastic Marxo–Sraffian agreeing, very sensibly, that Ricardo's writings contain not only too much enthusiastic support for free markets, but are much too fraught with ambiguity and contradiction, for him to be regarded as an authentic ancestor of Marxian economics, then the developments of recent decades would not exhibit such a self-serving aspect: just as they would not if one found an upholder of neoclassical orthodoxy, very reasonably, insisting that, despite some traces of neoclassical ideas, there are too many intimations of conflicting Marxian ideas in his writings for Ricardo to be regarded as a forerunner of Neoclassicism. But, of course, such sensible concessions are just what one does *not* find. What in fact we have been confronted with is the building up of Ricardo, by conflicting admirers, aided by this unprecedentedly sumptuous edition, into a major, original, superconsistent, charismatic figure, in order that they can show him off – in, of course, utterly contradictory terms – as an ancestor of themselves. (Already James Mill's campaign 130 years previously had long ago seen to it that Ricardo's name appropriated a number of the original ideas, in the air at that time, of which he was by no means the sole or earliest originator.) It is the challenge of Sraffa's and Dobb's editing which must bear much responsibility for the conversion of Ricardian studies into an interminable, 'bitterly contested paternity suit' (Peach, 1993, p. 303).

One can only hope that, after decades of this kind of scholarship, repulsion and boredom may be setting in. Much more positive signs may, however, be detected of healthier and more realistic possibilities for Ricardian studies in Dr Terry Peach's *Interpreting Ricardo*, which could, and should, mark a turning-point. Peach starts from the essential *sine qua non* for any interesting historical treatment of Ricardo, that is, the recognition of the serious and profound inconsistencies in his writings, and of the impossibility of setting him up as the super-consistent champion of a coherent body of thought – Marxo-Sraffian, Chicago-Classical or Shackelian-Neoclassical. We have shown that there are ample biographical explanations of why Ricardo never achieved adequate consistency. Peach, in fact, has had the courage to insist on 'a portrayal of a man capable of quite startling inconsistencies and errors', and on refusing 'to fudge a pleasing consistency when it became clear that none existed' (1993, p. xii). 'There are times' – Peach has said – 'when it becomes impossible to take texts seriously and impose consistency on an author'. Contradictory hagiographers are much too inclined 'to carry the search for textual consistency beyond the bounds of reason' (1990, pp. 761 and 764). Much of economic theorizing has long consisted of the analysis of omniscient economic agents. Some historians of economic thought would turn their subject into the study of the omniscient agent by the logically infallible economist.

VIII

In particular should be questioned the extravagant boosting of the reputation of the economist who, more than any other, was responsible for propagating a kind of labour theory of value just at the very historical juncture when the increasing role in production of capital, technology and multifarious new skills, was becoming a major and obvious secular trend; and just when, moreover, there was ready to hand a developing tradition of scarcity, utility and even productivity analysis in the works of the natural law writers, as well as in those of Galiani, Turgot and Condillac. George Stigler noticed how even 'Say's approach was fundamentally much more modern than that of his English contemporaries' – notably Ricardo (1965, p. 304). Also much more 'modern', as Stigler called it, and, at the same time, much more traditional – were Bentham, Bailey, W. F. Lloyd and other English, early-nineteenth-century opponents of the Ricardian labour theory. (By all means question monopolistic tendencies and the distribution of income under 'capitalism', as Adam Smith had done; but for this purpose a labour theory of value is neither necessary nor desirable.)

For decades the Royal Economic Society's sumptuous Sraffa–Dobb edition gave Ricardo's *œuvre* a supremely privileged position. The most starkly relevant contrast was with the works of Malthus. What George Stigler called 'the triumph of Ricardo over Malthus' seemed to be reflected in the editions, or non-editions, of their writings. At last, after 30 years or more, thanks to the invaluable work of Patricia James, John Pullen, E. A. Wrigley and others, this imbalance has been corrected. It is now time to question fundamentally the nature of the alleged Ricardian 'triumph' over the sensible empiricism of the mature Malthus and to recognize its largely disastrous methodological effects.[14]

IX

Ricardo, still today, remains an extremely important economist. His methodology and his often hyper-abstract ambiguities possess a peculiar appeal for late-twentieth-century academics, whether unreconstructed Marxists or uncritical, anti-empirical neoclassicals. With most of Marxian political economy having disappeared into the dustbin of history, and even with some Marxo-Sraffians eager to jettison the labour theory of value, today it is Ricardo's methodology which constitutes his most dangerously active heritage. For Ricardo still is – as he long has been – the Founding Father of 'anything goes' abstractionism; of the contempt for empirical discipline; of the 'unrealism-of-assumptions-doesn't-matter' school of thought – and especially of the assumption of omniscience – originally and explicitly introduced by Ricardo. Today it is this particular intellectual Augean stable which is so badly in need of a spring-clean. It must, however, in all fairness, in conclusion be remembered that today's methodological fallacies and fantasies are not, to any large extent, the fault of Ricardo. He seems, rather, to have been, when he started, something of an innocent abroad, whose inconsistent ideas, both originally, 170 years ago, and again in recent decades, fell into the hands of people too keen on exploiting them for their own ideological purposes, and who had to pretend that the inconsistencies were not there. It is now the task of those engaged in Ricardian studies, at long last, to try to rescue what is rescuable by restoring him to – what Dr Peach calls – 'his own surroundings'.

NOTES

1 An earlier version of this paper was delivered at a conference in Sardinia in September 1983 and was published in *Gli economisti e la politica economia*, ed. P. Roggi, 1985, pp. 323ff. This version contains considerable additions, subtractions and alterations.

2 On 'versions' of the history of economic thought, see Hutchison, 1978, chapter 8. Probably the most comprehensive and persistent version of the history of economic thought has been that of the Marxians – a version launched by the prophet himself. Most of the leading economists in the history of political economy have been fitted into the Marxian version somehow or other, either as heroes or as villains or bogeymen. An obvious bogeyman, against whom ideological warfare has often been, and still is being, waged, is William Stanley Jevons, who made so bold as to reject Ricardo, and was the spokesman for what Maurice Dobb called 'the Jevonian Revolution'. More than a decade ago Jevons was accused of harbouring a 'project to derive iron laws of income distribution' (White, 1982, pp. 32ff.). But no significant evidence has been offered that such a 'project' can fairly be ascribed to Jevons, even at the earliest stage of his writings as a 21-year-old in Sydney (see Hutchison, 1982b).

   Another interesting treatment, in the opposite direction, is that where Ronald Meek sought to groom the great Turgot for a starring role in the Marxian scenario as one of the major precursors of the theory of historical stages. But Turgot, in his remarkable paper *Valeurs et Monnaies*, showed himself an important pioneer of that Marxian bogey, the neoclassical theory of value and utility. To an orthodox

Marxian this unfinished paper is an unfortunate, or even embarrassing, aberration, on the part of a distinguished forerunner of a key aspect of Marx's thought. For, in Marxian theory, the historical, or historicist, analysis of stages and classes must be essentially linked with a labour theory of value. Ronald Meek, therefore, condemned Turgot's arguments in *Valeurs et Monnaies* as 'tortuous and unclear', and, without a shred of evidence, put forward the quite unjustifiable speculation that

> the essay remained unfinished . . . because Turgot could not see any way round the difficulties involved.
>
> (1973, p. 79)

Meek went on to find it

> interesting that a man of this calibre should have believed that a utility-based theory of value was perfectly compatible with a 'paradigm' not essentially dissimilar from Smith's.

But, of course, Turgot's subjective utility approach to value, which, on important points, anticipates closely some of the main ideas of both Walras and Menger, may be, for non-Marxians, perfectly compatible, logically and politically, with a historical analysis of stages and classes. Moreover, Turgot's treatment of value, in terms of subjective utility, logically reinforced his support for economic freedom and individualism, while Adam Smith's value theory conflicted fundamentally with his libertarian political philosophy.

What may be noted is the ploy of devaluing, or even dismissing, one or other of an economist's writings, if its message does not fit in with the role assigned to him in some macro-interpretation, or 'version' of the history of economic thought. In this case, the remarkable work *Valeurs et Monnaies* is dismissed for its inconsistency and incompleteness because the theory of value and utility which it advances is incompatible with the proto-Marxian role into which Meek was trying to fit Turgot.

It seems unlikely that the Marxian version of the history of economic thought will fade away without a generation change, in spite of the total and ignominious real-world collapse of Marxian political economy in 1989–91. As Ernest Gellner put it: 'Never in the history of human conflict has there been such a dreadful thrashing' (1993).

In a recent review (1992) of another series of huge volumes on Marxian economics, it is explained that they provide 'further proof that only Stalinism died in the great revolution of 1989–91. The Marxian critique of capitalism will long survive it' (J. E. King, 1992, p. 1008). What indeed is provided here is 'further proof' – if needed – that the main Marxian theories and 'critiques', as Imre Lakatos long ago observed, are devoid of empirical content and simply not refutable by *any* historical events:

> Has, for instance, Marxism ever predicted a stunning novel fact successfully? Never! It has some famous unsuccessful predictions. It predicted the absolute impoverishment of the working class. It predicted that the first socialist revolution would take place in the industrially most developed society. It predicted that socialist societies would be free of revolutions. It predicted that there will be no conflict of interests between socialist countries. Thus the earlier predictions of Marxism were bold and stunning but they failed. Marxists explained all their failures: they explained the rising living standards of the working class by devising a theory of imperialism; they even explained why the

first socialist revolution occurred in industrially backward Russia. They 'explained' Berlin 1955, Budapest 1956, Prague 1968. They 'explained' the 'Russian–Chinese conflict. But their auxiliary hypotheses were all cooked up after the event to protect Marxian theory from the facts.

(1978, vol. 1, p. 6; and Hutchison, 1981, p. 21)

Now the Marxists have even 'explained' the total collapse of the Marxist political economies in 1989–91, which is shrugged off simply as the death of 'Stalinism'. A 'critique' of capitalism might, however, be regarded as seriously undermined by the collapse of the socialist alternative, which, for much of the twentieth century, provided an essential support for that 'critique'. To continue to advocate (and predict) the violent and total overthrow of 'capitalism', when one's cherished alternative has completely collapsed, and there is nothing viable to put in 'capitalism's' place, may seem profoundly and disgracefully irresponsible, originally on the part of Marx, and now, very much more so, on the part of his twentieth-century followers.

For decade after decade the leading pioneers of Marxian economics in Britain and the USA drew their inspiration from what they imagined to be, and represented as, the triumphantly successful economic achievements of the USSR and other Marxian regimes. In particular, during the quarter of a century under Stalin, it was believed and proclaimed by these leading Marxian authorities that the great Marxian alternative form of economy was being created, which would outperform Western capitalism *because* it was based on Marxian theoretical foundations, including some form of the labour theory of value.

For what were called 'Marxist–Leninist–Stalinist' economics not only provided the alternative to 'capitalism', they constituted and embodied, for decade after decade, the prevailing versions of Marxian economic theories and ideas. Ronald Meek, for example, as late as 1973, after describing Stalin as 'a serious scientist', who possessed 'a mastery of the *method* of Marxism', went on to insist that Stalin's *Economic Problems of Socialism in the USSR* '. . . the appearance of which in 1952 had a liberating effect . . . may well remain the basis for serious scientific work on the operation of the law of value under socialism for some time to come' (1973, pp. xxx and 284). Soon after, with regard to the theory of value, Meek explained: 'The path from Ricardo to Sraffa, however, was not a wholly direct one. It also led through Marx and the Marxists' (1974, p. 257). It also led – one might add – through Stalin and the Stalinists. Almost all the leading Marxist economists from the 1930s to the 1960s can be quoted in enthusiastic support of Stalinism.

3 An interpretation of Ricardo's economics which is, in important respects, somewhat similar to that of Professor Samuel Hollander, has come from Professor Morishima who explains how a knowledge of the history of economic thought may be a disadvantage in formulating the kind of interpretation of Ricardo's writings at which he himself has arrived:

> I have never been a historian of economic thought but have been an economic theorist throughout my life. With such a speciality, I believe, I am allowed to concentrate solely on . . . main works; and by making this constraint I am able to read these works more deeply and more rigorously than specialists in the history of economic thought.

(1989, p. 3, quoted by Peach, 1993, p. 285n)

Professor Paul Samuelson, however, may also be regarded as a very highly distinguished exponent of the mathematical 'speciality' of which Morishima is a master; and Samuelson writes (regarding Ricardo's criticism of Adam Smith) of 'the economists' world, blinded by Ricardo's reputation for brilliance and unable to recognize in his murky exposition the many non-sequiturs contained there'. Samuelson goes on to explain how 'Ricardo wrote so badly as to provide that quantum of obscurity sufficient to evoke academic attention and overestimation' (1992, pp. 1 and 10). That Ricardo wrote so badly, certainly far from providing grounds for criticism, or for detracting from his fame, *has constituted the main foundation, not only for the various sharply contradictory interpretations of his writings, but also for the tremendous acclaim for his extraordinary profundity*, from those whom Samuelson describes as 'the mob' [*sic*] of Ricardian hagiographers' (1992, p, 10).

4 See *The Sunday Times*, 27 December 1992, Section 4, p. 3.

5 Professor Aksoy, in his interesting but inconclusive book (1991) seems to leave wide open the question of the criteria by which Ricardo's writings should be judged. Aksoy's closing chapter is entitled 'The Hermeneutical Significance of Multiple Interpretations', and takes as very seriously relevant to the appraisal of *The Principles of Political Economy and Taxation* the hermeneutical and deconstructivist doctrines of Gadamer and Derrida. Whether or not there is 'one true meaning' to Ricardo's *Principles*, the existence of highly contradictory interpretations, seems, according to reasonable, widely-held criteria, to point to profound inadequacies, *either* on the part of Ricardo, *or* of his contradictory interpreters (or both). The three authorities who contribute a joint 'Foreword' to Aksoy's book seem to share the author's inconclusiveness.

6 The first edition of *The Principles* reads:

> The amended condition of the labourer, in consequence of the increased value which is paid him, does not necessarily oblige him to marry and take upon himself the charge of a family – *he may, if it please him*, exchange his increased wages for any commodities that may contribute to his enjoyments. . . . But although this might be the consequence of high wages, yet so great are the delights of domestic society that in practice it is invariably found that an increase of population follows the amended condition of the labourer.
>
> (I, p. 406, italics added)

In the third edition the words italicized above, 'he may if it please him', are replaced by 'he will in all probability' spend more on his own enjoyments. It is anybody's guess as to what Ricardo *really meant*, or whether the upshot of this passage is *simply* that: 'Anything may happen'. The contrast between what the labourer 'will in all probability do' and what 'it is invariably found' happens in practice, points in opposite directions and it is left quite obscure how far the 'invariable' increase in population will leave any room for the higher expenditure on enjoyments (*v.* Hutchison, 1952, p. 240).

7 See the letter to James Brown of Newcastle of 13 October 1819 (VIII, p. 100):

> We all have to lament the present distressed situation of the labouring classes in this country, but the remedy is not very apparent to me. The correcting of our errors in legislation with regard to trade would ultimately be of considerable service to all classes of the community, but it would afford no immediate relief: On the contrary I should expect that it would plunge us into additional difficulties. If all prohibitions were removed from the import of corn and many other articles, the sudden fall in the price of corn and those other articles, which could not fail to follow, would ruin most of the farmers, and many of the manufacturers: and although others would be benefited, the derangement which such measures would occasion in the actual employments of capital, and the changes

which would become necessary, would rather aggravate than relieve the distress under which we are now labouring.

This *might* be taken to imply a denial that what would 'ultimately' be beneficent long-run equilibrating forces will, in fact come through, against shorter-run, possibly cumulative, adverse disequilibrating forces. (*v.* Hutchison, 1953a, p. 270)

8 As Professor Paul Samuelson has observed regarding Ricardo '. . . from his 1814 entrance into microeconomics until his death in 1823 [he] makes almost no progress in resolving the self-created ambiguities and problematics'. On the other hand Ricardo was, to the end, capable of intellectual somersaults, or striking out in new directions (as over machinery). Again, as Samuelson noted: 'Inside Ricardo there was a von Thünen and a J. B. Clark striving to be born' (1987, pp. 459–60).

9 For further evidence of Ricardo's reluctance or misgivings about entering parliament, see his letters of 20 December 1816 (No. 196) and 29 September 1818 (No. 274).

10 Mark Blaug's verdict on Ricardo's contribution on economic policy is difficult to contest. Regarding the Poor Laws: 'he not only favoured their abolition but also approved of harsh administration . . . so as to mitigate their worst effects on the economy. Unfortunately, as he confessed to a friend, he was woefully ignorant of the practical details of the subject' (1986, p. 119). Moreover, 'he never clearly analysed the mechanism by which the Poor Laws were supposed to stimulate population growth'.

Blaug's masterly conclusion requires full quotation:

> The great fascination of Ricardo's system is its peculiar combination of an unusually high level of abstraction with an equally unusual emphasis on the immediately practical deductions that can be drawn from the analytical model. In short, Ricardo has always served economists with a paradigm example of how one can join rigour and relevance within one and the same framework. Nevertheless, when one carefully examines his policy proposals, they turn out to be vaguely formulated and hedged about with extensive qualifications: they lack precision, they lack any judgements of quantitative magnitudes, they conflate the distinction between clock-time and analytical time, and they fail to confront the political problems of implementation. If this is our leading example of policy-oriented economics, we have nothing to be proud of.
>
> (1986, p. 125)

Apart from the area of financial policy, where he had genuine first-hand knowledge and expertise, Ricardo failed – pretty comprehensively – to follow the maxim of Sir John Hicks that 'theory gives one no right to pronounce on practical problems unless one has been through the labour, so often the formidable labour, of mastering the relevant facts' (1983, p. 361). It is noteworthy that Professor George Stigler thought that 'Ricardo's policy recommendations were profoundly good but his theory was not of the highest quality' (1965, p. 303). Stigler added in a footnote: 'T. W. Hutchison flunks him' – referring to my 1952 review article. Assuming that 'flunking' Ricardo means excluding him from the highest class of all-time great economists, which includes Adam Smith, Alfred Marshall and very few others, I still 'flunk' Ricardo and am delighted to find myself in the company of Mark Blaug, particularly regarding the vital area of economic policy. Incidentally, I still subscribe to the broad judgements of 1952, which I have tried to formulate and support in subsequent writings. The inclusion of this early article would unnecessarily and unduly extend the Ricardian content of this book.

11 Professor Hollander writes:

In his work on *Epistemics and Economics*, G. L. S. Shackle urged that a theory ought to be 'a classificatory one, putting situations in this box or that according to what *can happen* as a sequel to it. Theories which tell us what *will* happen are claiming too much. This position, I maintain, was precisely that of Ricardo.

(1979, p. 640)

The implications of Professor Shackle's views on predictability in economics, as Professor K. E. Boulding has observed, 'lead only to total despair' (1973, p. 1374) – at any rate regarding the prospects for deriving any policy-guidance from economic theorizing. Anyhow, the contrast, in the passage quoted, between 'what can happen' and 'what will happen', is hoplessly fuzzy regarding the question as to whether, or how, economic theories, and predictions derived from them, are to be regarded as falsifiable (or not). The title of one of Professor Shackle's books, *Economics for Pleasure*, is indicative of his deep scepticism regarding the derivation of any policy guidance from economic theorizing. But Ricardo (and James Mill) ardently and confidently believed in *Economics for Policy* – not for *Pleasure* – and that is why Ricardo entered Parliament. Furthermore, Professor Shackle repudiates to a highly significant extent – and probably to some extent justifiably – the applicability to economics of the aims, methods, and criteria of the natural sciences. On the other hand, as Dr Sraffa has maintained, mathematics and the natural sciences exercised a 'decisive influence on Ricardo's characteristic cast of mind' (X, p. 35). Moreover, in his conception of laws, and in other comparisons, Ricardo repeatedly affirms the close parallels in aims, methods, and achievements, between the science of political economy and the natural sciences. The relation between accumulation and economic progress, was, Ricardo maintained, 'as certain as the principle of gravitation' (VI, p. 204). In fact, it would be difficult, regarding the fundamental issues of the methodology of economics, to think of two eminent writers *farther apart* than Ricardo and that charming nihilist, Professor Shackle.

12 Brian Pollitt has traced the comradeship between Sraffa and Dobb back, at least, to 1925 (1988, p. 58). They visited Russia together on two occasions. Dobb was delighted to find that the Marx–Engels Institute had recently published a complete edition of the works of Ricardo which has sold 5,000 copies 'on advance orders alone' – (doubtless later a great and inspiring example to the two pilgrims).

Maurice Dobb, the outstanding pioneer of Marxian economics in Britain was throughout its existence, and long after, a totally committed supporter of the Stalin regime in the Soviet Union, hardly ever permitting himself a syllable of serious criticism until the last years of his life. Ernest Mandel, the eminent Trotskyist, pointed out how Dobb 'has always faithfully interpreted the official theses of the leading circles in the USSR' (1968, p. 552). Indeed, in the early 1950s, at the time of the publication of the Ricardo edition, Dobb was suggesting that well before the end of the century the Soviet Marxist regime would, in vital respects, have raised the economic performance of the USSR well above those of leading Western countries (*v.* Hutchison, 1981, pp. 84–7). In my review article (1952, p. 421) I remarked that the Sraffa–Dobb edition might just as well have been sponsored by the Moscow State Publishing House as by the Royal Economic Society, by whom it had been commissioned. It seems now that this somewhat jocular observation contained more truth than I may naively have realized at the time.

13 Possibly the sheer sumptuousness of the Sraffa–Dobb edition, and the elaborate care of its scholarship, were to some extent envisaged as serving as an imposing 'front', or bait, to attract bourgeois admirers who would go on to swallow the message which Dobb believed that he and Sraffa had so 'conclusively' established regarding the labour theory of value and 'the true line of descent' in the history of

economics, from Ricardo to Marx (bypassing, of course, Mill and Marshall). At any rate, few fundamental questions were raised amid the enthusiastic eulogies. I might just claim, however, that while expressing 'gratitude and delight' at such 'paragons of editorial scholarship and the publisher's art', which the successive volumes of the Sraffa–Dobb edition represented, I did also attempt, however, crudely and inadequately (and, in any case, utterly in vain), to suggest one or two fundamental questions which might have been worth raising (see my 1952).

14 Cambridge (England), however, has usually managed to excel itself on the subject of Ricardo. It could well be maintained that the only, and certainly the only serious *bêtise*, in the whole vast, magnificent *oeuvre* of Alfred Marshall, is his treatment of Ricardo (inspired somewhat, presumably, by an urge to pour a genteel douche of Cambridge cold water on Jevons). Worked over by Alfred, Ricardo emerges, of course, 'as so uncriticisable as to be almost Marshallian' (Hutchison 1952, p. 423).

Keynes, the original enthusiastic moving spirit behind the Royal Economic Society's edition, began (according to Harrod) by describing Ricardo as 'the most distinguished mind that has found economics worthy of its powers' (Harrod, 1951, p. 328). This judgement seems to date from an early 1920s' version of his paper on Malthus. In a later version Keynes was to complain that the dominant influence of Ricardo 'has been a disaster to the progress of economics' (1972, p. 98); while in *The General Theory* it was maintained that 'Ricardo offers us the supreme intellectual achievement, unattainable by weaker spirits, of adopting a hypothetical world remote from experience as though it were the world of experience and living in it consistently' (1936, p. 192) – which seems to exaggerate somewhat Ricardo's consistency, but not his far-reaching lack of realism. Presumably, by 1936, Keynes would have been keener on sponsoring an edition of Malthus, than of Ricardo. It is not quite clear, however, how far Keynes's portrayal of Ricardo's method and mentality corresponds with what Joan Robinson was later to describe as 'the precious heritage' of Ricardo's 'habit of thought' (1973, p. 266). And so, on to the achievement of Sraffa and Dobb, 'conclusively' establishing that the true Ricardian–Marxian 'line of descent' bypassed Alfred Marshall; followed, at some distance by Lord Eatwell's conclusion as to how the editorial introduction to Ricardo's *Principles* helped provide 'logically sound foundations for the Marxian theory of value and distribution' (1979, p. 144).

REFERENCES

Aksoy, E. G. (1991). *The Problem of the Multiple Interpretations of Ricardo.*
Bharadwaj, K. (1988). 'Sraffa's Ricardo', *Cambridge Journal of Economics*, 12, pp. 67ff.
Blaug, M. (1983 and 1986). 'Ricardo and the Problem of Public Policy', *Economic History and the History of Economics*, pp. 115ff.
Boulding, K. E. (1973). Review of Shackle, *Epistemics and Economics, Journal of Economic Literature*, II, pp. 1374ff.
Deane, P. (1978). *The Evolution of Economic Ideas.*
Dobb, M. H. (1939). 'Scientific Method and the Criticism of Economics', *Science and Society*, pp. 389ff.
Eatwell, Lord. (1979). 'Dobb, Maurice H.', *International Encyclopaedia of the Social Sciences*, vol. 18, p. 142.
Gellner, E. (1993). *Times Literary Supplement*, 16 July, p. 3.
Harrod, R. F. (1951). *The Life of J. M. Keynes.*
Hicks, Sir John. (1979). *Causality in Economics.*
Hicks, Sir John. (1984). *Classics and Moderns.*

Hollander, J. H. (1904). 'The Development of Ricardo's Theory of Value', *Quarterly Journal of Economics*, 18, pp. 455ff.

Hollander, S. (1979). *The Economics of David Ricardo*.

Hutchison, T. W. (1952). 'Some Questions about Ricardo', *Economica*, 19, pp. 415ff.

Hutchison, T. W. (1953a). 'Ricardo's Correspondence', *Economica*, 20, pp. 263ff.

Hutchison, T. W. (1953b). 'James Mill and the Political Education of Ricardo', *Cambridge Journal*, VII, pp. 81ff.

Hutchison, T. W. (1978). *Revolutions and Progress in Economic Knowledge*.

Hutchison, T. W. (1981). *The Politics and Philosophy of Economics*.

Hutchison, T. W. (1982a). 'Turgot and Smith', *Turgot, Economiste et Administrateur*, eds C. Bordes and J. Morange, pp. 35ff.

Hutchison, T. W. (1982b). 'The Politics and Philosophy in Jevon's Political Economy', *Manchester School*, pp. 366ff.

Keynes, Lord. (1972). *Collected Economic Writings*, vol. X, pp. 71ff.

King, J. E. (1992). *Review of Marx and Modern Economic Analysis*, ed. G. A. Caravale, *Economic Journal*, 102, 413, pp. 1006ff.

Lakatos, I. (1978). *Philosophical Papers*, 2 vols, eds. J. Worrall and G. Currie.

Mandel, E. (1968). *Marxist Economic Theory*, trans. B. Pearce.

Meek, R. L. (ed.) (1972). *Precursors of Adam Smith*.

Meek, R. L. (1973). *Studies in the Labour Theory of Value*, 2nd ed.

Meek, R. L. (ed.) (1974). 'Value in the History of Economic Thought', *History of Political Economy*, 6, pp. 246ff.

Morishima, M. (1989). *Ricardo's Economics*.

O'Brien, C. C. (1982). *The Observer*, 5 September, p. 7.

Peach, T. (1990). 'Samuel Hollander's Ricardian Growth Theory', *Oxford Economic Papers*, 42, pp. 751ff.

Peach, T. (1993). *Interpreting Ricardo*.

Pollitt, B. (1988). 'The Collaboration of Maurice Dobb in Sraffa's edition of Ricardo', *Cambridge Journal of Economics*, 12, pp. 55ff.

Ricardo, D. (1951–5). *Works and Correspondence*, 10 vols.

Robinson, J. (1973). *Collected Economic Papers*, vol. 4.

Robinson, J. and Eatwell, J. (1973). *An Introduction to Modern Economics*.

Rogin, L. (1956). *The Meaning and Validity of Economic Theory*.

Samuelson, P. A. (1978). 'The Canonical Classical Model of Political Economy', *Journal of Economic Literature*, 18, pp. 1415ff.

Samuelson, P. A. (1987). 'Sraffian Economics', *The New Palgrave: A Dictionary of Economics*, 4, pp. 485ff.

Samuelson, P. A. (1992). 'The Overdue Recovery of Adam Smith's Reputation as an Economic Theorist', *Adam Smith's Legacy*, ed. M. Fry, pp. 1ff.

Stigler, G. J. (1965). *Essays in the History of Economics*.

Stigler, G. J. (1981). Review of Hollander, S., *The Economics of David Ricardo*, *Journal of Economic Literature*, 21, pp. 101ff.

Stigler, G. J. (1990). 'Ricardo or Hollander?', *Oxford Economic Papers*, 42, pp. 765ff.

White, M. V. (1982). 'Jevons in Australia: a Reassessment', *Economic Record*, pp. 32ff.

5

'RICARDIAN POLITICS': ANOTHER VERSION OF RICARDIAN HAGIOGRAPHY?[1]

I

We have had Ricardo, the sometimes trenchant (but sometimes wavering) champion of classical free-market political economy, as earlier expounded by Lionel Robbins, and more recently, in Chicagoan terms, by George Stigler. We have had, too, as claimed by Maurice Dobb (perhaps the more decisive editorial comrade of Piero Sraffa) the Ricardo from whom 'the true line of descent' in our subject ran on to Marx and the labour theory of value, by-passing Marshall and the other *bourgeois* neoclassicals.[2] We have had, also, more recently, from Samuel Hollander, Ricardo as the late-twentieth-century, non-predicting, academic taxonomist and methodological follower of George Shackle. Moreover, we have had Ricardo the brilliant methodological innovator, who not only has been hailed as having 'discovered the technique of economic analysis', but who, according to Joan Robinson, bequeathed – especially to Cambridge Marxians and Marxo-Sraffians – 'a precious heritage – Ricardo's habit of thought' (1973, p. 266). (Another Ricardian methodological heritage has been, of course, the Ricardian vice.) For decade after decade these various, and often quite contradictory Ricardos have been hagiographically extolled and expertly, obstinately and dogmatically fought for. Now (1991) we have something entirely different: Ricardo the major, original, overlooked, radical political thinker.

II

According to Professors Milgate and Stimson (hereafter M and S), Ricardo's 'extensive' writings on politics contain a 'lucid and considerable' body of political ideas, which exhibit 'a novel and sophisticated linkage of arguments for democratic reform', and for 'a systematic and democratic platform' (1991, pp. ix, 13 and 17). Ricardo's politics are claimed to 'come off well' . . . 'even when measured against John Stuart Mill, who alone among the philosophical radicals is usually said to have avoided the shortcomings of both Bentham and his father' (1991, p. 16). Moreover, compared with Bentham and James Mill,

107

'Ricardo was in a better position to harness the science of political economy to the science of politics, if only because neither Bentham nor James Mill could seriously be described as having been in command of a theoretically informed version of economic science' (p. 16).[3] Quite apart from the fact that Bentham *can very seriously* be described as having been in command of a fundamentally superior version of 'economic science', as compared with that of Ricardo, M and S never actually explain precisely how Ricardo 'harnessed' his versions of economics to his 'science of politics'. The exaggeration, in fact, begins right at the start when a comparison is vaguely suggested or hinted at between Ricardo's work on politics and the writings of Smith, Marx, Schumpeter, Keynes, Hayek and Friedman (p. ix).

M and S next complain of the 'caricatures' of Ricardo 'which fill the secondary literature' (p. xi). The two alleged 'caricatures' of Ricardo complained of are, first, that portraying his very close intellectual relationship with James Mill; and, secondly, that emphasizing his seriously excessive and unqualified reliance on highly abstract and unrealistic 'models'. M and S attempt to diminish the importance of the relationship between Mill and Ricardo, which was so crucial in the development of Ricardo's political ideas and career – not to mention in the early formation of his economic theories and ideas, and later in the writing of *The Principles* – by producing their own counter-caricature, by alleging the existence of a 'dominant notion' that, as regards his political ideas and activities, Ricardo was 'little more than James Mill's marionette (or perhaps his amanuensis)' (p. 3).

The most important quotations, with which M and S seek to demonstrate the existence of this 'dominant notion' of Ricardo as some kind of 'marionette', or, perhaps, 'amanuensis', come from James and John Stuart Mill (pp. 3–4, n. 3). What James Mill said is that 'during the greater part' (a qualification omitted by M and S) of his dozen or so years of friendship with Ricardo, he (James Mill) was Ricardo's 'confidant and adviser' regarding almost all his thoughts and purposes, public or private (v. Ricardo's *Works*, vol. IX, p. 390). To suggest that having a confidant or adviser on most of one's private and public concerns turns one into a 'marionette' or 'amanuensis' is misleading and exaggerated.[4]

It may be noted, at this point, that there is one important feature of M and S's account of Ricardo which they share with Samuel Hollander, their predecessor as a hagiographic interpreter of Ricardo. (Actually, Hollander is not so much as mentioned by M and S, although they devote much space to Ricardo's economics, while Hollander discussed at some length Ricardo's politics.) In order to aggrandize, and exaggerate, the importance, originality and achievement of Ricardo, M and S, though not denying his 'encouragement', attempt repeatedly to diminish the role, and exclude the importance of James Mill in Ricardo's career – which is much more unjustifiable with regard to Ricardo's political ideas and career even than it is with regard to his economic theories.

As regards Ricardo's pronounced tendency to excessive and unrealistic abstraction – in spite of his obviously keen ambition to pronounce on real-world policy-making – M and S point to Henry Brougham as the originator of this 'tradition', or 'familiar portrait' (p. 6), with his remark in Parliament about Ricardo having apparently 'dropped from another planet' (1991, p. 4). Brougham, who was, in fact, quite well disposed towards Ricardo, and helped to fix his seat in Parliament, was directing some justifiable criticism at the highly abstract and unrealistic assumptions which Ricardo was employing in opposing, in the House of Commons, protection for agriculture, by claiming that if only the corn laws were removed and the national debt reduced, Britain's 'progress in prosperity would be beyond the power of imagination to conceive . . . its prosperity and happiness would be incomparably and almost inconceivably great' (1952, vol. V, p. 55).[5] When the parliamentary context is supplied, Brougham's criticisms seem quite well founded; and even his rather fanciful enquiry about whether Ricardo had 'dropped from another planet' does not seem seriously beyond the limits of parliamentary rhetorical licence. In fact, mentally, Ricardo *had* just dropped from another planet: a mental or 'model' planet which he himself was the first economist to explore and exploit, but which has been constantly visited, and for 'long periods' lived in by countless, 'model'-building economists ever since: an extra-terrestrial, timeless planet, the inhuman inhabitants of which are virtually perfect in knowledge, mobility and immediate adjustability: a planet where so many processes, which take ages in our real world, happen 'immediately': a planet the conditions of which may be very easy for economists to assume, but the actual workings of which are very difficult to imagine. (For Ricardo and the perfect knowledge postulate, *v.* Hutchison, 1978, pp. 48–9 and 200–1.)

The basic mistake of M and S in their attempt to refute criticisms, from Brougham to Schumpeter, of Ricardo's excessive use of oversimplified abstractions, derives from their total failure to recognize that his busy, real-world career in the City and Parliament, together with his driving interest in policy conclusions, could not, and did not, save him from falling into the errors which inevitably follow from what M and S refer to as 'the Ricardian Vice' of 'applying the conclusions of the most abstract and unreal models directly to reality' (p. 11n). This was precisely Brougham's (and Schumpeter's) well-justified criticism.

III

Since M and S repeatedly emphasize how 'extensive' and largely 'overlooked', as well as how 'novel and sophisticated', Ricardo's writings, or parts of them, are, it would surely have been helpful for the reader if they had listed, for him or her, just what and where the texts are to be found of the works, on behalf of which such claims are being made. Presumably, it is not Ricardo's writings on economic or social policies (such as the Poor Laws) which are being referred to as largely 'overlooked', when we have, on the one hand, the eloquent defence of Lionel Robbins (1949), and, on the other hand, the masterly and robust critique of Mark Blaug (1986) (this latter work not cited by M and S).

The actual texts of Ricardo's political writings – none of them written for publication – consist, first, of a couple of eight-page 'Discourses', 'which' – as Sraffa tells us, but M and S do not fully – 'Ricardo wrote at the instance of Mill as an exercise in speech-making before entering Parliament' (1952, vol. V, p. 492). These two eight-page items, much the lengthiest of Ricardo's writings on politics, are duly listed by M and S. Beyond these sixteen pages, Ricardo's political writings consist of a number of letters and speeches, or rather pages, paragraphs and passages, from letters and speeches, which need a lot of tracking down. Moreover the total 'extent' of these letters and speeches, and parts thereof, is difficult to estimate precisely, owing partly to the flexibility of the term 'politics'. My own estimate, using Sraffa's index, would be, that *about fifty pages* – though not providing room for all and every kind of Ricardo's 'political', or near-'political', observations – would have sufficed to include all his points and ideas on the problems of political reform. If an appendix of this order of magnitude had been included, readers would have been able to assess for themselves Ricardo's allegedly 'overlooked', but 'extensive', 'novel', 'sophisticated' and 'systematic' contributions – and perhaps come to a very different valuation. If the actual texts were too much to expect, then, at least, a list of page-references could have been provided, indicating just where these remarkable writings are to be found, among the four or five volumes of letters and speeches. The fact is that, as a description of Ricardo's political writings 'exiguous' would be a much more accurate adjective than 'extensive'.

Since M and S are specially concerned to elevate the role of Trower, and of his correspondence with Ricardo, as compared with that of James Mill, M and S seem, or purport, to provide a list of page-references covering the Ricardo–Trower exchanges in note 51, p. 31. Unfortunately, this list, while not even being complete, is very seriously exaggerated and misleading, much more so, even, than their claim that Ricardo's political writings, as a whole, are 'extensive'. (All this can be confirmed from Sraffa's index, *Works and Correspondence*, vol. XI, 1973, pp. 59–60, 80–5 and 105.)[6]

In assessing the importance and fruitfulness of Ricardo's exchanges and relationship with Trower, as compared with his relationship and exchanges with Mill, especially regarding politics, it must obviously be emphasized that, while Trower was a layman stockbroker, possessing, according to Sraffa, 'no claim to literary fame in his own right', Mill, by any standards, remains a formidable figure in the history of political thought.[7] It is quite inadequate and misleading to state that Mill 'encouraged' Ricardo, without adequately emphasizing his role as mentor and tutor, over many years, since their first meeting some time before the correspondence began. In fact, M and S go on to assert that 'providing encouragement is not the same thing as providing the substance of an argument' (1991, p. 145). In the case of the Mill and Ricardo exchanges on politics, political economy and economics, this is largely a false distinction. Mill did not simply encourage Ricardo to become an MP, and then to remain silent, or to say whatever came into his head (or because the House of Commons was the best club in London). Mill 'encouraged' Ricardo to enter the House of Commons in order that he should expound particular political and politico-economic views and doctrines; and Mill coached, tutored, advised and exercised Ricardo in the formulation, substance and presentation of these approved doctrines. Nor did Mill simply 'encourage' Ricardo to write a book of 'Principles of Political Economy' *any* 'Principles', such as those expounded by Lauderdale and Malthus, and in the later writings of Bentham on the subject (which were, arguably, far superior to those of Mill and Ricardo). Though Mill was not concerned with much of the detailed substance of Ricardo's *Principles*, he knew from his earlier close association with Ricardo that the latter would follow the broad approach with regard to such central theoretical issues as (1) a macroeconomic analysis of saving and investing which followed closely – if not, of course, absolutely precisely – the lines laid down in Mill's *Commerce Defended* (1808); and (2) the hard-line doctrines of wages, population and 'corn' outlined by Mill in his *Essay of the Impolicy of a Bounty on the Exportation of Grain* (1804), from which, as Professor Ingrid Rima has convincingly shown, the central Ricardian distribution problem was derived, since 'analytically speaking, the behavior of the distributive shares was Mill's chief concern in this essay' (*v*. Rima, 1975, pp. 115 and 118; and Hutchison, 1978, p. 31).

Moreover, an outstanding feature of the Mill–Ricardo exchanges is the constantly repeated, enthusiastic agreement which each expressed with the other's views, not only to each other, but when Ricardo writes off to Trower and Malthus about Mill's *History of India*. This impressive measure of enthusiastic agreement is quite compatible with Ricardo's probing requests for further explanations. These were two intellectually determined and argumentative men who would certainly not have shrunk from vigorous disagreement if they had seen anything important to disagree about.[8]

Dr Sraffa's phrase about the composition of Ricardo's two 'Discourses' on politics, that these were written 'at the instance' of James Mill applies significantly, though to a varying extent, to much or most of Ricardo's work and career in political economy and politics, after his meeting with Mill, that is: (a) to his career in parliament; (b) to his education in political thought and ideas; (c) to the writing and *some* of the content and broad approach of *The Principles*; and (d) to the broad approach, direction and framework of several of his main economic theories.

It must certainly be agreed as quite conceivable that a highly original and important contribution *might* be contained in very brief writings. A slow-working, careful, perfectionist author might produce a very small but highly significant opus. But Ricardo, instructed, and extremely over-confidently encouraged and urged on by Mill, was quite the opposite of slow-working, cautious and perfectionist. Thanks partly to Mill, as M and S emphasize, 'the rapidity with which Ricardo developed his thinking about politics was nothing if not spectacular' (p. 22). Ricardo's letters and 'Discourses' on politics followed almost concurrently with the spectacularly rapid development of his thinking (as was similarly the case with his writings on political economy). Unfortunately, however, spectacular rapidity in thinking and writing, about highly complex subjects, may take a heavy toll in terms of crucial inconsistencies, ambiguities and loose ends, when indulged in by someone starting almost from scratch, in middle age, and of 'poor education' – (as Donald Winch has put it, 1983, p. 87) – who insisted, with no excessive modesty, that, as a writer, he was an 'amateur'. For Ricardo, moreover, unquestionably an exceedingly quick learner, thinker and writer, even the spectacular rapidity of the development of his ideas, both on economics and politics, was not spectacularly rapid enough, given the vastness and complexity of the questions he raised for himself, and the tragically few years he was granted to resolve them.

IV

One of Ricardo's two political 'Discourses' is concerned with the demand for secrecy of the ballot, a reform certainly then calling for vigorous support from most of those with genuine democratic leanings. Ricardo's warm and enthusiastic rhetoric on this issue is highly commendable but can hardly be said to amount to a very significant or original contribution to political thought. The other of the two $7\frac{1}{2}$-page political 'discourses' dealt with the much broader, longer-run issue of the reform of the franchise. It is easily the most important item in Ricardo's political *oeuvre*. Here the central, fundamental question was just how far the franchise should be extended, and just how 'dangerous' the consequences of different kinds and degrees of extension might be. Actually, Ricardo seems to have been somewhat uninterested in this vital question and even to have considered rather unimportant the precise degree of extension (*v. Works*, 1952, vol. V, pp. 484–5; and note 10 below). Indeed, regarding the desirable extent of the electorate Ricardo wavered from one ambiguity to another (just as he had wavered regarding wages and their 'natural' level). On a number of occasions he uttered extremely optimistic calls for apparently sweeping extensions to the franchise, though restricting himself to vague generalizations which avoided any attempt to define, reasonably clearly and precisely, the extent of the electorate he was recommending. On one occasion he demanded 'a full, fair and equal representation of the people in the Commons' House of Parliament'[9] (*Works*, vol. V, 1952, p. 484). At other times, however, Ricardo repeatedly insisted on the vague but probably massive qualification that 'the rights of property should be held sacred', and that the franchise, therefore, should never be extended to anyone 'against whom it could justly be alleged that they considered it their interest to invade them' (ibid., p. 501). *Ricardo never undertook to tackle the problem as to just how this vast, vague and, for him, absolutely vital qualification, was to be, or could be implemented, in practice, in an actual reform of the electoral law.*

In some ways the nearest Ricardo came to providing a comprehensive but extremely concise formula for meeting the leading political and constitutional problem of the day, was in a letter to Trower of 16 June 1818. Here Ricardo very succinctly indicated his acceptance of the proposal put forward by Sir Samuel Romilly, which was: 'to extend the suffrage to the house-holder. To limit the duration of Parliaments to three years, and to vote by ballot' (*Works and Correspondence*, 1952, vol. VII, p. 273). Ricardo added: 'This is all the reform I desire.' ('Household suffrage', it might be explained, could have meant either quite a lot or pretty little.) Anyhow, though M and S mention this letter of Ricardo's to Trower to the effect that Ricardo 'stated his support' for Romilly's scheme, they unfortunately do not *quote* Ricardo, in particular his decisive statement: 'This is all the reform I desire.' Sir Samuel was not a radical but a moderate Whig, who enjoyed none of the illumination – dubiously claimed for Ricardo by M and S – from being 'in command of a theoretically informed version of economic science'. But in his nearest attempt at an adequately precise formula Ricardo simply echoed the non-economist Whig, Sir Samuel Romilly.

As an example, however, of the kind of policy, support for which should, according to Ricardo, have called for exclusion from the franchise, may be cited a resolution brought before the House of Commons in 1820 – by a Mr Maxwell MP – to alleviate the distress of large numbers of handloom weavers by taxing power looms and applying public money to providing lands for the destitute unemployed. The merits and demerits of such a proposal are certainly controversial. It should be noted, however, that Ricardo categorically denounced this measure because it would 'violate the sacredness of property, which constitutes the great security of society' (*Works*, vol. V, 1952, p. 68). Presumably, according to Ricardo, anyone inclined to vote, directly or indirectly, for such a relief measure, should have been excluded from the franchise. As Ricardo put it, to take from him 'the conviction of each capitalist that he will be allowed to enjoy unmolested the fruits of his capital, his skill, and his enterprise . . . is at once to annihilate half the productive industry of the country' (ibid., p. 501). Mr Maxwell MP obviously did not belong to what Ricardo called 'the reasonable part of the country' which deserved the franchise.

The problem of interpreting and elucidating Ricardo's various views and qualifications regarding the extension of the franchise, is illustrated in the penultimate paragraph of his paper on Parliamentary Reform. He first emphasizes:

My own opinion is in favour of caution, and therefore I lament that so much is said on the subject of Universal Suffrage. I am convinced that an extension of the franchise, *far short of making it universal*, will substantially secure to the people the good government they wish for.

(ibid., p. 502, italics added)[10]

Again, M and S, deplorably, give no quotation of Ricardo's support for a franchise *'far* short' of universal. Instead, on the basis of an optimistic quotation concerned with the longer term, or 'permanent' possibilities, they maintain that Ricardo 'proposed as an *immediate* reform of parliament the expansion of the elective franchise *just short of universal suffrage'* (1991, p. 37, italics added). Thus M and S present a quite unbalanced and misleading account of Ricardo's views. Ricardo's actual insistence on 'caution', and an initial measure 'far short' of universality, is transformed by M and S into a proposal for an 'immediate' reform 'just short of universal suffrage'. This gets Ricardo's views upside down and inside out with regard to his rosily naive and optimistic notions on longer-term possibilities, as contrasted with his very cautious and limited ideas as to 'immediate' reform.

Certainly, as regards the longer-term, or more 'permanent' possibilities, Ricardo expressed the most naively optimistic, and even Utopian views, maintaining that the wonderful effects of the initial, cautious measure (*'far* short' of universality) in bringing about 'good government', and the almost Utopian fruits thereof (such as 'prosperity and happiness . . . incomparably and almost inconceivably great') would 'satisfy the reasonable part of the public' who really wanted simply 'good government' rather than Universal Suffrage for its own sake: 'Give them good government, or let them be convinced that you are really in earnest in procuring it for them, and they will be satisfied, although you should not advance with the rapid steps that they think would be most advantageously taken' (ibid., p. 502).

Ricardo, in fact, seems here to regard a rapid, far-reaching extension of the franchise as unnecessary. The vast numbers excluded by a franchise 'far short' of universality would (according to Ricardo) be so thoroughly satisfied, that they would be very patient about further demands. Moreover, on the other hand, the almost inconceivable prosperity brought about by 'good government' would provide 'the means of so rapidly increasing the knowledge and intelligence of the public, that, *in a limited space of time*, after this first measure of reform had been granted, we might, with the utmost safety, extend the right of voting for members of Parliament to every class of people' (ibid., pp. 502–3, italics added). 'A limited space of time' is a pretty vague phrase, probably concealing considerable naive over-optimism.

V

In their Conclusion, after a considerable discussion of the labour theory of value, M and S sum up as follows:[11]

Ricardo single-mindedly advocated full democratic participation within the *existing* capitalist scheme. It was not necessary first to consult the degree to which individual intellectual and moral education had spread among the mass of the population before conferring upon them the franchise, it could safely be achieved there and then in England, in 1819.

(1991, p. 149, authors' italics)

The two main conclusions stated here are quite unjustifiable:

1 Ricardo did *not* advocate 'full democratic participation within the *existing* capitalist scheme . . . there and then'. He repeatedly advocated 'caution', emphasizing vital, if vague, qualifications regarding the sacredness of property. He only envisaged a widely expanded franchise when some great and widespread increase in wealth had been achieved, and, even then, doubted whether any great expansion would then prove necessary.

2 Ricardo did *not* hold that: 'It was not necessary first to consult the degree to which individual intellectual and moral education had spread among the mass of the population before conferring upon them the franchise.' As M and S themselves earlier explained: 'Ricardo spoke with such conviction of the need "to teach the labouring classes that they must themselves provide for those casualities to which they are exposed" ' (1991, p. 62).

What Ricardo was hoping for was that 'the labouring classes' would learn middle-class self-reliance and at the same time learn to restrict family size. Drastic pressure should be applied – as such learning processes might be protracted – in the form of the abolition of the Poor Law, which abolition was essential for the eventual great, widespread rise in the standard of living. It is obviously fantastic to regard these pre-conditions as existing 'there and then, in England in 1819'. The reform of the Poor Laws did not come until 1834 and would have been regarded by Ricardo as inadequate since he wanted abolition.

When M and S go on to assert that Ricardo 'never once seems to have entertained a doubt that capitalism could survive democracy' (p. 149) such an assertion must imply either (or both) his considerable political naiveté, and/or their own excessively simplistic concept of 'capitalism'. Those using this concept are in danger of neglecting or underestimating the economic, political and social transformations which 'capitalism' (unlike the recently collapsed Marxist systems) has been able to survive, throughout its history. In Britain it was only after half a century, or more, of economic and political transformation that a new version of 'capitalism' was ready for even a highly qualified kind of 'democracy'.[12]

VI

Another remarkable claim by M and S is that they 'provide evidence that Ricardo reached his own conclusions independently, and indeed before, the publication of James Mill's essay on Government (1820) . . . which according to received wisdom was supposed to have provided Ricardo with his politics' (1991, p. 18). Again, M and S fail to explain from whom, and by whom, this 'received wisdom' was ever 'received': certainly not from or by any scholar since 1952, when the Ricardo–Mill correspondence was first published. This correspondence shows that after the publication of the *Principles* in April 1817 (and a holiday in Europe in the summer months) Ricardo was now considered ready, by his mentor James Mill, for a crash course in politics. This course was to prepare him for parliamentary debate regarding the major issue of political reform. Fortunately, Mill's own mammoth, almost encyclopaedic, *History of British India* was appearing in a month or two, at the end of the year.[13] This was Ricardo's textbook, of which Mill immediately rushed him an advance copy, before publication. As Mill modestly explained, the work 'afforded an opportunity of laying open the principles and laws of the social order in almost all its more remarkable states, from the most rude to the most perfect with which we are yet acquainted' (19 October 1817, *Works and Correspondence*, vol. VII, pp. 195–6). Ricardo's copy of the History (18 December) came to him as something of a revelation: 'If I before had had doubts of what legislation might do, to improve society, I should have none after reading what I have read of your book' (18 December 1817, *op. cit.*, pp. 227–9).

These exchanges with Mill were the initial, and main component – together, of course, with the monstrous textbook so promptly provided – of Mill's spectacularly rapid crash course in politics. M and S describe this very important exchange with Mill as 'short' (which is quite unjustifiable when they elsewhere describe Ricardo's exchange with Trower, a year later, as 'extensive'). What Ricardo then got from Mill was crucially *formative* – unlike anything he ever got from Trower. Moreover, Mill's letters were supplemented by the textbook, and, when Ricardo was in London in the following spring, by discussions with Mill 'almost daily', on long walks in Kensington Gardens, during which they were joined by Trower.[14]

The vital stage of the Mill–Ricardo correspondence took place in the second half of 1817, nearly a year before the brief Ricardo–Trower exchanges on politics.[15] M and S do indeed recognize that Ricardo's correspondence with Mill, at this time, 'impinges directly on the question of representative government' (1991, p. 97). Certainly Ricardo was a rapid learner who put an acute question or two to his mentor. It seems, however, like a rather desperate attempt to put a cart before a horse for M and S to maintain that Ricardo 'reached his own conclusions', in his exercises written for Mill in late 1818 (or in the letters to Trower, approved by Mill of about the same date) *because* these exercises and letters were written before 1820 when Mill's essay on *Government* appeared. Ricardo's textbook was the multi-volume *History of British India*, which he began to study at the end of 1817. It is extraordinary that M and S seem quite unaware of the vital role of this phenomenal work in Ricardo's political education, and it is still more extraordinary, that, as easily the most important work in the development of Ricardo's political ideas, it is not even mentioned in their bibliography.

VII

It is time now to press home the question as to just what Ricardo's 'conclusions' consisted of – which are described by M and S as 'systematic', 'novel' and 'sophisticated', and which have been so long 'overlooked'. This question is crucial for assessing M and S's initial promises regarding the remarkably fruitful links between Ricardian economics and 'Ricardian politics':

> What sets Ricardian politics apart, what makes Ricardo more than just another economic adviser, is what he has to contribute to democratic theory proper. Furthermore, in the hands of Ricardo, economic theory itself had something to contribute to the strictly political question of the organization of the polity as well.
>
> (1991, p. 15)

> We shall spell out in some detail the manner in which Ricardo drew this connection between democratic theory and political economy.
>
> (p. 17)

M and S simply do not deliver on this magniloquent promise: first of all for the very simple reason that Ricardo himself did not deliver on it, and probably would never have claimed that he had so delivered. Certainly, there are some kinds of links between Ricardo's political economy and his approach to politics, in that he wanted political reform, above all, so as to obtain the great economic reforms, which he regarded as the test of 'good government', as he conceived it, and which, in their turn, would soon produce extraordinary prosperity.

Some of Ricardo's main political, or semi-political conclusions, as far as they seem to emerge are:

1 A strongly critical, or even hostile, attitude towards landlords for (as Adam Smith put it) 'reaping where they never sowed'; though Ricardo, at one point, indignantly denied such an attitude.

2 A rather incidental claim for a certain wisdom in the labouring classes, because they denied that the introduction of machinery never could damage their interests; an *aperçu*, which M and S, in spite of widespread Ludditism, seem to suggest might have justified their enfranchisement, in Ricardo's eyes. At the same time, of course, Ricardo entertained such a profound fear, regarding 'that increase of population which was so apt to take place among the labouring classes', that he held that the abolition of the Poor Laws was a matter of great urgency if 'any distinction of ranks', or incentives to capital accumulation, were to survive.

3 An extreme insistence that 'the rights of property should be held sacred';

117

which would require the disfranchisement of anyone who might support any relief from public funds for the unemployed.

4 The insistence by Ricardo that the reform formula of the moderate Whig, Sir Samuel Romilly, was 'all the reform I desire'?

'Conclusions' such as these seem neither 'novel' nor 'sophisticated'. They do seem to suggest waverings, wobblings, contrasts and conflicts of view, which Ricardo never successfully resolved in the tragically few years available to him. If there are other truly novel and sophisticated conclusions which emerge from Ricardo's political writings it is difficult to identify them in, and extricate them from, *Ricardian Politics*.

VIII

M and S have put forward another version of Ricardian hagiography. Using one of the oldest ploys in the controversial game, they proceed to demolish various exaggerated Aunt Sallies, of their own manufacture, which they variously describe as 'the dominant notion' (p. 3), 'the received opinion' (p. 6), 'this tradition' (p. 6) or 'received wisdom' (p. 18).

Like the two leading contradictory *economic* hagiographies of Ricardo, that of the Marxo–Sraffian, anti-neoclassical cult, and that of the academic abstractionist, pro-neoclassical-and-general-equilibrium theorists, M and S require for their political version the imposition on the texts of a degree of consistency which simply is not there. Unlike, however, the imaginative political version of M and S, the Ricardian economic hagiographers had at least *some* substantial texts (of more than seven to eight pages per item) which were intended for publication. They thus imposed coherence and consistency on texts for which at least *some* measure of such qualities was indeed being claimed, when they were put out under such a title as ' *The Principles of Political Economy and Taxation* '.

M and S, on the other hand, piece together their 'systematic' version of 'Ricardian politics' by piecing together letters, and extracts from letters and speeches, which – without adequately listing or identifying them – they repeatedly describe as 'extensive', but which do not seem even approximately to deserve such an adjective, when one can identify the original texts from which the version is constructed.

The attempt to impose a measure of 'system', or consistency, on a version constructed from such bits and pieces, involves the hagiographers in excluding anything contradictory as not 'worth quoting'; or by the simple but ruthless use of the blind eye: as when M and S apparently failed to notice – and certainly failed to quote – Ricardo's categorical acceptance of the reform of the franchise, put forward by the moderate Whig, Romilly, as 'all the reform I desire'; or when, somehow, Ricardo's emphasis on 'caution', and support for a franchise 'far short of universal', is transformed into a proposal for 'an

118

immediate reform of parliament' consisting of 'the expansion of the elective franchise just short of universal suffrage' (1991, p. 37).

Rapidity in assimilating ideas, and originality and acuteness in his political comments, is certainly not being denied to David Ricardo, especially after he had got into Parliament and was observing the passing political scene. Nor should it even be forgotten that if, instead of dying so prematurely, he had been granted another decade or two, to compensate somewhat for his late intellectual start in life, Ricardo's ideas might well have developed in all sorts of interesting directions.[16] Finally, even the most dogmatic and opinionated teacher may have learnt something from such a sharp-minded and quick-learning pupil, who had enjoyed some success, and much real-world experience, in the City and Parliament.

As they stand, however, at no point do Ricardo's political writings begin to justify the kind of claims and adjectives, advanced on their behalf by Professors Milgate and Stimson.

NOTES

1 The first version of this piece was given as a paper at the History of Economic Thought Conference at Exeter in September 1992. Somewhat acrimonious exchanges followed with the authors of the book criticized. This revised version appeared in the *History of Economics Review*, no. 19, Winter 1993, pp. 1ff.

2 See the preceding paper.

3 M and S pronounce a very unfavourable and totally unjustified verdict on Jeremy Bentham's economic writings. This is quite in accordance with classical conventional wisdom. Their dismissive treatment, however, rests on the sole basis, or sole mention, of the *Manual of Political Economy*, from among some twelve to fifteen extant economic works by Bentham. This is rather like assessing the work of Shakespeare while totally ignoring all his plays except, say, *The Two Gentlemen of Verona*. The *Manual* was written at an early stage of the eighteen years (*c.* 1786–*c.* 1804) in which he was writing on economics, during which time his views, on some major issues, changed fundamentally. According to M and S, Bentham could not 'seriously be described as having been in command of a theoretically informed version of economic science' (1991, p. 16). M and S add that his *Manual* 'is not a systematic treatise on the subject' (p. 16). It is difficult to define, at all precisely, what, in, say, 1804, a 'theoretically informed version of economic science' would have amounted to. It is perfectly reasonable to maintain, however, that in his later works – such as, for example, *The True Alarm* (1804) – Bentham showed himself to be in possession of far superior and sounder basic theories, than, subsequently, did James Mill and Ricardo, regarding the two fundamental and central questions of: (1) utility and value; and (2) saving and investing (including forced saving). Regarding utility and value, Bentham provided a superb critique of Smith's confused and confusing treatment of utility, value and the water-and-diamonds paradox (*v.* 1954, vol. 3, pp. 83–90). Regarding saving and investing, Bentham delivered an equally superb criticism of the Turgot–Smith savings-*is*-investing doctrine which became the cornerstone of the more rigid and dogmatic versions of classical macroeconomics (*thanks to James Mill and Ricardo*, who came to the rescue of the Turgot–Smith doctrine just when it had been under serious criticism, in the first quarter of the nineteenth century, from Bentham, Lauderdale, Thornton,

Blake and others, not to mention the sometimes inconsistent views of Malthus). It is, of course, highly misleading of M and S to state that 'Ricardo's opinion' on saving and investing 'represented the conventional wisdom on the subject among the classical economists' (p. 75) – unless this statement is a tautology. Certainly, on saving and investing Mill and Ricardo followed Adam Smith, but in the first quarter of the nineteenth century they may well have been in a minority of leading economists.

Anyhow, it was Mill and Ricardo who recommended to Dumont – against the editor's inclinations – that Bentham's *True Alarm* should be suppressed. Incidentally, it seems probable that Ricardo managed to lose the only copy of the original English manscript (*v.* Stark's Introduction to *Bentham's Economic Writings*, 1952, vol. III, pp. 17–18). This recommendation of Mill and Ricardo must rank as probably the most disastrous and dogmatic act of censorship in the history of the subject. Not, of course, that *The True Alarm* is finished, flawless work. But political economy in the nineteenth century, in particular with regard to two of the basic theories, of utility and value, and of saving and investment (both flawed and inadequate in the classical and/or Ricardian versions of political economy), would surely have been fundamentally enlightened and advanced by Bentham's work. It may not only have been, according to Keynes, a tragedy that Ricardo won out over Malthus. It may have been a much greater tragedy that Ricardo and Mill got away with suppressing Bentham. Needless to add, what Professor Paul Samuelson (1992, p. 10) describes (somewhat abrasively) as 'the mob' of Ricardo's gushing, but completely contradictory, admirers, supporters and hagiographers, has never condescended to take the slightest notice of Bentham's finest economic writings – which their hero helped to suppress.

4 James Mill, writing a few days after Ricardo's sudden death, may well have overstated, in some ways, the extent of his role as 'confidant' and 'adviser' of Ricardo. With regard, however, to what we are here concerned with, that is, the development of Ricardo's ideas and writings on political economy and politics, Mill *understates* his role, in that he was, on important points, not simply an adviser and confidant, but a tutor or instructor.

5 In the following year (7 March 1821) Ricardo was again describing to MPs the effects of the free import of corn: 'The prices of corn would be reduced immediately, and agriculture might be distressed more than at present. But the labour of this country would be immediately applied to the production of other and more profitably commodities . . .' (*Works*, vol. V, 1952, p. 82). Everything happens 'immediately', according to Ricardo, as he presents to his fellow parliamentarians one of his 'strong cases' in which masses of agricultural workers and their families are represented as moving off 'immediately' into other industries. Again, Brougham's comments were amply justified. No one with their feet quite firmly planted on this planet could have assumed that such a model was adequate (*v.* Hutchison 1953a, pp. 269–70). Barry Gordon quotes Brougham as describing Ricardo as arguing 'without duly taking into account in practice the condition of things . . . as if a mechanician were to construct an engine without taking into consideration the resistance of the air in which it was to work, or the strength and its weight and the friction of the parts of which it was to be made' (Gordon, 1976, p. 3; Brougham, 1839, p. 189; and M and S, 1991, pp. 4–5). Possibly as a result of Brougham's criticisms, Ricardo seems to have become more cautious subsequently, when, in his pamphlet on *Protection for Agriculture*, he recommended abolition of the corn laws by gradual stages, 'with a due regard for temporary interests' (*v. Works and Correspondence*, vol. IV, 1952, p. 266).

M and S go on hotly to defend the realism of 'the classical economists' against

Samuelson's 'ridiculous' claim that they 'lived during the industrial revolution, but scarcely looked out from their libraries to notice the remaking of the world' (p. 55, n. 25). Generalizations about 'the classical economists' must be viewed with caution, or even scepticism, as all too often tendentious regarding an imprecisely defined body of economists, who differed widely on both theory and method. It is, however, certainly *not* ridiculous to point out that after the enlightened eighteenth-century approaches to value theory of the Natural Law school in terms of utility and scarcity, and of Galiani, Turgot and Condillac, in terms of utility, subjectivity and expectations, it was blindly retrogressive of some leading British classicals to turn to a labour theory, as, most dogmatically and emphatically, did James Mill and Ricardo. Just at the very historical juncture when technological change was rendering more and more irrelevant a labour theory of value – which, as Adam Smith had observed, long before, applies only, without the most awkward quali-fications and intellectual contortions, in a beaver-and-deer-hunting society – Mill and Ricardo chose to 'shunt the car', not only onto the wrong lines but backwards. At least Marx had a *kind of* excuse, that, as a propagandist and agitator he was trying to use a labour theory of value for ideological and agitational purposes. Attempts to use the labour theory for any kind of positive explanation, or predic-tion, surely received their richly-deserved, final, and humiliating come-uppance in 1989–91 – after nearly two centuries of far-fetched qualifications and useless apologetic argumentation. It was only *some* of the English classicals who vastly over-worked the 'labour' approach to value – as, most emphatically, did Ricardo and James Mill.

6 From the index it can be ascertained that, according to Sraffa – and contrary to the claim of M and S – there were no letters between Ricardo and Trower on any significant political subject in 1816 or in 1817. According to Sraffa's Index, exchanges between Ricardo and Trower on 'Political Reform' began in the first half of 1818 and lasted until January 1819. Inspection confirms that Sraffa's Index is not guilty of any significant omissions. Ricardo's contribution, in fact, to the exchanges on politics between Ricardo and Trower amounted to five letters, written over nine months, that is, to a very small fraction, in terms both of extent and time, of what M and S suggest.

On the other hand, the relevant exchanges with James Mill, in late 1817 and the first quarter of 1818, took place a year earlier than those between Ricardo and Trower, and possessed an importance for the development of Ricardo's political ideas quite unmatched by the exchanges with Trower. From Ricardo's side there were about four to five significant political letters to Trower, which – like the two 'Discourses' – served as exercises, under Mill's surveillance, to round off his crash course on politics, and prepare Ricardo for parliamentary debate. Of course, in 1816 and 1817, such topics as, problems in the Royal Family, the Poor Laws and Provident Associations, had come up, but it would be very misleading to include such comments under any significant political heading (as Sraffa's index confirms by their omission).

7 Not content with seriously exaggerating the extent of Ricardo's exchange with Trower, M and S make an extraordinary suggestion regarding its quality and importance, to the effect that there is some significant 'correspondence', or 'parallel', between Trower and Malthus and between their exchanges with Ricardo on politics and political economy respectively: 'To his close friend and adversary on economic questions, Malthus, corresponded another close friend and adversary on political questions, Hutches Trower' (1991, p. 13). M and S then go on to explain that it 'would be a misrepresentation to claim a status for the Trower–Ricardo correspondence on politics quite as grand as that Keynes claimed for the parallel

Ricardo–Malthus correspondence (namely that it was "the most important literary correspondence in the whole development of Political Economy")' (p. 14). It is indeed gracious of M and S to concede that the Ricardo–Trower correspondence on politics is '*not quite* as grand' (italics added) as the justly celebrated Ricardo–Malthus correspondence on political economy. Except for the utterly trivial and banal fact that Ricardo exchanged letters with both of his friends, Malthus and Trower, there, is, of course, no 'correspondence' or 'parallel' whatsoever: the two exchanges are not in remotely the same class.

8 M and S are so intent on their attempt to distance Ricardo from James Mill that they involve themselves in what may seem an outright contradiction. They quote Ricardo (1991, p. 62) as speaking 'with such conviction of the need "to teach the labouring classes that they must themselves provide for those casualties to which they are exposed" ' (*v. Works*, vol. VII, 1952, p. 248, and vol. I, p. 107). Only two pages later, however, M and S are discussing Mill's views about the education of the labouring class, from which, of course, they immediately seek to distance Ricardo by proclaiming: 'There is nothing in Ricardo, for example, about needing to educate men and women to correct opinions or about having them emulate "those virtuous families of the middle rank" that Mill advocates' (p. 64). It was just the essentially 'middle-rank' virtues of independence and self-reliance, which, just two pages previously, M and S had quoted Ricardo as emphasizing the need 'to teach the labouring classes'. Certainly there may be a second-order difference regarding the particular 'middle-rank' virtue of independence and self-reliance referred to in these two quotations. But it seems rather desperate, if not contradictory, to try to insist on any profound clashes or disagreements between Ricardo and Mill in this area.

9 In a speech at the 'Westminster Reform Dinner' of 23 May 1823, Ricardo proposed the toast of 'a full, fair, free and equal Representation of the People in the Commons' House of Parliament'. This enthusiastic rhetoric was hardly matched by the much less than clear-cut words with which Ricardo continued regarding the extent of the franchise:

> A numerous class of persons in this country thought that it should be extended to the whole of the people; others thought it would be sufficiently extensive if given only to householders. Between these two opinions there was much debatable ground; he did not think this a point of such essential importance, as some appeared to consider it, and in his opinion there would be sufficient security for good government if the Elective Franchise was extended no farther than to those who paid direct taxes, or who were fairly called householders.
>
> (*Works*, vol. V, 1952, pp. 484–5)

This seems to combine restrictions far short of unversality, along the lines of Sir R. Romilly's scheme, which he had accepted five years previously, together with a certain indifference to the question of the extent of the franchise, provided 'good government' was somehow secured (rather underwhelming enthusiasm for what M and S call 'full participatory democracy').

It is unfortunately typical that while M and S find Ricardo's rosily enthusiastic words – about 'a full, fair, free and equal representation of the people' – to be 'worth quoting', they do not consider 'worth quoting' Ricardo's support for something like the unradical proposal of the moderate Whig, Sir Samuel Romilly; nor Ricardo's suggestion that the question of the extent of the franchise was *not* 'a point of such essential importance' (*v.* 1991, pp. 123–4).

10 The contrast between the emphatic caution of Ricardo's views on short-term political reform and his longer-term extreme optimism as to the compatibility of

universality (or near-universality) of the (adult male) franchise with what he regarded as 'good government', is part of a broader contrast between the marked emphasis on class conflict which pervades much of his economics (or what M and S call 'his vision of conflictual economic relations') and, on the other hand, the naive optimism of much of his longer-term political rhetoric implying far-reaching harmony (or harmonizability) in the political arena. This contrast between his proto-Marxism and his proto-Bastiatism is one of the fundamental incoherences in Ricardo's so rapidly developed views which never got clearly reconciled or resolved in the tragically few years available to him. Certainly, if Ricardo had been granted another active decade or two, he might have somersaulted in all sorts of directions, as he did over the effects of machinery; and some of these directions *might* have been quite opposed to the ideas of his original mentor, Mill.

11 In the course of their discussion of the labour theory of value M and S (p. 146) refer to, and paraphrase, a rather jocular remark of mine, from a review article of 1952, regarding the Stalinist orthodoxy of the day and the Sraffa–Dobb interpretation of Ricardo's theory of value. It is not for me to try to explain the precise relevance (if any) of this reference to M and S's line of argument. The suggestion might, however, perhaps be ventured that it would have been considerably less irrelevant of M and S – than referring to my 1952 review – to have cited, and even expressed some slight measure of agreement with, my 1953 article (revised 1978) entitled 'James Mill and the Political Education of Ricardo'. Stressing Ricardo's 'healthy doubts' and 'much native insight', I quoted at length a critical question directed by Ricardo at Mill: 'Are we to fix our eyes steadily on the happiness of the governed, and pursue it at the expense of those principles which all men are agreed in calling virtuous?' (see Hutchison, 1978, p. 39). M and S quote this paragraph (less lengthily) in discussing the problems of Mill's and Ricardo's utilitarianism (1991, p. 97). We seem to have come to very similar conclusions, both noting, as M and S put it: 'Unfortunately, there is no record in these letters showing that the enlightenment which Ricardo requested from Mill was forthcoming' (p. 97). My quotation and comment seem to demonstrate that at least one commentator, who emphasized the tremendous influence of Mill on Ricardo, nevertheless appreciated quite clearly that Ricardo was neither a 'marionette' nor an 'amanuensis'.

12 M and S claim that Ricardo wanted 'full democratic participation'. The expansion of the franchise to anything approaching such an extent was, in particular in Britain, almost inevitably accompanied by, among other measures, the granting of a significant legal status and powers to trade unions. In fact, in Britain, the Second Reform Bill (1867) was demanded and granted very much for the purpose of recognizing legally such a status and powers for the unions of 'the aristocracy of labour'. As Dicey put it, what the new voters, enfranchised in 1867, wanted, and very soon got, was 'a means for obtaining legislation (such, for example, as a modification of the combination laws) in accordance with the desires of trade unions' (1905, p. 253; see Hutchison, 1966, pp. 13–16, and 1981, pp. 24–32).

As for Ricardo, he never expressed anything like Adam Smith's view of wage-bargaining as heavily biased in favour of the employers and their monopsonistic practices. He put his faith in unrestricted competition on *both* sides of the labour market, proclaiming in the *Principles*: 'Like all other contracts wages should be left to the fair and free competition of the market' (*Works and Correspondence*, vol. I, p. 105; see Hutchison, 1978, p. 47). He elaborated his views in a letter to McCulloch, opposing the Combination Laws:

In spite of these laws masters are frequently intimidated, and are obliged to comply with the unjust demands of their workmen. The true remedy for combinations is perfect liberty on both sides, and adequate protection against violence and outrage. Wages should be the result of a free compact, and the contracting parties should look to the law to protect them from force being employed on either side; competition would not, I think, fail to do the rest.

(*op. cit.*, vol. VIII, p. 316)

Certainly, at times, Ricardo gave expression to a radical side to his not very coherent political and social views, which put him, however, much nearer a kind of hard-right, libertarian radicalism, than the kind of soft-left, democratic radicalism ascribed to him by M and S: especially when, for example, he was emphasizing in his maiden speech in parliament, 'that increase of population which was so apt to take place among the labouring classes'; or when he was chuntering on to Trower about how, without the abolition of the Poor Laws, 'the population and the rates would go on increasing in a regular progression till the rich were reduced to poverty, and till there would no longer be any distinction of ranks'. (Incidentally, this last foreboding seems to cast a pretty sick light on 'the modern version of the doctrine of class equality', which – according to M and S's splendid peroration – Ricardo 'brought forward' (1991, p. 149; see also *Works and Correspondence*, 1952, vol. V, p. 1, and vol. VII, p. 125; also Hutchison, 1978, p. 47).

13 For Mill it was so urgent that his pupil should get started on his '*History*' as soon as possible, that he sent him a pre-publication copy, without index or maps, and saved two precious months in the development of his pupil's political education. By January 1818, Ricardo was apparently into the third, huge volume of the work; see Mill's letter to Ricardo of 3 December 1817. On Mill's extraordinary *History of British India*, see Duncan Forbes, 1951; Hutchison, 1978, pp. 37–40; and William Thomas's edition of the work, 1975.

14 Regarding Ricardo's discussions with Mill on their walks together in Kensington Gardens in May 1818, see his letter to Malthus of 25 May, when he expressed the hope that Malthus might join them, and suggests that they would soon make a radical out of him if he did. Trower also joined these walks, making the exchanges 'three-cornered' – as Thomas describes the exchange of letters on politics. (See following note.)

15 William Thomas (1979, p. 126) describes the Ricardo–Trower exchanges on politics as part of a 'three cornered' exchange:

> Mill urged Ricardo to set down his thoughts on the subject, and Ricardo, complying reluctantly, *because it was a subject on which he knew little*, began to try out his views in letters to his friend Hutches Trower. . . . Ricardo, *primed by Mill*, tried to convert Trower, sometimes showing Mill his letters and Trower's replies. From this three-cornered correspondence *it is clear that Ricardo inclined to a moderate position on reform . . . sharing Trower's fears about popular ignorance and the danger it posed to property.* . . . To Ricardo, this meant enfranchising 'all reasonable men', or those who could be relied on to preserve property [italics added].

In his recent and comprehensive treatise on *The Philosophic Radicals*, Thomas, quite appropriately, casually mentions Ricardo several times, but, also quite appropriately, devotes altogether some three to four pages, out of 453, to his political writings. It may be observed, that, of the 150 pages of M and S on '*Ricardian Politics*' a considerable proportion are devoted to the politics of James and J. S. Mill, Bentham, Burke, Mackintosh, Place and others, while another considerable proportion is devoted to Ricardo's economics. The title of the book is a misnomer.

16 After a further forty years of contradictory hagiography the following conclusion regarding Ricardo's political economy seems also quite justifiable regarding his political ideas: 'The overriding fact surely is that Ricardo came, with tragic discontinuity, to the end of his own personal "long run", in no state of even relatively

stable or neutral intellectual equilibrium. Moreover, the "dynamic" process of development was crammed into so comparatively few years that no decisive trends in his thinking get much chance of emerging definitively' (Hutchison, 1953a, p. 265).

REFERENCES

Bentham, J. (1952). *Jeremy Bentham's Economic Writings*, 3 vols, ed. W. Stark.

Blaug, M. (1986). *Economic History and the History of Economics*.

Brougham, Lord. (1839). *Historical Sketches of Statesmen who Flourished in the Time of George III*, 2nd Series.

Collini, S., Winch, D., and Burrow, J. (1983). *That Noble Science of Politics*.

Dicey, A. V. (1905). *Lectures on the Relation between Law and Public Opinion*.

Eatwell, Lord. (1979). 'Maurice Dobb', *International Encyclopedia of the Social Sciences*, vol. 18, pp. 142–4.

Economist, The. (1951). p. 501.

Forbes, D. (1951). 'James Mill and India', *Cambridge Journal*, October, pp. 19ff.

Gordon, B. (1976). *Political Economy in Parliament, 1819–1823*.

Hollander, S. (1979). *The Economics of David Ricardo*.

Hutchison, T. W. (1952). 'Some Questions about Ricardo', *Economica*, vol. 19, November, pp. 451ff.

Hutchison, T. W. (1953a). 'Ricardo's Correspondence', *Economica*, vol. 20, August, pp. 263ff.

Hutchison, T. W. (1953b). 'James Mill and the Political Education of Ricardo', *Cambridge Journal*, vol. VII, no. 2, pp. 81ff.

Hutchison, T. W. (1966). *Markets and the Franchise*, Institute of Economic Affairs, Occasional Paper 10.

Hutchison, T. W. (1978). *On Revolutions and Progress in Economic Knowledge*, ch. 2, 'James Mill and Ricardian Economics: a Methodological Revolution?', pp. 26ff.

Hutchison, T. W. (1981). *The Philosophy and Politics of Economics*, ch. 2, 'The Market Economy and the Franchise, or 1867 and All That', pp. 23ff.

Hutchison, T. W. (1985). 'On the Interpretation and Misinterpretation of Economists', in *Gli Economistie la politica economia*, ed. P. Roggi, pp. 323ff.

Keynes, J. M. (1933). *Essays in Biography*.

Milgate, M. and Stimson, S. (1991). *Ricardian Politics*.

Mill, J. (1858). *History of British India*, ed. D. Winch.

Mill, J. (1966). *Selected Economic Writings*, ed. D. Winch.

Mill, J. (1975). *History of British India*, introduced by W. Thomas.

Mill, J. S. (1924). *Autobiography*, World's Classics, ed. H. J. Laski.

Pollitt, B. H. (1988). 'The Collaboration of Maurice Dobb in Sraffa's Edition of Ricardo', *Cambridge Journal of Economics*, vol. 12, March, pp. 55ff.

Ricardo, D. (1951–73). *Works and Correspondence*, ed. P. Sraffa with the collaboration of M. H. Dobb, 11 vols.

Rima, I. (1975). 'James Mill and Classical Economics: a Reappraisal', *Eastern Economic Journal*, vol. 2, pp. 113ff.

Robbins, L. C. (1949). *The Theory of Economic Policy in English Classical Political Economy*.

Robinson, J. (1973). *Collected Economic Papers*, vol. IV.

Samuelson, P. A. (1992). 'The Overdue Recovery of Adam Smith's Reputation as an Economic Theorist', in *Adam Smith's Legacy*, ed. M. Fry, pp. 1ff.

Schumpeter, J. A. (1942). *Capitalism, Socialism and Democracy*, 3rd ed.

Stigler, G. J. (1965). *Essay in the History of Economics*.

Thomas, W. (1975). 'Introduction' to *History of British India*, by James Mill.

Thomas, W. (1979). *The Philosophical Radicals*.

Thweatt, W. O. (1976). 'James Mill and the Early Development of Comparative Advantage', *History of Political Economy*, vol. 8, pp. 207ff.

Winch, D. N. (ed.) (1966). *Selected Economic Writings*, Chapter III, 'James Mill and David Ricardo', pp. 179ff.

Winch, D. N. (1983). 'The Cause of Good Government', in Burrows, J., Collini, S. and Winch, D. N. *The Noble Science of Politics*, pp. 91ff.

6

THE POLITICS AND PHILOSOPHY IN JEVONS'S POLITICAL ECONOMY[1]

I

For Jevons, as, until quite recently, for almost all economists, political economy was first and last a fruit-bearing subject concerned, above all, with the alleviation of real-world problems of poverty, insecurity and efficiency. The recent idea of 'much of economic theory' being pursued for no better reason than its providing 'a good game',[2] would have seemed to Jevons extremely odd and unacceptable. Therefore, his political and philosophical assumptions, or presuppositions, are of importance and interest for understanding his writings on political economy. New material on this subject has recently become available in the seven volumes of his *Papers and Correspondence* edited by Professor Black (1972–81), hereafter referred to as *P & C*.

Though he was deeply interested in, and a major writer on, philosophy and scientific method, Jevons did not include politics among the extraordinarily wide range of subjects which he studied, and to which he made important and original contributions. Later in life he remarked in a letter to his brother:

> About politics, I confess myself in a fog . . . I prefer to leave *la haute politique* alone, as a subject which admits of no scientific treatment. I have enough to think and write about which I can somewhat understand without troubling myself about things which I cannot understand.
>
> (14 November 1878; *P & C*, vol. IV, p. 293)[3]

The presuppositions from which Jevons started, as shaped by his temperament, upbringing, and family and social background, were based on a sturdy individualism and an enthusiastic confidence in freedom of trade. But there was another significant empirical component in Jevons's individualist and libertarian views, derived from observations and experience in his youthful, Australian days, where, as a government employee in Sydney, he saw something of politics at the grass-roots. In a letter to his cousin, H. E. Roscoe, Jevons gave his impressions of democratic politics in the young colony of New South Wales:

Politics here are in a very singular state; Responsible Government was inaugurated as they grandly express it about six months ago ever since which unfortunate event the colony has been perpetually in the agonies of Ministerial Crises. The new responsible Ministers have resigned or been kicked out two or three times already, three elections have taken place in Sydney within about 8 months and our new Parliament has debated for weeks together without passing a bill. It is all carried on nearly next door to us at the Mint and we sometimes turn into the gallery of an evening to have a bit of fun and hear the Ministerial and Opposition benches abusing each other.

(21 October 1856; *P & C*, vol. II, p. 247)

Later, dissatisfaction with his own quangoid job led Jevons to complain: 'I have learned to detest the Government Service' (9 October 1858; *P & C*, vol. II, p. 343).

It is hardly surprising, therefore, that when, at this time, problems of the New South Wales railways were the subject of controversy in the press, the young Jevons came out strongly against government investment policies. For he was never likely to have entertained the presupposition, which subsequently seems to have been involved in some Cambridge versions of 'welfare' economics, of an omniscient and benevolent government – (directed either, on the one hand, by the products, sent out 'with cool heads but warm hearts', of Marshall's Economics Tripos, or, alternatively, as embodied in such highly praised figures, in their own day, as Stalin and Mao).

Professor Black's new edition provides further evidence as to how the problems of the New South Wales railways and land policies constituted the starting point for Jevons's first steps in political economy. In this respect he was following the same path as other pioneers of marginal analysis and 'neo-classical' economics in the nineteenth century, such as Dupuit, Lardner, Ellet and Launhardt.[4] English classical theory was largely useless and impotent before the emerging, and increasingly important, problems of railways and public utilities, so that new tools and new ideas were required. Any reasonable assessment of 'neoclassical' economics, or of Jevons's pioneering contribution to the 'Jevonian revolution' – as M. H. Dobb called it – must recognize this highly practical, real-world starting-point; and that it is only on the basis of neoclassical concepts that economists can make any contribution to the analysis of real-world problems of this kind.

As regards the practical politics of railway investment, the well-founded fears of the 21-year-old Jevons regarding probable governmental over-investment and mismanagement misled him, to some extent, into over-simplification. He proceeded to condemn

. . . that extraordinary declaration of the Governor-General's that a rail-way need not necessarily be capable of paying any profits, since indirect benefits to the population may repay its cost. This I maintain to be completely false in principle, for the reason that the money returns of the railway, though not the object of its construction, as in private concerns, furnish, when the fares are adjusted to the maximum paying rates, an exact measure of the benefits conferred, direct or indirect.

(10 February 1857; *P & C*, vol. II, p. 265)

The youthful Jevons was, however, very reasonably apprehensive about the probable waste and corruption of open-ended government spending on public works when he insisted:

Now, though a debt which has been incurred by productive expenditure is very different from the nonproductive debts of Great Britain and other countries, it behoves us carefully to preserve this difference, and to spend not one pound upon public works which will not be probably paying 5 per cent interest in value, within a reasonable number of years, say five years to come.

(*P & C*, vol. II, p. 266)

Jevons proceeded to ask a very justifiable question regarding the American example:

In the States, too, the lines of railway are, I believe, projected and executed by private speculators, Yankee men of business, of well-known foresight and cuteness. Does the general success of government works in this colony or any other colony whatever, warrant us in supposing the same economy and foresight will be employed, or the same success attend the Government railway undertakings at present in question?

(*P & C*, vol. II, p. 267)

II

However, if the youthful Jevons started with ruggedly individualistic and anti-governmental presuppositions, he set out also with profound social sympathies and a warm concern about the problem of poverty. As I have noted elsewhere regarding the teenage Jevons:

Jevons used to go for long walks through the poorest parts of the Dickensian London of the early fifties looking at 'the condition of the people'. He writes (*aet.* 17) that the book he wants most to obtain is that wonderful pioneer social survey, Mayhew's *London Labour and London Poor*, 'the only book I know of to learn a little about the real condition of the poor in London'.

(Hutchison, 1953, p. 33)

Among Jevons's early projects was one described as *Notes and Researches on Social Statistics or the Science of Towns, especially as regards London and Sydney*. In an article on 'The Social Cesspools of Sydney' published in *The Sydney Morning Herald* (7 October 1858) he remarks:

> To a person of humane feelings, . . . the sight and acquaintance of social ills, has the same lively, although painful, interest that a rare and terrible bodily disease has to the devoted physician. . . . A great city is to him a thing worthy of deep research and reflection . . . that man who can witness all the phases of a city unmoved, and uninterested, is himself a criminal, a slave of pride and evil feelings. . . . It seems to me that he who bears a right feeling towards his fellows, should feel a very lively and exciting interest in many subjects social and sanitary.[5]

It is interesting to find Professors Walsh and Gram, in a recent study which favours classical and Marxian rather than neoclassical problems and concepts, comparing the young Jevons with a rather idealized view of Engels and Marx:

> The similarity of the tone of Jevons's social observation with certain great passages in *Capital* and with Friedrich Engels's *The Condition of the Working Classes in Britain*, is so striking that *one could sandwich a passage from Jevons between a couple of those of Marx or Engels without any sharp change of feeling or style being obvious*.

> (1980, p. 125, italics added)[6]

The main empirical, contemporary-historical starting point, 'vision', or original 'model', of Engels's and Marx's political economy was based on Manchester in the early 1840s, and continued to retain limitations stemming from the political and economic framework of that time and place. To some significant extent, London and Sydney in the 1850s provided a starting-point for Jevons. But it was also one where policies regarding railways and public works posed important practical, real-world problems, and the concepts and analysis devised for dealing with these problems had a very wide generality.

III

The middle years, indeed the greater part, of Jevons's quarter-century career as an economist (1857–82) were a time of major transition in politics and economic policy in Britain, as well as containing the turning-point, or 'revolution', associated with his *Theory of Political Economy* (1871). Jevons's ideas on economic policy and the role of government developed with the times. In fact, Professor Hayek regards Jevons's last work, *The State in Relation to Labour* (1882), as 'the end of the liberal era of principles' as had been upheld by the classicals (1973, p. 59). But Jevons should not be regarded as abandoning his earlier stress on freedom so much as recognizing the pressure of the qualifications which historical and institutional changes were bringing. Admittedly, Joseph Chamberlain in 1892 invoked the name of Jevons to justify utilitarian interventions by government, attributing to him the doctrine that 'the State is justified in passing any law, or even in doing any single act, which without ulterior consequences adds to the sum of human happiness'. But Chamberlain was *slightly* misrepresenting Jevons.[7]

Anyhow, regarding Jevons's last book, *The State in Relation to Labour*, his closest economist friend, H. S. Foxwell of Cambridge, a very severe critic of Ricardian *laissez-faire*, wrote to Jevons, just before its publication, as follows:

> I hope to find that you have taken up – well I won't say a Socialistic position, because some dislike the word: but at all events a position from which you recognize the obligation of the individual to society, and the necessity of some control, in the public interest, of his endeavours to secure his private gain. The more I read about the condition of labour, the more convinced I am of the necessity and advantage of organization and control. It vexes me to hear the authority of Political Economy always appealed to by the selfish rich on the other side. I don't think it will be so much longer, from what I see of the younger generation of economists.
>
> (10 April 1882; *P & C*, vol. V, p. 186)

Jevons replied two days later: 'Judging from what you say I fancy the new book will almost exactly meet your views' (p. 187).

The major turning-point in economic policy and political economy of the late 1860s and early 1870s can be seen as linked with the Reform Bill of 1867, support for which was also connected, to an important extent, with pressure for more liberal trade union legislation, which duly followed in the Acts of 1871 and 1875. The two Acts reinforced by that of 1906, laid the foundations of modern trade union power in Britain.

Though describing himself to his brother Herbert (28 December 1865), as 'not a democrat', with little positive enthusiasm for the impending electoral reform, Jevons considered that 'any reform bill that is likely to pass . . . may lead to many real improvements' (*P & C*, vol. III, p. 150). Certainly Jevons was apprehensive about the increase of the power of trade unions, because he did not believe that they could raise wages and that they might well reduce investment, or else squeeze consumers. In fact, Jevons foresaw what is believed by many today, economists and non-economists alike, to be a socially damaging excess of power on the side of the unions. His proposals included the promotion of competition as well as some form of cooperation or profit-sharing:

> The rate of wages, and the demand and supply for labour are things which cannot be regulated at the will of anyone. They depend upon the natural advantages of the country or the locality, the abundance of capital attracted to the trade, the course of foreign commerce, the state of the money market, and many other causes. Trades unions cannot alter or govern those things; they cannot, therefore, raise wages at all in

the long run. They may seem now and then to gain an advantage of five or ten per cent, but they cannot tell how much capital they drive away from a branch of trade by each strike or forced concession. . . .

I beg to join my small voice to that of men like Mr. Mill . . . who say that a new era will open to the workmen of England when they take measures for sharing in the possession, management, and profits of capital. They cannot do without capital, and therefore they ought, themselves to hold and enjoy a large portion of it. . . .

I am often inclined to think that the masters are to blame for the difficulties they encounter with their men. It is because the masters are always thought to be making secret, but vast profits that their men display profound distrust in all negotiations. . . . The sooner publicity is substituted for secrecy the better for the interests of all. It will then be practicable to combine the interest of masters and men by the division of all profits exceeding a certain fixed amount. . . .

(*P & C*, vol. III, pp. 137–8 and 143)

Subsequently Jevons concluded:

It follows that supposing all trades to form unions, as the workmen themselves wish, that each trade will be benefiting itself at the expense of all other trades; that consequently there can be no considerable advantage to any workmen whatever.

(*P & C*, vol. VI, p. 72)

Jevons's latest views were expounded in *The State in Relation to Labour* (1882) when he concluded with regard to trade unions:

One result which clearly emerges from a calm review is that all classes of society are trade unionists at heart, and differ chiefly in the boldness, ability and secrecy with which they push their respective interests.

(p. vi)

This final work of Jevons is especially distinguished by its cautious and moderate empiricism and fallibilism, and by a fundamental rejection of dogma. The book contains some brlilliant and well known passages, expressing his philosophical standpoint, which may be thought well worthy of requotation. Here are virtually his last published words in his lifetime:

It is clear that there can be no royal road to legislation in such matters. We cannot expect to agree in our utilitarian estimates, at least without much debate. We must agree to differ, and though we are bound to argue fearlessly, it should be with the consciousness that there is room for wide and *bona fide* difference of opinion. We must consent to advance cautiously, step by step, feeling our way, adopting no foregone conclusions, trusting no single science, expecting no infallible guide. We must neither maximise the functions of government at the beck of quasi-military officials, nor minimise them according to the theories of the very best philosophers. We must learn to judge each case upon its merits, interpreting with painful care all experience which can be brought to bear upon the matter.

Moreover, we must remember that, do what we will, we are not to expect approach to perfection in social affairs. . . . Tolerance therefore is indispensable . . .

(p. 166)

IV

We noted the earnest social concern and commitment, with and from which the young Jevons started his work as a political economist, alongside his strongly libertarian presuppositions. There was even a strain of missionary fervour in his ambition (*aet.* 22):

> To be powerfully good, that is to be good, not towards one or a dozen, or a hundred, but towards a nation or the world, is what now absorbs me. But this assumes the possession of the power.

(*P & C*, vol. II, p. 307)

As Adam Smith would have warned, ambitions for such wide-ranging benevolence have their dangers. But, for Jevons, this powerful ethical, or missionary drive was not so much – as it was a decade later for Marshall – a religious substitute, but rather a religious complement. Moreover, with Jevons, as with Marshall, though not with all Marshall's successors, missionary fervour was balanced by three vital checks: (1) a genuine, strenuous concern to find out empirically about the lives of the poor and those to whom he was aspiring to do good; (2) an insistence on the discipline of careful empirical testing, as far as possible; (3) a fundamental cautious and critical fallibilism regarding the principles of science.

Jevons's critical fallibilism is powerfully stated, with regard to political economy, in the section on 'The Noxious Influence of Authority' at the end of his *Theory* (1871):

> There is ever a tendency of the most hurtful kind to allow opinions to crystallise into creeds. Especially does this tendency manifest itself where some eminent author, enjoying power of clear and comprehensive exposition, becomes recognised as an authority. His works may perhaps be the best which are extant upon the subject in question; they may combine more truth with less error than we can elsewhere meet. But 'to err is human', and the best works should ever be open to criticism. If, instead of welcoming inquiry and criticism, the admirers of a great author accept his writings as authoritative, both in their excellence and in their defects, the most serious injury is done to truth. In matters of

133

philosophy and science authority has ever been the great opponent of truth. A despotic calm is usually the triumph of error.

(1871–1911, pp. 275–6)

Jevons went on to maintain that in the physical sciences authority had lost its noxious influence: 'Chemistry, in its brief existence of a century, has undergone three or four complete revolutions of theory'. On the other hand, regarding political economy, because of the anti-empirical dogmatism of 'the orthodox Ricardian School':

Our science has become far too much a stagnant one, in which opinions rather than experience and reason are appealed to.

He concluded:

In Science and philosophy nothing must be held sacred . . . no body and no school or clique must be allowed to set up a standard of orthodoxy which shall bar the freedom of scientific inquiry.

(p. 276)

Jevons's philosophical caution and critical fallibilism are expressed very clearly in *The Principles of Science* (1874). He emphasizes two vital 'characteristics of the scientific mind'. The first of these is 'perfect readiness to reject a theory inconsistent with fact'. Jevons emphasized:

It would be a mistake to suppose that this candour has anything akin to fickleness; on the contrary, readiness to reject a false theory may be combined with a peculiar pertinacity and courage in maintaining an hypothesis as long as its falsity is not actually apparent. There must, indeed, be no prejudice or bias distorting the mind, and causing it to pass over the unwelcome results of the experiment. There must be that scrupulous honesty and flexibility of mind, which assigns adequate value to all evidence; indeed, the more a man loves his theory, the more scrupulous should be his attention to its faults.

(2nd edition, 1887, p. 586)

The second requirement, or characteristic, of the philosophic mind, according to Jevons:

. . . is that of suspending judgement when the data are insufficient. Many people will express a confident opinion on almost any question which is put before them, but they thereby manifest not strength, but narrowness of mind. . . . Hence it is most frequently the philosophic mind which is in doubt, and the ignorant which is ready with a positive decision.

(p. 592)

Jevons quotes a philosophic hero of his, Michael Faraday:

Occasionally and frequently the exercise of the judgment ought to end in *absolute reservation*. It may be very distasteful, and great fatigue to suspend a conclusion, but as we are not infallible, so we ought to be cautious.

(quoted, p. 592)

Jevons emphasizes the much greater difficulties of the social or moral sciences as contrasted with the physical sciences:

Those who attempt to establish social or moral science soon become aware that they are dealing with subjects of enormous perplexity. Take as an instance the science of political economy. If a science at all, it must be a mathematical science, because it deals with quantities of commodities. *But as soon as we attempt to draw out the equations expressing the laws of demand and supply, we discover that they have a complexity entirely surpassing our powers of mathematical treatment.*

(p. 759, italics added)

Jevons goes on to ridicule Auguste Comte's notion of laws of development and concludes that: 'A science of history in the true sense of the term is an absurd notion' (p. 961).

V

Jevons's philosophical fallibilism, which has some important common elements with the doctrines of Sir Karl Popper, provides the essential epistemological foundation for an authentic libertarianism. In any case, one obvious conclusion must be that the contrast could hardly be more profound than that between the cautious, critical, empirical fallibilism of Jevons, and the confident, *a priorist* dogmatism of James Mill and Ricardo, with their claims to certainty and their comparisons of their 'laws' of the science of political economy, with the laws of physics.[8] Stark also is the contrast with the extreme claims for introspection and 'apodictic certainty' of some Austrians, notably Wieser and Mises. But starkest and most profound of all is the contrast with Marxian dogmatism, based on the infallibilist scientism of Engels, and the comparison of Engels and Marx of historical laws with the laws of physics. From this infallibilist philosophy of science there followed the insistence on the one-party state of Stalin, Mao and other Marxian leaders, which some of the most authoritative Marxian economists supported so long and so faithfully. As Sir Isaiah Berlin was informed in Leningrad regarding the infallibility of the Leninist–Stalinist system:

We are a scientifically governed society and if there is no room for free thinking in physics – a man who questions the laws of motion is so obviously ignorant or mad – why should we Marxists, who have

135

discovered laws of history and society, permit free thinking in the social sphere?

(Berlin, 1980, p. 170)

Jevons's modest, fallibilist conception of the relation between the science of political economy and economic policy and that, on the other hand, which 'we Marxists' hold, could hardly be more widely and fundamentally different.

A further obvious conclusion regarding Jevons's ideas on economic policy is how doubly unfounded and erroneous are such statements as that: 'For the neo-classicals *laissez-faire* became a dogma' (Robinson and Eatwell, 1973, p. 47). We have seen that Jevons, the neoclassical pioneer of what M. H. Dobb called 'the Jevonian Revolution', was fundamentally and philosophically anti-dogmatic. Even if Jevons had supported *laissez-faire*, it would not have been as a dogma. *It was for Ricardo that laissez-faire was something of a dogma. Moreover, Jevons's later view also marked an abandonment of laissez-faire.*

Finally, we should emphasize regarding economic policy and political economy that the *mood* in which theories and policy conclusions are advanced, dogmatic or undogmatic, cautious and critical or sweepingly confident, *a priorist* or empirical, infallibist or fallibilist, is of fundamental intellectual and political significance for the application of economic knowledge to policy, and of as much importance as the purely economic technicalities. Insistence on *a priorist* dogmas, 'apodictic certainty', and Marxian scientistic infallibilism in political economy, point directly towards totalitarianism and the one-party state. For all his healthily sceptical doubts regarding the efficiency of democratic processes, opposition to one-party dogmatism was the most fundamental political–philosophical principle for which Jevons stood.[9]

ADDENDUM

In 1982 Mr White concluded his contribution to our exchanges by stating that on 'another occasion' he would return to his unsupported attribution to Jevons of a 'project to derive iron laws of income distribution'. Over a decade later, this attribution (which I described as 'an elaboration of the once fashionable Marxistic interpretation of the neoclassicals') still remains as far as I am aware quite untrue. Instead, turning away from Jevons's economics, Professor White has switched the direction of his vendetta by accusing Jevons of 'racism', which he now alleges 'pervades his work, including *The Theory of Political Economy*'. I could hardly disagree more strongly than I do with such accusations. I am not, however, dealing with them further at this point since they have no serious relevance to the above paper. But in 1994 I intend to send some comments on Professor White's attack to the *History of Economics Review*, where his 'Note' first appeared (1993, 19, pp. 79ff.).

NOTES

1 This paper appeared in a Jevons Centenary number of *The Manchester School of Economic and Social Studies*, December 1982, vol. 50, pp. 366ff.

2 See Hicks, 1979, p. viii.

3 However, according to his son, Jevons showed some interest in politics in his Manchester period and got up a petition 'which it was intended to present to the Prime Minister, protesting against the title of "Empress of India" having been conferred upon Queen Victoria'. (See Keynes, Volume X, 1972, p. 154.)

4 Jevons bought Lardner's book (*Railway Economy*, 1850) very early in his studies of Political Economy, on 22 April 1857). A week later, in his personal diary, he notes that he is 'busy considering the subject of roads and internal communication in a financial point of view' (*P & C*, vol. VII, p. 118). Dupuit's 'Memoirs' were discovered much later and found to be 'most luminous and valuable' (*P & C*, vol. IV, p. 249). See also Hutchison, 1953, pp. 35–6. Additional very interesting material regarding Jevons's earlier interests in political economy in respect of the controversial questions of land and railway policy in New South Wales, has become available in *P & C*, especially volumes II and VII. Incidentally, it now seems to have been incorrect of me to have described (see 1968, p. 258) Jevons's *first* article as opening with the words: 'Freedom for all commercial transactions is the spirit of improved legislation'.

5 See the pioneering essay of J. A. La Nauze in his *Political Economy in Australia*, 1949.

6 The only reservation regarding Walsh and Gram's comparison of Jevons with Marx and Engels must be that nowhere does Jevons indulge in the kind of 'racist' abuse which characterizes some of the writings of Marx and Engels, in particular, in the case of Engels with regard to the Irish, in his famous *The Condition of the Working Classes in Britain* (Addendum, 1994).

7 On Joseph Chamberlain's quotation of Jevons in the House of Commons and on Hayek's judgement that Jevons's *The State in Relation to Labour* marked 'the end of the liberal era of principles', *see* Hutchison, 1978, p. 100n.

8 For further evidence regarding the dogmatic over-confidence of James Mill and Ricardo, see Hutchison, 1978, Chapter 2.

9 When acknowledging the receipt of the typescript of this paper, Professor Collison Black called my attention to an article by M. V. White, 'Jevons in Australia: a Reassessment' (*Economic Record*, March 1982, pp. 32ff.). Mr White rightly emphasizes the stimulating influence, in 1856–7, on the 21-year-old Jevons, of the railway controversy in New South Wales at that time, and, in particular, of the contribution by Professor M. B. Pell of Sydney, 'On the application of Certain Principles of Political Economy to the Question of Railways' (see also *P & C*, vol. I, pp. 25–6, vol. II, pp. 236 and 285, and vol. VII, p. 8). Mr White's very useful account of Pell's paper helps to confirm the point that, with Jevons, as with other pioneers of marginal and neoclassical analysis, such as Dupuit, Lardner, Ellet and later Launhardt, it was the increasingly important problems of railways and public utilities, in the face of which classical and Ricardian analysis was largely useless, which stimulated new ideas about price theory in the middle decades of the nineteenth century.

However, Mr White goes on to attempt some challenging conclusions, for which he presents very little or no evidence, and for which very little, or none whatever, seems to exist, while, in some cases, there is obviously overwhelming evidence to the contrary. Thus, (1) Mr White sets up as 'the conventional view', the notion 'that Jevons's time in Australia had little significance for the development of his economic theory' (p. 44). Mr White offers no evidence for the existence of any significant number of writers maintaining this 'conventional view'. Incidentally, nearly thirty years ago, I wrote regarding Jevons in Australia (1953, p. 34, not 1966 as *per* Mr White): 'It is easy to trace back to their Australian origin the seeds of what were to be his three main contributions to economics'. (2) Mr White, on the other hand, presents a peculiarly Australo-centric view of Jevons's intellectual development which apparently fails to allow, either for any important intellectual development by Jevons outside Australia, which he left at the age of 23; or that he subsequently revised, quite fundamentally, his views on the principles of policy, as compared with those he expressed in letters as a 21–23-year-old in Sydney. (3) Mr White also appears to assume that because he has validly demonstrated the importance of Pell's paper for Jevons in 1856–8, he is entitled to deny completely the importance of Lardner's work for the *Theory of Political Economy*, which Jevons himself explicitly stressed. There seems to be here a rather dogmatically exclusivist *non-sequitur*. (4) Mr White also refers to 'the Jevonian project to derive iron laws of income distribution', repeating the words 'iron laws' as though these were terms which Jevons would have accepted. But no significant evidence is offered that such a project can fairly be ascribed to Jevons, even as a 21-year-old. Moreover, if Jevons, at the age of 21–23, ever entertained such a project – which seems very questionable – the derivation of any 'iron laws' in economics would subsequently have been comprehensively rejected by him, as is perfectly clear from *The Principles of Science*, a fundamental work completely unmentioned by Mr White. (5) Mr White also ascribes extreme views to Jevons on state intervention in the economy without any mention of *The State in Relation to Labour*. Presenting Hamlet without the Prince – and the Ghost – would be a comparatively comprehensible exercise. Throughout the *SRL* Jevons repeatedly maintains, both in principle, and in specific cases, that there are theoretical and practical possibilities for beneficent state intervention. On the other hand, according to Mr White, it was one of Jevons's 'basic premises', *from which he 'was never to depart'* (p. 33, n. 8, italics added) that 'any' exchange transactions 'required no intervention by the State *so as to balance unequivalent transactions*' (p. 33). The *SRL* contains repeated and total refutations of Mr White's statements.

REFERENCES

Berlin, Sir Isaiah. (1980). *Personal Impressions: Selected Writings, Volume IV* (edited by Henry Hardy), London, Hogarth Press.

Black, R. D. Collison (ed.) (1972–1981). *Papers and Correspondence of William Stanley Jevons, Volumes I–VII*, London, Macmillan, in association with the Royal Economic Society.

Hayek, F. A. (1973). *Law, Legislation and Liberty, Volume I*, London, Routledge & Kegan Paul.

Hicks, Sir John. (1979). *Causality in Economics*.

Hutchison, T. W. (1953). *Review of Economic Doctrines, 1870–1929*, Oxford, Oxford University Press.

Hutchison, T. W. (1968). 'Jevons, W. S.', in *International Encyclopedia of the Social Sciences, Volume 8*, New York, Crowell, Collier and Macmillan.

Hutchison, T. W. (1978). *On Revolutions and Progress in Economic Knowledge*, Cambridge, Cambridge University Press, Chapter 4.

Jevons, W. S. (1871). *Theory of Political Economy*, 4th edition 1911, London, Macmillan.

Jevons, W. S. (1874). *The Principles of Science*, 2nd edition 1877, London, Macmillan.

Jevons, W. S. (1882). *The State in Relation to Labour*, London, Macmillan.

Keynes, John Maynard. (1972). *The Collected Writings of John Maynard Keynes, Volume X:*

Essays in Biography (edited by E. Johnson and D. Moggridge), London, Macmillan, for the Royal Economic Society.

La Nauze, J. A. (1949). *Political Economy in Australia: Historical Studies*, Carleton, Melbourne University Press.

Robinson, Joan, and Eatwell, John. (1973). *An Introduction to Modern Economics*, London: McGraw-Hill.

Walsh, V., and Gram, H. (1980). *Classical and Neoclassical Theories of General Equilibrium*, Oxford, Oxford University Press.

7

THE JEVONIAN REVOLUTION
AND ECONOMIC POLICY IN
BRITAIN[1]

I

The turning-point in economic theory in Britain which may be described as the Jevonian revolution occurred at roughly the same time as a major turning-point in economic policy in Britain. Though either of these turning-points could conceivably have occurred without the other, they are clearly inter-connected in that they influenced and interacted on one another as regards the particular forms they took. That they both occurred around 1870 in Britain is surely not entirely coincidental.

The long re- or e-volution in the economic role of government in Great Britain which has continued through succeeding waves, on one sector or another of the front, since the high tide of the 'classical', individualist, competitive market economy began perceptibly to recede, may be dated from somewhere around 1870. This seems, in round figures, to be the most generally suitable starting-date from which this long, vast continuing process may be traced. A few years either side of our round figures we have two significant events in economic ideas and two in politics. As we have already noted, in economic ideas there was (1) in 1869, Mill's retraction regarding the wages fund, which signified a general decline in the credibility of the classical distribution doctrines. This decline had also gradually been coming about regarding the empirically most important element in the classical account of distribution: the hard-line Ricardo–Mill version of the Malthusian population and natural-wage doctrine, for which, however, no precise date of any spectacular recantation can be fixed. Secondly (2) in 1871 there was Jevons's attack on the Ricardo–Mill value doctrines, and the development of his final utility theory, in his *Theory of Political Economy*, which work also contained – what was much more significant in terms of policy developments – a sweeping attack on the Ricardo–Mill doctrines of wages and distribution.

Either side of these two dates there were two political events with profound consequences for the subsequent development of economic policy: (1) the Second Reform Act of 1867; and (2) in 1871 (and 1875) the trade union legislation on which the subsequent rise to power of the unions was founded.

In favour of a later starting-point than 1870 for the long policy revolution, it could be argued that it was not until the 1880s that the new trend really become unmistakable, with a marked rise in public expenditure. But, as we shall see, a definite shift in the current of ideas about economic policy is perceptible in the 1870s.

On the other hand, with regard to economic policy-doctrines, one could argue that a considerably earlier date might be taken, which would bring in J. S. Mill and Book V of his *Principles*, since Jevons, Sidgwick and Marshall on some points hardly go beyond Mill, and on one or two points perhaps not as far, regarding possible developments in economic policy. But it can be countered, first, that though in some respects the post-1870 economists do not immediately go beyond Mill, in more important ways they do; and furthermore, that Mill can be regarded as concerned much more with prophetic hopes than with operational policies. It may be putting it rather strongly to say, as Clapham did, that 'Mill remained to his death in 1873 only the philosopher who raises a standard' (1932, vol. II, p. 391). But two major fundamental conditions put all Mill's discussion of economic policies in a different mood from the proposals which gradually began to gather force after 1870: (1) before 1867 there was no feasible electoral base for the sort of proposals Mill was discussing, especially with regard to redistribution in general and progressive inheritance duties in particular; (2) as Mill himself believed and assumed when writing his *Principles*, 'the great Malthusian difficulty', as Cairnes called it, continued to inhibit proposals aimed at general improvement in the condition of the people.[2]

It is the combination of the new electoral base and the lifting, or what was believed or realised to be the lifting, of 'the great Malthusian difficulty', that made for a new epoch in policy, bit-by-bit transforming prophetic aspirations and speculations into feasible policy proposals.

To assert that around 1870 a turning-point in economic policy occurred is not to deny or overlook the amount of legislation regarding factory conditions, hours of labour, public health and other fields which had been put through in the preceding decades. But this was largely concerned with creating a *framework* for a free-market or *laissez-faire* economy, not so much with intervening in its processes or results. This distinction is not clear-cut, but it helps to account for the nature of the turning-point with which we are here concerned.[3]

A further development, almost simultaneous with these, was the premonitory forebodings – as expressed in Jevons's *Coal Question*, for example – regarding Britain's relative economic position in the world, which was at its peak in the mid-1860s, and which later, towards the end of the century, was to give rise to much debate regarding economic policy, and in particular regarding the principles of commercial policy.

There is one further preliminary regarding the relations between economists' policy proposals and criticisms and the actual historical changes in economic policies. Economists may either provide the basis of positive predictions relevant for new kinds of policies, or they may act persuasively on the public's or the politicians' attitudes and values, or choice of new objectives, or of much higher levels of old objectives. Whichever sort of influence they may have, all one seems able to say is that for better or worse economists have sometimes kept roughly in step with changes in public or political opinions or aspirations; sometimes they have been a step or two behind; and sometimes they have been a leading force. In the period with which we are here concerned, they seem at least to have been in step, and sometimes a step or two ahead.

All the same, though no simple general thesis about economists will probably stand up for long, in studying their policy proposals it does seem that we are concerned with the proof of the whole intellectual pudding of economics, in that, *according to what might reasonably be regarded as economists' own tenets*, this lies in the improved prescience or heightened success of economic policies which may result from 'what economists do'.

II

Jevons appears as something of a revolutionary, or at any rate as claiming to be a revolutionary, on a central point of theory. On the subject of the role of government he was, if not a 'revolutionary', at least a transitional figure both chronologically and doctrinally. Chronologically he is almost too neatly so. His writing career covered exactly the quarter of a century from 1857 to 1882, pretty precisely bisected by our year 1870. It is not suggested that in or about that year Jevons underwent a sudden Pauline conversion from his earlier adherence to the strictest individualist principles, to his later position, for which he is better known, as, in Clapham's description, 'a cautious empirical innovator' who 'watched with critical impartiality the inroads of the state on individual liberty in the early '80s' (*op. cit.*, pp. 390 and 439). In fact, it can hardly be shown that anything in the way of a change of view by Jevons took place on any important *specific point* of economic policy or the role of government. It is rather that, as the 1870s wore on, more cases occurred to him which seemed to call for governmental action, or at least for detailed empirical examination, and which were no longer to be disposed of by a sweeping application of *laissez-faire* principles.[4]

In his first publication in Australia in 1857, the 22-year-old Jevons had begun by proclaiming comprehensively that 'freedom for *all* commercial transactions is the spirit of improved legislation'.[5] In particular, the earlier Jevons was a strong champion of Malthus and of the more rigorous interpretation of his doctrines in terms of self-help. Jevons considered it worth repeating in 1869 that 'the British Poor Law of 1834 is one of the wisest measures ever concerted by any government' (1883, p. 192). (Twenty-three years later Marshall, though agreeing that the poor law was justifiable in its own day, was to reject the whole basis of that law for *his* day.) Though he supported the Education Act of 1870, Jevons was not only opposed to any extension of state action with regard to health services for the poor but was against private medical charities in that they discouraged self-help.

As regards external commercial policy, for Jevons in 1869 free trade was an unquestioned and almost unquestionable article of faith:

> Freedom of trade may be regarded as a fundamental axiom of political economy; and though even axioms *may* be mistaken, and any different views concerning them must not be *prohibited*, yet we need not be frightened into questioning our own axioms. We may welcome *bona fide* investigation into the state of trade, and the causes of the present depression, but we can no more expect to have our opinions on free trade altered by such an investigation than the Mathematical Society would expect to have the axioms of Euclid disproved during the investigation of a complex problem.
>
> (*op. cit.*, p. 182)

The earlier and more severely individualistic strain in Jevons comes out especially in his treatment of taxation. He expressed concern in 1870 that 'the working class so long as they make a temperate use of spirituous liquors and tobacco pay a distinctly less proportion of their income to the state, and even intemperance does not make their contribution proportionally greater than those of more wealthy persons' (1870, p. 34).

In his main work on taxation, his pamphlet *The Match Tax* (1871), Jevons expressed some regret at the repeal of the tax because he wanted to retain taxes on articles of wide popular consumption, rejecting the Malthusian–Ricardian argument about the effects on wages of taxing 'necessaries'. Jevons figured out statistically that the burden of taxation was then very roughly proportional, but that – as he had complained the previous year – half the taxes paid by the poor were from alcohol and tobacco. These were not only avoidable but ought to be avoided. The great exponent of the utility approach to the problems of value and price came down very firmly in favour of proportional taxation on all except paupers:

> The more carefully and maturely I ponder over this question of taxation from various points of view, the more convinced I always return to the principle, that all classes of persons above the rank of actual paupers, should contribute to the state in the proportion of their incomes. I will not say this is a theoretically perfect rule. From feelings of humanity we might desire to graduate the rate of contribution and relieve persons who are comparatively poorer at the expense of those who are comparatively richer. But we must beware of obeying the dictates of ill-considered humanity. If we once professedly enter upon the course of exempting the poor, there will be no stopping.
>
> (1905, p. 235)[6]

However, already in 1870 Jevons was envisaging massive increases in public expenditure at the local (though not at the national) level. Calling for the reform of local taxation to meet the new needs, Jevons wrote:

> *There is sure to be a continuous increase of local taxation.* . . . All the more immediate needs of society, boards of health, medical officers, public schools, reformatories, free libraries, highway boards, main drainage schemes, water-suppliers, purification of rivers, improved police, better poor law medical science – these, and a score of other costly reforms must be supported mainly out of the local rates.
>
> (1883, p. 202, italics added)

It is in his Introductory Lecture at University College in 1876 that a shift in Jevons's attitude seems to become prominent. Even here he began by duly noting that 'it is impossible to doubt that the *laissez-faire* principle properly applied is the wholesome and true one'. But the spread of urban industrialism and its all-pervasive 'externalities', or neighbourhood effects, led Jevons to predict: 'It seems to me, while population grows more numerous and dense, while industry becomes more complex and interdependent, as we travel faster and make use of more intense forces, we shall necessarily need more legislative supervision' (*op. cit.*, p. 204). He called for a new empirical branch of economics:

> If such a thing is possible, we need a new branch of political and statist-ical science which shall carefully investigate the limits to the *laissez-faire* principle, and show where we want greater freedom and where less. . . . I am quite satisfied if we have pointed out the need and the probable rise of one new branch, which is only to be found briefly and imperfectly represented in the works of Mill and other economists.
>
> (*op. cit.*, pp. 204–6)[7]

Jevons then proceeds to give an example, representing a blend of paternalism and externalities, with regard to slum clearance and public housing:

> I am quite convinced, for instance, that the great mass of the people will not have healthy houses by the ordinary action of self-interest. The only chance of securing good sanitary arrangements is to pull down the houses which are hopelessly bad, as provided by an Act of the present ministry, and *most carefully to superintend under legislative regulations all new houses that are built.*
>
> (1883, p. 205, italics added)

Jevons went on a year or two later to suggest increased public expenditure over a wide range of elementary paternalist or public goods and services, such as libraries, museums, parks, municipal orchestras and meteorological services, claiming that these were 'unsanctified by the *laissez-faire* principle'.[8]

More widely, following up his remarks on public housing, Jevons suggested a further move into the field of town and country planning, by laying heavy emphasis on what he called 'the general interests of the public' as against those of private individuals:

Our idea of happiness in this country at present seems to consist in buying a piece of land if possible, and building a high wall round it. If a man can only secure, for instance, a beautiful view from his own garden and windows, he cares not how many thousands of other persons he cuts off from the daily enjoyment of that view. *The rights of private property and private action are pushed so far that the general interests of the public are made of no account whatever.*

(1905, p. 206, italics added)

On nationalized or state enterprise Jevons had written as early as 1867 a sentence anticipatory of his later empirical and experimental attitude: 'My own strong opinion is that no abstract principle, and no absolute rule, can guide us in determining what kinds of industrial enterprise, the State should undertake and what not' (1883, p. 278). After praising the Post Office, he called for the taking over of telegraph services, though when this was done in 1870 he condemned the financial arrangements. Later Jevons advocated a state-run parcel post (1879), but unlike Walter Bagehot, he was strongly opposed to nationalization of the railways (1874).[9]

In his final and admirable book, *The State in Relation to Labour*, published in the year of his death, Jevons dealt with consumer protection and government inspection, factory legislation and hours of work, and trade union legislation.

He returned again, long before the days of mass motoring and air travel, to the mounting importance of externalities and neighbourhood effects with the development of urban industrialism and with the threats to freedom deriving from the complex technology of affluence:

So intricate are the ways, industrial, sanitary, or political, in which one class or section of the people affect other classes or sections, that there is hardly any limit to the interference of the legislator. . . . It is impossible in short that we can have the constant multiplication of institutions and instruments of civilisation which evolution is producing, without a growing complication of relations, and a consequent growth of social regulations.

(1882, p. 14)

Regarding hours of work, Jevons argued that legislators up till then had 'in fact, always abstained from interfering with the liberty of adult men to work as long or as short a time as they like'. But he went on: 'I see nothing to forbid the state interfering in the matter . . . neither principle, experience, nor precedent, in other cases of legislation, prevents us from contemplating the idea of State interference in such circumstances' (*op. cit.*, pp. 64–5).

In fact, ten years later (1892) in the House of Commons, championing an eight-hour bill for miners, Joseph Chamberlain, in his radical socialistic, or at any rate, interventionist phase, quoted Jevons in support of his case, though in terms of very general utilitarian principle: 'The State is justified in passing any law, or even in doing any single act, which without ulterior consequences adds to the sum of human happiness.' Chamberlain drew a contrast, as he put it, with 'the strict doctrine of *laissez-faire* which perhaps 20 years ago [i.e., *c.* 1870] was accepted as preferable'.[10]

It is for its magnificently eloquent, often-quoted statements of an empirical, experimental anti-*a priori* approach to policy questions that Jevons's *The State in Relation to Labour* is famous. Jevons indeed is a forerunner of Sir Karl Popper both in his conception of scientific method in his *Principles of Science* and consequently also in his advocacy of empirical, piecemeal social experimentation.

Jevons's proposals for increasing governmental action are almost entirely confined to the heading describable as Inadequacies of Individual Choice, with its subheadings (a) paternalism, (b) ignorance, (c) externalities or 'neighbourhood effects', and (d) public goods and services.

Under the heading Monopoly and Restrictive Practices there is only a little in Jevons, including, for example, his treatment already mentioned of nationalization. But there is also his discussion of trade union monopolies, which he regarded with serious forebodings. He did not, however, propose to undo the favourable legislation of 1871 and 1875, and is curiously optimistic about the future of trade unions. He asks whether 'the lawgiver ought not simply to prohibit societies which tend towards such monopoly'. But he concludes in the negative (1882, p. 101).[11]

Under the other main headings for state intervention there is almost nothing to be found in Jevons. As we have seen, with regard to distribution and redistribution, one of the main fields opened up in the last quarter of the nineteenth century, Jevons seems to have remained strictly, even severely, classical, especially regarding proportionality in taxation.

On the great twentieth-century subject of the Monetary Framework and Macroeconomic Policy, on which before 1900 there were only some anticipatory rumblings, there is hardly an inkling in Jevons, in spite of the fact that he was a pioneer of research into business cycles and price index-numbers. With regard to the then orthodoxy, Professor Fetter has pointed out that 'in his philosophic approach to the limitations of any metallic standard Jevons soared on a high speculative level'. Fetter goes on to quote Jevons: 'But in itself gold-digging has ever seemed to me almost a dead loss of labour as regards the world in general – a wrong against the human race, just such as is that of a government against a people in over-issuing and depreciating its own currency.' Yet Fetter concludes that Jevons, 'either because he was the pure scientist unconcerned with policy-making, or because as a child of an era he was not prepared to fight its myths and its idols, made no public suggestion for a better standard, although he wrote but did not publish a proposal for a tabular standard of value' (1965, p. 248). Also, in spite of his great interest in cyclical fluctuations Jevons held to the Turgot–Smith 'saving-is-investing' doctrine, the basis of 'classical' theory in the Keynesian sense (1878, p. 22).

Finally, under the heading of Commercial Policy, External Economic Relations, or Britain and her Relative Position in the World Economy, Jevons, in his first and brilliant book, *The Coal Question* (1865), had uttered, at the very peak of Britain's relative economic standing in the world, a prescient warning, if rather over-anxious in the shorter term, that our occupation of this supreme position as the workshop of the world might prove highly transient.[12] Before the end of the century the problem of the weakening of Britain's relative economic position was to give rise to much policy debate. But Jevons reasserted in his last work, as Marshall was to do later, his firm adherence to free trade principles.

III

The historical and institutional critics of classical political economy in the 1870s and early 1880s, who come next, were mostly more concerned with theories and methods than with policy. There seems to be little on policy questions in Cliffe Leslie, for example, except with regard to Ireland. But Arnold Toybnee (d. 1883), a figure of some influence in Oxford, 'one of the noblest of the rising generation', as Marshall called him (1925, p. 152), perceived the politico-economic disequilibrium that had come about with the extension of the suffrage: 'Wealth is in the hands of the few rich, the suffrage in the hands of the many poor; in the concentration of wealth and the diffusion of political power lies a great danger of modern society.' Toynbee saw the importance of this politico-economic conjuncture for the problem of distribution, which he affirmed 'is the true problem of political economy at the present time' (1894, pp. 212 and 250).

Toynbee laid down the principles for state action in the following two propositions: '*First*, that where individual rights conflict with the interests of the community, there the State ought to interfere; and *second* that where the people are unable to provide a thing for themselves, and that thing is of *primary social importance*, then again the State should interfere and provide it for them' (1894, p. 216).

In this connection, almost simultaneously with Jevons, Toynbee raised the question of public housing, or 'the dwellings of the people', a subject

upon which it is difficult to understand why so little is said . . . I do not hesitate to say a community must step in and give the necessary aid. These labourers cannot obtain dwellings for themselves; the municipalities, or the State in some form, should have the power to buy up land and let it below the market value for the erection of decent dwellings.

(*op. cit.*, pp. 217–18)

Toynbee was arguing from the point of view of a Tory or even imperialist socialist: 'We demand that the material conditions of those who labour should be bettered, in order that, every source of weakness being removed at home, we, this English nation, may bring to the tasks which God has assigned us, the irresistible strength of a prosperous and united people' (1894, p. 221).

As regards Walter Bagehot there is not much to say here. We have noted his support for railway nationalization (1865).[13] In his major field of the monetary framework Bagehot seems to have provided or buttressed the orthodoxy of the day which was to survive until 1914 or 1931. Regarding the position of the Bank of England, as Professor Fetter puts it: 'In the eyes of Bagehot banking statesmanship and the profit motive were to be happily married, and his great service to the next half century of central banking was that he convinced his countrymen that this was an honourable union blessed by the laws of free trade' (1965, p. 271).

One year after Jevons's death Sidgwick's *Principles of Political Economy* appeared. These principles run very much on the general lines of Mill, but are more precise and penetrating at some important points. First, Sidgwick brings more precision regarding externalities and public goods: 'There is a large and varied class of cases in which private interest cannot be relied upon as a sufficient stimulus to the performance of the most socially useful services because such services are incapable of being appropriated by those who produce them or who would otherwise be willing to purchase them.'

He then mentions the lighthouse example, as had Mill. Sidgwick goes on to note, however: 'It does not follow, of course, that wherever *laissez-faire* falls short governmental interference is expedient.'

Regarding commercial policy Sidgwick certainly moved away from anything resembling a dogmatic *laissez-faire* position: 'The foundations on which the old short and simple confutations of Protection were once logically erected have been knocked away. . . . The fashion which still lingers of treating the Protectionist as a fool who cannot see – if he is not a knave who will not see – what is as plain as a proof of Euclid, is really an illogical survival' (1887, p. 448).

But the new principle of the most fundamental importance introduced by Sidgwick, though he himself did not develop the consequences, was his proclamation of the 'right' distribution of produce as a second main objective of government policy or 'the art of political economy', alongside increased production:

> We may take the subject of Political Economy considered as an Art to include, besides the Theory of provision for governmental expenditure, (1) the Art of making the proportion of produce to population a maximum . . . and (2) the Art of rightly Distributing produce among members of the community, whether on any principle of Equity or Justice, or on the economic principle of making the whole produce as useful as possible.
>
> (1883, p. 403)

However, like, generally, his classical predecessors, Sidgwick takes equality of sacrifice to imply proportionality in taxation and holds this to be 'the obviously equitable principle', going on to oppose progression and the redressing of inequalities of income by taxation:

> Most economists hold that any such communistic tendency should be rightly excluded in the adjustment of taxation; and that whatever Government may legitimately do to remedy the inequalities of distribution resulting from natural liberty should be done otherwise than by unequal imposition of financial burdens. And this is, in the main, the conclusion which I am myself disposed to adopt; but I must interpret or limit it by one important proviso which seems to me necessitated by the acceptance of the principle that the community ought to protect its members from starvation – a degree of communism which, as we have seen, is legally established in England.

> (1883, p. 562)

As regards the monetary framework, Sidgwick, in a chapter entitled 'Cases of Governmental Interference to Promote Production', raises some fundamental questions regarding what he calls 'currency'. He holds that the state 'ought to guard so far as it can against fluctuations in the value of the medium of exchange. It can only do this, however, to a very limited extent' (*op. cit.*, p. 453). Regarding the position of the Bank of England, Sidgwick questioned the orthodox acceptance of the happy marriage of private profit and social interest advocated by Bagehot:

> When we consider merely from an abstract point of view the proposal to give a particular joint-stock company an exclusive privilege of issuing notes, the value of which will, in the last resort be sustained by the authority of Government, without subjecting its exercise of this privilege to any governmental control whatsoever; it certainly appears a very hazardous measure.

> (1883, p. 462)

Finally, at this point mention should be made of Foxwell's monograph of 1886, *Irregularity of Employment and Fluctuations of Prices*. This was the outstanding anticipation at this time of what was to be the overriding problem and concern – between wars – of much of the first half of the twentieth century. Foxwell starts from the 'conviction, continually increasing in strength, that uncertainty of employment is the root of evil of the present industrial system'. He foresaw and emphasized the growing popular concern for 'social security': 'I cannot venture to say what would be the general opinion of the working class upon the point; but my own feeling would be that when a certain necessary limit had been reached, regularity of income was far more important than amount of income' (1886, pp. 7 and 17). Certainly Foxwell's lecture is more notable for its attempt to shatter complacency about a major problem for policy, and to establish the reduction of the irregularity of employment as an objective, than for the particular remedial measures he proposes. But after analysing the effects of changes in the value of money, Foxwell concludes in favour of stability of the price level, or rather a slightly and steadily rising level.

IV

In considering Alfred Marshall's ideas on policy one might, as with Jevons, try to discover and apply some pattern of development, though in Marshall's case the pattern would presumably be the different though very familiar one of a transition from an earlier, youthful, reformist enthusiasm to a much more cautious and sceptical attitude later on. There is quite a lot of evidence for this sort of pattern with regard to Marshall, though there do seem to be one or two important exceptions or irregularities. There are also, in any case, due to his delays of many decades in publishing his ideas, considerable chronological difficulties in trying to trace out at all definitely or precisely *any* simple lines for Marshall's intellectual development.

However, we may suitably start with his early paper of 1873, 'The Future of the Working Classes', which provides a glowing statement of early aspirations and which begins, incidentally, with an enthusiastic tribute to Mrs Harriet Taylor Mill for her contribution to the chapter of the same title in her second husband's *Principles*.

Marshall warms up in the manner of Marx, by citing contemporary blue books on such mid-Victorian industrial phenomena as 'lads and maidens, not 8 years old, toiling in the brickfields under monstrous loads from 5 o'clock in the morning till 8 o'clock at night'. He goes on:

> Our thoughts from youth upwards are dominated by a Pagan belief . . .
> that it is an ordinance of Nature that multitudes of men must toil a
> weary toil, which may give to others the means of refinement and
> luxury, but which can afford to themselves scarce any opportunity of
> mental growth. May not the world outgrow this belief, as it has out-
> grown others? It may and it will.

(1925, pp. 107–9)

It certainly has, nearly a hundred years later, in some very privileged parts of the world; though whether the parallel cultural accompaniments would have met with Marshall's approval seems highly doubtful. Economically, in fact, Marshall was never at all unrealistic or revolutionary. He denounced the socialists 'who attributed to every man an unlimited capacity for those self-forgetting virtues that they found in their own breasts', and whose schemes 'involve a subversion of existing arrangements according to which the work of every man is chosen by himself, and the remuneration he obtains for it is decided by free competition' (*op. cit.*, p. 109).

It was in his social, cultural and educational hopes that Marshall seems to have been, and for some time to have remained, rather over-optimistic. He saw that education and technological progress could and would raise the earning powers of the masses and reduce hours and physical toil. It was with regard to what would be done with the time and energy left over that Marshall may seem to have been unrealistic. He envisaged a country which

> is to have a fair share of wealth, and not an abnormally large population. Everyone is to have in youth an education which is thorough while it lasts, and which lasts long. No one is to do in the day so much manual work as will leave him little time or little aptitude for intellectual or artistic enjoyment in the evening. Since there will be nothing tending to render the individual coarse and unrefined, there will be nothing tending to render society coarse and unrefined. Exceptional morbid growths must exist in every society; but otherwise every man will be surrounded from birth upwards by almost all the influences which we have seen to be at present characteristic of the occupations of gentlemen; everyone who is not a gentleman will have himself alone to blame for it.
>
> (*op. cit.*, p. 110)

After this early statement of Marshall's social visions, it seems more convenient to continue by subject headings than entirely chronologically, partly for the reason previously mentioned of Marshall's delays in publication, and also because Marshall, unlike Jevons, contributed at different times proposals regarding most or all of the main sectors of possible governmental action in the economy.

First, let us take the four-part heading, Inadequacies of Individual Choice, under which all or most of Jevons's contributions were made.

On grounds both of paternalism and externalities Marshall strongly advocated, from his paper of 1873 onwards through the decades, increased public spending on education: 'The difference between the value of the labour of the educated man and that of the uneducated is, as a rule, many times greater than the difference between the costs of their education. . . . No individual reaps the full gains derived from educating a child' (*op. cit.*, p. 118). Subsequently Marshall was to emphasize the economic dangers to Britain of lagging behind Germany in technical and scientific education.

As regards housing, though not recommending subsidies in the same way as Jevons or Toynbee, Marshall in 1884 advocates government controls on movement into slum areas: 'To hinder people from going where their presence helps to lower the average standard of human life, is not more contrary to economic principle than the rule that when a steamer is full, admission should be refused to any more even though they themselves are willing to take the risk of being drowned' (*op. cit.*, p. 148). Later (1902), as contrasted with Toynbee and Jevons, Marshall was to proclaim that 'municipal housing seems to me scarcely ever right and generally very wrong. Municipal free baths seem to me nearly always right' (*op. cit.*, p. 445).

In his paper 'Economic Chivalry' (1907) Marshall suggests with regard to town planning:

> The State could so care for the amenities of life outside of the house that fresh air and variety of colour and scene might await the citizen and his children very soon after they start on a holiday walk. Everyone in health and strength can order his house well; the State alone can bring the beauties of nature and art within the reach of the ordinary citizen.
>
> (*op. cit.*, p. 345)

In this essay, in which he proclaims 'Let the State be up and doing', Marshall emphasizes especially 'the imperative duty to inspect and arbitrate', taking as an illustration 'the careless treatment of milk': 'Let the government arouse itself to do energetically its proper work of educating British farmers up to the Danish standard, if not beyond; and of enforcing sanitary regulations in critical matters such as this' (*op. cit.* p. 337).

It is under this broad general heading also that we might mention Marshall's abstract criticisms in the *Principles* of the doctrine of maximum satisfaction (Book 5, Chapter 13), where he seems to suggest taxing goods the production of which is subject to diminishing returns and subsidizing increasing return industries out of the proceeds. But though Marshall emphasizes that his conclusions 'do not by themselves afford a valid ground for government interference', these rather excessively abstract propositions may have produced more confusion than enlightenment.

Our next main heading, Poverty, Distribution, and Redistribution, certainly was of major concern to Marshall. As he told the Royal Commission on the Aged Poor (1893): 'I have devoted myself for the last 25 years to the problem of poverty, and . . . very little of my work has been devoted to any enquiry which does not bear on that' (1926, p. 205).[14]

Marshall emphasized to the Commission the lifting of 'the great Malthusian difficulty' and the change in the nature of the problem compared with the beginning of the century:

> You can trace the economic dogmas of present Poor Law literature direct from those times; and the doctrines which they laid down I think were fairly true in their time. The doctrine is that if you tax the rich, and give money to the working classes, the result will be that the working classes will increase in number and the result will be you will have lowered wages in the next generation; and the grant will not have improved the position of the working classes on the whole. *As regards this a change has come, which separates the economics of this generation from the economics of the past*; but it seems to me not to have penetrated the Poor Law literature yet; and this is the main thing that I desire to urge. That

change insists upon the fact that if the money is so spent as to increase the earning power of the next generation it may not lower wages.

(1926, p. 225, italics added)

On the question of progressive taxation we have seen that Jevons and Sidgwick were opposed, as was the Irish public finance expert C. F. Bastable. Mr Shehab in his valuable book states that in the 1890s and before, Marshall also 'was preaching against it', though especially later, and as late as 1917, aged seventy-five, he was to come out strongly in favour. But Mr Shehab's evidence for Marshall's earlier opposition to progression is based simply on a footnote in Clapham, which recalls that 'in his lectures in the 1890s Marshall used to tell his pupils that graduated income taxation would weaken the chief pillar of the tax's yield, collection at source'.[15] This does not seem to amount to outright opposition to progression in principle. Admittedly also – though Mr Shehab does not cite this – Marshall himself wrote in 1909 that he had for fifteen years 'somewhat eagerly' opposed death duties, because they checked the growth of capital, but that now he considers them 'a good method of raising a large part of the national revenue'. On the other hand, though admittedly his later statements are much more explicit, Marshall had proclaimed as early as 1889 for example: 'I myself certainly think that the rich ought to be taxed much more heavily than they are, in order to provide for their poorer brethren the material means for a healthy physical and mental development' (1925, p. 229).

Subsequently Marshall was certainly moving more explicitly, though still cautiously, towards progression in his Memorandum (1897) to the Royal Commission on Local Taxes. However, for the theoretical case in favour of progressive taxation, such as it was, one would have to go to Edgeworth's paper of the same year (1925, vol. II, pp. 63ff.). By 1907 Marshall is praising his contemporaries in that: 'Our age has reversed the old rules that the poor paid a larger percentage of their income in rates and taxes than the well-to-do' (1925, p. 327).

His 1917 paper, one of his last, is much his most forthright statement on progression, expressing the hope that 'the various advances towards graduation made before the war will be sustained and developed after it' (1925, p. 350).[16]

It may be of some interest also to note that in so far as Mr Shehab's view is justified that Marshall only moved more explicitly in his later years towards advocating progression, it would mean that he made this move in spite of the fact that through the various editions of his *Principles* he seemed to put less and less weight and trust in the concept of utility or any possibility of its measurement. Marshall, at any rate, seems to have moved with the times, though there is not necessarily anything virtuous in doing that.

Marshall's most important and definitive discussion of policies against poverty comes in the last chapter of the *Principles* in a section added in the fifth edition (1907). Marshall writes:

The inequalities of wealth though less than they are often represented to be, are a serious flaw in our economic organization. Any diminution of them which can be attained by means that would not sap the springs of free initiative and strength of character and would not therefore materially check the growth of the national dividend, would seem to be a clear social gain. Though arithmetic warns us that it is impossible to raise all earnings beyond the level already reached by specially well-to-do artisan families, it is certainly desirable that those who are below that level should be raised, even at the expense of lowering in some degree those who are above it. *Prompt action is needed in regard to the large, though it may be hoped, now steadily diminishing, 'Residuum' of persons who are physically, mentally, or morally incapable of doing a good day's work with which to earn a good day's wage.* . . . The system of economic freedom is probably the best from both a moral and material point of view for those who are in fairly good health of mind and body. But the Residuum cannot turn it to account.

Marshall is ready for vigorously paternalist measures. He holds: 'A beginning might be made with a broader, more educative and more generous administration of public aid to the helpless. . . . *The expense would be great: but there is no other so urgent need for bold expenditure*' (1920, pp. 714–15, italics added).

I shall deal very briefly with the next main heading, Monopolies and Restrictive Practices. This again was a major concern of Marshall. It is one of the main themes of *Industry and Trade*. (Incidentally, it really is ludicrous to suggest that economists only got interested in monopolistic problems in the 1930s.) In his paper of 1890, 'Some Aspects of Competition', Marshall wrote:

It is clear that combinations and partial monopolies will play a great part in future economic history; that their effects contain much good as well as much evil, and that to denounce them without discrimination would be to repeat the error which our forefathers made with regard to protection. . . . *It is a matter of pressing urgency that public opinion should accustom itself to deal with such questions.*

(1925, p. 289, italics added)

But Marshall has little to suggest in the way of remedies and countermeasures, most of his discussion being concerned with state regulation and nationalization, to the second of which he was usually vigorously opposed. This is no criticism of Marshall. In the nearly eighty years that have passed since Marshall was examining the subject, it has hardly proved possible to propose systematic policies, based on tested coherent theories. Nor has price theory, including the analysis of imperfect and monopolistic competition developed in the 1930s, shown itself to be of great assistance in propounding answers to this problem.[17] The next major section for state action, although it really came to a head in the second quarter of this century, is that of the Monetary Framework,

154

Aggregate Stabilization, Employment or 'Macroeconomic' Policy, or the comprehensive process described by Sir John Hicks as 'the Nationalization of Money'. Not that Marshall's proposals from the vantage, or disadvantage, point of the 1970s seem very extensive or relevant. Generally, for reasons examined by Professor R. C. O. Matthews (1986), Marshall in about 1900, unlike Foxwell and other contemporaries, did not consider that the problem of unemployment was growing more serious. Marshall's various suggestions regarding these problems are scattered through half a century of papers and memoranda. But perhaps the single most compact or systematic treatment, on very simple lines, is in his short paper to the Industrial Remuneration Conference of 1885, not collected in the *Memorials*, of which some sentences were eventually quoted in *Money, Credit and Commerce*, 1922. Marshall posed the question: 'How far do remediable causes influence prejudicially (a) the continuity of employment, (b) the rates of wages?' He sees the main remediable causes as 'chiefly connected in some way or other with the want of knowledge', and proceeds to discuss nine remedies, some of which today certainly seem of rather marginal relevance – such as avoiding vagaries of fashion in dress, especially female dress, countering excessive secrecy in traders by publishing income-tax returns in local newspapers, treating fraud more severely, and encouraging the growth of moral feeling against gambling, especially among the young. More significant seem his proposals for further research by economists on short-term fluctuations and for the development of economic forecasting:

> I see no reason why a body of able disinterested men, with a wide range of business knowledge, should not be able to issue predictions of trade storms and of trade weather generally, that would have an appreciable effect in rendering the employment of industry more steady and con-
> tinuous . . . though the time has not yet come for putting it [this proposal] into practice.

> (1885, p. 181)

Undoubtedly Marshall's main suggestions were in the monetary field, though they did not go far. First he proposed that: 'Arrangements must be made with the Bank of England, *or otherwise*, for raising the normal limit of the ultimate cash reserve of the nation. . . . It would not do much, but it would do a little towards steadying the money market directly and industry indirectly (*op. cit.*, p. 179).

Finally, Marshall made his proposal, which he elaborated on a number of other occasions, that the government 'should publish tables showing as closely as may be the changes in the purchasing power of gold; and should facilitate contracts for payments to be made in terms of units of fixed purchasing power'. He considered (1887) that this would do something to reduce price fluctuations and therefore fluctuations in employment: 'The only effective remedy for them is to be sought in relieving the currency of the duty, which it

155

is not fitted to perform, of acting as a standard of value; and by establishing, in accordance with a plan that has long been familiar to economists, an authoritative standard of purchasing power independent of the currency' (1925, p. 188). However, in reviewing this list of Marshall's remedies for aggregate fluctuations, or his proposals for macroeconomic policy either through rules or authorities, we have perhaps merely made it plain how completely different a world Marshall was living in, as regards the objectives and techniques of economic policy, from the world of the second half of the twentieth century.[18]

When we came to our last heading, Britain's External Commercial Policy and her Relative Economic Position in the World, quite often in perusing Marshall's writings of about three-quarters of a century ago we may feel how little has changed, and how similar are the problems, the warnings and the admonitions, which Marshall handed out to those heard in Britain most days, and especially most weekends, in the 1950s and 1960s. Certainly Britain's economic position in the world and her slower rate of growth relative to other countries were of major concern to Marshall and an important theme in *Industry and Trade*.

Perhaps the most significant illustrations of this point are in two letters written at the end of 1897 to the Master of Balliol, concerning a strike in the engineering industry. The contrast with other optimistic expressions of Marshall about the rapidly increasing economic chivalry of unions and management in Britain is rather remarkable. Marshall writes of the strike: 'If the men should win, and I were an engineering employer, I would sell my works for anything I could get and emigrate to America. If I were a working man, I would wish for no better or more hopeful conditions of life than those which I understand to prevail at the Carnegie works now.' In his next letter (5 December 1897) Marshall summarizes his views in the following paragraphs:

(i) This is the crisis of our industry. For the last twenty years we have indeed been still progressing; but we have been retrograding relatively to the Americans and to the nations of central Europe (not France, I think) and to Eastern lands.

(ii) The causes are partly natural, inevitable, and some are, from a cosmopolitan point of view, matters of satisfaction.

(iii) But one is unmixed evil for all, and a threat to national well-being. It is the dominance in some unions of the desire to 'make work' and an increase in their power to do so.

(iv) And there is another like it. It is the apathy of many employers and their contentment with inferior methods, until driven out of the field or threatened severely, at least, by more enterprising foreigners.

He goes on to speak of 'the laborious laziness' in many British workshops (1925, pp. 398–400).

Later Marshall makes the suggestion, as had Jevons in his *Coal Question* a generation before, of time running out for Britain: 'There is an urgent duty upon us to make even more rapid advance during this age of economic grace, for it may run out before the end of the century (*op. cit.*, p. 326). With the aid of two world wars it, of course, ran out before the end of the half-century.

Marshall returned to the theme, in quite vehement terms, in a letter of 20 January 1901:

> The Christian Socialists did, I believe, a great deal more good than harm: but they did harm. Their authority has been used with great effect by those mean, lazy and selfish men who since 1860 have done so much to undermine the vigour and honest work of English industry, and have removed her from the honourable leadership which she used to hold among the nations. . . .
>
> Fifty years ago nine-tenths of those changes, which have enabled the working classes to have healthy homes and food, originated in England. But, speaking generally, anything which was not English was really dearer than the English, though bought at a lower price. We owed our leadership partly to accidental advantages, most of which have now passed away. But we owed it mainly to the fact that we worked much harder than any continental nation. Now, on the average, we work less long and not more vigorously than our fathers did: and, meanwhile, the average amount of thoughtful work done by the German has nearly doubled; and a similar though less marked improvement is to be seen in other countries. Americans and Germans jeer at the way in which many of our businessmen give their energies to pleasure, and play with their work; and they say, truly as I believe, '*unless you completely shake off the habits that have grown on you in the last thirty years, you will go to join Spain*'. . . .
> It is, I believe, a fact that there is scarcely any industry, which has changed its form during the last ten years, in which we are not behind several countries; and that every Teutonic country, whether behind us or in front of us, is on the average growing in vigour of body and mind faster than we; and that, because there is none of them that is not less self-complacent than we are, less afraid to meet frankly and generously a new idea that is 'competing' for the field. . . .
>
> Our real danger is that we shall be undersold in the product of high class industries, and have to turn more and more to low class industries. There is no fear of our going backwards absolutely, but only relatively. The danger is that our industries will become of a lower grade relatively to other countries: that those which are in front of us will run farther away from us, and those which are behind us will catch us up. This might be tolerable if peace were assured; but I fear it is not. Here I am very sad and anxious. . . .
>
> I think therefore that the first step towards a right use of wealth within the country is the taking an [*sic*] unaggressive position among nations.
>
> (*op. cit.*, pp. 392–4)

Marshall considered the remedy of protective tariffs, then being energetically canvassed, in his 'Memorandum on Fiscal Policy' of 1903, surely one of the finest policy documents ever written by an academic economist, the publication of which apparently was only dragged out of him five years after it was written. Marshall regards 'the future of England with grave anxiety'. Though he had recognized the force of the infant industries argument for protection for less developed countries, Marshall comes out firmly and categorically against the senile industries argument for protection for Britain; nor is he enthusiastic about the imperialist element in the tariff programme, which might turn out to be too favourable to (what were to become) the white dominions. He emphasizes the dangers of retaliation in view of the urgency of Britain's demands for imports, and the possibilities of political mismanagement. Free trade, Marshall says, 'diminishes the money value of political power'. He notes that Britain is falling behind in certain new industries such as electrical engineering and chemicals (1926, pp. 365ff.).[19] Marshall, in this remarkable Memorandum, finally warned regarding 'the solid strength' of Britain's trade unions: 'Perhaps *her greatest danger* is, that they be tempted to use that strength for the promotion of the interests of particular groups of workers, at the expense of wider interests, as the landowning classes did when they had the power' (*op. cit.*, p. 396, italics added).

Thus, though Marshall was keenly aware of the looming problem of the changing relative economic position of Britain, his influence, and that of other economists in the opening years of this century, probably helped to retain Britain's mainly free trade policy for another two to three decades. In fact, Marshall was certainly cautious about putting forward sweeping or drastic policy proposals. Although Keynes (of all people) has remarked that 'Marshall was too anxious to do good', he had strictly limited and disciplined ideas about the role of the academic economist as well as a conscientious grasp of that vital kind of knowledge which consists in an awareness and acceptance of the extent of one's ignorance. 'Why should I be ashamed to say that I know of no simple remedy?' (1925, p. 387) Marshall once exclaimed. Here is a notable contrast with the attitude of some of his classical predecessors as also with his successors in the half-century after his death.

Of Marshall's younger period Lord Annan has written:

> The seventies and eighties were years in which the prevailing political ethos, the system of duties and privileges on which institutions were built, and the economic structure, were all being criticised by the younger school of liberals, by the Fabians and the imperialists. Alfred Marshall did not abandon the moral sciences for economics by accident; economics became for him the study which bore most obviously on moral problems.
>
> (1951, p. 243)

Though in his later years Marshall became very sceptical about state intervention (in the form, for example, of nationalization) he moved with the times with regard to the great transition from classical proportionality to progressive taxation, expressing stronger support for the latter as he grew older, and urging that the proceeds be devoted to increasing social and educational expenditure on the poor.[20]

V

The move to progressive taxation in this country, which began very gradually to gather momentum from the 1890s onwards, has obviously led on to a transformation of economic policy in the twentieth century. Whatever one may think about the justice of this change, or the desirability of the distribution to which it has led, in order to assess it fairly a comparison must be drawn with the kind of distribution which would have obtained if the classical proportionality principle, and, for example, J. S. Mill's *dictum* that progressive taxation was 'a mild form of robbery', still dominated. In this change, the importance of Edgeworth's work must be emphasized. Edgeworth argued for the minimum sacrifice principle, that is, 'that *ceteris paribus* the sum of privation or sacrifice caused by taxation should be a minimum. Therefore, if a certain amount of taxation has to be raised . . . the *prima facie* best distribution is that the whole amount should be paid by the wealthiest citizens' (1925, vol. II, p. 130).

Certainly Edgeworth strenuously qualified this principle with regard to the danger of 'checking accumulation', and denied it any revolutionary significance. But he was justified in holding that his new principle marked 'an important theoretical difference', and, in fact, the thin end of the wedge of progressive taxation became firmly inserted in this country at the time Edgeworth was writing. As the most learned subsequent critic of progressive taxation has stated with regard to its introduction: 'The author who had in this connection the greatest influence in the English-speaking world was F. Y. Edgeworth.'[21] We are not, of course, concerned here either with the ethical and political evaluation, nor with the logical or empirical validity of the arguments from utility analysis of Edgeworth and other neoclassicals. Nor would we try to estimate the actual political weight and effect of these doctrines in gradually transforming taxation, relative to other political or electoral factors. We are simply concerned with them as evidence of the political intentions of the 'neoclassicals' who can be said to have first raised, fundamentally and effectively, basic questions of equity in taxation and distribution. Dr Shehab's conclusion is worth quoting:

> The development of this progressive distributional theory at the close of the last century and the beginning of the present one is particularly instructive. Whether we accept it in the form Edgeworth developed, or that of Cannan which attempts to associate welfare with equity, and interprets the latter in terms of the former, or in Professor Pigou's

synthesis, we arrive at the same goal; namely the higher taxation of the rich in order to ameliorate the inequality of income distribution, and to procure optimum welfare. This end, it will be observed, is the same ultimate objective at which Socialists aim. Thus, for the first time, and after a whole century of *laissez-faire*, which the economists professed completely to support, the coalescence between academic discussion of tax distribution and popular demands was accomplished, a coalescence which the prominence of *laissez-faire* in English economic thought previously made inconceivable.

(1953, pp. 208–9)[22]

The new concern with the problem of poverty also led on to concern in the 1880s and 1890s with what was discerned as one of its main causes, that is 'irregularity of employment' and with relief works to counter this problem. These public works were supported by Marshall in 1886 and were to be defended in 1908 by Pigou who in his inaugural lecture challenged the Ricardian dogma by which they had been so effectively opposed for much of the nineteenth century. As José Harris, in her distinguished study of social policy from 1886 to 1914, points out:

The formation of new Liberal ideas on unemployment policy was merely an aspect of a much wider revolution in the Liberal attitude to social administration which occurred during the 1900s; a revolution in which many Liberals were consciously forced to abandon those principles of 1834 which have hitherto been the sheet-anchor of our social economics. This change in the Liberal approach to social problems had many origins, both intellectual and pragmatic. *Theoretically it was made possible by certain shifts of emphasis, in orthodox economics, particularly the teaching of Alfred Marshall* that gratuitous payments to persons in need did not necessarily depress wages, nor discourage thrift, nor act as an incentive to reckless procreation; they would instead raise wages, because the increased wealth of the working classes would lead to better living, more vigorous and better educated people, with greater earning power, and so wages would rise.

(1972, p. 212, italics added)

In fact José Harris goes on to maintain: 'By 1914 fatalistic acceptance of the inevitability of the trade cycle and doctrinaire prejudice against the relief of unemployment seemed to have largely passed away' (*op. cit.*, p. 5). Thus, after 1870 the leading economists in England, on questions of policy and the role of government in the economy, may be said, for better or for worse, to have moved with the times, in respect to the great changes which, at first gradually, but with gathering momentum, were to transform the role of government in the economy. These changes had already gone a considerable distance by 1914. Two major theoretical ideas, one negative and one positive, were basic

to the new policy-doctrines as contrasted with those of their classical predecessors: the first was the complete abandonment, so far as Britain was concerned, of the natural wage doctrine and the rejection of any hard-line content
in the Malthusian–Ricardian theory about population and wages. This
opened up the problems of poverty and unemployment. The second idea was
the introduction, or revival, of the utility concept, with the impetus it gave –
justifiably or otherwise – towards the replacement of the classical principle of
proportionality in taxation by progression. As Edwin Cannan justifiably
claimed:

> The economist of to-day is far less hostile to socialism in general than his
> predecessors of the classical school. . . . The doctrine of marginal utility
> stamps as economical many things which could formerly be recom-
> mended only on 'sentimental' or non-economic grounds. . . . Assuming
> needs to be equal, modern economics certainly teaches that a given
> amount of produce or income will 'go further' the more equally it is
> divided. The inequality of the present distribution has no pretension to
> be in proportion to needs.
>
> (1917, p. 319)

This survey breaks off rather unevenly around the turn of the century. But we
cannot conclude without a brief reference to the work of Pigou which represents the peak, or climax, of the neoclassical discussion of economic policy in
England. We can be very brief because we are citing later (Chapter 9, Section
IV [cf. Note 1]) Pigou's views in the 1930s on the economic role of government, which pointed ahead towards the mixed economy of the roughly two
decades following the Second World War; and we have also reviewed elsewhere Pigou's earlier comprehensive treatment of economic policy in his
Economics of Welfare (Hutchison, 1953, pp. 283–93).

The Economics of Welfare is built around the concept of the national income or
dividend, and might be said, therefore, *in that respect*, to be 'the leading
modern example of the approach to economics adopted in *The Wealth of
Nations*' (Hutchison, 1953, p. 285).

However, Smith and his followers concentrated almost entirely on *production*.
For Pigou, equally important with its production, or size, are the *distribution* of
the national income, and its *stability* – and the stability of employment –
through time.

On distribution, Pigou laid it down as:

> evident that any transference of income from a relatively rich man to a
> relatively poor man of similar temperament, since it enables more
> intense wants to be satisfied at the expense of less intense wants, must
> increase the aggregate sum of satisfaction. The old 'law of diminishing
> utility' thus leads securely to the proposition: Any cause which increases
> the absolute share of real income in the hands of the poor, provided

that it does not lead to a contraction in the size of the national dividend from any point of view, will, in general, increase economic welfare.

(1929, p. 91)

Regarding stability of income and employment, it should be remembered that the *Economics of Welfare* originated in a study of the causes of unemployment, in which field Pigou was a pioneer, having attacked (1908) the Ricardo–Treasury view against public investment long before Keynes. Only subsequently (1924) was the treatment of stability of incomes and employment separated off by Pigou in a separate volume on 'Industrial Fluctuations'.

Concentrating, in its later editions, on production and distribution the *Economics of Welfare* comprehensively reviewed

the main problems of economic policy arising in Britain in the first quarter of the twentieth century: the control of monopoly, cooperation, the public operation of industry, industrial peace, conciliation and arbitration, hours of labour, methods of wage payment, employment exchanges, interference to raise wages, minimum wages, sliding scales, rationing, subsidies, the redistribution of income, and a national minimum standard of real income.

(Hutchison, *op. cit.*, pp. 285–6)

In subsequent years Pigou's views have been *extremely* differently described and criticized. It is easy to understand that modern libertarians regard his contribution to ideas on economic policy as a fatal step, breaking with the Smithian tradition, along the road to the bureaucratically dominated, interventionist economy – just as Professor Hayek has described Jevons's later views as constituting a fatal turning-point and compromise with the principles of the free economy. On the other hand, it is hardly reasonably comprehensible that, at the other extreme, Professor Joan Robinson should describe Pigou as – apart from a number of cases which he treated as exceptions – laying down *laissez-faire* as 'a rule, which in general could not be questioned' (1973, p. 47).[23]

Pigou's general attitude to economic policy and the role of government, including policies against unemployment in the 1930s, was very near to that of Keynes – possibly, regarding many details, rather more interventionist than that of Keynes. This, of course, was fully acknowledged by Keynes who agreed (1937) that 'when it comes to practice, there is really extremely little between us' (1973, vol. XIV, p. 259).

But there were two important principles in respect of which Pigou (like Marshall and other neoclassicals) differed from Keynes, and still more from many of Keynes's followers.

Though Pigou, like Marshall, had started on the study of economics with glowing hopes of what this study could contribute to human betterment, social reform, and the relief of poverty, they both matured into a healthily sceptical

162

attitude towards the ability and willingness of politicians to implement the policy proposals of economists with requisite ingenuity and integrity. As we have seen, Marshall had come to regard as a major virtue and advantage of free trade – whatever theoretical cases could be constructed against it – that it 'diminishes the money value of political power'.

As regards Pigou, certainly following the First World War, he became heavily sceptical regarding the motives and competence of politicians in all fields of policy, including the economic and financial field. This scepticism even went so far as to incline him to support returning to gold at the old parity, and to profound long-run apprehensions about monetary management, by politicians. In his presidential address to the Royal Economic Society Pigou complained:

> The ambition, I have claimed elsewhere, of most economists is to help in some degree, directly or indirectly towards social betterment. Our study, we should like to think, of the principles of interaction among economic events provides for statesmen data, upon which, along with data of other kinds, they, philosopher kings, build up policies directed to the common good. How different from this dream is the actuality!
>
> (1939, pp. 220–1)

Of course, the expression of such uncompromising views about politicians, regardless of party and patronage, are hardly well calculated to forward one's name towards the Honours List or the House of Lords. However, Pigou's political scepticism perhaps expresses a measure of realism often lacking in subsequent decades.

There is also a second point regarding the contribution of the leading English 'neoclassicals' on the subject of economic policy. They set, on the average, an admirably high standard of caution and modesty. Of course it was not that Jevons, Sidgwick, Wicksteed, Marshall, Pigou or even Edgeworth, upheld some kind of lofty intellectual unconcern with the economic problems of the real world, or were not sufficiently anxious 'to do good' (which Keynes, in fact, accused Marshall of being 'too anxious' to do). What the great English neoclassicals possessed was a degree of genuine awareness of the limitations of economic knowledge which has not generally been attained by economists of other periods and schools. Some 'classicals', some 'Keynesians', and most 'Marxists', naively unaware of the extent of their own ignorance, have entertained and encouraged quite presumptuous and exaggerated ideas about the extent of economic knowledge and the guidance which it can provide for policy. But Jevons (in his later years), Leslie, Bagehot, Sidgwick, Marshall, Pigou and Edgeworth, possessed a realistic insight into the nature of economic knowledge and of its application to the problems of economic policy-making which has not been equalled by any other comparable group of economists, and was certainly far superior to that of their Ricardian predecessors with their comparisons with Newton and Euclid and the laws of physics.

NOTES

1 This item is a considerably revised version of an article which appeared in *History of Political Economy*, Fall 1969, pp. 231ff. It appeared as Chapter 4 of *On Revolutions and Progress in Economic Knowledge*, 1978 (Cambridge University Press and Gregg Revivals).

2 J. E. Cairnes's essay of 1870 on 'Political Economy and *Laissez-Faire*' was something of a landmark. Cairnes, who is sometimes described as 'the last of the classical economists', maintained that political economy was then 'very generally regarded as a sort of scientific rendering' of the *laissez-faire* maxim, which he asserted 'has no scientific basis whatever'. Cairnes was *primarily* concerned with a methodological point, that is, with claiming a politically neutral, scientific character for the subject. Cairnes certainly stressed 'those violent contrasts of poverty and wealth' in the England of his time, and maintained that 'the rich will be growing richer; and the poor, at least relatively, poorer'. But when considering reforms such as cooperation he objected that 'at bottom *the great Malthusian difficulty* would remain'. (See 1873, pp. 232ff.; and 1874, pp. 340 and 348, italics added.)

3 We may cite Professor E. J. Hobsbawm in his *Industry and Empire*, as taking 'around 1860' as 'the peak of British *laissez-faire*', of which '*the foundations . . . crumbled in the 1860s and 1870s*' (1969, pp. 226 and 237, italics added).

4 I would say now that it was a considerable underestimate on my part of the change which took place in Jevons's views on the economic role of government, to have said merely that he 'may have somewhat modified' them (1968, vol. VIII, p. 258).

5 W. S. Jevons, 1857 (italics added).

6 In his *Primer of Political Economy*, 1878, Jevons upheld the proportionality principle in the name of equality: 'Equality consists in everybody paying, in one way or another, about an equal percentage of the wages, salary, or other income which he receives.'

7 In *The Theory of Political Economy* Jevons discusses at some length, as 'negative values', the problems of 'the sewage of great towns, the foul or poisoned water from mines, dye-works, etc.', or what would now be regarded as polluting 'externalities'. He supposes: 'Two adjacent landowners, for instance, might reasonably agree that if A allows B to throw the spoil of his mine on A's land, then A shall be allowed to drain his mine into B's mine' (1879, p. 132).

8 It should be noted, however, that, long before Jevons, Nassau Senior had urged government action with regard to housing and also with regard to public amenities like parks and museums. See his *Lectures 1847–1852* and M. Bowley, *Nassau Senior and Classical Economics*, 1949, pp. 266–72.

9 See his paper 'The Railways and the State' (1874) in *Methods of Social Reform*, 1883.

10 See J. L. Garvin, 1933, vol. 2, p. 534; J. H. Clapham, vol. 3, 1938, p. 397; and W. S. Jevons, 1882, p. 12. Chamberlain slightly misquotes Jevons. I am indebted to Mr W. H. Richmond of the University of Queensland on this point.

11 Regarding labour legislation in general Jevons commented: 'The great lesson which we learn, and it is an impressive one, is that legislation with regard to labour has almost always been class-legislation. It is the effort of some dominant body to keep down a lower class, which had begun to show inconvenient aspirations' (*op. cit.*, p. 34).

12 See also Jevons's warning of 1869: 'I shudder to think what might be the effect of any serious impediment to our future progress, such as a long-continued war, the competition of other nations, or a comparative failure of our own material resources' (1883, p. 193).

13 In *The Economist*, 7 January 1865, under the title 'The Advantages that would

Accrue from an Ownership of the Railways by the State'. See J. H. Clapham, 1932, vol. II, p. 189.

14 Previously (1884), Marshall had called for a break with the old Poor-Law attitude fostered by Ricardian economics: 'Being without the means of livelihood must be treated not as a crime, but as a cause for uncompromising inspection and inquiry'. (See José Harris, 1972, p. 119.)

15 F. Shehab, 1953, p. 199; and J. H. Clapham, 1932, p. 40.

16 In a letter to *The Times* (16 November 1909) Marshall had given his blessing to Lloyd George's Budget of 1909 with its proposals for supertax and for taxing land values: 'In so far as the Budget proposes to check the appropriation of what is really public property by private persons, and in so far as it proposes to bring under taxation some income, which has escaped taxation merely because it does not appear above the surface in a money form, I regard it as sound finance. In so far as its proceeds are to be applied to social problems where a little money may do much towards raising the level of life of the people and increasing their happiness it seems to me a Social Welfare Budget. I do not profess to have mastered all its details; but on the whole I incline to think it merits that name.' See also the letter to Lord Reay of 12 November 1909 (1925, p. 464), in which Marshall strongly defended 'welfare spending': 'The notion that the investment of funds in the education of the workers, in sanitation, in providing open air play for all children etc. tends to diminish "capital" is abhorrent to me.'

17 *Industry and Trade* is Marshall's longest work and is devoted to the theme of 'the limited tendencies of self-interest to direct each individual's action on those lines, in which it will be most beneficial to others'. This work has been almost completely neglected by Marshall's successors, some of whom have charged 'the neoclassicals' with concentrating on perfect competition. It was only with the supersession of the Ricardo–Mill value theory, and the use of the marginal concept by the neoclassicals, that the analysis of monopoly and monopolistic conditions could begin to develop.

18 In a letter to *The Times* (15 February 1886) Marshall expressed some sharply anti-Ricardian support for relief works: 'It is often said that political economy has proved that outdoor relief must do more harm than good: I venture to question this. . . . Works that are not in themselves necessary, but are undertaken in order to give employment, should be such as can be suspended at any time. The pay should be enough to afford the necessaries of life, but so far below the ordinary wages of unskilled labour in ordinary trades that people will not be contented to take it for long, but will always be on the look-out for work elsewhere. I for one can see no economic objection to letting public money flow freely for relief works on this plan.' Later (1908) Marshall referred to unemployment as the symptom of a disease and went on: 'No doubt we ourselves, society at large, are responsible for the existence of this disease more than the victims of it are. And we ought not to be afraid of very large expenditure of public and private funds in removing or lessening the causes of the disease' (1925, p. 447, italics added). Thus Marshall ranged himself against the lingering Ricardian dogmas both regarding the Poor Laws and public relief works.

19 Though Marshall wrote this Memorandum in 1903 he did not publish it until pressed to do so in 1908. In his Prefatory Note Marshall explains that 'this Memorandum is written from the point of view of a student of economics rather than an advocate of any particular policy. I have not held back my own conclusion on the questions to which my attention was directed. But I have endeavoured to select for prominence those considerations which seem at once important and in some danger of being overlooked whether they tell for or against my conclusions.'

On publication Marshall was attacked by Bonar Law for having adopted a 'frankly partisan' attitude to the issue. Marshall, with a kind of mild exasperation protested in a letter to *The Times* (23 November 1908): 'No one can be sure that he has acted up to his intentions and Mr. Bonar Law would have been within his rights if he had said that I had failed to act up to my purpose of preserving a non-partisan attitude. But he was not justified in the explicit statement that I had frankly adopted a partisan attitude.'

20 Mrs R. McW. Tullberg (1975, p. 77) has stated that in an earlier version of this essay (1969), I had demonstrated that Marshall 'had little to contribute to this renewal of State concern with the alleviation of poverty'. I don't think my essay *did* demonstrate this (or tried, or *should* have tried, to demonstrate this). But certainly my emphasis on this subject has changed somewhat: partly from reading the distinguished work by José Harris quoted here; but also because of the realization that the significant comparison with regard to Marshall's proposals for policy changes is *not* with the vast transformation that has come about *subsequently, following two world wars*, but with *the attitudes of Marshall's immediate predecessors*. Here they represent the insertion of the thin end of a massive wedge, or a vital first step.

21 F. A. Hayek, 1960, p. 517. Dr Shehab in his scholarly monograph also ranks Edgeworth's paper 'The Pure Theory of Taxation' as the most important contribution by an economist to the introduction of progressive taxation (1953, p. 208). We cannot agree (nor, presumably could Professor Hayek and Dr Shehab) with Professor George Stigler's verdict that: 'After utility theory began to appear in the 1870s, it took no important part in any policy-oriented controversy up to World War I' (1973, p. 312).

22 Dr Shehab is referring, of course, to *laissez-faire* in *distribution*, which was certainly upheld in a pretty thoroughgoing form by Ricardo.

23 According to Professor Robinson: 'For fifty years before 1914 the established economists of various schools had *all* been preaching *one doctrine*, with great self-confidence and pomposity – the doctrine of *laissez-faire*' (1972, p. 2, italics added).

REFERENCES

Annan, N. (1951). *Leslie Stephen.*
Bowley, M. (1949). *Nassau Senior and Classical Political Economy.*
Cairnes, J. E. (1873). *Essays in Political Economy.*
Cairnes, J. E. (1874). *Some Leading Principles of Political Economy.*
Cannan, E. (1917). *Theories of Production and Distribution,* 1893, 3rd ed.
Clapham, J. H. (1932–8). *An Economic History of Modern Britain,* vol. II and vol. III.
Edgeworth, F. Y. (1925). *Papers Relating to Political Economy,* 3 vols.
Fetter, F. W. (1965). *The Development of British Monetary Orthodoxy 1797–1875.*
Foxwell, H. S. (1886). *Irregularity of Employment and Fluctuations of Prices.*
Garvin, J. L. (1933). *Life of Joseph Chamberlain.*
Harris, J. (1972). *Unemployment and Politics 1886–1914.*
Hayek, F. A. (1960). *The Constitution of Liberty.*
Hayek, F. A. (1973). *Law, Legislation and Liberty,* vol. I.
Hobsbawm, E. J. (1969). *Industry and Empire,* Pelican ed.
Hutchison, T. W. (1953). *Review of Economic Doctrines 1870–1929.*
Hutchison, T. W. (1968). 'Jevons', in *International Encyclopedia of the Social Sciences,* vol. 8.
Jevons, W. S. (1857). 'Comparison of the Land and Railway Policy of New South Wales', in *Empire,* Sydney.

Jevons, W. S. (1870 and 1962). 'Economic Policy', (1870) in *Essays in Economic Method*, ed. R. L. Smyth.

Jevons, W. S. (1878). *Primer of Political Economy*.

Jevons, W. S. (1879 and 1911). *Theory of Political Economy*, 2nd ed. and 4th. ed.

Jevons, W. S. (1882). *The State in Relation to Labour*.

Jevons, W. S. (1883). *Methods of Social Reform*.

Jevons, W. S. (1905). *The Principles of Economics and Other Papers*, ed. H. Higgs.

Keynes, J. M. (1973). *The Collected Writings*, ed. D. E. Moggridge, vol. XIV.

Marshall, A. (1885). Paper to the Industrial Remuneration Conference in *Report of the Proceedings and Papers*.

Marshall, A. (1919). *Industry and Trade*.

Marshall, A. (1920 and 1961). *Principles of Economics*, 8th ed., ed. C. W. Guillebaud, 2 vols.

Marshall, A. (1925). *Memorials*, ed. A. C. Pigou.

Marshall, A. (1926). *Official Papers*.

Matthews, R. C. D. (1968). 'Why has Britain had Full Employment since the War?', *Economic Journal*, Sept. 1968, pp. 555ff.

Pigou, A. C. (1929). *Economics of Welfare*, 3rd ed.

Pigou, A. C. (1939). Presidential Address, *Economic Journal*, 49, pp. 215ff.

Robinson, J. (1972). 'The Second Crisis of Economic Theory', *Papers and Proceedings of the A.E.A.*, vol. 62, pp. 1ff.

Robinson, J. and Eatwell, J. (1973). *An Introduction to Modern Economics*.

Senior, N. W. (1847 and 1852). *Lectures on Political Economy*.

Shehab, F. (1953). *Progressive Taxation*.

Sidgwick, H. (1883 and 1887). *Principles of Political Economy*, 1st and 2nd eds.

Stigler, G. J. (1973). 'The Adoption of the Marginal Utility Theory', in *The Marginal Revolution*, ed. R. D. C. Black, A. W. Coats and C. D. W. Goodwin, pp. 305ff.

Toynbee, A. (1894 and 1905). *Lectures on the Industrial Revolution*.

Tullberg, R. McW. (1975). 'Marshall's Tendency to Socialism', *History of Political Economy*, vol. 7, pp. 75ff.

8

FROM 'DISMAL SCIENCE' TO 'POSITIVE ECONOMICS': A CENTURY-AND-A-HALF OF PROGRESS?[1]

I

In the title suggested for this paper by the Recorder of Section F the most significant component seems to be the question mark at the end: '. . . Progress?' for a baffling initial problem in trying to review the last 150 years of change, growth, or perhaps 'progress', in political economy and economics, is presented by the uncertainty and ambiguity of the criteria for assessing growth or progress in this context. The problem is somewhat similar to the index-number problem familiar to economists, but considerably more complex and controversial. It is also considerably more complex and controversial to try to assess progress, or the growth of knowledge, in economics and the social sciences, than it is in the natural sciences. This is because economics and the social sciences have a crucially significant, though often overlooked, historical dimension, which the natural sciences do not possess to anything like the same extent: that is, they are not complicated, as economics is, by historical and institutional changes in their subject-matter, and in the significant questions and answers about it.

Certainly, in economics, one can confidently point to vast increases in the stock and flow of factual knowledge, historical and statistical, and also in the range and refinement of analytical, and especially mathematical, techniques and abstract models. But, though some growth in these two respects is probably necessary, it is surely not sufficient for progress in an empirical science, and especially one in which most of the practitioners have entertained, and continue to entertain, as a prime aim and claim – though recently by no means so unanimously as previously – the guidance of policy or a significant contribution to less unsuccessful policy-making. For increases *simply* in factual knowledge, and/or in the range and refinement of analytical techniques, do not necessarily yield the kind of progress in explanation, or – in some at least minimal sense – in predictive potential, which is necessary for a science with the aims and claims which political economy or economics has had, and is having, made for it.

Indeed, the much enlarged stock of factual knowledge, and the much more numerous, powerful or refined techniques available in 1981, as compared with 1831, *may* be of relatively little use for reaching scientific explanations of the main, real-world problems at the later date, and *may* even explain these problems less adequately, and provide less useful predictions, than the much smaller stock of factual knowledge, and the much smaller range of techniques available in 1831, helped to provide at the earlier date. This may be the case if the economic world has, in the meantime, become more complex, unpredictable and difficult to explain.

Of course, if the aims and claims made for economics by its practitioners are rejected or reduced, then the requirements for 'progress' in the subject may become much more flexible. Sir John Hicks has recently observed: 'There is much of economic theory which is pursued for no better reason than its intellectual attraction; it is a good game' (1979, p. viii).

In so far as this is the case, the assessment of 'progress' in economics may well become even more uncertain and relaxed. Indeed such claims might become comfortingly irrefutable.

The attempt might also be made to apply Lakatos's concept of how, in the progress of a scientific subject, a 'growth of knowledge' can be said to take place, when a new theory not only explains and predicts all that the previous theory explained and predicted, but *more*. It may be that Lakatos's concept of the growth of knowledge is less difficult to apply to the physical sciences, in terms of which it was developed. But it seems doubtful how successfully, or unambiguously, it can be applied to the development of *historical* subjects, concerned, that is, with material which has a historical dimension such as real-world economics undoubtedly has. For, in such subjects, *two* kinds of changes are important, which render highly problematic any assessment of the growth, let alone 'progress', of scientific knowledge or of a scientific discipline. Not only are there vital changes in valuations regarding the interest or importance of different problems, which, in economics, would derive mainly from changes in policy importance. There are also significant, positive, historical or institutional changes, which alter economic reactions and behaviour, particularly via changes in experience, information, expectations and processes of learning and unlearning, which may crucially transform, or complicate, economic processes, and render obsolete, or more inadequate, previous explanations and theories.

A more or less adequate explanation or theory, at an institutionally or historically earlier, and perhaps simpler and less complex stage, may become quite inadequate and misleading as experience, information and institutions change.[2] To meet such changes, what are earlier put forward as 'general' economic theories have increasingly to be adapted or qualified by *ad hoc* strategems, to the point perhaps of virtual taxonomic emptiness. For with subjects that possess a significant historical dimension, the task is not, as with the more developed natural sciences, one of giving fuller and fuller explanations or answers regarding the more or less constant, stable or unchanging behaviour of the physical world: the generalizations and explanations of political economy and economics, except for the flimsiest and least substantial, have frequently to be adapted to historical, institutional, informational and expectational changes, or to new or growing complexities in the subject-matter. Economists share, in significant measure, the fate of Sisyphus.

The progress or regress of economics and economic knowledge, in so far as it may be regarded as both a scientific and historical subject, must be distinguished from the (not entirely unrelated) processes involved in the ups and downs in public prestige and influence which economics and its practitioners have undergone, depending on whether or not they appear to be able to provide convincing answers to the main policy problems of the day. In periods of economic success in Britain, like the 1850s and 1860s, and, somewhat similarly, the 1950s and 1960s, there will be a tendency for economists to claim, and be granted, credit for this success, on behalf of a politico-economic theory around which a convincing range of consensus is likely to have gathered, with fundamental disagreements in abeyance. In periods, on the other hand, of striking economic *unsuccess*, like the 1970s, there are more likely to be fierce and fundamental disagreements, so that the subject and its practitioners suffer in influence and prestige, either because they do not seem to have an adequate answer to current problems, or because they have too many sharply conflicting answers. Previously orthodox theories may have become institutionally obsolete and the new challengers may not have established their credibility.

With this brief warning about the difficulties of attempting an answer to the question mark in the title of this paper, we shall now examine a set of four snapshots, posed at roughly half-century intervals, that is, at around 1831, 1881, 1931 and 1981. This is all that can be attempted by way of setting up the issues for those bold enough to attempt an answer regarding the 'progress', over the last century and a half, of Section F's subject.

II

Section F was not a founder section of the BA. According to Adam Sedgwick, the President of the Association at its 1833 meeting in Cambridge, 'this self-formed section' was created, that year, with some 'irregularity' (British Association, 1834, pp. xxvii–viii; see also Royal Statistical Society, 1934, pp. 4–8). The leading founders (or culprits) were Richard Jones, Malthus and Babbage. The title of the new section was simply 'Statistics', of which economic statistics was simply a part. 'Economic Science' was not allowed into the forefront of the title until twenty-five years later, in 1856, at a time when the prestige of the new science of political economy had reached something of a peak.

At its foundation, the ground which the Association's President somewhat grudgingly conceded to Section F comprised: 'What may be called the raw material to political economy and political philosophy; and by their help the lasting foundations of those sciences *may be perhaps ultimately laid*' (1834, p. xxviii, italics added).

Sedgwick was afraid that in admitting a human, moral, political or social subject, the British Association would be deserting 'the secure ground' which it had marked out for itself. He argued:

> The things with which the Association had to do were the laws and properties of matter and with these alone; the nature of the human mind was utterly beyond their province; the sciences of morals and politics were elevated far above the speculations of their material philosophy. . . . When we enter on these higher generalisations, that moment they are dissevered from the objects of the Association, and must be abandoned by it.
>
> (1834, p. xxviii)

Those among the early pioneers of Section F who were primarily interested in political economy, were surely not as negatively sceptical as Sedgwick regarding the longer-run scientific possibilities of their subject. But several of them, like Richard Jones and Malthus, *were* highly sceptical of the new, abstract, deductive method of Ricardo, and also were very dubious about the extremely confident claims for their new doctrines put forward by James Mill and McCulloch, for example. In helping to found Section F, Jones and Malthus were expressing an emphasis on the need to build up the empirical and statistical base of their subject. They may at some points have moved towards a kind of 'naive' empiricism, in questioning the excessive Ricardian claims. But it is surely incontrovertible that they were thoroughly justified in seeking to develop economic statistics, and thus to build up the empirical foundations of the subject. Anyhow, in Section F, they were balanced by Nassau Senior, who upheld the method of deduction from a few fundamental assumptions, but was much more cautious than the Ricardians about applications to policy.

Thus at the time when the Section was launched, three views may be distinguished regarding the possible programme and prospects for a science of political economy.

First, there was the negativist scepticism of Adam Sedgwick regarding the possibility of any 'scientific' treatment of economics, or of other human, moral or social subjects, in anything like the same ways, or in accordance with the same criteria, as those upheld by the main branches of natural science, around which the British Association had been founded.

Secondly, at the other extreme, there was the pretentious confidence of the Ricardians and McCulloch about their new science, with their claim of epistemological parity with the most advanced natural sciences.

Thirdly, and in the middle, there were the mainly, but not entirely, empirical economists, prominent in the foundation of Section F, who rejected, on the one hand, extreme negative scepticism regarding the possibilities of economic science, and, on the other hand the excessive pretensions and abstractions of Ricardo, James Mill or McCulloch.

Whatever may be concluded today regarding the longer-run balance of wisdom between these three programmes or viewpoints, there is no doubt that it was the second view which flourished over the next two or three decades. Outside Section F, among political economists, and increasingly among the public élite, much of this period was a time of growing confidence in the new science of political economy. Smith was acknowledged as the great founder. But in the ensuing half-century since *The Wealth of Nations*, immense progress was held to have taken place. That was the view of the two Mills and McCulloch, who exercised such a powerful influence. Admittedly there were some deep disagreements on value and distribution between the Ricardians and the Oxford–Dublin school of Senior and Whately, who were much closer to French and German theories. But – except for Malthus – there was widespread agreement on classical macroeconomics, as well as on the deductive method and, above all, on the general principles of policy. Of course, in the background – or the 'underworld' as Keynes called it – there were socialist and historical critics. But thanks largely to the influence of the Mills and McCulloch, a version of classical orthodoxy was gaining great influence and authority. To some extent this authority was obtained, not by weight of numbers, for those were very small, but by a kind of circular, self-sealing argument: the orthodox, authoritative doctrines were those of the serious, responsible economists; while the serious, responsible economists were identifiable as those who held the orthodox, authoritative doctrines. James Mill fairly explicitly adopted such an argument in his remarkable paper of 1836 entitled 'Whether Political Economy is Useful?' – to which question his answer was, of course, an extremely confident affirmative (1966, pp. 371ff.).

Especially ambitious claims came from the followers of Ricardo, and from McCulloch, who insisted on intellectual parity between the laws of physics and the laws of distribution of the new science of political economy. As McCulloch claimed:

> The errors with which Political Economy was formerly infected have now nearly disappeared, and a very few observations will suffice to show that *it really admits of as much certainty in its conclusions as any science founded on fact and experiment can possibly do.*
>
> (McCulloch, 1824, p. 75, italics added)

Moreover, the doctrines of the new science were regarded as so indisputably well founded that they could suitably be imparted to children. Indeed, Mrs Marcet's *Conversations on Political Economy*, which went through numerous editions between 1816 and 1839, was prescribed by Ricardo for his daughters. This work, as Schumpeter has observed, 'presents many of the most important tenets of the Ricardian school' (1954, p. 477). As Schumpeter (writing in the 1940s) goes on:

> Not for a moment did Mrs Marcet doubt not only that the definitive truth about economics and economic policy had been discovered at last, but also that this truth was so delightfully simple as to be capable of being taught to every schoolgirl. This frame of mind was then common and is highly characteristic of that age – exactly as a similar frame of mind is common among modern Keynesians and not less characteristic of our own age.

However, in 1831, though well on the upswing, classical political economy had not yet come to full fruition or the peak of its prestige in this country. That was to come in the three decades following the great reform of the franchise in 1832. The structure of the classical free market economy was completed, through, notably, the new Poor Law of 1834, the Bank Act of 1844 and the abolition of the Corn Laws in 1846. A relative peak of prosperity for the British economy was to follow in the 1850s. Some further features of this 1831 snapshot may be noticed.

First, everything was, quantitatively, on a miniature scale compared with today. The number of economists in the country – depending, of course, on how this somewhat problematic term is defined – would perhaps hardly have equalled the number today in a single, medium-sized modern university department. The same applied to the number of publications. There were no specialist journals, and not to be any for decades. As regards the stocks and flows of factual material, these, compared with today, were minute, whether in the form of historical and institutional material, or of economic statistics, which were confined mainly to certain trade returns and to the three or four population series after 1801.

Secondly, among the founders of Section F, and among economists generally, academics, though prominent, were not dominant. Chairs of Political Economy had been founded at Oxford in 1825, in Cambridge in 1828, and in Dublin in 1832. But academics did not dominate the subject to anything like the extent they were to do a century later, in the 1930s.

Thirdly, at this period, just when the British economy was achieving a unique supremacy in the world, so British economists were pre-eminent in the field of political economy, certainly in their own eyes, but in the eyes of others too. In fact, as Schumpeter has said of this period, 1790–1870: 'Barring a few lonely peaks abroad, England easily comes out first in the period's performance. In fact that period was the specifically English period in the history of our science', (1954, p. 382). Or, as T. H. Huxley put it (1868), political economy was 'an intensely Anglican subject'.

Two further points to be noticed at this stage refer to different aspects of the title of this paper.

The term 'positive economics' has come to possess a rather varied and uncertain content. But what might be regarded as the initial, core principle involved in the concept of 'positive' economics is the insistence on a fundamental distinction between positive and normative. This distinction, though not always easy to observe, and in some senses perhaps impossible to maintain, remains, as far as it goes – which is quite a long way – essential for the clarity which it is an intellectual and professional duty to strive after.

The introduction of this positive–normative distinction into political economy dates from just those years of the early 1830s when the BA, and Section F, were being launched. In Smith and Ricardo, the adjective 'natural' had shed a kind of normative–positive ambiguity over much of early classical political economy, which it was surely an important step forward to begin to dispel. This fundamental clarificatory work was due, in the first instance, mainly to Whately and Senior, both prominent in the early years of Section F (Whately 1832, pp. 20–4). 'Positive economics', in this important initial sense, was, therefore, a classical and not a neoclassical innovation.[3]

Another sense of this multifaceted concept of 'positive economics' is concerned with the view that economics can be, and is, a science in the same full sense as the most advanced natural sciences, and has already produced fully comparable theories and laws. We have noted above the two extremes, of Sedgwick, on the one hand, doubting whether such an epistemological possibility could, or would, ever be realized regarding human, moral, political or social subjects; and, on the other hand, the extreme claims of the Ricardians and McCulloch for the laws of their new science, and for full epistemological parity with the natural sciences. But here distinctions and discriminations are vital: between, on the one hand, claims to full epistemological parity of *already achieved results*; and, on the other hand, the moderate views, shared by the economist founders of Section F, that the empirical 'methods', discipline and criteria of the natural sciences can and should be followed in political economy, as far as the material allows, which is significantly far – without, of course, it being claimed, or hoped, that theories, laws, explanations and predictions, on a par with those of the natural sciences, were being, or would be, achieved.

A decade later, political economy was described by Carlyle (in *Past and Present*, 1843) as 'The Dismal Science'. However, over the next couple of decades, the policies of 'dismalness', or austerity, were to be followed by the British economy achieving a *relative* strength in the world unequalled before or since, while the living standards of the British people, at least by conventional standards, rose well above those of comparable countries. Of course, one may reject this kind of 'success', as conventionally measured, or one may deny that the application of the theories of the 'dismal science' played any effective part in achieving these outstanding results. But most economists would not find all the implications of such rejections, or denials, easy to accept.

III

Moving on half a century to 1881, one finds that the subject has gone through a large part – though not quite all – of a kind of cycle.

English classical political economy had moved to the climax of its prestige and influence in the 1850s and early 1860s. By means of a simple but effective *post hoc ergo propter hoc* argument, the extraordinary success of the British economy as 'the workshop of the world' had been more or less credibly transferred to boost the prestige of the dominant 'Anglican' version of the science of political economy. Pointing to the world leadership of the British economy at this time, Nassau Senior, who at different periods of his career played a prominent part in Section F, proclaimed to an admiring Frenchman: 'It is the triumph of theory. We are governed by philosophers and political economists' (Senior, 1878, vol. I, p. 169).

Meanwhile, the intellectual foundations for the prestige of the subject with the intelligent élite of the day, was provided by J. S. Mill's lucid, authoritative and masterly exposition of its principles.

However, quite suddenly in the middle or late 1860s, there had come a collapse in confidence and credibility. The causes may be found in various directions. Long-standing theoretical inadequacies were rendered more acutely serious by historical and institutional changes, at the same time as what was taken to be the subject's simple policy message of *laissez-faire* was being increasingly called in question by new political forces, which began to take their share of electoral power as a consequence of the second reform bill of 1867.

The point of departure for this 'revolution', or turning-point, is often taken to be Jevons's utility theory of value. Jevons, a great BA man, who delivered several of his most important papers to Section F, had first expounded his utility theory at the 1862 meeting of the Association. But no notice of Jevons's arguments was taken until they appeared in his *Theory of Political Economy* of 1871.

In fact, it seems that it was the problems raised by the increasingly serious institutional obsolescence of the classical distribution theory, which were probably the prior and more important theoretical cause of the collapse in credibility, and of the rapidly mounting crisis, of classical political economy. In particular, institutional changes were calling in question the significance of both the natural wage theory and the wages fund doctrine. When, in 1876, the centenary of *The Wealth of Nations* came round, profound disagreements were expressed about the state of the subject in respect of its theory, methods and policy doctrines. Jevons himself declared 'the state of the science to be almost chaotic'. J. E. Cairnes, often described as 'the last of the classicals' discerned in 1870, 'signs of a belief that Political Economy had ceased to be a fruitful speculation' – a complete reversal of James Mill's confident claims of a generation earlier. Later Walter Bagehot, in the 1870s, contrasted the prestige of, and enthusiasm for, political economy in the earlier part of the century:

'At that time economists indulged in happy visions; they thought the attainment of truth far easier than we have since found it to be' (Hutchison, 1953, pp. 5–7).

Indeed, such was the distrust of the subject that in 1877 Francis Galton published a paper in the *Journal of the Royal Statistical Society* entitled 'Considerations Adverse to the Maintenance of Section F', in which he castigated the 'unscientific' nature of the Section's discussions and complained that they lacked the degree of consensus requisite in a scientific subject, which should reach conclusions 'that all minds are obliged to accept'.

In a notable presidential address to Section F at Dublin the following year J. K. Ingram agreed that:

An important crisis in the history of our Section has taken place . . . and this is what lends a peculiar gravity to the incident – such a step could hardly have been taken if the general mass of the intelligent public entertained strong convictions as to the genuinely scientific character of political economy.

(1878, p. 14)

This intellectual crisis, or depression, of the 1870s was mainly a British phenomenon, just as classical political economy itself had been. In other countries, where English classical theories had never achieved the same dominance, the subject moved into the neoclassical era without the kind of 'revolution', or crisis in credibility, which occurred in Britain – though a major *Methodenstreit* ensued in Austria and Germany.

Anyhow, by 1881, signs of a new upswing were (or are, with hindsight) discernible, centred round what came to be called 'neoclassical' theory. Jevons died in 1882. But Alfred Marshall was already at work on his *Principles* and took over the Cambridge chair in 1885. A generation change had taken place, usually an important element in fundamental new developments in the subject.

But political economy, or 'economics', as it was about to be called, could no longer be described as an 'intensely Anglican' subject. British predominance was beginning relatively to decline. Important new schools of economic theory had begun to emerge in the 1870s in Vienna and Lausanne. Moreover, the academic influence was about to increase significantly, both as regards numbers of personnel, and intellectual criteria, a development marked in this country, a decade or so later, by the foundation of the London School (1895) and by the specialist Economics Tripos in Cambridge (1903). Numbers, however, were still very small. Cairnes, back in 1870, had estimated that there were fewer than 100 students of political economy in the whole of London.

The stock and flow of statistical and historical factual material was growing, thanks especially to some of the pioneer neoclassicals, notably Jevons, with the great advance he achieved in price index numbers. Moreover, economic history was emerging as a specialist subject. But unfortunately, this

176

development was largely separate from economics; so that, apart from Marshall's own individual efforts, a mutual, two-way enrichment of history and theory failed to ensue.

In due course, the theoretical advance was not confined to microeconomics. By the 1880s, concern with cyclical fluctuations and with irregularity of employment as a cause of poverty, was increasing markedly in Britain. In the second half of the nineteenth century much of the pioneer work on cyclical fluctuations and macroeconomic instability had been done in France and Germany – for example, by Juglar, a visitor to Section F. But 1886 was notable for two events in this field in Britain. First, there was the publication by Foxwell, Marshall's lieutenant in Cambridge, of his study of irregularity of employment, in which he described this problem as the most serious policy problem of the day. Secondly, in the same year, Joseph Chamberlain circularized local authorities recommending the setting up of relief works in times of high unemployment. Quantitatively, the effects of Chamberlain's measure were trivial. But intellectually, it marked an important break with Ricardian policies and was cautiously approved by Marshall.[4]

IV

Before coming to the present day, I would like to glance rapidly at the BA centenary year, 1931, when, because of the great economic crisis of that year, some of the more elderly of today's economists were, perhaps over-optimistically, first getting engaged with the subject of Section F.

Again, over the previous half-century since 1881, something of an intellectual cycle can be discerned as having taken place, though this does not stand out as clearly as in the preceding and succeeding periods. The year 1931 came just about halfway through that era of almost continuous violent upheaval between 1914 and 1945, when First World War, post-war, great slump, pre-war and Second World War followed one another with only fleeting interludes in between – a period, incidentally, which coincided almost exactly with the career of Keynes as an economist.

The economic world of the inter-war years was dominated by the breakdown of the monetary standard, together with very serious instability and unprecedented levels of unemployment (for which official statistics were now regularly available). As we have seen, for several decades before 1914, increasing concern had been shown with the business cycle and the unemployment problem. But this had been against a background of *comparative* economic stability, and 'a stable general culture', as Pigou had called it – in particular, the kind of stability provided by a more or less accepted and assured monetary framework and standard. For a time, in the 1920s, an attempt was made to get back to this framework of monetary stability; 1931 saw the end of this attempt.

Economic theory in this country in the 1920s, though hardly itself in a state of explicit crisis, was not manifestly mastering the fundamental and massive institutional changes taking place in the political economy of the post-war world. Neoclassical microeconomics, and, in particular the treatment of monopolistic, oligopolistic and imperfect markets, was, in Cambridge, being shunted away from the historical and institutional methods of Marshall's *Industry and Trade*, into a *cul-de-sac* of increasingly arid geometrical abstraction. As regards macroeconomics, though progress was being made with the study of cyclical fluctuations, the subject was not equipped to confront with credibility the tornado which struck in late 1929. Moreover, there were funda- mental ambiguities and inadequacies in the logical links between the two branches of theory ('micro' and 'macro' as they were soon to be described).

Nevertheless, with hindsight, it is clear that by 1931 what was to be known as 'the Keynesian Revolution' was already under way, though it only came to full fruition, with the first 'Keynesian' budget, ten years later in war-time Britain. But already by 1929 Keynes had claimed, without *much* exaggeration, that the majority of British economists supported his opposition to the Treasury or classical view that public works would then simply 'crowd out' private investment, and do little or nothing to relieve unemployment.

For some years after 1931, thanks to the intellectual confidence and optimism generated by Keynes, economists could plausibly convince them- selves that they were on their way to solving the basic economic problems con- fronting mankind – unemployment and economic instability. The kind of excited euphoria generated by such an intellectual upswing is demonstrated in the quite rhapsodic, Wordsworthian terms in which one of the senior Nobel Laureates has described the 1930s. In the midst of the great Depression, with unemployment everywhere at unprecedented levels, and with Stalin and Hitler gaining alarmingly in power, nevertheless, so rosy were the intel- lectual–political vistas then opening up, Professor Paul Samuelson tells us, that:

> Bliss was it in that dawn to be alive.
> But to be young was very heaven.

In any event, in the 1930s, an expansion in the numbers of economists in Britain was under way, considerable in relation to previous low levels, but still relatively very small compared with what was to come two to three decades later. But more than at any other time, in the years before the Second World War in Britain, the subject was dominated by university economists. At the time of 'the Keynesian Revolution', outside the universities, in government, banking and industry, there were in Britain only one or two isolated individuals described as 'economists'.

V

Finally, we reach 1981. Again, in the preceding half-century, since 1931, part of an intellectual cycle is discernible, more clearly so than in the case of

1881–1931, and having some similarities with the cycle of, roughly, 100 years previously. In the 1950s and 1960s there was certainly a remarkable intellectual boom of confidence in the subject, comparable with the English classical boom of about a century before. Again in the 1970s there was something of an intellectual depression or even a persisting 'crisis'. Whether by 1981 the elements of a new upswing, in one direction or another, are now discernible – as could be claimed regarding 1881 – remains debatable.

The remarkable period of real-world economic success, throughout most Western countries, which lasted from shortly after the Second World War down to about the middle 1960s, was certainly *post*-Keynes, and was widely acclaimed, by Keynesians, to be *ergo propter* Keynes. In Britain the spectacular fall in unemployment, compared with the inter-war period, generated more confidence in the validity and operational power of the prevailing economic doctrines than had existed for 100 years. This optimism regarding the solution of the unemployment problem was then extended – by, for example, Sir Roy Harrod, Lord Kaldor and other Keynesians – to the long-standing, if, by many, newly-discovered problem of Britain's relatively lower rate of economic growth, which was also confidently expected to yield to the ministrations of 'the New Economics' (see Hutchison, 1968, especially chapters 3 and 4).

Certainly this New Economics had shed, with contempt, all the puritanical, protestant-ethical 'dismalness' of English classical political economy. Spending one's way out of unemployment and low growth into the new age of affluence and plenty became an influential message, just at the moment when democratic appetites were coming to exercise more and more influence on economic policy through the electoral process. Even more clearly than the Keynesian doctrine proclaiming the power of governments to reduce unemployment, the new 'growthmanship' message seemed to provide the answer to politicians' prayers. In unprecedented numbers, economists began to be welcomed into Whitehall, Downing Street and the House of Lords.[5]

The expansive, liberating policy message was matched by an expansive, liberating methodological message. At this time – roughly describable as that of the 'silly sixties' – the 'positive' restraint and discipline, called for by a regard for the normative–positive distinction, as had been upheld in Cambridge by such past masters and disciplinarians as Marshall, Sidgwick and J. N. Keynes, was, in some fashionable circles, cast aside as an outmoded, 'positivist' repression, in favour of the liberating methodological doctrine that 'anything goes'.

Anyhow, the huge upsurge in the number of economists reduced all previous figures to insignificance. The expansion reached out far beyond the university base, which was itself then growing at an unprecedentd pace, and proceeded backwards into the schools, on an immense scale, and forwards into the civil service, finance and industry. However, though Keynes had revived the Anglican contribution to the subject, British economics was rapidly becoming a much smaller part of the world profession, which was dominated more and more from the USA.

179

Then, quite suddenly, in the late 1960s, came the collapse, in a manner comparable in *some* respects with the slump in the English classical doctrines of just 100 years previously.

Again, significant institutional changes had been accumulating, on this occasion affecting employment conditions, the powers of trade unions and inflationary expectations. These changes seriously aggravated long-standing theoretical limitations in the prevailing doctrines. Moreover, at this point, alarming and unprecedented economic phenomena began rather suddenly to appear, notably the combination of more and more serious inflation with a marked rise in unemployment. The question arose as to how far such new phenomena, long held to be more or less incompatible, called for revisions in the prevailing, confidently, and even in some cases dogmatically, held theories and policy doctrines, in which such quantities of intellectual capital had been invested over the previous decades. Just how fundamental were the revisions required by the new institutional and expectational facts? Of course, it is always possible, indeed almost easy, for *a priorists* impervious to empirical evidence, to add on another *ad hoc* patch to a cherished pair of general theoretical trousers. Pending a generation change, such will often be a wide-spread reaction in such intellectual crises.

Meanwhile, however, the theory and policy doctrines now challenging 'Keynesian' orthodoxy (which orthodoxy, in the form widely prevalent a quarter of a century after his death, Keynes himself might well have largely rejected) harked back, in some respects, to the classical model. The previous degree of consensus, which had been held together in the late 1950s and early 1960s to an important extent by the prevailing appearance of real-world economic success, proceeded to disintegrate. Disagreements were soon magnified. In times of economic difficulty or crisis, economists are usually ready to ascribe great influence to their opponents. Adherents of one 'general theory' began to accuse the other side of being responsible for unemployment; while adherents of the alternative 'general theory' accused the first of being responsible for inflation – or for 'Keynesian inflation', as it was called by one authority.

After about a decade of 'crisis' (this term was still being authoritatively applied to the state of the subject in 1980), can it now be said, in 1981, that a new intellectual upswing is discernible – as might have been claimed in 1881? As with the economy itself, downswings seem to have been followed fairly regularly by upswings. But it does not follow that a new upswing, or one resembling previous upswings, will follow on cue, on this occasion. Perhaps, for some time, a kind of persistent depression may ensue. But, of course, optimists of different persuasions discern the approach of dawn (unfortunately, at diametrically opposite points of the compass).[6]

Anyhow, it might be worthwhile to enquire just how far the kind of boom of prestige and influence enjoyed by the subject in the 1850s and early 1860s, and again in the 1950s and early 1960s, is either possible or desirable. In the real-world economy a boom, in spite of some inflation, brings more employment and makes many people better off than previously. But in intellectual booms, over-confident, inflated pretensions run the danger of causing more harm, in fostering subsequent political disillusion, than the gains, which may accrue from a growth of knowledge, do good. It should not, however, be denied that the great English classical and Keynesian 'booms' *did* produce, or were based on, *some* genuine growth of knowledge both of specially valuable relevance for a few decades, and even of *some* permanent significance. Unfortunately, however, the serious limitations of the original, general theoretical claims were overlooked in the course of the initial success and intellectual euphoria, and this, in turn, led on (with the epigoni taking over from the original founders), to dogmatic inflexibilities and over-simplifications, which were then undermined and rendered seriously obsolete by historical, institutional and expectational changes.

Therefore, what does *not* seem a promising line of advance is a new intellectual upswing based on a new exclusivist 'general theory'. We have had the classical and neoclassical general theories, and the Keynesian general theory. Also, for over 100 years, through the eras of Stalin and Mao, the Marxian general theory has gained adherents among economists. Something in the way of synthesis may be possible, but not in terms of a significant new general theory. What may rather be needed is not some 'general theory', adjusted in all directions to the possibilities of all times and places, but rather a much greater recognition of the historical and institutional dimensions of the subject, together with the development of a range of alternative theories appropriate for changing historical and institutional conditions.

VI

Meanwhile, through all the booms and slumps of the last 150 years, the stock of factual material, historical and statistical, and the range and sophistication of analytical techniques and models, has continued steadily to grow, probably at an increasing pace over the last half-century.

If scientific progress consisted simply of growth in these two components, or is defined in these terms, then progress has surely been continuing, and may confidently be expected to continue. But if, as we suggested above, economics has a significant historical dimension, as well as a heavy commitment to policy application, then whether 'progress' has taken place is a much more problematic question.

The President of the Royal Economic Society claimed last year, with perhaps not quite completely justifiable euphoria, that today 'economists are technically streets ahead' of those of a generation or two ago; and that 'the tools on offer to the policy-makers are getting more and more sophisticated' (Stone, 1980, p. 732). But, with historical and institutional change, new and unprecedented problems confront theory and policy. What if the 'streets-ahead' techniques, and the 'more and more sophisticated' tools are of limited, and perhaps increasingly limited, relevance for answering the new questions, both of theory and policy, which historical or institutional changes are producing? And what if, in spite of all this 'streets-ahead' sophistication, no reasonable degree of consensus – in fact, much less than existed earlier – emerges regarding the answers to what are considered the most important theoretical and policy problems?

Certainly it may be inappropriate to deny the progress of a subject simply because new policy problems are being created, or aggravated, in the real world, by the excessive appetites of politicians and public, which prove insusceptible to anything like agreed solutions – even if, in some cases, these excessive appetites have been stimulated by economists.

But can significant progress be claimed, if the subject provides less adequate answers, to what are regarded as the main problems of both theory and policy than earlier economists provided for the problems of their day – even though it might be claimed that the problems of today, especially the policy problems, but also some theoretical problems, are much more complex and intractable than those of earlier periods?

The precise answer to that particular conundrum may well not be of much importance. But what *are* of the greatest importance are questions of the nature and extent of economic knowledge and ignorance, and of what growth or progress in them it is realistic and responsible to suggest is likely. Such questions are not simply of academic, philosophical interest, though it would be philistine and obscurantist to neglect them even if that is all they were. It is of considerable public and political importance, if dangerous political disillusion is to be prevented, to assess how far any hopes for less unsuccessful economic policy-making can realistically and responsibly be based on the state and possible progress of economic knowledge. Such clarification may be considerably more feasible, and possibly just as valuable, as new theoretical work in economics, certainly than that considerable part of it which is apparently pursued simply as 'a good game'. It is an eminently suitable task for Section F.

Finally, let us recall that triangle of contrasting views about the scientific nature of Section F's subject, which was apparent at the time of the Section's foundation. First, outside Section F, there were the extremely excessive claims of the Ricardians for full epistemological parity with the most advanced natural sciences, not only regarding aims and 'methods', but in already achieved laws and results. Though somewhat similar pretensions were being advanced twenty years ago in the 1960s, at the peak of the mathematical and 'Keynesian' boom, such claims today have become very muted. More danger today is perhaps contained in the other kind of extreme, represented in 1833 by the then President, Adam Sedgwick, and today by a vocal group of sociologists, social philosophers and 'social scientists', as well as by some economists. Sedgwick suggested the kind of view, that it is not simply pretentious, in human and social subjects, to hope for similar laws, and the same degree of consensus as in the natural sciences, but that it is wrong even to attempt to pursue the same kind of 'methods' *and discipline* as far as they will go – which, over the last 150 years, has not been a negligible distance, even if *far* less than has often been claimed. The dangers of such an attitude are that it represents an over-reaction to the present 'crisis', and, more seriously, that it may encourage the abandonment of the element of scientific discipline – which should be common to natural and social sciences – in favour of the anarchy of 'anything goes'. Moreover, those who entertain such an attitude must *either* show satisfactorily just how it is compatible with the traditional aims and claims of the subject, still widely upheld, to provide significant guidance for policy, including less unreliable predictions, *or* they must explicitly jettison these traditional aims and claims.

So, in 1981, the moderate programme of the economist founders of Section F, 150 years ago, seems to retain its superior validity against its two competitors: that is, the programme of rejecting the pretentious claims and hopes for epistemological parity with the advanced natural sciences, in terms at any rate of explanations and predictions; and of seeking to continue building up the often-changing empirical foundations of the subject, in accordance with, and in acceptance of, the disciplines of scientific method, common to both social and natural sciences.

NOTES

1 This paper, in an abbreviated form, was delivered in September 1981 at one of the special symposia held to celebrate the 150th anniversary of the founding of the British Association for the Advancement of Science at York. It was published in a volume, edited by Jack Wiseman, entitled *Beyond Positive Economics* (Macmillan, 1983).

2 The labour theory of value, as treated by Adam Smith, provided a classic example of how a *comparatively* powerful theory is rendered obsolete, and deprived of its original power, and has increasingly to be qualified and complicated, in the face of institutional changes. The labour-embodied theory can be said to work powerfully 'in the early and rude state of society which precedes both the accumulation of stock and the appropriation of land'; that is, in a hand-to-mouth, hunting economy, where labour can reasonably be treated as homogeneous. As soon as the ideally simplified conditions of such a very primitive economy are complicated by institutional developments, including private property in land, the use of capital, and the emergence of different qualities of labour, then endless qualifications and adjustment have increasingly to be introduced into the theory, until it ends up either falsified or empirically vacuous.

Since this paper was written, the complete collapse took place of the Marxist economies of Eastern Europe, where the labour theory was preserved as the official, politically unfalsifiable dogma. The practically useless nature of the labour theory, together with the censorship of any value-theory based on idividual utility must have played, intellectually, an important role in the ignominious collapse of the Marxist economies. (Addendum, 1993.)

3 It could be maintained that the introduction of the normative–positive distinction was the achievement of leading Pre-Classicals, such as William Petty and, especially, Richard Cantillon. (Addendum, 1993.)

4 See T. W. Hutchison (1978), chap. 5, section VIII. In the history of macro-economics in England, 1836, 1886 and 1936 are highly important dates. The year 1836 is the date of the second edition of Malthus's *Principles*, the concluding paragraph of which – Malthus's last word, so to speak – emphasized the 'serious sum of human misery' caused by economic instability or cyclical fluctuations. Then the classical view, as represented, for example, by J. S. Mill, came to dominate in England, to the effect that macroeconomic instability was not a serious problem. It was just fifty years later that Foxwell, in Cambridge, stressed the great social significance of economic fluctuations and 'irregularity of employment' as 'the root evil of the present industrial régime' (and just another fifty years, of course, to *The General Theory*).

5 For the kind of guidance provided by the ennobled experts, see Hutchison, 1968. One – fortunately not quite typical – piece of advice from a Balliol pundit, shortly before being promoted, first to Dowining Street and subsequently to the House of Lords, related to investment policy, and the need for centralized controls: 'This was the way the Soviet obtained its results, and I doubt whether we can do better' (1963). For the influence of such views on leaders of the Labour Government in the 1960s, notably on R. H. S. Crossman, and the Prime Minister, Harold Wilson, *v.* Pimlott, 1993, pp. 198, 218, 236, 276, 302 and 304 (Addendum, 1993).

6 See, for example, the contrasting pronouncements of Lord Kaldor (1978) and Professor Minford (1980) referred to in Hutchison, 1981, pp. 258–9.

REFERENCES

British Association for the Advancement of Science. (1834). *Report of the Third Meeting, 1833.*

Foxwell, H. S. (1886). 'Irregularity of Employment and Fluctuations of Prices', in *The Claims of Labour*, ed. J. Burnett *et al.*

Galton, F. (1877). 'Considerations Adverse to the Maintenance of Section F', *Journal of the Royal Statistical Society* (September) pp. 468ff.

Hicks, Sir John. (1979). *Causality in Economics* (Oxford: Blackwell).

Hutchison, T. W. (1953). *A Review of Economic Doctrines, 1870–1929* (London: Greenwood Press).

Hutchison, T. W. (1968). *Economists and Economic Policy in Britain, 1946–1966* (London: Allen & Unwin).

Hutchison, T. W. (1978). *On Revolutions and Progress in Economic Knowledge* (Cambridge University Press).

Hutchison, T. W. (1981). *The Politics and Philosophy of Economics* (Oxford: Blackwell).

Ingram, J. K. (1878). 'The Present Position and Prospects of Political Economy', reprinted in *Essays in Economic Method*, ed. R. L. Smyth (1962) pp. 41ff. (London: Duckworth).

Lord Kaldor (1978). *Further Essays in Economic Theory* (London: Duckworth).

McCulloch, J. R. (1824). *A Discourse on the Rise, Progress, Peculiar Objects and Importance of Political Economy.*

Malthus, T. R. (1836). *Principles of Political Economy*, 2nd ed.

Mill, J. (1966). 'Whether Political Economy is Useful?' (1836) in *Selected Writings*, ed. D. Winch (Oliver & Boyd, 1966) pp. 371ff.

Minford, P. (1980). 'The Nature and Purpose of UK Macroeconomic Models', *Three Banks Review* (March) pp. 3ff.

Pimlott, B. (1993). *Harold Wilson*, paperback ed.

Royal Statistical Society. (1934). *Annals 1834–1934.*

Samuelson, P. A. (1946). 'Lord Keynes and the General Theory', reprinted in *The New Economics*, ed. S. Harris (London: Dobson, 1948) pp. 145ff.

Schumpeter, J. A. (1954). *History of Economic Analysis* (London: Allen & Unwin, 1965).

Senior, N. W. (1878). *Conversations with M. Thiers, M. Guizot, and other Distinguished Persons during the Second Enpire.*

Stone, Sir Richard. (1980). 'Political Economy, Economics and Beyond', *Economic Journal*, 90 (December) pp. 732ff.

Whately, R. (1832). *Introductory Lectures on Political Economy*, 2nd ed.

Part II

SUBJECTIVISM, METHODS AND AIMS

9

NOTES TOWARDS THE IDENTIFICATION AND HISTORY OF 'SUBJECTIVISM' IN ECONOMIC THEORY[1]

I. QUESTIONS OF IDENTIFICATION AND DEFINITION

It seems desirable to start with some questions about identification and definition because profound obscurities and disagreements seem to surround the term 'subjectivism', even, or especially, among the adherents of that school of thought of which an insistent emphasis on the vital and fundamental significance of its own 'subjectivist' approach is its outstanding characteristic (see below, section VIII).

Looking through the *Oxford English Dictionary* at the various usages and definitions of 'subjective' and 'subjectivism' (and of 'objective' and 'objectivism') the following points may be significant for economists:

'Subjective': i.e.: 'having its source in the mind'; . . . 'related to the thinking subject'; . . . 'Objective': i.e.: 'external to the mind'; . . . 'real', . . . 'material' as opposed to 'subjective'.

In another paragraph we have:

'Subjective': i.e. 'pertaining or peculiar to an individual subject or his mental operations'; . . . 'depending upon one's individuality or idiosyncrasy'; . . . 'personal', 'individual'.

So 'subjective' has, on the one hand, its 'mental' or psychological aspect, and, on the other hand, its individualistic aspect.

We emphasize that we are concerned solely with identifying a definition of 'subjectivism', or 'subjectivist', *which is clarificatory or useful in appraising the history of economic thought and theory*; *not* with any more general, philosophical defintion of the term. I would propose that a 'subjective' or 'subjectivist' theory should not *simply* be regarded as concerned with the choices, and actions of individual consumers, producers and investors, etc. 'Subjective' or 'subjectivist' theories must also be concerned with decisions and choices which involve significant 'mental' or 'psychological' processes. It follows that theories concerned with individual decisions and choices which are automatic,

189

or even quasi-mechanical, are not 'subjective' theories properly so-called. In other words, 'microeconomic' theories are not necessarily 'subjective', or 'subjectivist', just because they are concerned with the decisions and choices of individuals, *when* these individuals are assumed to possess full knowledge (or '*Allwissenheit*', to use Carl Menger's term) and to be acting under conditions of certainty, when decisions and choices are more or less automatic and therefore involve little or nothing in the way of mental or psychological processes, because based on 'objectively' given knowledge.

Individuals' tastes may all, of course, be different, just as their heights, weights, eyesights, hearing and allergies may be different, and, indeed, much of their physical, mental and psychological make-up. If, however, a consumer, investor, or any other kind of economic agent, is assumed to be some kind of maximizer or optimizer, and to possess all the precise and certain knowledge necessary for his maximizing or optimizing, then, since his decisions and choices will be, or become, more or less automatic, or mechanical, and hardly involve any 'mental' or psychological processes, then, the study of, or theories about, such consumers or investors, under these assumptions, can hardly be regarded as 'subjective' or 'subjectivist'.

Much of traditional, 'mainstream', or orthodox economic theorizing and analysis has, of course, for nearly two centuries, that is, since Ricardo, been based on assumptions about the knowledge of economic agents, and the absence of uncertainty, which have excluded 'subjectivism'. In fact, it was this very exclusion and simplification (or over-simplification) which made possible the development of the kind of deductive theory or analysis, by the classicals and neoclassicals, which, by many historians of thought, is regarded as the most solidly progressive achievement in the history of political economy and economics.

II. FROM THE SCHOLASTICS TO THE PRE-CLASSICALS

In the Scholastic and Pre-Classical periods, before the assumption of full knowledge and the exclusion of ignorance and uncertainty took over a pervasive and explicit role, much of the theorizing and analysis about values and prices recognized, or assumed, the subjectivity of the decisions and choices of economic agents. Even though the Scholastics seem to have used an objective concept of utility as an essential, quasi-substantial ingredient of goods, the more penetrating writers recognized that market values and prices were dependent on the estimates of ignorant, foolish or 'irrational' human beings. As was observed by the leader of the very important Salamancan school, Diego de Covarrubias (1512–77) (who was later quoted by two of the greatest Italian pioneers of economic analysis, Davanzati and Galiani):

> The value of an article does not depend on its essential nature, but on the estimate of men, even if that estimate be foolish.
>
> (*v.* Grice-Hutchison, 1952, p. 48; Hutchison, 1988, p. 16)

Here the 'subjective' nature of the decisions and choices of economic agents seems to be clearly recognized by Covarrubias. At the same time the 'objectivity' of the utility concept, maintained in some scholastic writings, was fading out in the analysis of the pioneer Italian and French theorists, from the late seventeenth on to the early nineteenth century. As Langholm has observed, regarding the 'psychological' nature of the utility concept expounded by this succession of great writers:

> The success of the value theory which was to be developed, in the line extending from Montanari through Galiani to the Italian and French economists of the eighteenth and early nineteenth centures, is in no small part explained by its emphasis on utility as a psychological experience, playing down considerations of the properties in goods which cause men to desire them.
>
> (Langholm, 1979, p. 144; Hutchison, 1988, p. 255)

Certainly the theory or analysis of value and price developed by these major writers may be described as genuinely 'subjective', not (or not simply), however, because of the erosion of the more objective scholastic concept of utility, but because this theory, or analysis, was not dependent on a simplifying assumption of full, or perfect, knowledge and the absence of uncertainty.

The leading exponents of the Natural Law school in the late seventeenth and eighteenth centuries, emphasized the same vital point about the ignorance or errors of choosers and decision-makers in real-world markets. As Samuel Pufendorf, for example, insisted, in his important analysis of 'use' (or utility), value and price:

> now the use of a certain thing is defined not merely from the circumstance that it truly helps to preserve or to make pleasurable our existence, but in addition that it contributes some pleasure or ornament *even though this be in the sole opinion of certain men.*
>
> (1931 [1660], p. 65, italics added; Hutchison, 1988, p. 98)

Other writers of the natural law tradition emphasized such subjective determinants of choice as 'fancy' and 'fashion', as well as sheer ignorance.

Gershom Carmichael (1672–1729), the founder of the Glasgow school of moral philosophy, and therefore a kind of intellectual grandfather – *via* Francis Hutcheson – of Adam Smith, maintained that for a good to have a price it must possess a certain usefulness, or 'aptitude', either actual *or imagined*:

> Generally, the price of things depends on these two elements: *scarcity* and *the difficulty of acquiring* them. Moreover, scarcity can be derived from two things, the number of those demanding the good or service, and the 'aptitude', or usefulness, which they think it contains. . . .
>
> (1724, p. 247n; Hutchison, 1988, p. 193)

191

The 'never-to-be-forgotten' Francis Hutcheson (1694–1746), the successor of Carmichael, distinguished 'natural' use from use based on custom or fancy (which is, or was to become, a difficult distinction to maintain):

> By the use causing a demand we mean not only a natural subserviency to our support, or to some natural pleasure, but any tendency to give satisfaction, by prevailing custom or fancy, as a matter of ornament or distinction, or in the more eminent status; for this will cause a demand as well as the natural use.
>
> (1755, vol. II, pp. 54–5; Hutchison, 1988, p. 195)

Finally, among the leading exponents of the Natural Law doctrines, mention should be made of Jean Jacques Burlamaqui (1694–1748), the Swiss philosopher. Burlamaqui included in utility, as a determinant of demand, value and price, not only 'real utility but also that which is only arbitrary, or imagined, like that of precious stones' (1773 and 1783, p. 225; also Hutchison, 1988, p. 322).

The Natural Law theory of value and price, with its 'subjective' elements, passed from Pufendorf to Adam Smith *via* Carmichael and Hutcheson; and from Pufendorf to Léon Walras *via* Burlamaqui and Auguste Walras. As Walras (senior) explained:

> The doctrine, which I am about to present to my readers on the nature of wealth and the origin of value, is so little new or modern, that it has been set out a long time ago in a work on public law, written in French and published on the frontiers of France. I wish to mention the *Élements du droit naturel* by Burlamaqui.
>
> (1831, p. 209; Hutchison, 1988, p. 323)

Subjectivity, however, did not survive in Walrasian theory. Nevertheless, though inheriting almost identical doctrines of value and price, Adam Smith and Auguste and Léon Walras made significantly different uses of their inheritance. But neither Smith nor Léon Walras preserved or paid much attention to the subjective element of their inheritance.

III. CONDILLAC: THE MASTER OF SUBJECTIVISM

In the works of some of the leading Pre-Classical writers a 'subjective' approach is apparent not only in the treatment of value and price, as in the Natural Law theory, but also, where a recognition of ignorance and uncertainty is difficult to avoid, in the discussion of problems of money and of profit.

A fuller historical account of 'subjectivity' in economic theory would provide a more detailed account than is attempted here of the ideas of two of the greatest economists of the Pre-Classical (or any other) period: Pierre de Boisguilbert (1646–1714) and Richard Cantillon (16??–1734). Boisguilbert, though a pioneer of the equilibrium concept and assumption, was also especially concerned with the agricultural sector of the French economy (of course, overwhelmingly the major sector) and its catastrophic instability – and hence the uncertainty and ignorance which dominated decisions and choices, and seriously aggravated the huge fluctuations in prices, on the one hand, and in investment and cash-holdings (or 'liquidity preference') on the other hand.

Cantillon, while laying many of the foundations on which the classicals were to build (though they were in ignorance of his work) was also a pioneer of abstraction in economic theory, notably with regard to ethics and politics. But Cantillon's abstraction was disciplined and limited, and he recognized the ubiquity of uncertainty, especially with regard to the role of entrepreneurs, as represented in the key example of wholesalers and dealers who bought to resell at a profit, but who 'can never know how great will be the demand' (1931, p. 51; Hutchison, 1988, p. 169).

In *any* history, however, of subjectivism in economics there is one great writer from the Pre-Classical period whose work calls for a much fuller account than that of anyone else, before or since. The publication of *Le Commerce et le gouvernement considérés l'un à l'autre*, by Étienne Bonnot, Abbé de Condillac (1715–80), took place in February 1776, about one month before that of *The Wealth of Nations*. Condillac's work constitutes the high peak of value and price theory in Italy and France and the outstanding expression of the subjectivist emphasis of the Pre-Classicals. It was to be roughly two hundred years before the subjectivist basis of economic theory was developed so clearly, and consequentially as it was by Condillac. (See Hutchison, 1988, pp. 324ff.)

Condillac's first interests and writings were concerned with philosophy and epistemology. A follower of Locke, he developed a 'sensationalist' epistemological theory, according to which human knowledge was built up from the sense data of individuals. His economic theory was based on, or followed closely from, his fundamental epistemological principles. It was a comparatively short step from the theory that knowledge was derived from sensations, or sense data, to a subjectively-based economic theory which derived value from the utility of goods as estimated by (often ignorant) individuals. Condillac rejected fundamentally the idea of objective value advanced by the physiocrats.

Probably the most important of the fundamental principles of the physiocrats – and of many subsequent economists – on which they built their theoretical constructions, and which Condillac rejected as fundamentally misleading, was that which postulated a kind of 'rationalistic', full knowledge, and even certainty, together with *objective* values. Condillac started from the prevalence of uncertainty, ignorance and error, in human decisions. His theory of knowledge was fundamentally fallibilist, and he rejected the kind of dogmatic infallibilism proclaimed by the physiocrats (and, among subsequent economists, by the Austrian, Ludwig Mises). As Isabel Knight puts it:

Condillac always stressed 'the relative, the subjective, the historical, and the empirical' (1968, p. 259).

Condillac's book, *Le commerce et le gouvernement*, is divided into two parts, theoretical and practical. But the foundation and centrepiece of his work is his theory of value and price, presented in the first chapter. The values of goods were derived from needs, and were based on the utility of goods, on the one hand, and on scarcity or abundance, on the other hand. But scarcity and abundance were not objectively known – nor also were future needs and utilities – but had to be subjectively estimated from a position of uncertainty and ignorance with regard to both present and future needs:

> The utility being the same, the value would be greater or less depending only on the scarcity or abundance, if this degree was known with precision. . . .
>
> But this degree will not ever be known. It is, therefore, principally on opinion that the greater or less value [of goods] is founded.
>
> (1776, pp. 9–10)

Condillac was concerned with the main real-world problem in France at that period, extreme fluctuations in the price of grain, or the subsistence of the people. With fluctuating grain harvests and stocks, *opinion*, or expectations, were very obviously the key determinants of values and prices. Ignorance could produce panic, which could produce huge swings in prices: 'It is clear that the value of grain may increase in proportion to the extent that opinion exaggerates the dearth' (p. 11).

As Professor Knight puts it:

> . . . a governing principle of Condillac's entire economic theory is that it is the opinion, not fact, which determines everything. . . .
>
> Thus everything important in economics – including, as we shall see, productivity, labor, money – rests on value, defined as a subjective opinion, which varies relative to the same object not only according to general circumstances but according to the person who has the opinion.
>
> (1968, pp. 236 and 248)

Condillac regarded markets as, primarily, places where information and experience could be obtained regarding the supplies and demands for different goods:

> One sees again that prices can only be settled in markets because it is . . . only in markets that one can judge the extent of the abundance or scarcity of goods, relatively to one another, which determines the respective prices. . . .
>
> (p. 31)

> We see that the government strikes a blow at agriculture and commerce every time it undertakes to fix the prices of goods.
>
> (p. 29)

As regards the profits of the entrepreneur, Condillac emphasized the element of uncertainty. He took the example of an entrepreneur-farmer and indicated the vast range of uncertainties which confronted him: notably the average crop which a piece of land would produce and the market price this crop would fetch, together with the crops his neighbours would be producing. When considering the introduction of an innovation 'his speculations were even more uncertain' (p. 384). Manufacturing entrepreneurs had to estimate and speculate regarding the prices of raw materials, wages, tastes and the number of their competitors. Fashion and luxury tastes introduced further uncertainties. Following Boisguilbert, Condillac also stressed the vital role of uncertainty and ignorance with regard to the demand for money: 'There is always a certain quantity which does not circulate; such as is put in reserve as a resource in case of an accident' (p. 99).

Similarly with regard to the foreign exchanges, Condillac was probably indebted on this subject to Cantillon, who had emphasized the influence of ignorance and psychological factors (*v.* p. 270).

Condillac's work might be regarded as the last word – from France, at any rate – before the publication of *The Wealth of Nations*. With the beginning of the Classical period in Britain the subjectivist assumptions and insights of the Pre-Classicals tended, to a large extent, to be forgotten. Nor, after 1870, with the dawn of the Neo-classical era, were these insights rapidly rediscovered and re-developed in the masterly and consequential terms in which Condillac had presented them. In 1993 it is the best of news for serious students of the History of Economic Thought that Dr and Mrs Eltis are preparing an English edition of Condillac's masterpiece.

IV. THE CLASSICAL ECLIPSE

The Classical regress from, or eclipse of, the recognition of subjectivity may be said to have started with Adam Smith's confusing treatment of what he called 'value in use', at the end of chapter 4 of Book I of *The Wealth of Nations* (published about a month after Condillac's masterpiece). 'Value in use' is treated by Smith as a kind of objective, or quasi-objective, biological value, so that goods like diamonds 'which have the greatest value in exchange have frequently little *or no* value in use' (Smith, 1976, p. 44, italics added). Smith crucially alters the meaning of use, or 'value in use', or utility, from that of his predecessors, Pufendorf and Carmichael, and, to some extent, from that of Francis Hutcheson, by omitting to mention that it is use 'in the sole opinion of certain men', or the use which 'they think it contains', which is a fundamental determinant of the value and price of a good. In any case, utility, use, or 'value in use', has a considerably less important role to play in Smith's theory of value than it had in the work of his great predecessors, whether those of the Natural Law school, or the major Italian and French writers on value of the seventeenth and eighteenth centuries.

195

Not, of course, that Smith carried through any radical or consequential elimination of the subjectivity of economic decisions and choices from *The Wealth of Nations*. There is certainly no explicit assumption of full knowledge, or *'Allwissenheit'*, behind the operations of the invisible hand. Smith specially emphasized, for example (as had Cantillon), ignorance with regard to profits: 'Profit is so very fluctuating that the person who carries on a particular trade cannot always tell you himself what is the average of his annual profit' (1976, vol. I, p. 103).[2]

Virtually total eclipse came with Ricardo and his explicit assumption of full knowledge as an essential, 'natural' component, or prerequisite, of economic theory:

> Whilst every man is free to employ his capital where he pleases he will naturally seek for it that employment which is most advantageous; he will naturally be dissatisfied with a profit of 10 per cent, if by removing his capital he can obtain a profit of 15 per cent.
> (1951, vol. I, p. 88; see also Hutchison 1937, p. 637; 1978, pp. 200–1)

In an earlier letter to Malthus, of 1811, on international payments, Ricardo acknowledged the full postulate of *'Allwissenheit'* as fundamental to his method.

> The first point to be considered is, what is the interest of countries in the case supposed? The second what is their practice? Now it is obvious that I need not be greatly solicitous about this latter point; it can clearly be demonstrated that the interest of the public is as I have stated it. It would be no answer to me to say that men were ignorant of the best and cheapest mode of conducting their business and paying their debts, *because that is a question of fact and not of science, and might be urged against almost every proposition in Political Economy.'*
> (1952, vol. VI, p. 64; Hutchison 1938, p. 121; 1978, p. 48, n. 28;
> italics added)

With J. S. Mill, the huge simplification of the full knowledge postulate, and the exclusion of ignorance, uncertainty and subjectivity, is slipped in quite casually. In economic theory man is treated 'solely as a being who desires to possess wealth, and who is capable of judging of the comparative efficacy of means for obtaining that end' (1844, p. 137).

Moreover, Mill saw this full knowledge postulate as an essential component of 'competition', which, in turn, was essential for the very existence of political economy as a science (a 'science', that is, which, of its nature, excluded ignorance, uncertainty and subjectivity). For 'only through the principle of competition has political economy any pretension to the character of a science' (1909), II, IV, 1; Hutchison, 1978, p. 208).

V. NEOCLASSICAL INCONSISTENCIES

When Hayek claimed that 'every important advance in economic theory during the last hundred years was a further step in the consistent application of subjectivism', presumably the main component of the advances which he had in mind, was the replacement, after 1870, of the English classical value-theory, as a result of the 'marginal', or, in England, the 'Jevonian' revolution. A 'cost-of-production' theory of value was replaced by a theory based on utility or preference. It must, however, be insisted that though such a fundamental shift might be regarded as a potential advance in a 'subjective' direction, it remains highly questionable whether, or how far, any *consistent application of subjectivism* can be said to have taken place, either in Britain, Austria or Lausanne.

Just because there was a new and sharper focus on individual consumers and their 'tastes', no very significant steps were thereby, and necessarily, being taken in the consistent application of 'subjectivism', in so far as these individual consumers were being assumed to be in command of full, certain and precise knowledge of how much the consumption of each particular quantity, of each particular good, would bring them in utility, or would move them towards a 'superior' point on their indifference maps. To accept that the tastes of individuals differ is not necessarily to treat them as 'subjective'.

Not for nothing were the 'Neoclassicals' so called. They changed or transformed the theories of the Classicals, but *renewed the deductive method, based, fundamentally and above all, on the homo economicus, whose vital, methodolgically essential characteristic was not necessarily any acquisitiveness or materialism, but his full knowledge or 'Allwissenheit'*.[3] In fact, what followed after 1870 was not any 'consistent application of subjectivism', but rather a more pervasive, consistent and 'rigorous' application of the essentially non-subjective, full-knowledge assumption, as the concept and assumption of 'perfect' competition was refined. 'Perfection' in competition meant, most importantly, perfection in requisite knowledge. This 'perfection' in knowledge came to be summarized in the profusion of beautiful and precise curves and diagrams which increasingly swept so impressively across the pages of neoclassical textbooks and the blackboards of classrooms, portraying people's 'perfect' awareness (both *ex-ante* and *ex-post*) of every detail of what Pareto called their 'tastes and obstacles'. A fundamental implication of the whole apparatus was, of course, that the 'decisions' and 'choices' under study were between certainties, and therefore automatic, or even mechanical, and perhaps not properly describable as *real-world* 'decisions' or 'choices'. Just because, after 1870, the focus had shifted to *apparently* 'psychological' concepts like utility and tastes, and away from something material, like (for the most part) costs, it was an illusion to suppose that an advance had been made in the consistent application of 'subjectivism', so long as the fundamental postulate remained inevitably in place.[4] In due course it had to be recognized – or rediscovered, for Cantillon and Condillac had glimpsed the point – that costs too had to be regarded from an *ex-ante* and essentially 'subjective' viewpoint in most real-world models.

So when Ludwig Lachmann wrote of 'the subjective revolution of the 1870s', there seem to be some questions to ask. There may have been some fleeting hints or suggestions of subjectivity as in Jevons's famous denunciation of cost-of-production theories of value:

> The fact is, that labour once spent has no influence on the future value of any article: it is gone and lost for ever. In commerce bygones are for ever bygones; and we are always starting clear at each moment, judging the values of things with a view to future utility. Industry is essentially prospective, not retrospective; and *seldom does the result of any undertaking exactly coincide with the first intentions of its promoters.*
>
> (1879 and 1900, p. 164; italics added)[5]

But the brilliant rhetoric of Jevons was just a lightning flash in the mounting, encircling darkness. The 'Neoclassical' Edgeworth soon repeated the 'Classical' J. S. Mill's insistence that the assumption of competition (which necessarily included the assumption of full knowledge or '*Allwissenheit*') was an essential foundation for the subject as he understood it, from which followed the exclusion of 'subjectivism' (as we would suggest it should be defined).[6]

In contrast, however, with his claim about 'the subjective revolution of the 1870s', Ludwig Lachman was right on target when he observed: 'In a world of change the subjectivism of expectations is perhaps even more important than the subjectivism of preferences' (1977, p. 28). In other words, what is fundamental for a subjectivist treatment of economic actions is the kind of knowledge which individuals are assumed to possess, and that their knowledge is not regularly and perfectly certain and precise, which would make their decisions and choices automatic or mechanical. The explicit introduction of 'expectations' implies that these expectations are not always correct, and admits the possibility and significance of error, ignorance and uncertainty (and of subjectivity). Apart from a scattering of occasional introductions of the adjective 'expected' – mostly before such terms a 'profits', 'productivity' and 'prices' – the attempt at an explicit and systematic introduction of expectations had to wait for some decades, or even more than half a century, after 1870.[7]

VI. HOW CONSISTENTLY 'SUBJECTIVIST' WERE MENGER, WIESER AND BÖHM-BAWERK?

In recent years attempts have been made to distinguish sharply, as much more distinctly and consistently 'subjectivist', the contribution of Carl Menger from those of Jevons and Walras. Some such case is presented by a number of 'modern Austrians', and is emphasized even by Max Alter in his illuminating critical study, who seems to equate 'subjectivism' with 'methodological individualism'. It is far from easy, however, to discover any *very* consistent application of subjectivism on the part of Menger and his Austrian followers – though this depends, of course, on how the term 'subjectivist' is defined.

It is true that Menger, rather fleetingly, cited and quoted Condillac, though Jevons also did rather more enthusiastically. When, however, Menger, in a celebrated letter to Walras, marked off his theoretical approach from that of his French contemporary, he distinguished it by stressing his own Aristotelian concern with 'essences', and by rejecting Walras's use of mathematics. Menger is often a very difficult writer to interpret, even, or perhaps especially, for those who know some German, and sometimes he seems seriously inconsistent. Anyhow, at some points Menger quite explicitly excludes subjectivism, in the sense identified in this paper, from the main aims and achievements of theoretical economics. For Menger recognized and emphasized that human ignorance and errors seriously limited the applicability of what he called 'theoretical economics', which depends on the assumption of *'Allwissenheit'*:

> Even if economic men always and everywhere let themselves be guided exclusively by self-interest, the strict regularity of economic phenomena would none the less have to be considered impossible because of the fact, given by experience, that in innumerable cases they are in error about their economic interest, or in ignorance of economic conditions. Our historians are too lenient towards their scholarly opponents. The presupposition of a strict regularity in economic phenomena, and with this of a theoretical economics in the full meaning of the term, includes not only the dogma of ever-constant self-interest, but also the dogma of 'infallibility' and 'omniscience' of men in economic affairs.
>
> (1963, p. 84; Hutchison, 1981, p. 182)

What Menger calls 'theoretical economics' and its 'exact laws' are, therefore, generally limited to decisions undertaken by a kind of omniscient, automatic calculator, who is claimed to represent the generality of economic decision-makers:

> Error and imperfect knowledge may give rise to aberrations, but these are the pathological phenomena of social economics and prove as little against the laws of economics as do symptoms of a sick body against the laws of physiology.
>
> (1950, p. 216; see also L. H. White in Caldwell, 1990, p. 356)

Apparently, in Menger's Austria one was a 'sick' and 'pathological' case if and when one was not infallible and omniscient. Without the existence, however, of some such 'sickness' no processes of decision-making reasonably describable as 'subjective' could exist. For all such processes as F. H. Knight (1921) observed, would have become automatic and mechanical.[8] This limitation of Carl Menger's conception of 'theoretical economics' has been noted by Lawrence White, an enthusiastic supporter of 'Modern Austrian' ideas, who emphasizes that, according to Menger: 'Error and ignorance are excluded from economic prices which are the prices which would prevail in a fully arbitraged (no error) market' (v. Caldwell, 1990, p. 356).

Moreover, Dr Paul Meyer, in his valuable monograph, points out how Condillac, a century before Menger, had, on some points, provided a more consistent application of subjectivism (1944, pp. 248–9). Menger, for example, treated the concepts of 'scarcity', and of 'free goods', as objectively quantitative, whereas Condillac had regarded them as subjective estimates.

As regards Menger's two great successors, neither, as regards methodology, seems to have followed Menger very closely. Anyhow, Böhm-Bawerk made it very clear that, in his view, economic theory 'starts exactly as the historical school would have it start, with observations of actual conditions'. As regards the utility theory of value, Böhm-Bawerk asks, how did economists arrive at it?: 'By some soaring a priori speculation? Not at all. In the first place they simply observed how men, in practice, regard property' (1924, pp. 263–4).

Certainly, Böhm-Bawerk's 'ultra-empiricism' provided an excellent starting-point from which to draw subjectivist conclusions. This had been the great Condillac's approach. But Böhm-Bawerk did not push on in that direction.

Menger's other major successor, Friedrich Wieser, who was, for a time, considerably more influential than Menger, developed his own peculiar 'psychological method', which – such is the flexibility of the term – *might* be described by some as 'subjectivist'. Unlike Menger and Böhm-Bawerk, Wieser insisted strongly on fundamental differences between the natural and the social sciences. In fact, according to Wieser, the social, or human scientist started with a great advantage over the natural scientist:

> We can observe natural phenomena only from outside but ourselves from within. . . . This psychological method chooses the most advantageous position for observation. It finds for us in common experience all the most important facts of economy. . . . It finds that certain acts take place in our consciousness with a feeling of necessity. What a huge advantage for the natural scientist if the organic and inorganic world clearly informed him of its laws, and why should we neglect such assistance?

> (v. 1929, p. 17)

How far Wieser's 'psychological method' should be described as a type of 'subjectivism' hardly seems an important question. His 'psychological', or introspective method, however, with its pretentious claims to establishing 'laws' and 'necessities', for some time, probably, had considerably more influence on subsequent Austrian methodological ideas, than Menger's writings had. For Mises and the early Hayek (before his all-too-gentle and unobtrusive break with Mises) followed Wieser, both as regards a decisive methodological dualism, as between the natural and social sciences, and also with dogmatic claims regarding the necessity, or certainty, which Mises claimed for his doctrines – a claim which must leave the 'subjectivist' nature of these doctrines very doubtful.

VII. 'PSYCHOLOGY', ECONOMIC 'CRISES' AND SUBJECTIVISM

It is not among the leading upholders of Classical or Neoclassical orthodoxy, focused on their smoothly self-equilibrating models, based on correct expectations or foresight, and excluding ignorance and uncertainty, that advances in, or 'consistent applications of subjectivism', can be expected. The very concept of equilibrium and of smoothly, or automatically, equilibrating processes, implies compatibility and correctness of expectations, and leaves little or no room for uncertainty and ignorance. It is rather from those concerned with some kind, or aspect, of economic instability and disequilibrium, where problems of uncertainty are inherent and unavoidable, that subjectivist approaches or assumptions are more likely to be forthcoming: that is, with regard to problems involving profit, money, interest, fluctuations, instability and 'crises' (such as had in fact engaged the two major French masters, Boisguilbert and Condillac).[9]

As the nineteenth century progressed, the problems of economic 'crises', and of the acute and widespread unemployment, poverty and distress which they caused, became of increasingly unavoidable importance for economists concerned with real-world problems. Particularly when, as in England, the power of the vote was extended down to the poorer classes, such economic disasters could no longer be brushed aside as pathological abnormalities or 'frictions'. Let us look first, very briefly, at one or two of the earlier attempts at explaining economic crises in Britain.

At just about the time when Ricardo was explicitly launching the assumption of full knowledge on its long, vital and pervasive career, Sismondi was seeking to explain the new and very serious postwar economic 'crisis' in Britain, by emphasizing the growing complexity of economic activity, brought about by the spread of the division of labour, which had increased the ignorance of many producers as to the demand for their products.

Explanations, or partial explanations, in terms of ignorance and 'psychology' were advanced by various writers in the course of the nineteenth century, notably by Wilhelm Roscher the leader of the German Historical school (v. *Ansichten der Vokswirtschaftslehre*, 1861; Hutchison, 1953, pp. 364–5). As the focus shifted, later in the century, from crises to cycles, fluctuating 'psychological' factors were invoked as an explanatory element of the ups and downs of markets, especially in times of panic. For example, the Manchester writer, John Mills (1867), insisted on a thoroughly 'subjectivist' explanation when he remarked (in an almost Shackelian *aperçu*) that 'the malady of commercial crises is not in essence a matter of the purse but of the mind. . . .

Broadly defined, panic is the destruction in the mind of a bundle of beliefs'. (See Mills's paper on 'Credit Cycles and the Origins of Commercial Panics' in *Transactions of the Manchester Statistical Society*, 1867; Hutchison, 1953, p. 367.)

The most brilliant and influential writer on the 'psychological' fluctuations of markets was undoubtedly Walter Bagehot. In one of his salty epigrams, on the subject of financial panics, he proclaimed: 'One thing is certain, that at particular times a great many stupid people have a great deal of stupid money.' (Certainly Bagehot's *Lombard Street* does not seem to have shared the 'rational' expectations of Chicago.) Bagehot went on to link 'psychological' instability with cumulative upswings and downswings. (See 1873, chapter VI; Hutchison, 1953, p. 367.) Later Alfred Marshall, a great admirer of Bagehot, emphasized the same 'psychological' fluctuations of markets in explaining the business cycle, citing 'want of confidence' as 'the chief cause' of depressions (1961, pp. 710–11).

The problems of interest rates were also an area where uncertainty and erroneous expectations were obvious factors (though little discussed in Böhm-Bawerk's vast writings). Irving Fisher, however, especially in his early work, *Appreciation and Interest* (1896), observed how 'periods of speculation and depression are the result of inequality of foresight' (1896, pp. 75–8; Hutchison, 1953, pp. 275–6). Fisher here assumed that not all anticipations, or expectations, were correct (which could not fail to be the case if equilibrium was to be maintained). Shortly after Fisher, Knut Wicksell rather casually introduced expectations into his analysis of the market rate of interest, which, he observed, 'can clearly never be high or low in itself but only in relation to the return which can, or is expected to be obtained by the man who has possession of money' (1898 and 1936, trans. R. F. Kahn, p. xxv; Hutchison, 1953, pp. 236–7). It was not, however, until the late 1920s and early 1930s that Wicksell's successors in Sweden, Erik Lindahl and Gunnar Myrdal, introduced a more systematic analysis of expectations into the theory of money and the business cycle.

Finally may be mentioned two more fundamental, general criticisms of the basic postulates of political economy and economics regarding knowledge and ignorance – and, therefore, regarding 'subjectivism'. First, no historical survey of this subject, however brief, should omit the remarkable essay by Cliffe Leslie, the Irish historical economist, entitled 'The Known and the Unknown in the Economic World' (1879). We noticed above how Carl Menger had taunted the German historical critics of economic theory for their failure to notice the limitations imposed by the postulate of full knowledge, or *'Allwissenheit'*. Just four years previously, however, Cliffe Leslie had denounced what he described as 'the fundamental error of the *a priori* system', as that of 'confounding the unknown with the known in the economic world'. Leslie pointed out that:

The orthodox, *a priori* system thus postulates much more than a general desire of wealth. It postulates also, . . . full knowledge of the gains in different employments and such facilities of choice and change of employment. . . .

(1888, pp. 229–30; Hutchison, 1953, p. 323)

Secondly, over forty years later, examining closely the postulates of what Leslie had called 'the *a priori* system', F. H. Knight proceeded to 'placard', as he put it, 'the unrealities of the postulates of theoretical economics, not for the purpose of discrediting the doctrine, but with a view to making clear its theoretical limitations' (1921, p. 11). According to Knight, ignorance and 'uncertainty' emerged as 'the most important underlying difference between the conditions theory is compelled to assume and those which exist in fact' (p. 51). Subsequently Knight examined further 'the conditions' which he had maintained that 'theory is compelled to assume', as follows:

It is doubtful whether intelligence itself would exist in such a situation; in a world so built that perfect knowledge was theoretically possible, it seems likely that all organic readjustment would become mechanical, all organisms automatic.

(p. 268)

In this kind of nirvana it seems obvious that anything describable as entrepreneurial activity would disappear. What Knight presumably meant by insisting that 'theory is compelled to assume' this kind of nirvanic world of certainty and '*Allwissenheit*', must be that such an assumption was logically essential for the 'tractability' of the abstract deductive system, the conclusions of which were regarded by the orthodox deductivists as the great achievement of the science of political economy and economics.

Now it can, of course, be argued in defence of 'the orthodox *a priori* system' that quite a number of the decisions and choices made by real-world economic agents *are* made under conditions which, in fact, approximate reasonably closely – though never correspond *absolutely* – to the nirvanic conditions assumed by 'orthodoxy'. If, indeed *all* economic decisions and choices were always, or regularly, undertaken under such conditions, then, as Knight observes, human intelligence would have faded away – if it had ever existed – and some kind of robotic, automatic machines would have taken over. Certainly, anything describable as 'subjectivism' in decision-making and choices would not exist. In other words, it is ignorance and uncertainty, on a major scale, which necessitates both economic intelligence and 'subjectivism' in economic decision-making and choices. It might be thought that it is the decisions and choices requiring human intelligence, rather than, simply, robotic automaticity, which should be of major interest to economists. It would appear, moreover, that it is failures with regard to these decisions requiring intelligent, human judgement, which have led to the most catastrophic

203

economic disasters. Nevertheless, some fervent adherents of the abstract, *a priori*, deductive method have felt 'compelled' to try to retain the assumptions of nirvana, even for solving the real and serious problems of our real and human world (in the face, in fact, of the greatest depression and 'disequilibrium' of this turbulent century which took place in the early 1930s).

VIII. REVOLUTION IN THE 1930s

The 1930s were, of course, a time of almost unprecedentedly profound economic disequilibrium and political upheaval. After 1929, any fleeting hopes finally and totally collapsed for some eventual return to the kind of relative stability, and 'normalcy', which had prevailed in Europe before 1914. Never were the self-equilibrating postulates of full knowledge and the absence of uncertainty more obviously and alarmingly unrealistic. Certainly in the 1930s greater advances were forthcoming than in any previous (or, perhaps subsequent) decade in this century, in the recognition and application of subjectivism in economic theory. These advances may be said to have established a kind of intellectual bridgehead, which has survived through the retreat, of two decades or so, from the late 1940s, when a period of remarkable stability followed the Second World War.

The recognition of expectations served as a starting-point but no more than that. The gradual introduction of the adjective 'expected', or the casual mention of the 'expectations' of investors, consumers or other economic agents, hardly threatened the dominance of the postulates of full knowledge and the absence of uncertainty. As Ralph Hawtrey put it: 'The fact that all economic activity is governed by expectations has been universally taken for granted from the beginning' (1937, p. 349; Hutchison, 1953, p. 324). 'Taken for granted' here, as so often, means that expectations were disregarded and underestimated, because, in fact, they were usually assumed to be correct.

As noted in the previous section, a more explicit and systematic analysis of expectations in economic theory was launched in the 1920s in Sweden by Lindahl and Myrdal, following a suggestion from Wicksell. The introduction of the distinction between *ex-ante* and *ex-post* concepts, or of differences between anticipated and realized quantities, helped to clarify the distinguishing characteristic of positions of equilibrium.

Much the most prominent and influential role in the recognition and application of subjectivism in the 1930s came, of course, from much the most prominent and influential economist of that decade. Keynes had first claimed to differentiate his 'general' theory from 'the special case' assumed by his 'orthodox' predecessors, by observing that he denied that 'the economic system' was self-adjusting. He went on to discern that the causal characteristic of the self-adjusting system derived essentially from the unrealistically high level of correct and precise knowledge assumed to be possessed by those participating:

The orthodox theory assumes that we have a knowledge of the future of a kind quite different from that which we actually possess. This false realization follows the lines of the Benthamite calculus. The hypothesis of a calculable future leads to a wrong interpretation of the principles of behaviour which the need for action compels us to adopt.

(1937, p. 192)

It was not only in macroeconomics that the assumption of correct expectations, or the equality of *ex-ante* and *ex-post* quantities, was being criticized. Robert Triffin questioned the basic assumptions of monopolistic and imperfectly, or non-perfectly, competitive conditions, which maintained that the

subjective sales curve was merely the exact reflection of an objective sales curve, embodying the actual reactions of the market. In this way, the distinction between a subjective and an objective definition of demand becomes irrelevant; . . . the same sales curve is interpreted as representing identically both the expectations of the seller and the happenings on the market. . . . It must be recognized that the usual statement of equilibrium conditions is valid only when the entrepreneurs succeed in gauging correctly the shape of their sales curves.

(1940, pp. 63 and 66; Hutchison, 1953, p. 327)

It may be noted that we have not included in this section mention of any Austrian contributions in the 1930s to the consistent application of subjectivism in economic theory; although this was a decade of the most profound disequilibrium which surely called for such an application. Our omission is because Austrian contributions to subjectivist ideas in the 1930s were – as regards Mises, for example – non-existent or obscurantist; or else, though highly significant, were strangely muted (as in the case of Hayek) as we shall discuss in the next section.

As regards their consistent application of 'subjectivist' ideas, the three major Austrian leaders might, with extreme brevity, be summed up as follows: Carl Menger was a fundamentally inconsistent subjectivist; Ludwig Mises, though he had contributed importantly to the theory of money and business cycles, could, as regards his very emphatic and dogmatic methodological ideas, hardly be described even as 'an inconsistent subjectivist', in any defensible sense of the term; while Hayek, *after his methodological break with Mises*, in the 1930s, became a more and more masterly exponent of subjectivist ideas.

It is hardly surprising that the new 'Austrian' movement found considerable difficulty in identifying the precise sense and implications of the idea of 'subjectivism' which it was claiming, so forthrightly, to be its outstanding tenet and characteristic. These difficulties with the concept of subjectivism came very obviously to the surface in one of the various volumes of 'Austrian' essays published in the 1980s. Here we find Professor Karen Vaughn after claiming, rather surprisingly, that it was 'reasonable' to 'take subjectivism to be synonymous with praxeology', concluding, nevertheless, that 'there is no consensus on the meaning of the word' (1982, p. 28). A few pages later, Dr Stephen Böhm, in a contribution on 'The Ambiguous Notion of Subjectivism', while proclaiming 'subjectivism' to be 'one of the twin pillars, aside from methodological individualism, on which the edifice of Austrian methodology has come to rest' (p. 42), went on, rather apprehensively, to plead: 'At the risk of being stamped on for heresy I venture to propose that there are some important obscurities in the thesis that Austrians adhere to the principle of subjectivism' (surely a hint of almost Hayekian gentleness).

Ludwig Lachmann contributed a paper on 'Mises and the Extension of Subjectivism', which might be understood as concluding that Mises did not, in any way, 'extend' subjectivism, or its application, in any defensible meaning of the term. Lachmann noted that in the inter-war years, when Swedish economists sought to recognize the importance of ignorance and uncertainty by means of the concept of expectations – correct or incorrect – 'Mises, and most Austrians, took no interest', thus missing 'a golden opportunity to extend the scope of subjectivism' (*op. cit.*, 1982, p. 36). Lachmann went on to point out just what the alleged 'subjectivism' of Mises amounted to: 'It meant to him no more than that different men pursue different ends' (p. 37). This is to reduce 'subjectivism' (the great twin pillar of Austrian economic theory) to a pathetic triviality. Who would ever want to deny that 'different men pursue different ends', any more than that different men have different names and different physiques? Who is *not* a 'subjectivist' in this trivial sense?

IX. CONCLUSIONS

Some drastic methodological conclusions may be added which follow from the identification of 'subjectivist' economic theory with the recognition of uncertainty and ignorance, so long excluded by the tradition of classical and neoclassical abstract-deductive analysis since Ricardo, based on the assumption of full knowledge, '*Allwissenheit*', and certainty.

It is important to realize that the full-knowledge postulate was introduced, and *had to be introduced*, as an essentially required simplification, if the main edifice of classical and neoclassical theorizing was to be constructed. It seems to have been a long time before it was realized quite what a drastic abstraction, exclusion or simplification was involved. It was doubtless estimated, and presumably still is, that, though a considerable simplification is being perpetrated, some kind of far-from-insignificant 'approximation' has been achieved. Up to a point, it is, however, reasonable to complain, with Knight, that only 'automata' can be operating in such a simplified model (or, alternatively, 'ants' (Mises) or 'rats' (Buchanan)). The possible justification can only be that some human actions, in some of their aspects, may significantly and relevantly be compared with those of automata, ants and rats. Anyhow, as

Carl Menger (sometimes described as a 'subjectivist') fully agreed, his 'Exact Laws' depended on this kind of simplification – as do Mises's 'apodictic certainties' – (whether or not Mises himself conceded the point).

Condillac was a great pioneer of subjectivism in economics because he was an empiricist. In tackling the most important real-world policy issue of the France of his day (the catastrophic fluctuations in the prices of basic foodstuffs) he simply observed that it was ignorance and uncertainty about present and future supplies on the part of consumers, producers and wholesale-dealers, that were the essence of the problem. 'Subjectivist' economic theorizing – that is, theorizing which does not exclude by simplifying assumption, but seeks to take account of ignorance and uncertainty – *has to proceed empirically*, and by case-by-case analysis. As Ludwig Lachmann long ago suggested:

> Under these circumstances, what can the economist do but construct various hypothetical types of expectations conceived as responses to various hypothetical situations, and then leave the process of selection to empirical verification in the light of economic history?
>
> (1977, p. 67; quoted by Littlechild, 1982, p. 95)

We would only venture to emphasize that last condition of Lachmann's as essential: that is, selecting cases according to 'empirical verification in the light of economic history' rather than according to their tractability in terms of 'rigorous', abstract, mathematical analysis.

On this point, we had best let Professor Herbert Simon have the last word:

> There seems to be no escape. If economics is to deal with uncertainty, it will have to understand how human beings in fact behave in the face of uncertainty, and by what limits of information and computability they are bound.

A shift to the study of real-world decision-making, Professor Simon insists,

> requires a basic shift in scientific style, from an emphasis on deductive reasoning within a tight system of axioms to an emphasis on detailed empirical exploration. . . . Undoubtedly the uncongeniality of the latter style to economists has slowed down the transition. . . .
>
> (1976, pp. 147–8; quoted by Hutchison, 1978, p. 211)

Recognizing the importance of subjectivism in the study of economic decisions and actions has been of considerable, purely critical, value. If, however, such subjectivist studies in economics are to be advanced constructively, then inevitable methodological requirements must be accepted. 'Modern Austrians' are hamstrung in the constructive advance of subjectivist economics by their clinging so dogmatically to the method of abstract, *a priorist* deduction. If subjective decisions and actions are to be studied in economics, then, as Hayek was to indicate, in his crucial (if all-too-gentle) rejection of Misesian *a priorism*, it is to 'economics as an empirical science' that a decisive, methodological

207

'turn' must be made. Empirical and inductive methods must inevitably play a larger part, and the pursuit of the 'exact laws' of Menger, and of the 'apodictic certainties' of Mises, must be left to the devotees of vacuous mathematical filigree.

· NOTES

1 This paper was written in 1992–3 and has not been published before. In the earlier sections I have drawn heavily on Hutchison, 1988.

2 Denis O'Brien has got Adam Smith's treatment of value exactly right: 'Adam Smith laid the foundations for classical value theory. What he did and the way he did it, were to prove extremely important because he seems deliberately and consciously to have rejected the value theory which he inherited. He inherited a subjective value theory; and instead of developing this he largely substituted for it a cost of production theory. . . . The dismissal of utility as a determinant of value is justified by reference to the 'diamonds-and-water paradox' although, as we have seen, Smith solved this in his *Lectures*. It is interesting to see that Smith so far purges his analysis of the subjective elements as to redefine utility' (1975, pp. 78ff.; Hutchison, 1988, p. 366). It has occurred to me since 1988 that Francis Hutcheson's introduction of the term 'natural use' *may* have suggested to Smith his switch from a subjective to an objective concept of utility. As regards the inadequacy of human knowledge in pursuit of 'the great ends' of 'self-preservation' and 'the propagation of the species', Smith emphasizes, in *The Theory of Moral Sentiments*: 'it has not been intrusted to the slow and uncertain determinations of our reason, to find out the proper means of bringing them about' (1976, p. 77).

3 Gide and Rist in the 1909 edition of their *History* seem to have been one of the first to refer to the 'new school' as 'essentially Neoclassical', because it is based on the assumption of 'the *homo economicus* of the Classicals'. (See Gide and Rist, 1948, pp. 489 and 507–9.) The analytically vital characteristic of the *homo economicus*, of course, is not, or not only, his materialism, or his narrow or exclusive regard for his own interests, but to his full knowledge as an omniscient maximizer, operating 'ant'-like – as Mises put it – in a world without uncertainty. When, therefore, in recent decades, theoretical economists have sought 'imperialistically' to apply economic analysis to other political or sociological areas, it is the not-uncriticizable, simplificatory, or over-simplificatory notion of the 'ant-like' omniscient maximizer, to whom uncertainty is unknown, which has been exported.

4 On the various neoclassical concepts of utility and its possible measurability, see Stigler, 1965, pp. 84, 87, 117.

5 Böhm-Bawerk's typically terse version of the point Jevons was making in his famous passage about 'bygones being forever bygones', was: 'Das in-die Zukunft-gerichtet-sein der Wirtschaft.'

6 The classical and neoclassical assumption of 'competition', eventually refined as 'perfect' competition, usually included – and *had* to include for most analytical purposes – the assumption of full knowledge. Edgeworth followed Mill in observing that if competitive conditions, with full knowledge, of course, were superseded by some form of monopoly: 'Among those who would suffer by the new régime there would be one class . . . namely the abstract economists, who would be deprived of their occupation, the investigation of the conditions which determine value. There would survive only the empirical school, flourishing in a chaos congenial to their mentality' (1925, vol. I, pp. 138–9).

About a century later, the academic-mathematical abstractionist descendants of

Edgeworth seem, somehow, not only to have survived, but to have flourished, in terms of 'high status', in an academic, fantasy Utopia of omniscient ants, rats and automata (doubtless 'congenial to their mentality').

7 Professor James Buchanan has expressed doubts very similar to those raised here regarding what he described as 'the so-called subjective-value revolution', and as to whether there were 'any necessarily subjective elements' in 'the economic theory of Jevons, Menger and Walras'. Buchanan continued: 'There is nothing in neo-classical economic theory that precludes the universalized existence of simple reaction patterns of behavior on the part of all persons in the economy, reaction patterns that, even if more complex, are still analogous to those that might empirically describe the behavior of rats' (Kirzner, ed. 1982, p. 11). We would venture to emphasize: (1) that it is the assumption of full knowledge, and the absence of uncertainty, which transforms ignorant, uncertainty-ridden human beings into 'rats' (or, according to Mises, into 'ants': see following note); and (2) that, as both Menger and Knight unerringly observed, the assumption of full knowledge, or *Allwissenheit*, was *absolutely essential* for Menger's 'exact laws', for Mises's 'apodictic certainties' and, indeed, for the whole fabric of classical and neoclassical analysis. Of course, any political analysis of 'public choice' dependent on the full-knowledge assumption is concerned not with human beings but with rats, ants or automata.

8 Ludwig Mises described the world of perfect foresight as follows: 'Such a rigid system is not peopled with living men making choices and liable to error, it is a world of soulless unthinking automatons; it is not a human society, it is an ant-hill' (1966, p. 248; quoted by Littlechild, *op. cit.*, p. 86). It need only be added that, of course, Mises's own 'apodictic certainties' depend, necessarily on the assumption of 'automatons' or 'an ant-hill', as do Menger's 'exact laws' and, indeed, much of the entire fabric of classical and neoclassical theory. It is of some interest to notice the great Jacob Viner's criticism of Menger, which applies, obviously, much more widely than only to the Austrian leader. Regarding the *Methodenstreit*, Viner wrote: 'My fellow theorists tell me that the theorists won a definitive victory in this battle when Carl Menger, in the 1880s, demolished Gustav Schmoller. I cannot agree. I believe that the battle was mostly a sham one, and that while Schmoller certainly carried off no laurels, the ones that have ever since been bestowed on Menger for his victory in this battle are tinsel ones.' Viner goes on: 'The real challenge which Menger should have faced was not that of justifying in principle recourse to abstraction by economists, but of justifying in principle the particular extent and manner in which he and his fellow theorists practiced it' (1991, pp. 238–9).

9 I have taken most of the examples of 'subjective' ideas summarized in this section from Hutchison, 1953, chs. 20–2, pp. 320ff.

BIBLIOGRAPHY

Alter, M. (1990). *Carl Menger and the Origins of Austrian Economics.*
Bagehot, W. (1873). *Lombard Street.*
Böhm, S. (1982). 'The Ambiguous Notion of Subjectivism', in I. Kirzner, ed., pp. 41ff.
Böhm-Bawerk, E. (1924). *Gesammelte Schriften.*
Buchanan, J. M. (1982). 'The Domain of Subjective Economics', in I. Kirzner, ed., pp. 7ff.
Burlamaqui, J. J. (1773). *Élements du droit naturel*, 1783 ed.
Caldwell, B. J. (ed.) (1990). *Carl Menger and his Legacy in Economics.*
Cantillon, R. (1931). *Essai sur la nature du commerce en général*, ed. H. Higgs.

Carmichael, G. (1724). Annotations in revised ed. of *De officio hominis et civis*, by S. Pufendorf.

Condillac, E. B. de (1776). *Le commerce et le gouvernement*, in *Oeuvres* de Condillac, vol. 4, 21 vols., 1821–2.

Dolan, E. G. (ed.) (1976). *The Foundations of Modern Austrian Economics*.

Edgeworth, F. Y. (1925). *Papers on Political Economy*, vol. I.

Fisher, I. (1896). *Appreciation and Interest*.

Gide, C., and Rist, C. (1909 and 1948). *A History of Economic Doctrines*.

Grice-Hutchinson, M. (1952). *The School of Salamanca*.

Hawtrey, R. G. (1937). 'Alternative Theories of the Rate of Interest', *Economic Journal*, 47, pp. 436ff.

Hayek, F. A. (1937). 'Economics and Knowledge', *Economica*, n.s., 4, pp. 33–54.

Hutcheson, F. (1755). *A System of Moral Philosophy*, 3 vols.

Hutchison, T. W. (1937). 'Expectation and Rational Conduct', *Zeitschrift für Nationalökonomie*, VIII, 5, pp. 636ff.

Hutchison, T. W. (1938). *The Significance and Basic Postulates of Economic Theory*.

Hutchison, T. W. (1953). *A Review of Economic Doctrines 1870–1929*.

Hutchison, T. W. (1978). *Revolutions and Progress in Economic Knowledge*.

Hutchison, T. W. (1981). *The Politics and Philosophy of Economics*.

Hutchison, T. W. (1988). *Before Adam Smith*.

Jevons, W. S. (1879). *The Theory of Political Economy*, 2nd ed.

Keynes, J. M. (1937). 'The General Theory of Employment', *Quarterly Journal of Economics*, 51, pp. 209ff.

Keynes, J. M. (1956). *The General Theory of Employment, Interest and Money*.

Kirzner, I. (ed.) (1982). *Method, Process and Austrian Economics*.

Knight, F. H. (1921). *Risk, Uncertainty and Profit*.

Knight, I. F. (1968). *The Geometric Spirit: The Abbé de Condillac and the French Enlightenment*.

Kresge, S. (1992). Introduction to *The Fortunes of Liberalism*, by F. A. Hayek, pp. 1ff.

Lachmann, L. (1977). *Capital, Expectations and the Market Process*.

Langholm, O. (1979). *Price and Value in the Aristotelian Tradition*.

Leslie, C. (n.d.). *Essays in Political and Moral Philosophy*.

Littlechild, S. C. (1982). 'Equilibrium and the Market Process', in I. Kirzner, ed., pp. 85ff.

Marshall, A. (1961). *Principles of Economics*, 2 vols, ed. C. W. Guillebaud.

Menger, C. (1950). *Principles of Economics*, trans. J. Dingwall and B. F. Hoselitz.

Menger, C. (1963). *Problems of Economics and Society*, trans. F. J. Nock.

Mill, J. S. (1844). *Essays on Some Unsettled Questions of Political Economy*.

Mill, J. S. (1909). *Principles of Political Economy*, ed. W. J. Ashley.

Mills, J. (1867). 'Credit Cycles and the Origins of Commercial Panics', in *Transactions of the Manchester Statistical Society*.

Mises, L. (1966). *Human Action*, 3rd ed.

Myrdal, G. (1938). *Monetary Equilibrium*.

O'Brien, D. (1975). *The Classical Economists*.

Oxford English Dictionary (1971). Compact edition.

Pufendorf, S. (1660). *Elementorum jurisprudentiae universalis*, trans. W. A. Oldfather, 1931.

Ricardo, D. (1951–2). *Works and Correspondence*, ed. P. Sraffa, vols I and II.

Roscher, W. (1861). *Ansichten der Volkswirtschaftslehre*.

Simon, H. (1976). 'From Substantive to Procedural Rationality', in *Method and Appraisal in Economics*, ed. S. J. Latsis, pp. 129ff.

Sismondi, S. de (1819). *Nouveaux Principes d'économie politiques*, 2 vols.

Smith, A. (1776). *The Wealth of Nations*, eds. R. H. Campbell, A. S. Skinner and W. B. Todd (1976).

Smith, A. (1976). *The Theory of Moral Sentiments*, eds. D. D. Raphael and A. L. Macfie.

Stigler, G. J. (1965). *Essays in the History of Economics*.

Triffrin, R. (1940). *Monopolistic Competition and General Equilibrium Theory*.

Vaughn, K. (1982). 'Subjectivism, Predictability and Creativity', in *Method, Process and Austrian Economics*, ed. I. Kirzner, pp. 21ff.

Viner, J. (1991). *Essays on the Intellectual History of Economics*.

Walras, A. (1831). *De la nature de la richesse et de l'origine de la valeur*.

White, L. H. (1990). 'Restoring an "Altered" Menger', in *Carl Menger and his Legacy in Economics*, ed. B. J. Caldwell, pp. 313ff.

Wicksell, K. (1898). *Interest and Prices*, trans. R. F. Kahn.

Wieser, F. (1929). *Gesammelte Abhandlungen*, ed. F. A. Hayek.

10

HAYEK, MISES AND THE METHODOLOGICAL CONTRADICTIONS OF 'MODERN AUSTRIAN' ECONOMICS[1]

I

For some two-thirds of this turbulent century Friedrich Hayek poured out a stream of books, pamphlets, articles and reviews, primarily on various aspects of economics, but later more and more on related questions of philosophy, politics, the history of ideas and the theory of psychology.[2]

It may seem that on most subjects Hayek preserved a remarkable constancy of view. Here and there, however, in one or two key areas of great import- ance, quite profound shifts may be detected. One of these key areas is that of the fundamental assumption, or assumptions, of economic theory, a postulate or postulates, so basic that vital methodological questions are involved. To describe the most crucial phase of this fundamental shift, however, is not as straightforward a task as might be hoped. The first source of difficulties in attempting to set out a clear story arises because some of Hayek's scattered reminiscences, in the last decades of his long life, are somewhat imprecise, or involve conflicts regarding dates.

Secondly, and probably more seriously, Hayek's most important shift of view involved a significant break with his mentor Ludwig Mises, nearly twenty years his senior (at a time when that kind of seniority meant something much more than, and very different from, what it does today). Mises was, as Hayek himself put it, 'the chief guide' in the development of his ideas for ten years, in the crucial period from his early twenties until his early thirties. The extreme hesitations, restraint or 'gentleness', with which Hayek eventually announced his divergences from the views of his chief guide did not make for clarity and incisiveness.

A further aggravation of the difficulties of interpreting Hayek arises from the attempts, over the last decade or two, from the rise of what has been called 'Modern Austrian Economics', to propagate interpretations of Hayek's views which preserved, as far and as long as possible, the unity, consistency and coherence of this movement by minimizing differences, and by attacking, or claiming to 'refute', interpretations which seemed to detract from the coherence of the movement, or from the plausibility of its sometimes somewhat confusing version of its history.[3] Various schools or movements in the history of economics and political economy have sought to compose – or concoct – a version of the history of the subject in an attempt to build up prestige and coherence (see Hutchison, 1978, chapter 8). The Marxist version has obviously been one of the most persistent and elaborate of such attempts. Some versions are more obviously open to criticism than others. In the 'Modern Austrian' version the relationship between Hayek and Mises is vital, as also is the relationship between Hayek and Popper – with the two relationships pulling in diametrically opposite directions.

II

Let us start by recalling what must have been the main factors in the initial and early development of Hayek's ideas in the first fifteen years of his study of economics and his early career as an economist. When, in 1921, he chose economics as his subject, rather than psychology – 'perhaps wrongly', as he puts it – he had as his most authoritative teacher, Friedrich Wieser (Weimer and Palermo, 1982, p. 288). Later in the 1920s, Hayek was to edit Wieser's collected essays, contributing a most respectful introductory tribute to his 'revered teacher'. The first of these essays represented Wieser's most striking methodological statement, his denunciation of the youthful Schumpeter's 'positivism'. The importance of this essay of Wieser has not been sufficiently recognized by 'Modern Austrians' (possibly because it has only recently been translated into English, and possibly because of Wieser's sympathy with socialism and social reform).[4]

Introspection, or 'the psychological method', as Wieser called it, as contrasted with 'positivist' methods,

> finds that certain acts take place with a feeling of necessity. What a huge advantage for the natural scientist if the organic and inorganic world clearly informed him of its laws, and why should we neglect such assitance?
>
> (1929, p. 17)

Wieser maintained:

> For all actions, which are accompanied by a consciousness of necessity, economic theory need never strive to establish a law in a long series of inductions. In these cases we, each of us, hear the law pronounced by an unmistakable inner voice.
>
> (1927, p. 8)

In Hayek's first, concise and confident statement of his methodological views in 1935 we find a closely similar pretentiousness regarding the certainty, necessity or indisputability of the basic phenomena, or assumptions, of economics, and of their remarkable superiority in certainty to those of the natural sciences.

Regarding the crucial decade after the completion of his studies, Hayek has told us how, while employed in a temporary government office,

> good fortune brought it that I found myself there under the direction of another economist . . . who, for the next ten years, became the chief guide in the development of my ideas, Ludwig von Mises.
>
> (1984, p. 1)

Stephen Böhm, moreover, has referred to the intense methodological discussions in Mises's private seminar, which presumably must have left a deep imprint on the young Hayek (1989a, p. 204). Mises himself certainly developed very confident, even dogmatic views; and that his ten-year direction of the young Hayek's further education somehow stopped short of the hazy and flexible frontier between theory and methodology seems highly improbable. Of course, Hayek's methodological views never became 100 per cent identical with those of Mises, and possibly not with regard to the rather vague and imprecise terms, or concepts, of 'praxeology' and 'a priorism'. This difference, however, may have been more terminological than substantial, and may not have involved any very different degree of dogmatism, as between Wieser, Mises and Hayek, with regard to the 'unmistakable', 'unquestionable' and 'indisputable' quality which all three of them claimed for their basic postulates.

Mises certainly followed Wieser in insisting on the unquestionable insights yielded by introspection, as well as on the 'understanding' of the actions of others:

> What we know about our own actions and those of other people is conditioned by our familiarity with the category of action that we owe to a process of understanding of other people's conduct. To question their insight is no less impossible than to question the fact that we live.
>
> (1962, p. 71; Hutchison, 1981, p. 210)[5]

There is, of course, no question that useful, and even essential insights may *originate* with, or via, introspection. It is the dogmatic, pretentious claims (on behalf, presumably, of non-trivial insights) to 'unquestionability' and 'indisputability' which are so intellectually repulsive.

Indeed, it may be suggested that the similarity, or family affiliation, between the methodological views of Wieser, and those of Mises is closer than that between any of the three members of the original Austrian triumvirate and any other second- or third-generation Austrian.

Mises did not publish any full version of his methodological doctrines until 1933, with the first, previously unpublished, essay of his *Grundprobleme*. The complete Misesian conceptual framework, however, was not to appear until later. In 1933, though Mises insisted on the 'apodictic certainty' and *a priori*

214

nature of the truths on which the science of human action rested, he did not employ the term 'praxeologie'.[6] Anyhow, soon after the appearance of the *Grundprobleme*, Hayek published the following concise but comprehensive summary of his methodological tenets at this time:

> The essential basic facts which we need for the explanation of social phenomena are part of our common experience, part of the stuff of our thinking. In the social sciences it is the elements of the complex phenomena which are known beyond the possibility of dispute. In the natural sciences they can be at best surmised. The existence of these elements is so much more certain than any regularities in the complex phenomena to which they give rise that it is they which constitute the truly empirical factor in the social sciences.
>
> (1935, p. 11; quoted in Hutchison, 1981, pp. 213–14)

Professional philosophers may, of course, argue interminably about the differences between the *a priori* apodictic certainties of Mises, and what is 'known beyond the possibility of dispute' – according to Hayek. For economists, on the other hand, insistence on significant differences in epistemological status between various claims to certainty or indisputability, whether or not '*a priori*' – anyway, a highly ambiguous term – may justifiably be dismissed as a largely irrelevant philosophical quibble. The extreme closeness of Hayek (1935) to Wieser and Mises (without, of course, total 100 per cent identity of views) is surely obvious regarding the two fundamental points of: (a) the infallibilist irrefutability of 'the essential basic facts of economics'; and (b) the fundamental contrast and difference in nature between the methods and basic postulates of the social sciences and those of the natural sciences – a contrast drawn with about equally preposterous pretentiousness by Wieser, Mises and Hayek in favour of economics as a social science.

Neither Wieser, nor Mises, nor Hayek, was ever prepared to give some reasonably precise examples of these extraordinary 'unquestionable' or 'indisputable' propositions, so that critics could appraise them for their possibly trivial, vacuous, tautological or totally unrealistic character. What seems often to have been included, or slipped in, with these remarkable basic assumptions, was one of full or perfect knowledge.

We have stressed that the statement of Hayek (1935), which we have quoted, is virtually his only clear and explicit methodological statement until that date. He had, however, implicitly demonstrated his methodological inclinations in his two early books, *Monetary Theory and the Trade Cycle* (German, 1929, and English, 1933) and *Prices and Production*, English, 1931 and 1935). In these two books Hayek insisted that the theory of the trade cycle must be incorporated 'into the static system which is the basis of all theoretical economics' (1933, p. 98; Hutchison, 1981, p. 212). Ignorance and uncertainty must, as far as possible, be ruled out, for they are 'bound to have a devastating effect on theory', since they involve 'the sacrifice of any exact theoretical deduction' (1933, p. 96; Hutchison, 1981, p. 213). As Hayek put it in *Prices and Production*:

> . . . it is my conviction that if we want to explain economic phenomena at all, we have no means available but build on the foundations given by a tendency to equilibrium.
>
> (1935, p. 34)

Here Hayek was simply following Carl Menger (and also J. S. Mill, Edgeworth and F. H. Knight) in insisting that full knowledge was an essential, necessary component of the assumption of competition, on which the structure of orthodox, deductive 'theory' had long depended (see Hutchison, 1978, pp. 200–4).

III

At this point we must introduce a remarkable reminiscence from Hayek, first produced at a conference in 1977 and first published in 1982 (*aet.* 83). A lengthy quotation seems fully justified. Questioned about his views on Kuhn's work, Hayek explained:

> I was so much a Popperian long before Kuhn appeared that I've never been able to see that Kuhn 'refuted' much of Popper. But so far as the pure theory of knowledge is concerned, I have reservations. Not only Kuhn but Lakatos and Feyerabend have made the field perhaps a little more difficult than Popper ever acknowledged. But basically, I am still a Popperian. Indeed, I should tell you that, in a way, I was a Popperian before he published *The Logic of Scientific Discovery*. We were both, in the 1920s, constantly arguing with two types of people – Marxists and Freudians – who both claimed that their theories were, in their nature, irrefutable. Now the claim that a scientific theory should be beyond the possibility of refutation is, of course, very irritating. This led Popper to the conclusion that a theory that cannot be refuted is, by definition, not scientific. When Popper stated that in detail, I just embraced his views as a statement of what I was feeling. And that is why ever since his *Logik der Forschung* first came out in 1934, I have been a complete adherent to his general theory of methodology.
>
> (Weimer and Palermo, 1982, vol. 2, p. 323)[7]

This is certainly a robust, minimally qualified statement regarding his intellectual autobiography. It is, however, slightly puzzling that hardly the faintest traces of any Popperian ideas regarding refutability (or falsifiability) can, so far, be found in any of Hayek's writings before 1937. Quite the contrary, in fact. As we have just seen, nothing could have been more emphatically opposed to the Popperian principle about refutability than the ideas of Wieser and Mises as to how the basic axioms or postulates of economic theory were

216

'unmistakable' (according to Wieser); or 'impossible to question' (Mises); or, as Hayek himself, in 1935, put it, 'known beyond the possibility of dispute'. It remains curious that someone who, from an earlier stage, had been significantly inclined towards the falsifiability principle, could, in his clear, concise statement of methodological principles, in 1935, assert such a diametrically opposite view.

What may have happened was that the youthful Hayek, confronted in Vienna, as Popper had been, by the argumentative tactics of Marxists and Freudians, had then, perhaps even before he launched on his economic studies under Wieser, inclined towards the incisive critical principle eventually formulated by Popper. Then, perhaps about a decade and a half later, when emerging, on his move to London, out from under the dogmatic direction and guidance of Mises, he came upon the powerful statement in *Logik der Forschung* in 1934 (or, more probably, 1935) and was eventually emboldened even to hint publicly to Mises – though all too gently – of his break with his mentor's dogmatic certainties based on an oversimplified and vacuous assumption about knowledge.

IV

There have been conflicting signals regarding the precise date when Hayek read Popper's *Logik der Forschung*. As we have seen, on one occasion Hayek seemed to imply that he read the book as soon as it was published in 1934. In a letter to this writer, however, of 15 May 1983, Hayek stated that 'Economics and Knowledge' (1937) was written 'before I knew anything about Popper'. On the other hand, Sir Karl Popper has recently very clearly recollected that he and Hayek first met 'in September or October 1935', and that a week or so later the two discussed *Logik der Forschung*, Hayek having just read it 'with great care' (1992, p. 5).[8]

If Popper's recollection is correct, then the year 1935 had a twofold significance in the story of Hayek's profoundly changing views on the assumptions and method of economics. Early in the year he had published his clear and explicit statement of his methodological position – which closely followed the teachings of Wieser and Mises. Later in 1935 he read *Logik der Forschung* and discussed it with Popper.

The years 1935 to 1937 were certainly a time when the fundamental assumptions, or basic postulates of economics, especially those regarding knowledge and expectations, were being widely and intensely scrutinized by leading economists. First, there were the Swedish economists: notably Erik Lindahl and Gunnar Myrdal. In fact, Myrdal's work on *Monetary Equilibrium* appeared in German translation in 1931, in a volume edited by Hayek. The Swedes were especially concerned with correct and incorrect expectations and the *ex-ante* and *ex-post* distinctions. The year 1936 was, of course, when Keynes's '*General Theory*' appeared, which opened with a challenge to 'orthodox economics' which concentrated on 'a lack of clearness and generality in the premises' of economic theory (1936, p. v). Keynes perceived these defects as specially serious with regard to 'human decisions affecting the future', and the knowledge or ignorance on which these decisions were based.[9]

Hayek has described how:

> though at one time a very pure and narrow economic theorist, I was led from technical economics into all kinds of questions usually regarded as philosophical. When I look back, it seems to have all begun . . . with an essay on 'Economics and Knowledge' in which I examined what seemed to me some of the central difficulties of pure economic theory.
>
> (1967, p. 91)

Hayek's paper on 'Economics and Knowledge' was delivered as the presidential address to the London Economics Club in November 1936 and published early in 1937. Probably the most serious defect of the eight-and-a-half-page section on Hayek, in my chapter of 1981, was the excessive brevity of my treatment of this very important paper. There are, moreover, two specific corrections to be made. First, it was quite unnecessarily speculative to have introduced the problematic, biographical question of the possible *influence* of Popper's *Logik der Forschung*, mentioned in the first footnote of Hayek's article. It would have been, and is, quite sufficient to assert that, as between his immediately preceding, emphatically Wieserian and/or Misesian methodological statement of 1935, and his article published early in 1937, Hayek's views showed a decisive transformation in the direction of some of the main ideas in Popper's *Logik der Forschung*, whatever influence from that book, or from any other direction, may or may not have been at work.

In the above-mentioned letter to this writer of 15 May 1983, Hayek also stated that his 'main intention' in 'Economics and Knowledge' was 'to explain gently to Mises why I could not accept his a priorism'. Unfortunately, the message to Mises, which it was Hayek's 'main intention' to deliver in this celebrated article, was imparted so 'gently' that forty to fifty years later it had still not got through to most 'Modern Austrians', who, of course, found the fact of a vital, fundamental division of views between the two great patron saints of their movement difficult to accept. 'Economics and Knowledge', however, possessed the very rare significance in Hayek's more than sixty years of writing, of delivering a definite rejection – however 'gently' – of a fundamental doctrine of Mises. Certainly this rejection of *a priorism* also stamps 'Economics and Knowledge' as centrally and fundamentally methodological, though the precise content of the 'a priorism' which Hayek was rejecting remains somewhat ambiguous. In any case, however, the break with Mises, and with the claims about 'indisputability' in Hayek's own article of 1935, marked an essential first step in Hayek's move in the direction of Popper's views, with which, of course, Hayek never achieved complete identity, but which, in any case, lay in a diametrically opposite direction to those of Mises.

Hayek's opening sentences explain his methodological purpose and his concern with the 'assumptions and propositions about knowledge' underlying equilibrium theorizing. At once he drew a sharp and fundamental distinction between 'tautologies, of which formal equilibrium analysis in economics essentially consists, and, on the other hand, 'propositions which tell us anything about causation in the real world' (1949, p. 33). Hayek goes on to contend that:

> the empirical element in economic theory – the only part which is con- cerned not merely with implications but with causes and effects and which leads therefore to conclusions which, at any rate in principle, are capable of verification – consists of propositions about the acquisition of knowledge. . . .
>
> (p. 33)

In a footnote Hayek substituted 'falsification' for 'verification' in the above quotation, adding a reference to Popper's *Logik der Forschung*, 'passim'. This footnote need not, of course, signify that Hayek was *influenced* by Popper, but it must have been an acknowledgement that the central theme of his article was on closely similar lines to Popper's analysis of the relationship between falsifiability, tautologies and empirical content. Moreover, his (or rather Karl Popper's) replacement of 'verification' by 'falsification' was crucial for Hayek's argument, because tautologies, which he was criticizing for lack of empirical content, are, of course, in a way, verifiable, but not falsifiable.[10]

Hayek at once emphasized the wide-ranging importance of the assumptions made concerning foresight and knowledge for theories of duopoly and oligo- poly, as well as for those of money and industrial fluctuations, concluding: 'The situation seems here to be that before we can explain why people commit mistakes we must first explain why they should ever be right' (p. 34). (Hayek should also have added the issue of economic 'calculation' in a socialist economy as one where assumptions about knowledge were absolutely vital; but he didn't.[11]) Anyhow, Hayek is here, of course, completely reversing his earlier view, as stated in his first two books on monetary economics (1928 and 1931), that 'the static system' must be retained, which 'is the basis of all theoretical economics', and which included the assumption of 'a necessary tendency towards equilibrium', ruling out ignorance, the admission of which would be bound to have 'a devastating effect on theory'. Hayek glimpsed, in fact, how much deductive, and (especially) *a priori*, economic theorizing depends on the vastly simplificatory assumption of perfect competition, including full knowledge. Later, Hayek again emphasized how 'an exercise in pure logic', as performed by Misesian *a priorism*, simply produces empirically vacuous tautologies. In fact, in the mid-1930s there was considerable discus- sion among economists of the nature and role of tautologies in economic theor- izing. (I might mention, incidentally, that my own first two publications were mainly concerned with these questions (1935 and 1937a.) I was, therefore, bound to be specially interested, when reading 'Economics and Knowledge' towards the middle of 1937 – having read *Logik der Forschung* in 1936 – in the vital distinctions which Hayek drew – which, of course, were closely similar to some of the fundamental distinctions drawn by Popper in *Logik der Forschung*.)

It is also important to realize that, for several years before 1937, much discussion had been taking place among economists not only of the distinction between tautologies and explanatory and empirical statements, but also of the other main theme of 'Economics and Knowledge', that of the concept of equilibrium and the assumption of equilibrating tendencies.[12] Hayek's ideas on these subjects ran on similar lines to those of Johan Akerman, who complained of some writers that:

> They find the ideal of abstract description in the perfect logical circle. . . .
> The setting is thus *a priori* tautologous; it arrives at results which are exactly identical with the elements of thought which have been put into the argument.

> (1936, p. 118, quoted by Hutchison, 1937a, p. 87)

Whenever, precisely, Hayek read, *Logik der Forschung*, by the time he reached page 13, he would have met with the challenging statement: 'Ein empirisch wissenschaftliches system muss an der Erfahrung scheitern Können' ('it must be possible for an empirical scientific system to be refuted by experience'). Hayek might, perhaps, have recalled that the Marxian and Freudian systems were claimed to be not thus refutable, as was Mises's analysis of 'the pure logic of choice' (which actually is a misnomer for the logic of omniscient or automatic choice – which is not what most human choice resembles). Anyhow, resolved to break with Misesian claims to *a priori*, apodictic certainties, Hayek came out with the decisive summons: 'To economics as an empirical science we must now turn' (1949, p. 4). That is, economists should make a 'turn' away in the diametrically opposite direction from the dogmatic vacuities of Misesian *a priorism* – which then fudged the question of knowledge – towards 'economics as an empirical science' (as defined in terms of falsifiability by Popper). Surely this can reasonably be described as 'a U-turn'. We do not wish, however, to argue whether Hayek's turn was one of 150° or 180°. Anyhow, there is, of course, no need to be dogmatic about terminology; so if such a description as a 'transformation' is preferred, by all means let it be used.

V

In his article on 'Economics and Knowledge' of 1937 Hayek was concerned with a particular basic postulate of economic theory, albeit one with wide ramifications. Within three or four years of its publication Hayek's work was beginning to extend over a much wider range of subjects. His contributions to methodology were concerned with 'the study of society' and 'the social sciences', rather than focusing on specific assumptions of economic theory.

It would, of course, be ridiculously simplistic to expect that the ideas of a thinker so prodigiously erudite, and profoundly original, and engaged on such an exceptionally wide variety of intellectual fronts, would develop in terms of straightforward, rapid, unilinear advances. In fact, in the early 1940s, Hayek moved towards broader comparisons of the methods of the natural and social sciences, in 'The Facts of the Social Sciences' (1943) and in the mainly historical essays on 'The Counter-Revolution of Science' (1941) and 'Scientism and the Study of Society' (1942/1943/1944) dating from the early 1940s. Although Hayek still maintained a dualist position in comparing the methods and criteria of the natural and social sciences, it is important to recognize that these papers contained no signs of the preposterous Wieserian–Misesian pretences of knowledge, which had been reproduced by Hayek in 1935, regarding: (1) the certainty or 'knowledge beyond the possibility of dispute', on which economics and the social sciences are supposed to be based; or (2) regarding the distinct superiority, or greater reliability, of the basic propositions of economics, as compared with those of the natural sciences. These Wieserian–Misesian claims disappeared from Hayek's writings after 1935, as he moved further in the direction of Popper's views. (Surely, incidentally, on this much controverted issue of the similarities or differences in methods and criteria as between the natural and the social sciences, the only sensible position is somewhere in the middle, away from the extreme pretences of knowledge, or from over-simplified 'dualism', or 'monism'.)

Anyhow, the 'dualist' theme in essays on 'Scientism' and 'the Counter-Revolution of Science' (fascinating though these are as studies in the history of ideas) lasted barely a decade. By 1955 Hayek was reformulating his ideas on the methodology of the social (as contrasted with the natural) sciences, in terms of the complexity, greater or less, of different sciences, thus turning differences into one of gradual degree, abandoning the idea of a fundamental difference in kind. In fact, the idea of dualism had always been much more a German than an Austrian doctrine, and had been introduced into economics in Austria not so much by Menger as by Wieser (whose rather markedly German nationalist ideas have been critically remarked upon by the present occupant of the Vienna chair, Professor Streissler (1987)).

Hayek has explained how 'Popper's influence on me was great on the question of the methods of the natural sciences' (letter of 15 May 1983), and he had, indeed, proceeded to formulate his ideas in terms of the differences between more complex and less complex sciences, or studies. The two very important papers which marked his further fundamental break with Wieserian–Misesian ideas were 'Degrees of Explanation' (first published 1955; v. 1967) – which Hayek describes as 'little more than an elaboration of some of Popper's ideas' (1967, p. 4n) – and 'The Theory of Complex Phenomena' (1964).

Professor Stephen Böhm has recently observed that 'all Austrian subjectivists are staunch exponents of methodological dualism', adding, however, 'with the notable exception of Hayek'. Notable exception, indeed! Böhm confirms that Hayek 'in his neglected (among economists) later methodological work appears to narrow down the radical differentiation between the problems of the natural and social sciences to one of degrees' (1989a, pp. 65, 91). This sad neglect, it should be noted, has, of course, been most serious on the part of those 'Modern Austrians', who, of course, seek to draw a veil across or 'refute', writings which obviously contradict the *a priorist*, praxeological ideas of Mises.

A number of mainly non-Austrian writers have, however, succeeded in discerning these important later Hayekian developments. I first called attention in 1978 to 'the transition, which seems to be detectable over the decades in Hayek's methodological views, in a direction away from Mises and towards Popper' (1978, p. 841). Norman Barry (1979) also noted the Popperian component in Hayek's methodological ideas. Since my brief treatment in 1981, a number of other writers have emphasized Hayek's turn in the directions of Popperian views on both (a) falsifiability and (b) differences between the natural and social sciences: for example, Böhm (1982), Butler (1983), Klant (1984), Gray (1988), and, in her very thorough and profound study, Loy (1988).[13]

VI

In his introduction to volume IV of the *Collected Works* of Hayek (*The Fortunes of Liberalism*) the editor, Professor Peter Klein, remarks that 'the nature of the Mises–Hayek relationship is not fully understood' (1992, p. 13). Klein offers this observation as part of his account of how 'the modern Austrian school may have become split into opposing camps'. This is now obviously the case (and, incidentally, always should have been obvious since the emergence of the 'Modern Austrian' movement in the early or middle 1970s). As Klein states, three such 'opposing camps' may be distinguished:

1 There are the 'strict Misesians', who are social 'rationalists' and practice 'extreme a priorism'; and also oppose almost any and every kind of government activity. So this might be described as the Austro-anarchist sect.
2 There are the 'radical subjectivists', who follow the late George Shackle and Ludwig Lachmann, and 'who deny the possibility of *any* order in economic affairs' (because they deny the possibility of any prediction or predictability in economics) – and so may be described as 'Austro-Nihilists'.
3 There are the 'Hayekians', who emphasize spontaneous order and the limits of rationality (p. 13) (who have a solid claim to the adjective 'Austrian').

Certainly this lack of understanding of the Mises–Hayek relationship is fatal to the understanding of Hayek, especially regarding methodology and philosophy. Two obvious sources for this failure of understanding were mentioned above. First, the main source of misunderstanding, already discussed, was certainly Hayek's extreme gentleness and restraint in mentioning his break with Mises and the widening differences after 1937. A second main source of misunderstanding, which we shall discuss in section VII, has been the failure, or refusal, of 'Modern Austrians' to recognize the profound philosophical and methodological contradictions between different sections of their movement whose unity and coherence they were so concerned to preserve.

In order to minimize any differences between himself and his mentor of ten years, Hayek seemed to want to suggest that Mises did not really mean what he said: for example, he stated that the emphasis of Mises 'on the a priori character of theory sometimes gives the impression of a more extreme position than the author in fact holds' (1992, p. 148). At other times Hayek seems to be making excuses for Mises:

> For too long he had lacked the opportunity to discuss problems with intellectual equals. . . .
> Considering the kind of battle he had to lead, I also understand that he was driven to certain exaggerations like that of the a priori character of economic theory, where I could not follow him.
>
> (*op. cit.*, p. 158)

Just when and where Mises was deprived of opportunities of discussion with equals, and was 'driven to certain exaggerations', is not clear: presumably not in Vienna in the days of his famous private seminar.

Later on Hayek did indicate the profundity of his philosophical disagreement with Mises: 'One of my differences is over a statement of Mises on basic philosophy over which I always felt a little uneasy. But only now can I articulate why I was uncomfortable with it' (p. 142). This was written in 1978, when the author was 79, and five years after the death of Mises. Certainly, enlightened discussion operates under a certain handicap if philosophical differences can only be articulated when one of the parties concerned has long departed this world.

Anyhow, Hayek then goes on to quote Mises as asserting that liberalism 'regards all social co-operation as an emanation of rationally recognized utility' (p. 142). Hayek adds: 'The extreme rationalism of this passage, which as a child of his time he could not escape from, and which he perhaps never fully abandoned, now seems to me factually mistaken' (p. 142).[14] Hayek constantly seemed eager to minimize the differences between himself and Mises. In fact economists may consider differences regarding 'rationalism' as of minor importance considering the great and enthusiastic area of agreement on the policy issues of anti-socialism, and also the business cycle. But it was Hayek himself who insisted that the extreme rationalist in politico-economic and social thought is the most dangerous enemy of true liberty, a 'false individualist' who always tends to prompt 'the opposite of individualism, namely socialism or collectivism' (1949, p. 4).

In fact, one of Hayek's most important essays, though one of the least discussed, by 'modern Austrians', is his 'Individualism: True and False' (1949). In it he drew a fundamental distinction between two utterly contradictory types of individualism, and traced their development from the seventeenth and eighteenth centuries down to the second half of the nineteenth century.

True individualism,

> began its modern development with John Locke, and particularly with Bernard Mandeville and David Hume, and achieved full stature for the first time in the work of Josiah Tucker, Adam Ferguson, and Adam Smith. . . . In the nineteenth century I find it represented most perfectly in the work of its greatest historians and political philosophers: Alexis de Tocqueville and Lord Acton . . . while the classical economists of the nineteenth century, or at least the Benthamites or philosophical radicals among them, came increasingly under the influence of another kind of individualism of different origin.
>
> (1949, p. 4)

Hayek then goes on to explain how 'this antirationalistic approach' of 'true' individualism,

> which regards man not as a highly rational and intelligent but as a very irrational and fallible being, whose individual errors are corrected only in the course of a social process . . . is probably the most characteristic feature of English individualism.
>
> (pp. 8–9)

'False' individualism, on the other hand, stems from Descartes and 'is represented mainly by French and other Continental writers', and was outstandingly represented by 'the Encyclopedists, Rousseau, and the physiocrats' (p. 4).

One of the characteristics, incidentally noticed by Hayek (p. 10n) of the 'false', French individualists, was 'the anti-historical attitude of Descartes'. Correspondingly, one, of course, of the characteristics of the later, Ricardian classical economists, was the elimination of the historical element from Smithian political economy. There has also been, for the most part, a strong, anti-historical element in much of Austrian economics.

Anyhow, as Hayek continued, 'the classical economists of the nineteenth century, and particularly John Stuart Mill . . . were almost as much influenced by the French as by the English tradition' (p. 11). Unfortunately, Hayek never traced the development of false individualism on into this century. Presumably 'false' individualism did not, by some miraculous influence, disappear around the beginning of this century. Was it, possibly, that Hayek's gentle restraint made him shrink from pursuing his vital, politico-philosophical distinction into this century because he might have felt compelled to point the finger at his mentor Mises as an exponent of 'extreme rationalism' and 'false individualsm'? It might, of course, also have been that pursuing such a distinction, between 'Individualism: True and False', might have called attention, too obviously, to the contradiction between Hayek's own tendency towards a conservative Burkean traditionalism and his radical, somewhat 'constructivist' reformism, financially regarding the monetary system and politically regarding the constitution. All that I wish to point out here, however, is that Hayek's challenging analysis of 'Individualism: True and False' seems to have been noted, and eventually answered, very robustly, and even scathingly, on behalf of Mises, by the leading spokesman for pure Misesism, Professor Murray Rothbard ('Vice-President for Academic Affairs of the Ludwig von Mises Institute'). We shall discuss Rothbard's Misesian rejoinder to Hayek's 'Individualism: True or False' below in section VIII.

VII

For understanding Hayek and his much-misunderstood relationship with his ten-year mentor Mises, one must appreciate how closely, in his early career, Hayek followed Mises with regard to the two main problems which most engaged him down to about the late 1930s: (a) the Austrian, monetary over-investment theory of the business cycle; and (b) the debate over calculation and allocation in a socialist economy.

On both these subjects Mises had been an influential leader and had made important contributions, closely followed, and built upon, by the youthful Hayek. Serious flaws must, however, be noted in the Austrian ideas regarding both these issues.

(a) The Austrian, monetary over-investment analysis was, as regards diagnosis, important and widely held in central Europe in 1929, at the time of the onset of the great world slump. Unfortunately, however, regarding policy, both Mises and Hayek rigidly opposed, in principle, *any* attempt by means of monetary policy or public investment to counter one of the most savage and disastrous deflations of modern times, between 1930 and 1932 in Germany, which brought about an appallingly swift rise in unemployment. Whatever influence, if any, the Austrian doctrine may have exercised, the consequences in Germany, and for the world, from 1933 onwards, are well known. If Austrian economics seemed to lose ground in the 1930s the reason is obvious. As we have noted, when Hayek in an article of 1937 conceded in a footnote that 'desperate situations' might arise in which it was desirable to take measures to increase employment, it was rather too late (v. Hayek 1937, p. 64n).[15]

(b) As regards the debate on socialism, it may be worth observing, first, that the question as to how a socialist economy would, or could, achieve a more or less 'efficient' allocation of resources did not originate with the Austrian school, but with German historical economists, including even, in a rather jocular passage, Friedrich Engels (v. Hutchison, 1953, pp. 293–8; and 1981, pp. 14–16). Mises certainly deserves credit, however, for raising the issue so sharply in 1920. But the argument he employed was seriously exaggerated and over-simplified. Intermittently, underlying his argument is the extreme rationalist assumption of what Kirzner, rather misleadingly, calls 'static individualism', and also, of course, of so much economic theorizing since Ricardo of generally full, or even perfect knowledge. It is just too facile to demonstrate that socialist planners may not be able to improve on the allocation of competitive markets if everybody in those markets – more or less by definition – is equipped with full or perfect knowledge. At one point, for example, Mises raised the question of how a 'socialist commonwealth' would decide about investing in a new railway line. He explains that 'under a system of private ownership we could use money calculations to decide these questions' (1969, p. 104). Certainly 'money calculations' could be used, but they would not lead to correct or even efficient decisions without adequate knowledge on the part of the calculators. In fact, the Austro-nihilist wing, of the modern Austrian movement, led by Lachmann and Shackle, insisted that total unpredictability made any kind of economic 'calculation' (capitalist or socialist) impossible in any case. Mises, in fact, also failed to recall that it was precisely in the area of railway investment, in the pristine heyday of free-market capitalism in Britain, that some of the most immense and disastrous miscalculations had been perpetrated which plunged the whole economy into years of depression, bringing intense suffering to the poorest in the community (see Hutchison, 1938, p. 186).

It is just too facile simply to assume, or insist, that private entrepreneurs (or, for that matter as the Marxist, Maurice Dobb did, socialist planners) are *bound* to have the superior knowledge which would make either free markets, on the one hand, or socialist planning, on the other hand, work more effectively. It is, however, highly relevant to observe that private entrepreneurs will be much more powerfully *motivated* than government planners to seek out, collect and apply all relevant kinds of economic knowledge as a basis for less inaccuracy in the essential economic predictions. The factor of knowledge, *without reference to motivation*, has played too exclusively preponderant a role in some of the criticisms of socialist planning. In fact, the exaggerations and over-simplifications of Mises may actually have hindered rather than helped the acceptance of the profoundly important criticism of socialism which was eventually developed by Hayek, after, in the late 1930s he had broken with Mises.

VIII

We must now turn to the second source of misunderstandings of the Mises–Hayek relationship. This has been the unwillingness, after the launching of the 'modern Austrian' movement, for some of its prominent supporters, over-eager to preserve a veneer of unity, to recognize fundamental philosophical

226

and methodological differences and divergences – especially any between their two great leaders, Mises and Hayek; and especially, also, any conceivable influence of Karl Popper – the 'rabid' empiricist – on Hayek, which would be to concede a fundamental break with Mises.

To start with, the 'modern Austrian' movement adopted a quite extraordinary concept of 'Austrian' economics. As Professor Karen Vaughn has described, Mises, after arriving in the USA in 1940,

> . . . held a chair that was financed by the Volker Fund, a conservative organization that knew of his life-long anti-statist fight. At NYU he conducted a weekly seminar which, along with the publications flowing from his pen during the two decades following 1945, *was* the Austrian School in the United States.
>
> (Caldwell, 1990, ed., p. 396)

At this time, in the United States alone – not to mention Hayek in England – there were such unquestionable 'Austrian' economists, of the highest distinction, teaching or writing, as Haberler, Morgenstern, Rosenstein-Rodan, also the philosopher Felix Kaufmann and others, who disagreed profoundly with Mises on a number of issues of fundamental significance.

The bizarre notion that the teaching and writing of Mises *was* the Austrian school in the United States, and perhaps elsewhere, was supported, or propagated, in the opening manifesto of the movement, the volume *The Foundations of Modern Austrian Economics* (ed. Dolan, 1976). This was the first of a considerable number of 'Austrian' books of essays and conference-papers which appeared from the late 1970s and through much of the 1980s. Following the editor's introduction, the first paper in the 1976 volume was by Professor Murray Rothbard, and was entitled 'Praxeology: the Methodology of Austrian Economics'. This title was, of course, as highly questionable as the claim, or belief, that the teaching and writings of Mises *were* Austrian economics (or merely 'Modern Austrian', in the USA or anywhere else). As Professor Stephen Böhm has noted (and Professor Böhm enjoys the almost unique distinction, for a modern Austrian economist, of being an 'Austrian' in an unquestionable sense of the term): 'among the Austrians Mises was the sole advocate of praxeology' (1989a, p. 204n).[16]

Rothbard, however, quoted Hayek's Wieserian–Misesian statement of 1935, maintaining, not unreasonably as regards Hayek's views of 1935, *but no later*, that 'Friedrich Hayek trenchantly described the praxeological method in contrast to the method of the physical sciences' (1976, p. 27).

Neither the term 'praxeology', nor that of 'a priori', has a quite clear-cut meaning, so Rothbard's claim that the 'praxeological method' had come down from J. B. Say, Senior and Cairnes may or may not be regarded as accurate, while certainly implying that there is nothing uniquely 'Austrian' about it – it is, rather, a 'Cartesian' method, if an adjective must be found. Rothbard also, unwillingly or not, confirmed the total empirical emptiness of Misesian praxeology with regard to its assumptions about knowledge, because he simply replaced the usual assumption of full and perfect knowledge, which has pervaded so much of economic theorizing since Ricardo, with blank vacuity, in that he had no other assumption about knowledge or expectations to put in its place:

> Let us note that praxeology does not assume that a person has chosen the technically correct method. . . . All that praxeology asserts is that the individual actor adopts goals, and believes, whether erroneously or correctly, that he can arrive at them by the employment of certain means.

> (1976, p. 20)

It is no advance, but, if anything, a retreat, to replace the long traditional assumption of full or perfect knowledge by total emptiness. What Misesian, or 'Modern Austrian' praxeology succeeds in achieving is a quite unacceptable combination of dogmatic, 'apodictic certainties' with total empirical vacuity. Instead of being left with the traditional, full-knowledge 'theory', we are provided with the marvellously rich, enlightening and totally uninformative model – or Misesian 'apodictic certainty' – that people act with whatever tastes, and whatever kind of knowledge and ignorance, which they happen to possess. By rejecting Misesian *a priorism* or 'praxeology' in 1937 Hayek saved himself intellectually by turning, as he put it, 'to economics as an empirical science' (1949, p. 44).

In this first 'manifesto' volume (*The Foundations of Modern Austrian Economics*, 1976) Rothbard's opening essay on 'Praxeology: the Methodology of Austrian Economics' was followed by Israel Kirzner's paper, 'On the Method of Austrian Economics', which opened with the remarkable statement: 'One of the areas in which disagreement may seem to be non-existent is that of methodology' (1976, p. 40).

Kirzner seemed eager to cling to this idea of non-existent Austrian disagreement in continuing immediately to insist on 'the unique view of method shared by all [*sic*] Austrian economists' (1976, p. 40). (One would venture to hope that this 'Austrian' view is at least unique, though preferably non-existent, since it rests on such a profound contradiction.) This contradiction soon begins to become obvious as Kirzner courageously proceeds to explore Hayek's paper on 'Economics and Knowledge' (of nearly forty years previously). For Kirzner then goes on to interpret Hayek as having 'asserted that when postulating a tendency toward equilibrium, we do have to resort to a particular empirical proposition' (p. 48). This has to be a proposition about learning, i.e. that 'men gradually learn to avoid mistakes'. Moreover: 'Hayek stated very clearly that this is an empirical hypothesis' (p. 49).

The outright contradiction with Rothbard's insistence on the empirical vacuity, regarding knowledge, of Misesian praxeology, should be too obvious to need emphasis. For, as we have seen, a few pages previously Rothbard had insisted that no particular empirical proposition or assumption about knowledge or learning was necessary or made.

Kirzner also clearly revealed a further fundamental contradiction, which he recognized as 'something of a dilemma for the Austrian economist' (p. 48).[17] In fact, as is now recognized among non-Austrians, there has been not only a fundamental two-way split among Austrian economists, as between ultra-rationalist Misesians and anti-rationalist Hayekians; but a three-way split regarding, also, predictability and unpredictability. For Kirzner asserted, as an Austrian 'insight', that

> there is an indeterminacy and unpredictability inherent in human preferences, human expectations, and human knowledge. . . .
>
> Our dissatisfaction with empirical work and our suspicion of measure-ment rest on the conviction that empirical observation of past human choices will not yield any regularities or any consistent pattern that may be safely extrapolated beyond the existing data at hand to yield scientific theorems of universal applicability.
>
> (p. 43)[18]

If Kirzner was insisting here on total unpredictability (and the uselessness of market research) then there was an obvious conflict with Hayek's recognition that a kind of order emerged in a free-market economy. For unless one is assuming that this order emerged by pure chance or magic, *some kind of predictability must have been at work.* In fact, indeed, Hayek himself recognized that: 'as I am anxious to repeat, we still achieve predictions which can be falsified and which therefore are of empirical significance' (1978, p. 33).

It must at this point be noted, however, that at least one 'modern Austrian' eventually recognized the fundamental philosophical and methodological conflict between Hayek and his ten-year guide and mentor Mises. Rothbard may have, in 1976, shown no signs of discerning this fundamental conflict in his essay on 'Praxeology: the Method of Modern Austrian Economics'. Eleven years later, however, in time for the fiftieth anniversary of Hayek's 'Economics and Knowledge', and forty-two years after his 'Individualism: True and False', Rothbard, fully recognizing the great methodological gulf between the two champions of Modern Austrian economics, launched into a comprehensive and very hostile philosophical denunciation of Hayek (which seems to amount to a belated and indignant rejoinder to 'Individualism: True and False', though that important paper is not actually mentioned).

Much of Rothbard's brief but brilliant paper is devoted to restating, with admirable trenchancy and scholarship, the critical Schumpeterian or Jevonian case against the British classical economists, and, in particular against Adam Smith. On this theme we do not wish to add to what we have argued in the first paper in this volume (*v.* pp. 13ff, above).[19] Rothbard writes:

> In recent years Smith and his friends and colleagues, who constituted the Scottish Enlightenment of the eighteenth century, have come in to

scholarly fashion. One reason for this, and for F. A. Hayek's laudation of the Scottish Enlightenment, is precisely because the Scottish advocacy of freedom and free markets was cautious, limited, and all too moderate – a trait which was wrapped up in the irrationalism, the appeal to man's ignorance, to custom, and tradition, which was important for these Scots as well as for Hayek.

(1987; reprinted in Littlechild, ed., 1990, p. 43)

Rothbard champions the radicalism of the French rationalists in their opposition to both Church and State: 'They saw the State and Church as both irrationalist and tyrannical' (p. 43).

On the other hand, the 'Moderates' of the Scottish Enlightenment, according to Rothbard, 'believed in smiting the American rebels root and branch' (p. 44). Rothbard also ridicules: 'Hayek's favourite concept of events that "are the results of human action, but not of human design" '. He claims that the origins of this concept – expounded by Carl Menger, among others – lie 'in Calvinist apologetic' and emphasizes 'its closeness to Hegel's notorious concept of the "cunning of reason" ' (p. 44).

The profound and stark contrast between the philosophical and methodological views of Mises, on the one hand, and the post-1937 views of Hayek, on the other, could hardly have been more sharply drawn. Rothbard's counterblast against Hayek may seem in various respects unfair and misdirected. At least, however, his blunt, outspoken forthrightness may seem preferable to attempts to cover up blatant contradictions and incoherence with a smokescreen of ambiguity. Moreover, Rothbard demonstrated that, in the previous eleven years, he had learnt something important about Hayek (unlike, it seems, one or two other 'Modern Austrians'). For in 1976 Rothbard had quoted Hayek (1935) as the representative exponent of 'Praxeology', which he described as 'the Methodology of Austrian Economics'. But by 1987 he had realized that Hayek, after 1935, had, philosophically and methodologically, turned away, in fundamental respects from Mises – a turning which apparently some Modern Austrians, over half a century later, find almost impossible to accept.

IX

I remember very well my first meeting with Hayek. It was on the afternoon of Friday 11 May 1938, one of those days of horror and foreboding which punctuated the 1930s as the decade advanced: the day when Hitler marched his army into Austria. I was giving a paper to Hayek's seminar on methodology at the LSE. Afterwards Hayek invited me to dinner at the Reform Club. I remonstrated, as best I could, that he must have other, all-too-serious preoccupations that evening. But he insisted on going through with what he evidently regarded as a social obligation: I had sung for my supper, so I must have my supper, even if the world around us was falling apart. The impression was of a rigid, unflinching, officer-like sense of duty.

A deep and lasting effect must have been left on Hayek by his experience as a young officer in the Austrian army. He may, for some time, have carried some of his officer-like preoccupations into his peace-time academic career: in particular, that a junior officer must loyally follow his seniors. He was a young subaltern: Wieser was a general and Mises a colonel. Differences of judgement or opinion must *not* be asserted. This might perhaps help to explain Hayek's persistently uncritical attitude to the methodological peculiarities of Wieser and Mises. Eventually, however, after moving to London, in the (and his) early thirties, Hayek made so bold as to raise, very 'gently', a quite fundamental methodological question regarding the doctrines of his seniors, while perhaps harking back to some earlier ideas of his own regarding the intellectually unsatisfactory nature of inconceivably refutable 'theories', such as those of Marx and Freud (not to mention those of Mises).

Even when he had turned, however, there were hesitations and backward glances. But in the end he completed his struggle of escape. In so doing Hayek saved his own intellectual career and started on that long journey in which he made of his *Collected Writings* – as their editor has put it – 'an invaluable education in a subject which is nothing less than the development of the modern world' (Hayek, 1992, p. ix). Professor Stephen Kresge's historical emphasis is apt. In any case, however, this superb achievement would hardly have been possible if, in the 1930s, he had not broken philosophically with Wieser and Mises.

The greater, the more valuable and more lasting the cause that is being championed, the more unjustifiable it is to be content with arguments which, the deeper one digs, the more ill-founded and unacceptable they are revealed to be. The cause of political and economic freedom, to which Hayek devoted his intellectual career, could not, in the longer, or even in the shorter run, have been fought on the basis of the doctrines of his original teacher Wieser, or his mentor of a decade, Mises. Though it was a difficult and tortuous transition or escape, Hayek had to make it – or we would not have today the tremendous achievement so monumentally recorded in his *Collected Writings*. Unfortunately, however, very few Modern Austrians have followed Hayek, during the past decades, in making the break. Moreover they have not had the same excuse, in terms of personal embarrassment in breaking with a mentor, which Hayek had.[20]

NOTES

1 My first attempt at describing the development of Hayek's methodological and philosophical ideas consisted of a section of eight-and-a-half pages in a chapter on 'Austrians on Philosophy and Method since Menger': i.e. a survey reaching from Böhm-Bawerk and Wieser to Rothbard and Kirzner, which purported to

SUBJECTIVISM, METHODS AND AIMS

demonstrate the various contrasts and divergences in Austrian views. When this chapter was published in 1981 comparatively little had been written on Hayek, apart from Norman Barry's pioneer book. Since then there has been quite a flood of literature, both from members of the 'Modern Austrian' school (or schools) of thought, and from non-members, culminating in the first volumes of the *Collected Writings*. This revised and extended version tries to take account of the recent literature, as well as of a number of reminiscences from Hayek himself, in his later years. I would still venture to refer any interested reader to my earlier piece of 1981 and to the broader 'Austrian' context in which it was set. There are, however, one or two mistakes and inadequacies which I seek to rectify here. This revised and enlarged version also takes into account an attempt by a spokesman for the Modern Austrian movement to present a comprehensive 'refutation' of my earlier piece on Hayek (*v.* Hutchison, 1992).

2 In his essay on 'Statistical Studies in the History of Economic Thought' (1965), George Stigler introduced the idea of a writer's publishing span: i.e. the time between the appearance of his first publication and his last. In the nineteenth century Robert Torrens was quite outstanding with a span of fifty-four years (1804–58). In the second half of this century the span has often lengthened considerably. Hayek's span of sixty-four years (1924–88) seems to be the longest achieved by any major writer on economics.

3 In the first manifesto of modern Austrian economics, a volume of essays published in 1976 (ed. E. G. Dolan), a leader of the movement claimed the existence of 'the unique view of method shared by all Austrian economists'. By 1992 the editor of volume 4 of Hayek's *Collected Writings* was expressing doubts about 'the continuing vitality of the school' because it 'may have been split into opposing camps' (Hayek, 1992, pp. 12–13). These splits were obviously discernible in 1976.

4 On Wieser's methodological views, see Hutchison, 1981, pp. 205–7 and 213.

5 For Mises's Wieserian claims for introspection, see Hutchison, 1981, p. 210. The treatment of Menger by Mises is especially noteworthy. Though Mises refers to Menger's 'path-breaking' '*Untersuchungen*' he alleges that they suffer seriously from the empiricism and 'psychologism' of J. S. Mill. Moreover, Mises makes the extraordinary allegation that Menger's '*Untersuchungen*' 'do not start from modern formulations of subjectivist economics, but from the system, methodology and logic of classical political economy' (1933, pp. 20n and 67n). The intense, Misesist phobia of 'empiricism' is characteristic.

6 The term 'praxeology' or 'praxeological' only occurs in Mises's '*Grundprobleme*' of 1933 in a citation of a work by Slutsky, of which Mises expressed disapproval, though it may have provided him with the source of this term, employed by him later. In the English translation of 1960 the term 'praxeology' is introduced four times to render – though hardly to translate – such German terms as 'Soziologie', 'praktik' and 'gesellschaftslehre'.

7 In their discussion in the *New Palgrave Dictionary* of Hayek's methodological ideas, two leading spokesmen for the 'Modern Austrian' school make no mention of Popper and, of course, do not mention Hayek's own statement about Popper quoted above. Another 'Modern Austrian' enthusiast (R. N. Langlois) has explained how 'many modern Austrians are inclined to read Popper as a rabid empiricist noteworthy primarily for the bad influence he exerted on Hayek' (1982, p. 77). It took 'Modern Austrians' over forty years to admit that Hayek broke methodologically with Mises in 1937: that he broke with Mises by moving in the direction of Popper, that is, in the diametrically opposite direction, philosophically, to that of Mises, must have been too appalling to contemplate. The programme for the *Collected Writings* of Hayek has included a whole volume devoted to 'The Correspondence

between Karl Popper and F. A. Hayek'. The possibility of Hayek having been infected with philosophical rabies must have been extremely alarming. (One gathers, however, that this volume may not actually materialize, and Sir Karl himself doubts whether the correspondence is sufficiently significant to merit publication.) In any case, it is rather a waste of everybody's time for Garrison and Kirzner, in their *New Palgrave* article, to focus their attack on the exaggerated and misleading statement – which nobody ever seems to have made – to the effect that Hayek became a 'falsificationist': it is quite sufficient, in describing the break with Mises, to observe that Hayek was recognizing and insisting on a kind of essential empirical element denied by 'praxeology' (an *aperçu* symptomatic of intellectual rabies for 'many modern Austrians'). Anyhow, Fritz Machlup, a very genuine Austrian, has pointed out that Hayek, while recognizing the difficulties of 'complex' subjects, 'did not, however, deny the possibility of testing and falsifying propositions about such complex situations' (1979, p. 280).

It may further be worth emphasizing that the terms 'falsificationism' and 'falsificationist' suffer, like most words ending in '-ism' and '-ist', from serious ambiguities, and are often introduced to serve a polemical purpose. 'Falsificationism', in fact, has at least two main components which are conceivably separable.

(1) First, what may be called 'the falsifiability principle' maintains that, in the interests of clarity, it is necessary to make clear whether or not a theory, or system of theory, is to be understood as empirically falsifiable. For if it is not refutable by experience, 'a theory', as Hayek himself put it, 'is by definition not scientific'; or, as Popper asserted in his original statement of the principle, 'It must be possible for an empirical-scientific system to be refuted by experience' (1935, p. 13). Surely the falsifiability principle has taken on a profound importance at this time when pure, mathematical 'rigour', which, of course, excludes empirical refutability, is being proclaimed as the overriding criterion of economics; while, at the same time, a distinguished specialist on scientific method concludes that 'economics' may be 'best viewed as more akin to a branch of mathematics on the intersection between pure axiomatization and applied geometry' (Rosenberg, 1992, p. 252).

(2) A second element in the concept of 'falsificationism' is the proposal that theories should be seriously tested so that, if possible, (it often won't be), verdicts can be reached on their falsity, or otherwise. It is surely very difficult not to dismiss, as outright obscurantist, objections to such a proposal. Surely *attempts* to falsify theories are a valuable procedure for acquiring vital knowledge and identifying vital ignorance.

It seems, however, often to be assumed that if a 'verdict' of 'guilty of falsity' is reached on a theory or system the convicted criminal must be immediately whisked off to the electric chair and never heard of again. No such sentence necessarily follows. The whole analogy with a legal process is misconceived. There are no police, no executioners and no legally appointed judges or juries in free, 'scientific' communities. Any free individual can reopen and reconsider the case on a 'theory', however widely and authoritatively it may be regarded as having been 'convicted' of falsity. Moreover, especially in a subject which has a historical dimension, once-and-for-all tests, or attempts at falsification will often, or even usually, prove quite inadequate. Frequent empirical testing and retesting will be necessary, especially in macroeconomics, if historical–institutional changes may be taking place which may render a particular theory inapplicable or false. (One only needs to consider what has happened to the theory of foreign-exchange markets in this century.)

'Falsificationism', including the falsifiability principle, is, in both or all senses, a normative doctrine. Professor Uskali Mäki appears to suggest that it is so much the worse for this entire doctrine that economists often, or even usually, do not practise it. Not necessarily so. It is so much the 'worse' for economics, *though in two very different senses*. In so far as, after all reasonable efforts, economists so often *can't* achieve clear-cut falsifications of their theories, this implies that economics is a very 'problematic' subject, in which much remains speculative – which is, of course, not the fault of economists. In so far, however, as some economists *do not attempt* to formulate their theories in a falsifiable way, *or* to falsify, or test empirically, their theories, but are satisfied with claiming abstract, mathematical 'rigour', or 'apodictic certainty' for them, they are deluding themselves and their customers about the significance of their work. For as Mäki puts it, they are proclaiming economics to be a subject which 'is not systematically constrained by empirical evidence' (1992, p. 89).

Two unjustifiable suppositions, for which little or no evidence is produced, seem to be playing an exaggerated role in the falsification debate: (1) that serious efforts to test or falsify important theories are generally not, as far as possible, being attempted; and (2) that widespread attempts to falsify, if seriously pursued, would result in the wholesale destruction of existing theories – as suggested by Professor Wade Hands (1992, p. 62). It might be observed at this point that Professor Frank Hahn has recently asserted: 'I know of no economic theory which all reasonable people would agree to have been falsified' (1993b, p. 5). Though not often agreeing with Hahn on methodological issues, I think he is pointing with some exaggeration, to the more likely possibility, and is less distant from reality than the scare-mongers afraid of wholesale destruction. For whatever verdict may be reached on a theory, which will often be more or less inconclusive, its sentence, or treatment, is a question of sentencing policy. In macroeconomics there have been, for some time, two opposed theories, or types of theory, both of which might be regarded as having been falsified in some important cases, though the institutional and psychological conditions in which tests have taken place have frequently been changing. Meanwhile, one or other type of theory may well have appeared, in specific cases, to have been the least weak theory available to policy-makers.

8 According to Popper, Hayek told him that it was Gottfried Haberler who called his (Hayek's) attention to *Logik der Forschung*. Incidentally, my most valuable encouragement at that time (1937) came from Haberler – to whom I was, and remain, deeply grateful – as I do also to Oskar Morgernstern, the very distinguished editor of the *Zeitschrift für Nationalökonomie* of Vienna, then in a brilliant period (before the Nazi takeover of 1938) as one of the outstanding economic journals of its day, the very opposite, of course, of a sectarian publication. I shall always remain grateful for having had several of my early writings published in the Austrian *Zeitschrift*. This gratitude has made it more difficult to accept some recent distortions of the Austrian tradition.

9 See Hutchison, 1978, pp. 204–5. In his remarkable article of 1937 Keynes had written: 'I accuse the classical economic theory of being itself one of those pretty polite techniques which tries to deal with the present by abstracting from the fact that we know very little about the future. . . . The orthodox theory assumes that we have a knowledge of the future of a kind quite different from that we actually possess' (1937, p. 192). In his earlier writings (*Monetary Theory and the Trade Cycle* and *Prices and Production*) Hayek had, of course, tried to cling to this orthodox, 'static' theory. But in 1937, he joined Keynes in insisting on empirical reality – as contrasted with his guide and mentor, Mises. Surely 1937 was a vintage year with regard to the clarification of the basic assumptions of economics.

10 See the illuminating discussion by Boland of 'Falsifiability versus Verifiability' and

'Tautology versus Testability' (1989, pp. 47–8 and 131–2). Hayek observed that tautologies cannot be falsified empirically because they do not 'forbid' anything empirical (only contradictions in terms). As Popper put it: 'Not for nothing do we call the laws of nature "laws": the more they prohibit the more they say' (1935, p. 73). This statement was quoted in my 1937a (p. 651). It is delightful to find Dr Claudia Loy (1988, p. 202) reaffirming the importance of Popper's *aperçu*. According to Sir Karl this may well have been the first time he was quoted in English.

11 See Hutchison 1937b ('Note on Uncertainty and Planning').

12 See Hicks (1933) and Myrdal (1933). Hayek himself in 'Economics and Knowledge' was following up some of his earlier writings on intertemporal equilibrium and business fluctuations.

13 It is only some of the more inflexible and persistent 'Modern Austrian' spokesmen who continue to deny that Hayek moved in a Popperian direction in, and after, his famous article of 1937. On the other hand, Professor Stephen Böhm (1982, p. 50) has stated: 'It is important to note that Hayek's views on methodology have changed drastically since the late thirties and early forties . . . crudely put, in a direction away from Mises and towards Popper'. Butler (1983, p. 137) notes that Hayek's views on the social sciences 'underwent a significant change in the early 1940s. . . . He was originally of the view that the methods of the social and natural sciences were completely different. . . . However, in the meantime, Sir Karl produced a convincing explanation of the essential unity of all scientific method which forced Hayek to reconsider'. Professor J. J. Klant has observed of Hayek how, 'influenced by Popper, he shows himself to be clearly aware of the importance of the criterion of falsifiability' (1984, p. 79). Mr John Gray has described how Hayek 'came to adopt Popper's proposal that falsifiability be treated as a demarcation criterion of science from non-science. Again Hayek followed Popper in qualifying his earlier Austrian conviction that there is a radical dualism of method as between natural and social science' (1986, pp. 19–20). (Incidentally, it is rather disappointing to find Mr Gray maintaining that I have not correctly identified 'Hayek's real debts to Popper', when his sole quotation from Hayek in support of his own account – which is very sound as far as it goes – is identical to one of my quotations (in 1981) (except for Gray's addition of an erroneous and ungrammatical 's').)

Dr Claudia Loy, in her distinguished and very thorough study (1988, pp. 15–16) gives a precise account of how, 'under the influence of Popper, Hayek, towards the end of the thirties, gradually modified his methodological views'. Incidentally, Dr Loy also remarks in a footnote on the reverse influence of Hayek on Popper, which must almost certainly have occurred in the course of such a lengthy exchange. Presumably most of Popper's acquaintance with economics and political economy came via Hayek.

Finally, it should be added that Graf (1978), in his detailed and discerning study of Hayek's views on prediction, suggests that, at some points, Hayek moved significantly towards Popper's views.

14 Hayek went on to claim that it was 'greatly to Mises's credit that he largely emancipated himself from that rationalist–constructivist starting-point but that task is still to be completed' (1992, p. 142). Hayek does not indicate where the evidence for this emancipation of Mises is to be found. It hardly seems that this emancipation has been enjoyed by some of the leading spokespersons for the Misesian wing of the 'Modern Austrian' movement.

15 Hayek's belated political concern was potentially of very great significance if such appalling and immeasurable political consequences may flow from excessively severe deflation. Lionel Robbins later described the policy conclusions which he (and Hayek) drew from the Austrian monetary, over-investment theory as 'the

greatest mistake of my professional career', and 'as unsuitable as denying blankets and stimulants to a drunk who has fallen into an icy pond, on the ground that his original trouble was overheating' (1971, p. 154).

16 It is, however, a total non-sequitur on Böhm's part to conclude from his perhaps justifiable statement that 'among the Austrians Mises was the sole advocate of praxeology' that 'there was nothing to escape from for Hayek' (1989b, p. 204n). Hayek made it perfectly clear that (as we have already quoted) for the formative decade of his career as an economist Mises was 'the chief guide in the development of my ideas' – no exception being made for methodological ideas. For his further non-sequitur – that 'in his philosophy of social science Popper is arguably more indebted to Hayek than vice versa' – Böhm here produces no evidence or arguments whatsover.

A further example of a strange, and even incomprehensible delusion (deriving, perhaps from that of Rothbard) regarding 'praxeology' and 'Austrian methodology', was the proposal that 'for ease of exposition, the terms "praxeology" and "Austrian methodology" will be used interchangeably', even while it was warned that this usage 'should not be taken to imply that all Austrians adhere to the praxeological position' (Caldwell, 1982, p. 119). What kind of 'ease of exposition', or what conceivable kind of justification there could be, for this terminological hijack, it is difficult to conceive. A decade later, however, according to Caldwell: 'Mises' particular version of praxeology is best viewed as an historical oddity', because of his 'misguided foray into a priorism' (v. de Marchi, ed., 1992, pp. 141–2). Fortunately it is not our task to explain how Caldwell's latest pronouncement squares (a) with his 'ease of exposition' of 1982; (b) his 'flirtation' with a priorism of 1984 (v. Caldwell, 1984); and (c) Stephen Böhm's view that Mises was the sole 'praxeologist' among the Austrians.

17 The 'dilemma' admitted by Professor Kirzner in 1976 (to which I referred in 1981) has, in nearly two decades, never been faced by modern Austrians. And there have been other contradictions. Dr Claudia Loy (1988, pp. 188–90) comments very gently on the 'extreme polarities' and outright contradictions at the heart of 'Modern Austrian' doctrines about expectations, equilibrium and predictability. She describes it, very politely, as 'astonishing' that such contradictions have not led to any reforms of Misesian claims to certainty. This condition of long-persisting contradictions between rival 'apodictic certainties', without any accepted means of resolving such dilemmas, seems to point to a state of methodological bankruptcy.

18 It seems that the 'insight', as Kirzner describes it, of the total unpredictability of human preferences, expectations, knowledge and, presumably, actions, may rather have originated in Germany than Austria. Ludwig Lachmann, one of the major exponents of the 'impossibility-of-prediction' idea, may have got it from his mentor Werner Sombart, the German historical economist in Berlin (see the introduction by W. E. Grinder to Lachmann, 1977). Incidentally, if, according to this allegedly 'Austrian' doctrine, the preferences, expectations and knowledge of human demanders and suppliers, including also presumably their actions, are totally unpredictable, then no kind of comprehensible economic order, through markets or any other institution, can be possible.

19 According to Rothbard: 'Not only did Adam Smith not create economic theory, but his economics was a large and calamitous step downward from the heights of the Continental tradition' (op. cit., p. 42). Certainly Smith was very far from advocating either anarchism or extreme laissez-faire. As Jacob Viner long ago pointed out – but as is often not recognized by contemporary enthusiasts who take Smith's name in vain – he supported a very considerable agenda for government, including, most surprisingly, legal restrictions on interest rates. It must be recognized,

also, that, regarding two fundamental analytical principles, *The Wealth of Nations* is seriously flawed: i.e. with regard to (a) utility and value; and (b) his saving-is-investing doctrine (shared with Turgot but not Quesnay). It is the superb weight and wisdom of Smith's historical and institutional analysis, together with his understanding of human nature which makes his book the greatest ever written on its subject. As Hayek put it: 'I may perhaps venture the opinion that *for all practical purposes* we can still learn more about the behaviour of men from *The Wealth of Nations* than from most of the more pretentious modern treatises on "social psychology" ' (1949, p. 11, italics added). Perhaps, methodologically, the greatness of *The Wealth of Nations* demonstrates how *relatively* little academic and mathematical 'rigour' really matters for 'real-world' economics.

20 While finishing off the final draft of this paper I have read the latest pronouncements from one of the leaders of Modern Austrian Economics: this is *The Meaning of Market Process*, by Professor Israel Kirzner (1992).

Some signs may indeed at last be discerned that some of the profound contradictions which have beset, since its birth, the 'Modern Austrian' movement are just beginning to be realized. There are, however, no signs whatsoever that these contradictions are being faced with anything like the seriousness they deserve.

The first sign of something amiss comes on the first page of the Preface (p. ix) when we are informed of:

> attempts, made in certain radically subjectivist contributions, to declare Austrian subjectivism to be thoroughly and fundamentally inconsistent with appreciation for market-equilibrating tendencies. The author firmly believes these attempts, although made in the course of valuable efforts to further the Austrian approach, nevertheless to be profoundly unfortunate and mistaken.
>
> (Kirzner, 1992, p. ix)

Typically, no further explicit mention is made throughout the whole volume of these 'profoundly unfortunate' mistakes, nor to the identity of their perpetrators. It can, and must, however, at once be pointed out that 'market-equilibrating tendencies' must inevitably depend on the assumption of *some* mutual predictabilities (as, of course, must be the possibility of any civilized arrangements). The 'radical subjectivists' deduce, inevitably and correctly, the inconsistency of market equilibrating tendencies with the assertion of total unpredictability regarding human expectations, preferences, choices and actions. This assertion has been put forward by various 'Modern Austrians' since the origins of the movement; not only by the late Ludwig Lachmann, George Shackle and Jack Wiseman, but by Israel Kirzner himself in his essay of 1976 in the original volume of essays (*v.* section VIII above).

Indeed, in this very volume, while initially condemning the conclusion quite logically drawn from a main 'radical subjectivist' principle, or assumption, Professor Kirzner commends approvingly Shackle's summary of this principle in the following terms: 'Moreover the essential unpredictability of the future is itself partly the consequence of our complete certainty that the future will be shaped, in large part, by intrinsically unpredictable future human decisions (p. 22). There is, therefore, a total contradiction between Kirzner's austere condemnation of the 'profoundly unfortunate and mistaken' attempts of 'radical subjectivists' (p. ix), and the loyal full approval and support for the doctrine of total unpredictability (p. 122), which Kirzner has been propagating since the beginnings of the 'Modern Austrian' movement in the 1970s.

A *second* profound conflict or incompatability has also surfaced – only, of course, to be immediately brushed aside. At long last the fundamental contradiction between the methodologies of Mises and Hayek is being, at least *mentioned* by Professor Kirzner, initially as 'something of a paradox':

> There can be no doubt that, on key elements in the Misesian system, Hayek is no Misesist at all. For Mises the possibility of economic understanding rests entirely on insights achieved *a priori*; his *praxeological* view of economic science expresses this a priorism in consistent and unqualified fashion. Yet at a relatively early and pivotal stage in his career as economist, Hayek made it clear that he was unable to follow his mentor in this regard. For Hayek the possibility of economic regularities capable of being comprehended by science rests squarely on an empirical basis. Unaided human logic, for Hayek, is able to generate no systematic truths concerning economic processes.

(p. 120)

In other words, Hayek's verdict on Misesian praxeology was (from 1937 onwards) that it was and always has been, essentially and totally erroneous and inadequate – which it remains nearly sixty years later. Such a verdict, however, causes 'Modern Austrians' no concern at all: Kirzner goes on, in fact, to claim some 'uniquely shared understanding' between Mises and Hayek, based on 'subjectivism' – a leading Modern Austrian slogan as to the definition of which they themselves have expressed the deepest uncertainties and disagreements (*v.* above pp. 198ff.). Kirzner proceeds to develop a distinction which he describes as one between 'static subjectivism' and 'dynamic subjectivism'. Terminologically this distinction, and the introduction of the adjectives 'static' and 'dynamic', seem highly unsuitable and misleading. What 'static subjectivism' seems to amount to is omniscient 'subjectivism', under conditions of certainty, which should be recognized as no 'subjectivism' at all. Anyhow, it is Lionel Robbins who is held responsible by Kirzner for the development of 'static subjectivism', and, indeed, anyone who has confessed to 'especial indebtedness' and 'general assistance' from Mises – however brief or slight – cannot possibly be spared a fair modicum of criticism (see Robbins, 1932, Preface). But the original, crudest and most dogmatic example of 'static subjectivism' (if such an apparently contradictory term is permissible) is certainly Misesian praxeology, which, of course, is still being clung to, limpet-like, by some 'Modern Austrians', nearly half a century after it was rejected, though all too gently, by the greatest Modern Austrian of them all.

May it not now seem, in conclusion, that Hayek would have performed an even greater service to economists, Austrian and non-Austrian, if, in 1937 and all the subsequent years, instead of employing such extreme gentleness and restraint in moving away so fundamentally from the doctrines of his senior officer, he had – however embarrassing it might have been – spelt out his profound rejection quite bluntly, forthrightly and repeatedly? At least the nature of the Mises–Hayek relationship, so inadequately understood in some Austrian circles even today, might have emerged rather more clearly.

REFERENCES

Ackermann, J. (1936). 'Annual Survey of Economic Theory', *Econometrica*, 4, pp. 97ff.

Barry, N. P. (1979). *Hayek's Social and Economic Philosophy*.

Blaug, M. (1993). Review of I. M. Kirzner, 'The Meaning of Market Process', *Economic Journal*, vol. 103, pp. 757–8.

Böhm, S. (1982). 'The Ambiguous Notion of Subjectivism', in *Method, Process and Austrian Economics*, ed. I. Kirzner, pp. 41ff.

Böhm, S. (1989a). 'Hayek on Knowledge, Equilibrium and Prices', *Wirtschafts-politischer Blatter*, 36, pp. 201ff.

Böhm, S. (1989b). 'Subjectivism and Post-Keynesianism', in *New Directions in Post-Keynesian Economics*, ed. J. Phebey.

Boland, L. A. (1989). *The Methodology of Economic Model-Building*.

Butler, E. (1983). *Hayek*.

Caldwell, B. (1982). *Beyond Positivism*.

Caldwell, B. (1984). 'Praxeology and its Critics', *History of Political Economy*, 16(3), 263.

Caldwell, B. (ed.) (1990). *Carl Menger and His Legacy in Economics*.

Caldwell, B. (1992a). 'Hayek the Falsificationist? A Refutation', *Research in the History of Economic Thought and Methodology*, 10, pp. 1ff.

Caldwell, B. (1992b). 'Commentary', in N. de Marchi, ed., pp. 135ff,

De Marchi, N. (ed.) (1992). *Post-Popperian Methodology of Economics*.

Dolan, E. G. (ed.) (1976). *The Foundations of Modern Economics*.

Graf, H.-G. (1978). *'Muster-Voraussagen' und 'Erklärungen des Prinzips' bei F. A. von Hayek*.

Gray, J. (1988). *Hayek on Liberty*. 2nd ed.

Hands, W. (1992). 'Reply', in N. de Marchi, ed., pp. 61ff.

Hayek, F. A. (1933). *Monetary Theory and the Trade Cycle* (German ed., 1929).

Hayek, F. A. (1935a). *Prices and Production*, 2nd ed.

Hayek, F. A. (1935b). *Collectivist Economic Planning*.

Hayek, F. A. (1937 and 1949). 'Economics and Knowledge', *Economica*, 4, pp. 33ff.; and in *Individualism and Economic Order*, 1949, pp. 33ff.

Hayek, F. A. (1937). *Profits, Interest and Employment*.

Hayek, F. A. (1941). 'The Counter-Revolution of Science', 3 parts, *Economica* 8, pp. 9ff.; pp. 119ff.; pp. 281ff.

Hayek, F. A. (1942/1943/1944). 'Scientism and the Study of Society', *Economica*, 9, pp. 267ff.; 10, pp. 234ff.; 11, pp. 241ff.

Hayek, F. A. (1943). 'The Facts of the Social Sciences', *Ethics*, 54, pp. 1ff.

Hayek, F. A. (1949). *Individualism and Economic Order*.

Hayek, F. A. (1964). 'The Theory of Complex Phenomena', in *The Critical Approach to Science and Philosophy: Essays in Honor of Karl Popper*, ed. M. Bunge.

Hayek, F. A. (1967). *Studies in Philosophy, Politics and Economics*.

Hayek, F. A. (1974). *The Pretence of Knowledge*, Nobel Lecture.

Hayek, F. A. (1978). *New Studies in Philosophy, Politics, Economics and the History of Ideas*.

Hayek, F. A. (1983). Letter to T. W. Hutchison, 15 May.

Hayek, F. A. (1984). *Money, Capital and Fluctuations*, ed. R. McLoughrey.

Hayek, F. A. (1992). *Collected Works*, vol. IV, ed. P. G. Klein.

Hicks, J. R. (1993). 'Gleichgewicht and Konjunktur', *Zeitschrift für Nationalökonomie*, 4, pp. 441ff.

Hutchison, T. W. (1935). 'A Note on Tautologies and the Nature of Economic Theory', *Review of Economic Studies*, 2, pp. 159ff.

Hutchison, T. W. (1937a). 'Theoretische Ökonomie als Sprachsystem', *Zeitschrift für Nationalökonomie*, 8, pp. 636ff.

Hutchison, T. W. (1937b). 'Note on Uncertainty and Planning', *Review of Economic Studies*, 5, pp. 72ff.

Hutchison, T. W. (1938). *The Significance and Basic Postulates of Economic Theory*.

Hutchison, T. W. (1953). *Review of Economic Doctrines, 1870–1929*.

Hutchison, T. W. (1977). *Knowledge and Ignorance in Economics*.

Hutchison, T. W. (1978a). *On Revolutions and Progress in Economic Knowledge*.

Hutchison, T. W. (1978b). Reviews of books by L. M. Lachmann, G. P. O'Driscoll, M. Rothbard and J. Jewkes, *Economic Journal*, 88, pp. 240ff.

Hutchison, T. W. (1979). Review of Hayek, 1978, *Economic Journal*, 89, pp. 179ff.

Hutchison, T. W. (1981). *The Politics and Philosophy of Economics*.

Hutchison, T. W. (1992a). Contribution to *Meeting in Memory of Professor Friedrich von Hayek*, London School of Economics.

Hutchison, T. W. (1992b). 'Hayek and "Modern Austrian" Methodology: Comment on a Non-Refuting Refutation', *Research in the History of Economic Thought and Methodology*, 10, pp. 17ff.

Keynes, J. M. (1937). 'The General Theory of Employment', *Quarterly Journal of Economics*, 51, pp. 209ff.

Kirzner, I. M. (1976). 'On the Method of Austrian Economics', in *The Foundations of Modern Austrian Economics*, ed. E. G. Dolan, pp. 40ff.

Kirzner, I. M. (1992). *The Meaning of Market Process*.

Kirzner, I. M., and Garrison, R. W. (1987). 'Hayek, F. A. von', *The New Palgrave Dictionary of Economics*.

Klant, J. J. (1984). *The Rules of the Game*.

Lachmann, L. (1977). *Capital, Expectations and the Market Process*, introduction by W. E. Grinder.

Langlois, R. N. (ed.) (1982). 'Austrian Economics as Affirmative Science', in *Method, Process and Austrian Economics*, ed. I. M. Kirzner, pp. 75ff.

Leslie, T. E. C. (n.d.). *Essays in Political and Moral Philosophy*.

Littlechild, S. C. (ed.) (1990). *Austrian Economics*, 3 vols.

Loy, C. (1988). *Marktsystem und Gleichgewichtstendenz*.

Machlup, F. (1979). 'F. A. von Hayek', *Encyclopedia of the Social Sciences*, vol. 18, pp. 274ff.

Mäki, U. (1993). 'Social Conditioning of Economics', in *Post-Popperian Methodology of Economics*, ed. N. de Marchi, pp. 65ff.

Mises, L. (1933). *Grundprobleme der Nationalökonomie*.

Mises, L. (1960). *Epistemological Problems in Economics*, trans. G. Reisman.

Mises, L. (1962). *The Ultimate Foundations of Economic Science*.

Mises, L. (1981). *Socialism*, trans. J. Kahane, Liberty Classics.

Myrdal, G. (1933). 'Der Gleichgewichtsbegrift als Instrument der geldtheoretischen Analyse', in *Beitrage zur Geldtheorie*, ed. F. A. Hayek.

Popper, K. R. (1935). *Logic der Forschung*.

Popper, Sir Karl (1992). Contribution to *Meeting in Memory of Professor Friedrich von Hayek*, London School of Economics.

Robbins, L. C. (1932). *Essay on the Nature and Significance of Economic Science*.

Robbins, Lord (1971). *Autobiography of an Economist*.

Rosenberg, A. (1992). *Economics – Mathematical Politics or Science of Diminishing Returns?*

Rothbard, M. (1970). *Power and Markets*.

Rothbard, M. (1976). 'Praxeology: the Methodology of Austrian Economics', in *The Foundations of Modern Austrian Economics*, ed. E. G. Dolan.

Rothbard, M. (1987). 'Adam Smith Reconsidered', *Austrian Economics Newsletter*, 9(1), pp. 5ff.

Stigler, G. J. (1965). *Essays in the History of Economics*.

Vaughn, K. (1990). 'The Mengerian Roots of the Austrian Revival', in *Carl Menger and his Legacy in Economics*, ed. B. Caldwell.

Weimer, W. B., and Palermo, D. S. (1982). *Cognition and the Symbolic Process*, 2 vols.

Wieser, F. (1927). *Social Economics*, trans. A. F. Hinrichs.

Wieser, F. (1929). *Gesammelte Abhandlungen*, ed. F. A. Hayek.

11

A METHODOLOGICAL CRISIS?[1]

I

For over ten years, a 'crisis' in economics, or in economic policy, or economic theory, was widely discussed. In 1972 the then Presidents of the Royal Economic Society and of Section F of the British Association both voiced a profound dissatisfaction with the state and methods of research and teaching in the subject. Then there was the persisting world-wide policy crisis, with more than usually fundamental conflict in views about how to meet it. Then again, in 1981, there appeared an interesting collection of essays, by mainly American *illuminati*, proclaiming 'the crisis in economic theory', and exhibiting a significant number of completely contradictory points of view as to how it should be overcome (see Phelps Brown, 1972, and Worswick, 1972; also Bell and Kristol, 1981).

This decade or more of crisis talk followed one of the most extraordinary intellectual booms in the history of the subject, which had lasted through much of the preceding quarter-century, a period of confident pretensions and prestige comparable only with that of the English classical boom of more than a century before. As with the fluctuations of the real economy, some connections may perhaps be traceable between the illusions, excesses and duration of the preceding boom, and the severity, despondency and persistence of the ensuing depression. In any case, it might well be maintained that, intellectually, much of this despondency has been quite inappropriate. 'Crises' in economic theory may mark a very real kind of progress – a progress of ignorance, or of the realization of the real state of knowledge. A 'crisis' may constitute a much healthier intellectual condition than the preceding 'boom', with its excessive pretensions and pretences, and even fantasies, of knowledge, and of the power to plan and regulate. Economics, or political economy, is perhaps a subject which is only in a healthy condition when it is in a pretty profound depression, that is, when the true extent of ignorance becomes more apparent.

However, among the various aspects of this crisis, something describable as a methodological crisis may be discerned which has a fundamental bearing on the other more widely debated facets. The main feature of this methodological

241

crisis has been latent, though occasionally recognized, for a very long time, and may be traced back to Ricardo, the great pioneer of the method of abstract deduction and 'model'-building on the basis of extremely simplified assumptions. This kind of crisis was in fact identified, or its possibility raised, by critics of the Ricardian or 'classical' method, in the course of two previous upheavals in the subject. It was recognized in the 1870s by Cliffe Leslie and in the 1930s by Keynes and others.

This methodological crisis centres on the simplified assumption regarding knowledge, expectations and uncertainty – or certainty – first explicitly deployed by Ricardo. What Joan Robinson admired so enthusiastically as Ricardo's 'habit of thought' (1973, p. 266) amounts to the deductive manipulation pre-eminently – but of course not only – of this postulate regarding knowledge, expectations and certainty. This assumption is easily the most ubiquitous, as well as the most richly consequential, of the various simplifying assumptions about human behaviour employed by theoretical or analytical economists. It is clearly implicated not only with such fundamental concepts as those of competition, equilibrium, maximization or optimization, but also with concepts like the rate of profit for an economy. It has had a central role in the use of the deductive method and abstract model-building in economics. It is relied on in much classical and neoclassical, as well as (paleo- and neo-) Ricardian and Marxian analysis. It pervades and infests most textbooks, large parts of which, including most of the geometrical exercises, could not be compiled without it. Even some quite recent fashionable developments, like much of the immense expansion of the analysis of political or social choice (which is discussed below) are fundamentally dependent on the same kind of vastly simplified assumption, and, of course, subject to the limitations such a simplification imposes.

The most criticizable and unrealistic feature of 'The Economic Man' is not his materialism, or selfishness, which can be corrected for. His most fatal limitation, from the point of view of real-world applicability, is his omniscience. Moreover, it is this assumption about knowledge which keeps the analysis rigidly static, and it has to be abandoned if there is to be any advance towards a truly dynamic theory. As F. H. Knight observed, the presence, or absence, of uncertainty is 'the most important underlying difference between the conditions which theory is compelled to assume and those which exist in fact' (1921, p. 51). The methodological crisis, therefore, is not a crisis simply of one particular brand or school of economics, or of political economy of one or other political stripe. It is not a crisis simply of 'orthodox' economics, on the one hand, or of 'unorthodox' on the other, however these are defined. Perhaps the only kind of economics not today involved in this methodological crisis is historical or institutional economics, whose pioneer in this country, Cliffe Leslie, discerned just over a hundred years ago something of the underlying, or impending, problem in his remarkable paper 'The Known and the Unknown in the Economic World' (1879).

II

The abstract deductive method, as classically codified by Senior, and now-adays elaborated with vast displays of almost totally irrelevant mathematical rigour, was that of deducing conclusions, or predictions, from a small number of allegedly obvious, common-sense assumptions, of which overwhelmingly the most important regarding economic behaviour was, as Senior himself expressed it, that 'every man desires to obtain additional Wealth with as little sacrifice as possible' (1836, p. 28).

But nothing can be deduced regarding people's actions or decisions simply and solely from a generalization about their desires or aims. A further fundamental postulate has to be included that people have the requisite *knowledge* to fulfil this aim, or that their expectations regarding relevant historical developments turn out to be correct. It is extraordinary how far, for decade after decade, the essential role of this extreme assumption regarding knowledge, expectations and certainty was succesfully overlooked by the followers of the Ricardo–Senior method – classical, neoclassical and Marxian. The removal of this comprehensive simplification largely removed with it the possibility of deriving significant general conclusions or predictions about people's choices, decisions or behaviour by the method of abstract deduction from a small number of obvious, common-sense postulates. For as soon as one cannot, or does not, continue to assume that people make the single 'right' or maximizing decision, one has to discover and justify the particular decision which they will make of the virtually infinite number of 'wrong' ones.

Deductive analysis cannot significantly help in discovering which particular kind of ignorance, or erroneous expectations, may be operative. Either an assumption has to be introduced on the basis of 'hunch', or it has to be 'plucked from the air', to use Sir Henry Phelps Brown's expressive phrase (1972, p. 3); or it will have to be tentatively formulated as an empirical, historical or institutional proposition about patterns of behaviour, of much less generality than the traditional fundamental assumption. Inevitably, a considerable shift of method would be involved, for the significant kinds of uncertainty, the patterns of expectations and the kinds of ignorance and error are constantly shifting with historical and institutional change. As Herbert Simon has emphasized, research into conditions where uncertainty, ignorance and erroneous expectations prevail,

> requires a basic shift in scientific style, from an emphasis on deductive reasoning within a tight system of axioms to an emphasis on detailed empirical exploration. . . . Undoubtedly the uncongeniality of the latter style to economists has slowed the transition. . . .

> As economics becomes more and more involved in the study of uncertainty, more and more concerned with the complex actuality of business decision-making, the shift in programme will become inevitable. Wider and wider areas of economics will replace the over-simplified assumptions

243

of the situationally constrained omniscient decision-maker with a realistic (and psychological) characterization of the limits on Man's rationality, and the consequences of those limits for his economic behaviour.

(1976, pp. 147–8)

However, the Ricardo–Senior abstract-deductive method is, in many ways, much less expensive than the institutional and historical alternatives, both in research and in teaching and examining. So persistent attempts are made to justify its importance and prestige as the programme to which quantitatively and qualitatively a major share of research and teaching should be directed.

One long-standing argument to this end invokes the 'optimistic' idea (the adjective is, or was, Joan Robinson's) of successive approximations or decreasing abstraction. The idea is, or was, that one should start from some deliberately over-simplified case, introduce successive complications step by step, and so approach or arrive at the real world, or something usefully approximating to it. Up to a point, this kind of procedure seems sometimes to have worked out. It was used, for what it was worth, in the opening chapter of Ricardo's *Principles*, with regard to the extreme abstractions of his labour-embodied theory of value. Ricardo started by mentioning Adam Smith's primitive example of the beaver-and-deer hunting economy, and then attempted, surely not very usefully or successfully, to approach the real world by introducing some of the complications involved in the use of capital. Also, in his *Elements*, Walrus proceeded (less unsuccessfully) in a somewhat similar way, starting from the extreme simplification of two-party and two-commodity exchange, and introducing step by step the successive complications of production, capital and money.

But for the most part this 'optimistic' procedure just has not worked out at all fruitfully, and, as regards our fundamental assumption about knowledge, expectations and certainty, *it seems that it simply cannot work out*. No fruitful way has emerged of gradually relaxing the certainty assumption step by step, or of getting from the first approximation to a second approximation significantly less distant from the real world.

Perhaps the most far-fetched attempt to justify the continuing employment of extremely simplified assumptions is the confused and confusing doctrine that the unrealism of assumptions simply does not matter. With regard to our fundamental assumption about knowledge, expectations and certainty, the implication (not always recognized) of this extraordinary, but understandably long-fashionable, doctrine seems to be that the ignorance, erroneous expectations and uncertainty of the real world (as contrasted with the full knowledge, correct expectations and certainty assumed in the model) have negligible effects on real-world outcomes. There is even some obscurity as to how some of the most serious politico-economic problems of the real world, including aggregate fluctuations and unemployment, can arise if politico-economic decisions are generally governed by 'rational' expectations – a highly imprecise term, and one admitted by those who use it to be unrealistic.[2]

However, for decade after decade, exponents of the programme of starting from extreme abstractions, and either asserting that the utter unrealism of the assumptions simply does not matter or promising that, by successive approximations, gradually the significant complexities of the real world will be accounted for in the model, have attempted, or claimed, to overcome the obvious limitations imposed by the original simplification. Thirty or forty years ago, it was 'welfare' analysis, and before that imperfect competition, which, it was promised, would achieve a breakthrough. More recently some champions of general-equilibrium analysis have promised highly significant advances; to discuss them may require the highest expertise, but it takes little more than common sense and attention to past experience to see that they are hardly likely to be achieved.

It must, however, certainly be recognized that the kind of theory, or analysis, which has emerged from this fundamental simplification did yield some genuine and lasting advances in understanding, and in prediction or predictive potential, when applied loosely, discreetly and with restraint. If one does not take the view that over, say, the past two centuries economists, by the application of their theories and analyses, have almost completely failed to contribute to the task of less unsuccessful policy-making, then such contributions as have been delivered must surely, to a significant extent, have been derived from theories or models in some way dependent on this fundamental simplification.

But some four qualifications may be made. Firstly, the theories, analyses or models have often *not* been applied with discretion and restraint. The basic over-simplification involved has spawned other over-simplifications. For example, the concentration on optimization, or maximization, has led, on both sides of the political argument, to gross misconceptions as to the nature of real-world policy issues. It can hardly be denied that the idea originated by Smith and Turgot of general interdependence, and even of a kind of tendency towards equilibrium, has been profoundly illuminating, and even the elaborate development of general-equilibrium analysis by Léon Walras may have yielded valuable conclusions. But it now seems to be regarded as the outstanding contribution to the understanding of real-world policy issues, forthcoming from the 'considerable', or even 'major intellectual', achievement represented by contemporary hyper-rigorous and sophisticated GE analysis, that it has definitively demonstrated 'that leaving allocation to market forces will not guarantee an optimal solution'. Surely, however, no one except an extreme apriorist, or someone intoxicated by the exuberance of their own mathematical virtuosity, could ever have entertained such a misconception as to the nature of the real-world policy issue. Regarding claims that in the real world there is 'a beneficent role for the invisible hand' (Bell and Kristol, 1981, p. 185), the introduction of 'a guarantee of an optimal solution' is vastly irrelevant and misleading.[3] Though realizable in the fantasy world of omniscience and certainty, guaranteed optima and maxima will always be up in the mathematical–Utopian clouds, above a world in which ignorance, uncertainty and erroneous expectations are and will be, to put it mildly, of some importance. For anyone who happens to be interested in real-world problems, the immensely complex and largely empirical and institutional question is whether or not the invisible hand may, over large areas, perform somewhat less unsuccessfully, oppressively or even disastrously than the historically and politically available forms of government regulation. Plentiful recent evidence would appear to suggest that this is not too ambitious a target at which the invisible hand might frequently be allowed to direct itself.

Secondly, though a significant part of any contribution to more successful policy-making, which may have been forthcoming from formal economic theory or analysis, to some extent depended on one fundamental simplification regarding knowledge, expectations and certainty, this source of insight – such as it may have been – has surely long been exhausted. For perhaps something approaching a hundred years, this orange has been squeezed dry, and what has emerged since has been mainly the squeaking of mathematical pips. Of course, further insights of this broad elementary kind may continue to be forthcoming, and may even long continue to provide a major part of such policy guidance as may be based on formal economic theorizing or analysis. But it does not seem reasonable to expect or promise that any further new conclusions are likely to emerge from still more rigorous or refined analysis, mathematical or otherwise, which will be of relevance to real-world policy-making.

An interesting example of how the introduction of the perfect-knowledge assumption can rapidly produce an abundance of irrelevant, vacuous 'rigour', with a minimum of real-world applicability, is offered by some of the developments of public-choice analysis over the last two decades. Bruno Frey has pointed out how Schumpeter, using a predominantly institutional method, had anticipated nearly all the important contributions of contemporary public (or social) choice analysis (1981, pp. 126ff.). But Schumpeter included, and emphasized, the possibility of mistakes and fraudulence (i.e. that a significant number of people do get fooled a significant amount of the time). On the other hand, more recently the field had been taken over largely by 'rigorous' but irrelevant analysis based on the assumption of correct expectations or full knowledge. As a result, Frey maintains:

> Scientific journals containing articles on political economy – in particular *Public Choice* – have become less and less interesting to read for anybody who wants to know about the real world. . . .
> Schumpeter argues that unfair and fraudulent competition between parties and interest groups cannot be excluded if the analysis is not to end up as an unrealistic ideal. . . . But this is exactly where the axiomatic

public choice theory of party competition has come to! . . . As a result, most governments which have ever existed anywhere in the world are excluded from application of the models.

(1981, pp. 134 and 137)

Thirdly, the fundamental over-simplification, pushed precisely and rigorously to its logical conclusion, simply rules out many or most of the serious economic problems of the real world. Under these assumptions economic processes take place in a kind of historical and institutional vacuum. In particular, among the institutions excluded is that of money, or a money and banking framework, and even, perhaps, firms. So long as economic theory and analysis is kept bottled up, with mathematical rigour, in this vacuum, it can hardly be hoped that its contribution to the economic issues of the day will make progress.

Fourthly and finally, the simplified, or over-simplified, model, based on knowledge, certainty and correct expectations, may have been more of a justifiable simplification, or genuine first approximation, in the (in some ways) apparently less unstable world of a hundred years ago. Then, in this country, there was something approaching price stability, and something approaching that 'stable general culture' which Pigou assumed to be a presupposition of the economic theory and analysis of his younger days. A hundred to a hundred and fifty years ago, when according to T. H. Huxley political economy was 'a peculiarly Anglican subject', it may have been considerably less unjustifiable that the far-reaching assumption pervading so much of its theory and analysis was one which largely precluded instability. A comparatively stable price-level, and a comparatively stable 'general culture', may well have provided the climate in which knowledge and expectations, though far, indeed, from the requirements of the over-simplified assumption (with regard, for example, to the recurring crises of the business cycle) nevertheless diverged less completely and continuously from it, so that the assumption of perfect knowledge could more or less validly be regarded as a genuine 'first approximation'.

III

In the course of the crisis in economics which took place in the 1930s the fundamental postulate about knowledge, expectations and uncertainty came under serious scrutiny from a number of economists, including Keynes. Briefly in his *General Theory* (1936), and more forcefully in an article of 1937, Keynes emphasized how this fundamental over-simplification more or less assumed out of existence the very serious real-world problems which were supposed to be under examination. Denouncing the extreme unrealism of the fundamental assumption, Keynes described the edifice of theory based on it as 'a pretty polite technique' which 'tries to deal with the present by abstracting from the fact that we know very little about the future'; and further that 'the

247

hypothesis of a calculable future leads to a wrong interpretation of the prin-ciples of behaviour' (1937, pp. 186 and 192).

But taking his writings as a whole Keynes did not place the main emphasis of his criticism of what he called 'classical theory' on this fundamental over-simplification. Nor, for over a quarter of a century after his death, did Keynesian writers focus significantly on the limitations of this basic postulate. This fundamental line of criticism continued to be comparatively neglected, in spite of the writings of George Shackle, when, after the post-war adjustment process, a remarkable period followed of what looked like something approaching aggregate equilibrium, with very low levels of unemployment and only comparatively mild inflation. Criticism of the fundamental assump-tion regarding knowledge, expectations and uncertainty only re-emerged, among most Keynesians, with the profound maladjustments of the 1970s, and when a crisis in the subject itself was widely recognized.

Keynes himself had met simply by 'hunch' and brilliant improvisation the fundamental methodological problem to which he had called attention. He proceeded to introduce, at the relevant points, crucial assumptions regarding knowledge, expectations, uncertainty and maximization, basing these on his own insights regarding the particular processes and institutions of the Britain of his day, rather than on any more systematic investigation. There was nothing else he could have done in order to get the results he wanted. In this way he reached his conclusions: (1) on the impossibility, by cutting money wages, of achieving the cut in real wages required for a reduction of unem-ployment; and (2) as to how this necessary cut in real wages *could* be brought about by an expansion of aggregate demand. In this way Keynes presumably provided a relevant and serviceable theory *for the Britain of his day – especially at a time of catastrophically falling prices.* But it was very far from being a 'General Theory', because the assumptions regarding knowledge and expectations on which it was based were not general. Methodologically, Keynes was replacing a fundamental postulate which, although it constituted such an extreme over-simplification, nevertheless possessed, for what it was worth, a kind of broad generality, with assumptions which were inevitably much less general, and much more historically and institutionally limited, or relative.

Since Keynes, various attempts have been made to replace the classical general over-simplication with some other over-simplification, such as adaptive or rational expectations, so as to provide a basis for further abstract model-building. But as has been observed:

> It is one thing to reject the 'perfect knowledge' assumption, but it is another entirely different thing to make a case for any given alternative.
> (Meckling, 1978, p. 103; see Hutchison, 1981, p. 247)

For while there is only one way of being perfectly right, there are countless different ways of being somewhat or entirely wrong. The rational-expectations assumption, in its various forms, attempts to reconstruct the classical abstract-deductive method and conclusions. At least it has the virtue of recognizing the possibility that people may learn, and may possess knowledge as accurate as, or less inaccurate than, that of the government. But, *in its more extreme form*, the rational-expectations postulate is simply another sweeping over-simplification on which abstract-deductive analysis can elaborate and proliferate. It seeks to cope with the serious real-world questions, which it is presumed to be answering, by assuming that, in the main, they do not, or cannot, arise. That was how classical orthodoxy, as represented by J. S. Mill, treated the business cycle, surely a serious recurring problem of instability which was hardly compatible with strictly 'rational' expectations.

Moreover, there seems to be something of a paradox involved in reintroducing such an assumption as that of rational expectations at a time when the classical assumption, or condition, of something approximating to peacetime price stability may have disappeared for a long time to come, with constantly and very sharply changing rates of inflation the more realistic prospect. Furthermore, much more frequent changes in monetary institutions and their management have replaced what, down to about a decade ago, were relatively much less unstable arrangements. Patterns of expectations, and of reactions to changes, are bound to be frequently shifting, so that the historical and institutional element in economic processes, and in their explanation, obviously becomes increasingly important.

What has also not been sufficiently recognized is the profound methodological contrast between the structure of elementary microeconomics and that of the macroeconomics built up in the last half-century originally round Keynes's *General Theory*. The abstract-deductive method based on the fundamental Ricardian assumption of perfect knowledge, correct expectations and maximization under certainty, and drawing also on such basic generalizations as diminishing utility, and variable factor proportions, worked effectively in the construction of an elaborate edifice of general theory and analysis broadly applicable at widely differing times and places. It is based on a core of propositions of the widest generality, which yields conclusions, or allocation formulae, certainly somewhat tenuous in content, and sometimes reduced to tautologies, but which, for what they are worth, have some validity for Robinson Crusoe, a private firm or a socialist planner. There simply has not been discovered, and very probably does not exist, any such core of general propositions on which to build, or from which to deduce, a body of macroeconomic theory of comparable generality and significance.

It may be that this contrast between the structure and generality of microeconomics and of macroeconomics should not be pressed in the most absolute black-and-white terms. But it is certainly one of widely different shades of grey. Keynes attempted to fill the fundamental void in the foundations of his macroeconomics with what he called his 'Fundamental Psychological Law' regarding income and consumption, 'upon which we are entitled to depend with great confidence both *a priori* from our knowledge of human nature and from the detailed facts of experience' (1936, p. 96). Subsequently there were the various forms of 'Phillips curves'. But such propositions, though not useless, simply do not possess the generality and reliability, or alternatively the empirical content, to provide the basic postulates for a significant body of theory.

Finally, Paul Davidson may, of course, validly claim that:

> For members of the Post Keynesian schools the notions discussed above
> – historical time, uncertainty, expectations, political and economic
> institutions (especially money and forward contracts) – represent funda-
> mental characteristics of the world we inhabit – *the real world.*
>
> (Davidson, 1981, p. 171)

But if the problems to which these vital features of 'the real world' give rise are to be grappled with, then the change in methodological style, emphasized by Simon, will have to be more fundamental than it has been undertaken so far. What Joan Robinson so ardently admired as the 'precious heritage – Ricardo's habit of thought', which depended to a large extent on his assumption of perfect knowledge and correct expectations – will have to be jettisoned. The aim will also have to be abandoned of establishing or re-establishing a, or the, 'General Theory' of macroeconomics (which most Keynesians, post- or neo-, seem to suppose that Keynes originally discovered); that is, if it is genuinely intended to recognize 'historical time' as an essential part of the real economic world. It has recently been stated that 'Keynes insisted on treating every patient as a separate problem rather than as one of a series of standard cases.' The Keynes here under discussion was, of course, not Maynard, but his brother Geoffrey. Economists may not have to go as far as did the surgeon Geoffrey Keynes in treating every case, or economy, at each different time in its history, as a separate problem. But, to take account of the historical element and 'historical time', they will need, in macroeconomics, to go much further in Geoffrey's direction than did Maynard with his attempt at *The* (or *a*) *General Theory*.

IV

Our discussion up to now of the existence, nature and source of a 'methodological crisis' has proceeded on the basis of some implicit assumptions regarding the objectives of economics, or of what economists do. Such assumptions hardly ever come to the surface, and might be claimed to go without saying. But there can hardly be a crisis, methodological or otherwise, in a subject unless there are objectives which are not being adequately, and within the limits of the possible, attained. Certainly, no crisis, methodological or theoretical, needs to be held to exist *simply* because economists cannot provide more or less agreed solutions showing how the appetites and ambitions of politicians and public are reconcilable with existing, or acceptable, institutions.

But for most of the history of political economy and economics, from Adam Smith to Keynes (and especially *before* Smith in the period of those whom Schumpeter called the 'consultant administrators'), one would suppose that a, or the, overriding aim was to discover, or construct, theories which would contribute, directly or indirectly, to less unsuccessful policy-making. That has been the presupposition underlying this chapter. But although this traditional assumption dominated until recent decades, today there seems to be a good deal of vagueness, and even fundamental disagreement, about objectives (which confusion may be another facet of the methodological crisis). This intellectual situation seems to have been growing up gradually, but with a considerable acceleration in roughly the last quarter of a century, with the immense growth in the number of academic economists. Ten years ago Sir Henry Phelps Brown and G. D. N. Worswick were complaining powerfully that much of economic teaching and research, and much of that claiming and receiving the highest priority and prestige, was based on such extreme abstractions, so remote from reality, as to signify an abandonment of the traditional objective of economists to construct theories which could contribute to less unsuccessful real-world policy-making. More recently we have the authority of Sir John Hicks for the observation that 'there is much of economic theory which is pursued for no better reason than its intellectual attraction; it is a good game' (1979, p. viii).

Now there is no reason at all for supposing that any crisis, methodological or otherwise, exists, or need arise, with regard to the pursuit of 'good games', or with regard to 'economics for pleasure' (the title of one of George Shackle's books). As regards 'much economic theory', there is no need to question the further serviceability of the fundamental Ricardian simplification about knowledge, expectations and certainty, in so far as 'a good game' is the object of the exercise (like the game described by Mark Blaug as 'playing tennis with the net down'). In fact, 'the Ricardian habit of thought' will doubtless continue to be of great service in promoting 'good games'. But a methodological crisis has, and can only have, arisen if economic theorizing is regarded as furthering other objectives than that of providing 'a good game', such as contributing, in one way or another, to more successful real-world policy-making.

Now though one may possess one's own quite strong views as to what the aims of economics and economic theorizing ought to be, one should be firmly opposed to any dogmatic or censorious conclusions as to what should be the aims of other serious academic people, even if these amount to games-playing, or 'economics for fun', *provided that such an objective is quite clearly and frankly avowed.* In the first place, there are strong grounds in academic freedom for protecting serious academic interests which may, like pure mathematics, have no apparent relevance or relation to any kind of real-world fruitfulness or policy-making. Furthermore, it may be that the turn towards games-playing in 'much' of economic theory stems to some extent from a not completely unjustifiable scepticism about the contribution of further economic theorizing

251

to more successful real-world policy-making: either because such theoretical advances are more or less out of reach, or because, whatever advances in relevant economic theorizing *might* be achieved, these will inevitably come through – the present democratic policy-making process being what it is – in some crude, oversimplified form which might well bring more harm than good. Already, nearly fifty years ago, in his later, more sceptical years, the once highly optimistic Pigou was expressing profound pessimism about the market for economists' wares (1939, pp. 220–1).

Moreover, one should not be dogmatic as to what may or may not contain a contribution to more successful real-world policy-making. Eventually a model or theory, however abstract or simplified, *may* find a real-world applicability and policy relevance not discernible at the present time. There is a considerable grey area here in which it might be dangerous and damaging to eliminate over-censoriously new theoretical developments, even though they may appear extremely over-simplified and remote from the real world.

However, we cannot often establish this kind of case on behalf of Hicks's 'much' (and, it would seem, more and more) economic theorizing that is being pursued more or less as a good game. It *might* perhaps sometimes be got away with if there were sufficient explicit frankness as to how extreme and consequential were the degrees of abstraction and unrealism often being employed, and if the long record of unfulfilled promises of eventual, real-world fruitfulness was acknowledged, not only in respect of opposing or contrasting politico-economic theories but in respect of one's own. For whatever else it may, or may not, be able to achieve, or at least seek, academic economics should surely give the highest priority to maintaining standards of intellectual lucidity and frankness in research and teaching, in respect of the significance, and applicability to the real world, of its theories.

We have already mentioned the kind of intellectual fudging and mudging with regard to 'the very great practical importance' (or lack thereof) of recent refinements in general-equilibrium analysis. Similar questions may be asked about the extreme other-worldly abstractions of 'Neo-Ricardian' analysis, which shares to some extent with general-equilibrium analysis the same Ricardian over-simplification regarding knowledge and certainty. It can hardly be for any testable, empirical or predictive content which could contribute to policy-making in any kind of real-world economy that neo-Ricardian analysis has been so assiduously cultivated for two decades or more. Indeed its defenders can be found denouncing as 'instrumentalist' any appeal to such criteria – while also making use of the usual self-sealing protective ploy that critics cannot be understanding the ultra-refined intellectual *mystique* involved.

Unlike, however, general-equilibrium analysis, neo-Ricardian analysis possesses the distinctive and, to some, highly attractive feature of a highly charged ideological penumbra which diffuses a pungent aroma of politico-moralistic disapproval of the distribution of income in a market economy, as contrasted, apparently, with that in some kind of centrally regulated East-

European economy. Certainly the intensity of the ideological input contrasts strikingly with the tenuousness of the testable empirical or predictive output. But this blend of refined and arcane academic preciosity, with its overtones of austere politico-moralistic disapproval, obviously possesses powerful attractions for those for whom mere empirical reality comes in a very poor third. Anyhow the 'neo-Ricardian' analysis certainly scores very highly if the suggestion of value-judgements, or the diffusion of an ideological aroma, of one particular flavour or another, by those who regard their own expertise as entitling them to act as 'critics and judges',[4] is the main object of the exercise. There certainly need be no question of any 'crisis' in this particular sector of the subject if this is the only kind of objective being pursued.

Moreover even some of those who seem clearly to hold to the traditional aim of contributing (somehow) to real-world policy-making may well consider no kind of theoretical or methodological crisis to exist, *if* they are sufficiently confident in their own particular brand of theory to be able totally to disregard the wide range of contrasting or contradictory doctrines. For such economists, any crisis that exists is not theoretical or methodological, but one of public relations or public influence: that is, some other brand of theory is influencing policy, which derives, not from serious economists, such as themselves, but from 'cranks', 'amateurs', unprofessional 'dilettanti', non-mathematicians, or political ideologues of the wrong colour. Many Marxians, or neo-Ricardians, *some* neo- or post-Keynesians (or Keynesians, *tout simple*), *some* rational-expectations theorists, or general-equilibrium theorists (affirming confidently 'the very great practical importance' of their ideas), *some* Austrians, too, seem to share, more or less, the traditional aim of contributing to real-world policy-making; but they certainly do not seem prepared to recognize the existence of any methodological or theoretical crisis.

For example, a few years ago Lord Kaldor announced as follows:

> We are on the verge of evolving an integrated theory of inflation which should be capable of forging the tools necessary for securing prosperity combined with price stability, partly through intervention in commodity markets and partly through incomes policies in the industrial countries.
>
> (1978, p. xxxviii)

No reports seem to be to hand as to whether 'we' are now still 'on the verge', or have now crossed the verge. But there can surely have been no theoretical or methodological crisis for Lord Kaldor, or for those who agreed with him, while certainly he held wholeheartedly to the view that economic theorizing should contribute to more successful real-world policy-making.

V

Not only are there the obvious strident disagreements about policies and the theories underlying them; not only is there a great deal of vagueness and latent disagreement regarding the objectives of economic theorizing; there is just as much, or more, vagueness or disagreement among economists who apparently hold to the traditional objective of contributing to real-world policy-making, as regards how, or by what precise steps or methods, this aim can validly be approached. In some cases there seems to be a readiness to proclaim the traditional objective, while trying, at the same time, to cling to a kind of intellectual purity which effectively precludes the most important means by which theory *can* contribute to policy: that is, by improved prediction. But if one really wills the end of contributing to policy-making, one must recognize the possibility of really effective means to promoting this end, or public confusion will be further heightened.

The epistemological links between theorizing and policy-making are a large and complex area which belongs, at least in part, to philosophers. But only in part, because the vital task remains with economists of defining and interpreting the theories, arguments and propositions which have to be epistemologically assessed, as well as the objectives which policies are claimed to promote. On the subject of this demarcation question, a rather brusque exchange took place in the columns of *The New York Times* (3 January 1982), in the course of a debate on 'The Meaning of Social Justice', between the Keynesian, Nobel Laureate, Yale economist, James Tobin, and the conservative, individualist, Harvard philosopher, Robert Nozick. At one point Tobin felt moved to exclaim 'There's nothing more dangerous than a philosopher who's learned a little bit of economics.' To which Nozick replied, 'Unless it's an economist who hasn't learned any philosophy.'

Certainly the dangers from both of these types are immense. On the one side, the history of political economy and economics is full of examples of economists taking up, or making up, bits of philosophy, epistemology or methodology, to support their own particular brand of theorizing, or to boost their scientific prestige or professional status or influence. On the other side, that of non-economist philosophers, there may be failures in interpreting economic theories due to a lack of grasp of the full politico-economic context. Alternatively, philosophers may take too much at face value the first political economist they meet whose views seem politically sympathetic. Again, there are obvious dangers in applying some very general philosophical viewpoint without allowance for certain highly special characteristics of political economy and economics, notably its intense and continual involvement in political issues and even in party politics. In another direction, those philosophers of science who have constructed their methodological doctrines from the example of the natural sciences, especially physics, may put forward as positive analysis, or as methodological norms, ideas which are hardly applicable to economics, because – among other reasons – of its historical dimension. Alternatively, some philosophers seem to go over the top in the opposite direction, in denying *any* parallels between economics and the natural sciences as regards methods

254

or criteria, which may be even more dangerous than exaggerating the parallels and similarities.

But someone or other has got to take the risks and face up to the dangers, if a whole complex of fundamental questions is not to be left obscure and un-answered, questions to which reasonably sound answers are essential for the accomplishment of the traditional aims of the subject. These questions relate to precisely how contributions to less unsuccessful economic policy-making should be, or can be, derived from economic theories. There appears to be a great deal of disagreement and fuzziness on this question, in so far as it is explicitly dealt with.

One of the subjects on which both fuzziness and outright contradictions are frequent is that of prediction: whether it should be an aim or claim of econo-mists, and how far economists can claim to provide effective guidance for policy-makers if they entirely reject prediction (see Hutchison, 1977, chapter 2). Certainly the spectacle seems educationally dubious: distinguished pro-fessors of the subject proclaim the impossibility of effective prediction in economics, while some of their brightest pupils go straight off to posts as 'economists', in government or business, in which their prime task, which they will be paid to perform, will be to contribute vitally to the allegedly impossible.

But there is another question which is, perhaps, still more fundamental, which is concerned with the nature, or source, of the authority which a pro-fessional economist, or 'expert', can claim on the basis of his command of economic theory. At present there seems to be a growing rejection, as 'positiv-ist', of the kind of discipline which consists in requiring the formulation of theories in a testable, refutable or falsifiable way, and in seeking, as strenuously as is feasible, to test, refute and falsify. It is observed, quite correctly, that this is often or usually extremely difficult, or sometimes, practically speaking, outright impossible. (However, there is always the further (positivist?) norm, in the case of inadequate testing, of *withholding judgement*, which is impossible for politicians, but perfectly feasible for academics.)

Yet, while this kind of discipline is being rejected, no other effective code of discipline, such as roughly obtains in the natural sciences, is being proposed in its place, nor any 'principle of demarcation' as Popper called it. But because of its intense and unrelenting involvement in highly political, or party-political, issues, there is probably *no* subject claiming academic status which requires more urgently some kind of demarcation principle or code of discipline.

Nevertheless, some recent writings on the methodology of economics dis-play a marked and increasing support for methodological permissiveness, and a rejection of any discipline through testing, falsifiability and falsification, as well as the dismissal of prediction as an aim. A position is thus becoming established which amounts, virtually, to that of 'anything goes', or the methodological anarchism of Feyerabend, without his explicit, cheerfully irresponsible abandon. But it must be noted that Feyerabend, in proclaiming his message of 'anything goes', was quite explicitly concerned with undermining the public influence of natural scientists, who he thinks are too 'pushy', and whom he regarded as having grossly misused their influence and prestige. But if claims to scientific discipline, or the possibility thereof, are undermined, then simultaneously claims to influence based on some kind of scientific authority, and indeed science's *raison d'être*, are also undermined. Economists must face the dilemma that in so far as they reject such disciplines as are implied in the obligations of testing and testability, or falsifiability and attempting to falsify, with no other proposed disciplinary code existing, in a subject so intensely involved in party politics, they are undermining claims to influence or to some kind of 'authority'. Some, economists and non-economists, might heartily welcome such an abandonment, but hardly anyone would do so who holds that the main aim of economic theorizing is to promote more successful policy-making.

Past economists, from physiocrats and Ricardians onwards, have claimed, rightly or wrongly, but sincerely, that they were concerned with a 'scientific' *discipline* (even one producing 'laws') and have claimed public influence on that basis. If it now emerges that no attempts at discipline, or at demarcation of 'science' from 'non-science', can be valid, or worth attempting, then it hardly seems that any claims to influence or authority can be upheld.

However, we now conclude by putting forward another aim for economists, which might be regarded as especially appealing, or even obligatory, for academics: that is the maximum feasible frankness and clarity in stating the aims and objectives of their subject and their theorizing: and in stating how far these aims are being, or are likely to be, fulfilled, together with *the kind of discipline* on which their conclusions are based. This, in other words – to quote the concluding line of a recent study – is the aim of making economics 'a more honest science' (Caldwell, 1982, p. 252). This aim is perfectly complementary with the traditional aim of contributing to real-world policy-making, and seems even more essential for effective teaching. If it is to be advanced, much needs to be done.

ADDENDUM (1993)

I have considerably altered the rather tolerant attitude to games-playing in economic 'theorizing' expressed in section IV above. This change of view has been influenced somewhat by Professor Peter Wiles's comment in his 'Epilogue' to *Economics in Disarray* (pp. 293ff.). I have also been influenced by subsequent developments over the last decade; in particular, the courageous work of Klamer and Colander exposing the grossly excessive mathematical hijack of graduate education in economics in the USA.

In a trenchant passage Wiles wrote:

I deny, then, the 'strong grounds in academic freedom for protecting serious academic interests which may, like pure mathematics, have no relevance or relation to any kind of real-world fruitfulness, or policy-making', that lead Hutchison (chapter 1, p. 14) to allow scientists to play around without even the hope of a (1) serious or (2) useful outcome. I am saying *as a taxpayer* that the public funding of science should be more sceptical and more Philistine. What people do after hours with their already earned income is their own affair – and the recognition of *that* sufficiently preserves academic freedom.

(Wiles and Routh, eds, 1984, pp. 312–13)

Wiles is, of course, referring to the British case, where research and teaching in economics are funded to a much greater extent – though not entirely – by the taxpayer. Researchers are, of course, entitled to use funds raised privately for purposes agreed with sponsors, assuming that they, the researchers, 'come clean' about the aims and methods of their research. What is, however, most strongly objectionable is that the exponents of mathematical abstractionism seldom, if ever, state, and often do not seem to possess, any clear view, or definition, of their aims; nor do they usually attempt to outline with any clarity the methods they propose to use, and just how these methods would promote whatever aims they may adopt (notice, for example, the widespread and persistent fudging of the term 'theory').

As Donald McCloskey has observed, the aims and criteria of most mathematical economists have 'adopted the intellectual values of the Math Department', and have abandoned the values methodologically demanded by 'an empirical scientist' (1991, pp. 8–10). At the same time, no awareness is perceivable that the aims and criteria of pure mathematics are fundamentally different from those of an empirical discipline. (Incidentally the poverty of the intellectual defences of much of contemporary mathematical economics and econometrics is all too glaringly exposed by the irrelevant tirade on their behalf in *Economics in Disarray*.)

Two contributions of Wiles's 'Epilogue' deserve the warmest support: first, his opening proposition that 'the main thing that is wrong with economics is its disrespect for fact' (p. 293). (We assume that by 'economics' is meant *academic* economics and not the large section of the subject which is the 'real-world' economics of business and government.)

Secondly, there was Wiles's valuable contribution to the political sociology of economics and the dominant economic orthodoxy, which has produced such a serious *'deformation professionelle'*. Wiles called attention to the neglected, pioneering work of Benjamin Ward in *What's Wrong with Economics?* (1972). Along these lines there seems to be much research to be done.

NOTES

1 This paper was delivered at a conference on Economic Methodology held at New College, Oxford, in December 1982, and was – as explained above – published in a volume entitled *Economics in Disarray*, edited by Peter Wiles and Guy Routh.

2 Patrick Minford defends an extreme form of 'rational' expectations on the basis of the methodological justifiability of unrealistic assumptions: 'The rational expectations view has been widely criticised as "unrealistic", "not how people behave" . . . The answer is clear: *of course* it is unrealistic, it is meant to be. It is a very powerful assumption for generating predictions. This one assumption is a rich source of restriction in economic models. The criticism is quite simply irrelevant' (Minford and Peel, 1981, p. 3). Minford then expressed the view that the predictions generated by RE models had been 'rather successful' – a view around which it could hardly have been said that a consensus has formed. Earlier Minford had claimed: 'Within five years the standard macroeconomic model will be an equilibrium model in which expectations are formed optimally and contract arrangements respond to economic forces especially inflation' (1980, p. 24). It is not quite clear whether the rational-expectations assumptions are intended as 'negligibility' assumptions, 'domain' assumptions, or simply as heuristic, simplifying assumptions (to use A. Musgrave's valuable distinctions). But they seem in Minford's writings to represent the strongest form of the three, i.e. negligibility assumptions (see Musgrave, 1981; Hutchison, 1981, pp. 288–91).

3 See Hahn (1981) and Davidson (1981) contributions to Bell and Kristol, 1981, pp. 126, 137 and 157–8.

4 In support of the economist acting 'as a critic and judge', rather than as 'the positivists' passive and neutral observer', see Hollis and Nell, 1975, p. 241. With regard to 'High Theory', which, of course, today means 'High Mathematical Theory', the very serious advice of Alan Prest in his recent 'Letter to a Young Economist' should be pondered by young and old concerned with the state of the subject: 'The suggested Ph.D. thesis title "n solutions to $n-1$ problems" is a very promising theme for an academic career devoted to High Theory. Nowadays this is the super-highway to eminence and professional acclaim. And you will very quickly discover that your standing and status will rise in geometrical proportion to the irrelevance and obscurity of what you say and write. Abraham Lincoln was wrong here: you can fool all the people all the time – without much effort either' (1983, p. 131).

REFERENCES

Bell, D., and Kristol, I. (eds) (1981). *The Crisis in Economic Theory*.

Caldwell, B. (1982). *Beyond Positivism*.

Davidson, P. (1981). 'Post-Keynesian Economics', in D. Bell and I. Kristol, eds, *The Crisis in Economic Theory*, pp. 151ff.

Frey, B. (1981). 'Schumpeter, Political Economist', in H. Frisch, ed., *Schumpeterian Economics*, pp. 126ff.

Hahn, F. H. (1981). 'General Equilibrium Theory', in D. Bell and I. Kristol, eds, *The Crisis in Economic Theory*, pp. 123ff.

Hicks, Sir John (1979). *Causality in Economics*.

Hollis, M. and Nell, E. J. (1975). *Rational Economic Man*.

Hutchison, T. W. (1977). *Knowledge and Ignorance in Economics*.

Hutchison, T. W. (1981). *The Politics and Philosophy of Economics*.

Hutchison, T. W. (1992). *Changing Aims in Economics*.

Kaldor, Lord (1978). *Further Essays in Economic Theory*.

Keynes, J. M. (1936). *The General Theory of Employment, Interest and Money*.

Keynes, J. M. (1937). 'The General Theory: Fundamental Concepts and Ideas', *Quarterly Journal of Economics*, 51, pp. 209ff.

Knight, F. H. (1921). *Risk, Uncertainty and Profit*.

Leslie, T. E. C. (1879). 'The Known and the Unknown in the Economic World', in *Essays in Moral and Political Philosophy*, pp. 221ff.

McCloskey, D. M. (1991). 'Economic Science: a Search through the Hyperspace of Assumptions?', *Methodus*, 3, 1, pp. 6ff.

Meckling, W. H. (1978). 'Comment', in J. M. Buchanan and R. E. Wagner, eds, *Fiscal Responsibility in Constitutional Democracy*.

Minford, P. and Peel, D. (1981). 'Is the Government's Economic Strategy on Course?', *Lloyds Bank Review*.

Musgrave, A. (1981). 'Unreal Assumptions in Economic Theory: The F-twist Untwisted', *Kyklos*, 34, p. 377ff.

Nozick, R. and Tobin, J. (1982). 'The Meaning of Social Justice', in *New York Times*, 3 January.

Phelps Brown, Sir Henry. (1972). 'The Underdevelopment of Economics', *Economic Journal*, 82, pp. 1ff.

Pigou, A. C. (1939). Presidential Address to the Royal Economic Society, *Economic Journal*, 49, pp. 215ff.

Prest, A. R. (1983). 'Letter to a Young Economist', *Journal of Economic Affairs*.

Robinson, Joan (1973). *Collected Economic Papers*, vol. IV.

Senior, N. W. (1836). *An Outline of Political Economy* (new ed. 1951).

Simon, H. (1976). 'From Substantive to Procedural Rationality', in *Method and Appraisal in Economics*, ed. S. J. Latsis, pp. 129ff.

Worswick, G. D. N. (1972). 'Is Progress in Economic Science Possible?', *Economic Journal*, 82, pp. 75ff.

12

THE WISDOM OF JACOB VINER: 'OUTSTANDING ALL-ROUNDER', AND PROFOUND AND PERSISTENT METHODOLOGICAL CRITIC[1]

I

Using a cricketing metaphor, Lionel Robbins described Jacob Viner as 'the outstanding all-rounder of his time' (a very great time in economics):

> His talent was impressively many-sided. He made significant contributions to pure analysis. He enriched the literature of applied economics. He served his tour of duty as a public servant and adviser. He was a great teacher and a great scholar . . . probably the greatest authority of his age in the history of economic and social thought.
>
> (1970, pp. 2 and 6)

Some might feel disposed to argue that, in important respects, Joseph Schumpeter was the more enlightening historian of economic thought.[2] But the subject to be discussed here is certainly not that of the relative merits and demerits of the two supreme masters of the history of economic thought. What is being insisted on here is the addition of a seriously neglected dimension to Viner's 'all-roundness'. In his very first publication in 1917, and again, repeatedly, towards the end of his career after 1950, Viner engaged profoundly in methodological criticism, showing himself, again and again, seriously concerned with the methods, assumptions, condition and tendency of the subject.

II

Viner's first publication (as I have only very recently perceived) was an article on methodology. It was entitled 'Some Problems of Logical Method in Political Economy', and appeared in 1917 when he was 25. It seems to have been – with one possible exception, published at the age of 63 – the only work he ever wrote explicitly and exclusively devoted to methodology. He was concerned, in this youthful essay, with undertaking a vigorous defence of induction, and with launching a sharply critical attack on the leading classical

260

exponents of the abstract, hypothetical-deductive method, i.e., Senior, J. S. Mill and Cairnes.

Viner began with a call for radical methodological reform, asserting that 'in no other of its border-line problems does political economy so urgently require a recasting and reanalysis of its principles as in the problems of logical method in political economy' (1917, p. 236). Viner continued:

> The logical doctrines of the average economist are antiquated and inadequate to his needs. Furthermore, the literature of economic method is dominated by the writings of a group of economists who were at the same time logicians of a narrow and discredited school. These economists, influenced by their general logical dogmas, either rejected induction *in toto* as a possible method of economic research, or gave it only grudging admission as the veriest handmaid to the deductive method. . . . If the economist follows the old economic logicians in their rejection of induction, his own practice, generally better than his precepts, forces him into contradictions from which he finds only partial escape by belated and inconsistent concessions to a method of whose value he would at first admit nothing.
>
> (pp. 236–7)

> Unless a science is wholly abstract or hypothetical, it must therefore rely on inductive inferences for its fundamental general propositions, and must consist largely of inductive inference and the deductive application of such inference to narrower groups of instances.
>
> (p. 237)

Viner maintained that:

> the abstract economists exaggerate the possibility of obtaining a vast deal of knowledge from a system of deductions derived from an initial set of four or five propositions.
>
> (p. 235)

> Political economy has been too often described as if it were merely a 'pure' or a priori psychological theory of value and distribution. Of much greater importance to the economist than any 'pure' theory is the knowledge and understanding of the concrete facts of production, distribution, consumption, of the whole economic situation with all its causal processes.
>
> (p. 251)

Viner (citing the example of J. S. Mill) observed:

> Even those economists who were most decided in their contention that the abstract deductive method was the only one available to the economist made considerable use of these inductive methods in their economic

researches. In some cases their chief contributions to political economy were predominantly inductive in character.

(p. 253)

The vital point was the essential and inevitable role of induction.[3] In protesting against the excessive and misleading orthodox emphasis on pure deduction, and in thus stressing the role of induction, the youthful Viner's was (apart from the institutionalist critics) a lone voice. A decade and a half later the classical deductive view was still more forcefully re-stated by Robbins (1932) and Mises (1933). For a third of a century, however, Viner made no further protest on the subject of induction and deduction. That he by no means abandoned his inductive principles, however, seems to be indicated by the sub-title of his important work, *Canada's Balance of International Indebtedness: an Inductive Study* (1924). But, however unsatisfactory some of his auxiliary arguments may have been, it was surely a very regrettable loss that he ceased to fight his corner on methodology and, for over three decades, gave up his criticism of orthodoxy. What happened? Did, perhaps, the young Viner, as he advanced into and through his thirties, come to regard his radical methodological criticism as a brash indiscretion, and decide that it was professionally prudent to put aside childish things?[4] In terms of professional career advancement, methodological criticism has an obviously negative pay-off. Anyhow, Viner certainly did not repudiate his critical, methodological views, because a third of a century later he can be found expressing and developing closely similar arguments.

III

Looking through the two volumes of Viner's collected papers (1958 and 1991), only one item can be found, of some methodological significance, published before 1950. This exception dates from 1928 and was a contribution to a discussion on 'The Present Status and Future Prospects of Quantitative Economics'. Viner began in a very different mood from that of his youthful methodological radicalism of eleven years previously. Now his complaint is that

economists have not ordinarily appeared at their best when engaging in methodological discussion. Writers who in the ordinary course of events were mild, tolerant, catholic in their own practice, in a word 'sensible', were in their methodological preaching exceedingly prone to be dogmatic, bigoted, exclusivist.

(1958, p. 41)

Viner's particular methodological target was the enthusiastic preaching of new methods together with 'magnificent programs and manifestos'; to counter which he insists,

262

that never has there been a time in which a generation has made such vast strides that it could afford to discard or even to neglect the achievements of the preceding generations; that economics has never been demonstrably aided by methodological discussion, . . . [and] that methodological enthusiasms by distorting and throwing out of balance the curriculum of training for young economists . . . have done much harm to economics by promoting methodological fanaticism.

(pp. 41–2)

Viner here was not, of course, referring to the methodological enthusiasm for mathematical abstraction which emerged so powerfully after 1950, but to the case for 'quantitative economics', fashionable in the USA in 1928. We can, unquestionably, all join in denouncing dogma, bigotry, fanaticism and exclusivism, and it may possibly be that some kinds of methodological writing contain a higher concentration of such deplorable characteristics than do other kinds of economic writing. The important question, however, remains, as to whether there are vital methodological issues which seriously need to be addressed and widespread methodological practices and assumptions which call for severe criticism. At the age of 25 Viner obviously thought that there were such issues and assumptions, and, from the age of 57 to that of 70 and after, he was obviously to think so again.

IV

We must now jump ahead to 1950, by which date, it might be said, American economists were taking over the lead from the English; and from which date, also, might be traced a profound movement, under the guise of mathematics, towards much more widespread and extreme abstraction, together with what Viner, in 1928, had described as the process of 'distorting and throwing out of balance the curriculum of training for young economists'.

In 1950 Viner (now *aet.* 58) wrote a fundamentally critical review of the *Survey of Contemporary Economics*, edited by H. S. Ellis for the American Economic Association (AEA). Though commending the 'experiment', as he called it, as 'fairly successful', Viner remarked that the contributors: 'were chosen predominantly, perhaps wholly and deliberately, from among the safe, middle-of-the-road members of the profession, with respect both to their policy attitudes and their methodological predilections' (1958, p. 431).

Evidently this AEA survey had not produced the kind of critical, fundamental scrutiny which Viner thought was needed. He suggested, therefore:

that a large-scale 'review' of the methodological state of our discipline is a project which our Association might well take in hand as its next major experiment.

That such a survey is needed this very volume provides abundant evidence. There is scarcely a hint in it of discussion of how economists

263

should choose their premises. . . . One contributor cites in support of resort to a particular arbitrary assumption its use by another economist; that other economist, who happens also to be a contributor, in his own contribution concedes, with a frankness sufficiently uncommon to call for special commendation, that resort to that asumption, having as its only justification its ease of use, is a fundamental weakness in his own work.

(p. 434)

Viner concluded:

A philosopher has recently . . . complained that social scientists borrow their methods uncritically from other sciences instead of letting their subject matter determine their methods. Even this volume, I believe, provides considerable evidence supporting this criticism. We need seriously to examine to what extent the criticism is justified and to explore the availability of remedies.

(p. 434)

Methodological questions are connected, intricately and inevitably, with educational or curricular questions. In the same mid-century year Viner published his 'Modest Proposal for Some Stress on Scholarship in Graduate Training', a 'proposal' with important and profound methodological implications.

Viner began by defining 'scholarship' as 'nothing more than the pursuit of broad and exact knowledge of the history of the working of the human mind as revealed in written records' (1958, p. 369). Viner then identified the American graduate schools as the – or a – key sector in the economics profession. He described these schools as follows:

The graduate schools . . . train our college teachers as well as our researchers, and the graduate school faculties also teach in the colleges. The graduate schools, I repeat, tend to mould their students into narrow specialists, who see only from the point of view of their subject, or of a special branch of their special subject, and fail to recognize the importance of looking even at their own subject from other than its own point of view. These students then acquire their doctoral degrees on the strength of theses which have demonstrated to the satisfaction of their supervisors that they have adequately decontaminated their minds from any influences surviving from their undergraduate training in other fields than those occupied by their chosen discipline. They then find their way back to the colleges to transmit to the next generation the graduate school version of a liberal education, or how to see the world through the eye of a needle.

(p. 379)

Viner added the educational implication that

men who have been trained to think only within the limits of one subject, or only from the point of view of one subject, will never make good teachers at the college level even in that subject. They may know exceedingly well the possibilities of that subject, but they will never be conscious of its limitations, or if conscious of them will never have an adequate motive or a good basis for judging as to their consequence or extent.

(p. 380)

Viner concluded by insisting that: 'ways can be found to harmonize training in professional skills with training in scholarship. They must be found. They will be found' (p. 380).

Over forty years later Viner's over-optimism seems almost fantastic. Far from any ways of harmonizing 'professional' skills with scholarship in graduate training in economics, the problem has immensely worsened, and, given the academic-sociological factors, probably *cannot* be found without some kind of highly improbable institutional transformation. Anyhow, Viner's 'modest proposal' for reversing a blinkered, 'aggravated specialism', in favour of a broader, scholarly curriculum, is not simply a genteel plea for an infusion of 'culture'. The effects of economic policies are inevitably extremely wide and various in nature, and simply cannot be appreciated by those whose narrow, over-specialized training has imbued them with philistine, over-simplified views of the objectives and effects of economic policies. Viner certainly did not always agree with Hayek but he would certainly have applauded Hayek's statement that 'an economist who is nothing but an economist cannot be a good economist' – who was following in the tradition of J. S. Mill and Alfred Marshall, who observed that 'a person is not likely to be a good economist who is nothing else' (*v.* Kadish and Tribe, 1993, p. 144).

V

Viner's next methodological comments and criticisms were directed at the issue of permissible and impermissible abstract assumptions in economic theorizing. In his review article (1954) on Schumpeter's *History of Economic Analysis*, which incidentally, appeared in the same year as Friedman's famous essay 'The Methodology of Positive Economics', Viner claims that Schumpeter has: 'not made clear to what extent "good" economic analysis is dependent on the realism of its assumptions' (1958, p. 345).

He charges that, according to Schumpeter: 'scientific truth at times seems to include propositions which are factually untrue' (p. 345). He might well have cited, for example, the ubiquitous assumption of full knowledge and the absence of uncertainty, which has pervaded so much of microeconomic analysis since Ricardo.

Viner then observed that Schumpeter 'when defending resort to an acceptance of unrealistic assumptions . . . appeals to what he regards as appropriate parallels in other fields, especially physics' (p. 346). For Schumpeter had claimed that 'it is no valid objection to the law of gravitation that my watch that lies on my table does not move toward the centre of the earth, though economists who are not professionally theorists sometimes argue as if it were' (1954, p. 1031).

Viner rightly concluded that this frequent kind of defence of unrealistic abstraction is much too facile and complacent, commenting that

> the problems that may arise for economic analysis because the obstacles to the operation of its theoretical 'principles' are more omnipresent and in practice less removeable than are tables as obstacles to the operation of the law of gravity are not really explored.

> (p. 346)

This criticism of Schumpeter is all the more significant because, especially following the publication, in this same year, of Friedman's essay on the methodology of positive economics, the all too glib and presumptuous claim was to become all the more widespread that the unrealism of assumptions in economic theory did not matter.

VI

In the year following his review article on Schumpeter, Viner published what Professor Donald Winch has described as 'perhaps the best statement of his methodological position' (1983, p. 8).[5] This paper, 'International Trade Theory and its Present Day Relevance' (1955), was certainly Viner's fullest and richest methodological statement (at least since 1917) and it contains probably the most subversive criticism of what have since become widely prevailing methodological assumptions, or fashions. *It was not included in either of the two collections of his papers (1958 and 1991).* It really consists of two essays in one, the first starting from the question of the then, present-day 'relevance' of classical international trade theory; and the second proceeding to a thorough and wide-ranging analysis of the meaning and criteria of 'relevance' (of various types), and of the meaning and nature of 'theory' (a bewilderingly ambiguous term, of course, as used by economists). Viner goes on to examine how, methodologically, 'relevance' can be sought, and the supreme position it should hold in the intellectual priorities of economists. At one point in this paper Viner stated that 'my central theme is the relevance of economic theorizing' (p. 106), thus committing himself to the examination of two of the most problematic and controversial concepts in the discussion of the methodology of economics.

In an introduction to a collection of articles on International Economics (1951) Viner had argued regarding the classical theory of international trade:

> Despite my belief in its merits and its relevance during its period of dominance, I am convinced, however, that it would be a mistake to

carry its rehabilitation so far as to claim for it, even in its improved and modernized form, adequacy as a theory to guide policy in the present-day world. *The world has changed greatly. . . . The classical theory is not directly relevant for such a world, and it may be for such a world there is and can be no relevant general theory.*

(1955, p. 100 italics added)

Viner was thus advancing an emphatically historical-relativist view for which he proceeded to argue against the defenders of the relevance of the classical theory. He began by insisting that it was the availability of a relevant *general* theory that he was denying, and that he was not criticizing 'theorizing' as such, though he proceeded to expound a much broader and more inclusive concept of 'theorizing' and 'theory' than many economists employed even then, let alone today, forty years on. Viner described a 'general' theory as 'a comprehensive theory that embraces all the variables recognized as having major significance' and which 'operates with a considerable degree of analytical rigor, and which reaches conclusions that, if true, would be of some consequence' (p. 10).[6] Viner went on to claim that 'the great bulk of economic theorizing since it first began to be a professional activity has not been, has not pretended to be, and has not striven to be *general* theorizing' (p. 101).

Much of theory was 'partial', and much, 'especially in more recent years' was 'a search for quantitative correlations between statistical series' (p. 102). Though lack of generality can be a defect, and reduce reliability,

a theory that is formally indisputably 'general' may be without relevance for any time or any place, because the forces, the variables, it recognizes may not be the ones that are in fact important and may even be wholly fictitious and spurious.

(p. 102)

Observing that the classical theory of international trade assumed that national markets were 'basically competitive', Viner went on to challenge an often-quoted assertion of Edgeworth that 'the investigation of the conditions which determine value' depends essentially on the assumption of competition, and that if that assumption was, or had to be, abandoned, 'abstract economists would be deprived of their occupation' (pp. 102–3).

Viner concedes that 'in the present state of our skills, the assumption of competition is necessary for the prosecution of "general" theorizing', but denies that the competitive assumption is a prerequisite for 'partial', or other forms of 'theorizing' or 'theory', notably for what he calls 'empirical theorizing', which 'is useful whenever it produces useful results' (p. 104). 'Empirical theorizing', Viner asserted, is frequently used in the natural sciences, where, he points out, empirical regularities are much more frequently found; whereas 'findings of empirical economic regularities go stale

267

almost as fast as do eggs. . . . Only one pertinent exception comes to my mind. . . . Engels's Law' (pp. 104–5). Viner concludes:

> In consequence we have no logical justification for belief in the existence of important economic functions that are simple, stable through time and space and characterized by stable and fixed parameters.
>
> (p. 105)

Viner does not mention the possibility of resorting to economic *trends* as the bases for theorizing and prediction. In fact, real-world economists do base most of their predictions on trends, because they have little or nothing else on which to base them. Certainly it is vital to distinguish laws from trends, as Karl Popper insisted, but however severely academic methodologists may reject trends, for purposes of theorizing and prediction, a subject with a historical dimension, which also aims at assisting towards less unsuccessful, real-world policy-making, simply cannot avoid using trends – with as much care and insight as possible.

Viner then examines various 'universes of discourse', or intellectual forms or contexts, in which 'economic theorists operate' (p. 106). First, 'economic theory sometimes operates in a universe of intellectual play, without ulterior motives' (p. 106). (This is certainly a universe much more densely populated by economic 'theorists' in the 1990s than when Viner was writing in 1955.) In this area, 'rigor and elegance are here the only relevant tests of workmanship, and internal consistency the only test of validity of results' (p. 106). Economists, Viner added, may also engage in theorizing because of adherence to, or rejection of, a professional tradition. In assessing, however, the relevance of such earlier theorizing for understanding current reality, or for solving current problems of social policy, it is necessary constantly to beware of historical or institutional obsolescence:

> Even if the past theorizing was fully relevant for the period of its original blossoming, however, and this should never be taken for granted, it is in the abstract a reasonable presumption that it will have undergone considerable obsolescence with the passage of time.
>
> (p. 107)

Viner concludes that 'it is only for the universe of discourse in which economic theory is primarily an arena of intellectual play that the criteria of "good" theory are primarily "demonstration", "rigor", and "elegance" ' (p. 107). Moreover, regarding the duty of economists:

> Since what economists are 'kept' to do is to bring understanding of the nature and function of the economic process in the real world . . . there is a moral obligation on the part of the profession as a whole, if not on the part of every individual economist, and if not at every moment for any economist, to seek relevance and to assign high value to it. . . .

The only moral I draw for the individual economic theorist from the argument I have so far presented is that he has two intellectual obligations: first, to seek awareness of which universe he is operating in and to share whatever awareness he attains with his audience, and, second, in his relations with his public, and especially his students and his lay public, to avoid claiming for theorizing, which is governed . . . by surrender to play-impulses, anything more than accidental and partial relevance to the understanding of the real world and of the ways in which it can be changed for the better.

(p. 108)

Viner went on to add that 'the individual campus economist' is 'not ordinarily equipped with the comprehensive and up-to-date information necessary for intelligent solutions of immediate and specific problems' (p. 109).

Returning to the classical theory of international trade, Viner urged special 'caution' and 'major reservations' with regard to 'the welfare or "gains from trade" conclusions that the old school drew from their reciprocal-demand analysis' . . .

The idea, for instance, of being able to determine the optimum level of a tariff by relatively simple geometry on the face invites the type of incredulity that in another connection led Coleridge to ask: 'What should we think of one who said that his love of his wife was north-west-by-west of his passion for roast beef?'

(p. 120)

In fact, Viner was critical of how

economic theory tends . . . to conduct welfare analysis in terms of single objectives, assumed to represent simple and homogeneous quantities of welfare-stuff, such as 'gain', 'benefit', 'development', 'income' and so forth. . . .

In the actual course of policy-making in the real world, however, the monistic concepts that economic theory uses in its welfare analysis seem always to be catch-all labels for complex packages of objectives that the policy-maker in practice is forced to separate out and to weigh against each other when they conflict with each other.

(p. 121; v. Hutchison, 1964, pp. 165–6)

In concluding his assessment of the relevance of classical trade theory, Viner asked how much deviation between its assumptions and the facts the theory can stand, or how much flexibility is permissible (thereby suggesting an approximation to Karl Popper's falsifiability criterion):

There must be a limit somewhere. A theory elastic enough to withstand almost any degree of subversion of its premises must be a theory so good in general that it is not much good for anything specific.

(p. 125)

Regarding methods for attaining 'relevance' in theorizing Viner challenged one well-worn, orthodoxly recommended practice and suggested a very different approach. He noted how

> it is common practice to start with the simplest and the most rigorous model, and to leave it to a later stage, or to others, to introduce into the model additional variables or other variables.

> (p. 128)

All too often, this method of decreasing abstraction is not, and cannot be, followed through to any conclusion significantly closer to the real world. Viner goes on:

> I venture to suggest that the most useful type of 'first approximation' would often be of a radically different character. It would consist of a listing of all the variables known or believed to be or suspected of being of substantial significance, and a corresponding listing of types and directions of interrelationships between these variables. . . . Instead of beginning with rigor and elegance, only from this second stage on would these become legitimate goals, and even then for a time they should be distant goals, to be given high value only after it is clear that they can be reached without substantial loss of relevance.

> Such procedure, it would seem to me, would have some distinct advantages as compared to the more usual procedure on the part of theorists of starting – and often ending – with models that gain their rigor at the cost of unrealistic simplification.

> (p. 129)

Viner concludes powerfully:

> The final outcome of such a change in analytical procedure might well be a definitive loss in rigor and elegance at least for a long time, on the one hand, but a definite gain in scope for the useful exploitation of new information and of wisdom and insight on the other hand. Such a result, I hope and believe, would in most cases constitute a new gain in relevance for understanding of reality and for the promotion of economic welfare by means of economic theorizing.

> (pp. 129–30)

Viner could hardly have made his intellectual priorities clearer: empirical relevance had the highest priority for economic theorists, far overriding logical or mathematical rigor, and was attainable through 'wisdom and insight'. This methodological conclusion is the more authoritative in that Viner himself has been most widely regarded, by the highest authorities, as outstanding among economists for his 'wisdom'.

VII

Two years later Viner was again taking up the question of excessive, undisciplined abstraction in an article entitled 'Fashion in Economics'[7] (1957). He complained:

> I take for granted that we all agree that in all thinking some degree of abstraction is absolutely necessary – we can't take account of everything simultaneously. But some pursue, apparently, the maximum degree of abstraction, and some show no concern as to the particular pattern of their abstraction. They say, 'let us start from these assumptions', without thinking it important to argue why these assumptions and not some alternative set should be used. *There even occurs, in current economic literature, the proposition that lack of realism of assumptions does not, of itself, detract from their relevance, including, I take it, relevance to matters that are of concern to non-economists.*
>
> (1991, p. 193, italics added)[8]

Viner concluded this paper on 'Fashion in Economics' by calling attention to

> the great concern which our brightest and most promising younger economists show today for the aesthetic side of economics, for the formal rigor and elegance of their models, apparently at whatever cost in terms of relevance, realism, significance, except as economics is pursued as a form of art.
>
> (p. 197)

If that was Viner's comment on the 'Fashion' of the 1950s with regard to abstraction, what on earth would he have thought, or said, of the fashions of the 1980s and 1990s?

In his Wabash Lectures on 'Economics and Freedom' of 1959, Viner forty-two years later, relaunched his methodological attack of 1917 on the classical economists, an attack all the more noteworthy for being the only serious criticism he undertook of his favourite school. Holding that the English classicals 'erred through lack of realism' he went on: 'They relied too much on an abstraction as making relevant theorizing possible without resort to more than a minimum of systematic observation'; Viner further charged the classicals: 'that *even for their "economic man" they took too much for granted that he would have a clear and simple and accurate knowledge of what his economic interests were*' (p. 75, italics added).

Here, Viner's criticism penetrates right to the heart of the classical hypothetical-deductive method in economics, that is, regarding the vital assumption regarding knowledge and expectations. Obviously his strictures do not apply only to English classicals. Obviously, also, they do not apply to the leading English classicals *to anything like an equal extent*. They apply very little, if at all to Adam Smith, but quite devastatingly to Ricardo, and quite seriously to J. S. Mill, Senior and Cairnes.

We come finally to Viner's Ely lecture of 1962, entitled 'The Economist in History'. He began by remarking on his difficulty in deciding on a title for this lecture, remarking that he had considered calling it: 'Why has economics always had a bad press?' (1991, p. 227).

Viner's methodological criticism was again first directed at the English classical economists, on somewhat similar lines to those of his attack on Senior, J. S. Mill and Cairnes in his first-ever publication forty-five years previously. His fundamental methodological criticism of the English classicals contrasted strikingly with his generally highly restrained and uncritical attitude to this school.[9]

He began with a criticism which he had emphasized earlier, observing that the classicals worked 'from categorical premises treated as axiomatic', but 'did not, with a few notable exceptions, . . . check inductively for validity. . . . They also much exaggerated the extent to which serviceable and genuine axioms are available' (p. 235). Viner goes on to insist that:

if a professional group regards itself as having a message to deliver to others than its own members and makes any public claims in that respect, it thereby gives others the right to scrutinize the methods where-by that message was discovered, including the principles, or possibly prejudices, followed in choosing premises.

(p. 237)

At this point Viner displays a certain professional sensitivity in denying the right of economic historians to criticize economic theorizing even when their criticisms were virtually identical with those which he himself was quite rightly emphasizing. Anyhow, he concludes that neither the economic historian nor the economists have, with regard to basic postulates, *'given sufficient mental effort to the task'* (p. 237, italics added).

Viner then went on to reject the attempt by Walter Bagehot, often a discerning and pungent critic of the classicals, to offer a defence of classical methodology. Bagehot had written:

Modern economists know their own limitations; they would no more undertake to prescribe for the real world than a man in green spectacles would undertake to describe the colours of a landscape.

Viner (1991) commented:

Except for the small but important and esteemed group of economists who today live a completely happy life devoted to dalliance with elegant models of comely shape but without vital organs, how many present-day economists are there for whom Bagehot's statement is even approximately true?

(p. 238)

Viner then turned to the famous (or notorious) *Methodenstreit* between Menger and Schmoller, offering a remarkable, dissenting verdict thereon:

> My fellow theorists tell me that the theorists won a definitive victory in this battle when Carl Menger, in the 1880's, demolished Gustav Schmoller. I cannot agree. I believe that the battle was mostly a sham one, and that while Schmoller certainly carried off no laurels, the ones that have ever since been bestowed on Menger for his victory in this battle are tinsel ones.
>
> (p. 238)

Viner quite justifiably denied that Menger had ever faced 'the real challenge' regarding abstraction:

> The real challenge which Menger should have faced was not that of justifying in principle recourse to abstraction by economists, but of justifying the particular extent and manner in which he and his fellow theorists practised it.
>
> (p. 239)

Menger's defence of abstraction by economic theorists was based on an example from theoretical chemistry, which, Viner observes, 'begs most of the important questions' (p. 239).

One can only wonder what friends and colleagues of Viner, like Lionel Robbins and Fritz Machlup, and, indeed, his AEA audience at the Ely lecture, made of this verdict on Menger and the *Methodenstreit*. Little comment seems to have been forthcoming.[10] Viner's criticisms deserve full sympathy. How often have critics of the orthodox, abstract assumptions of economic theorizing been fobbed off with complacent banalities about how *some* abstraction is inevitable? Actually, the fact seems to be that in economics and political science, and subjects with a vital historical-institutional dimension, the scope for useful abstraction – as distinct from vacuous academic games-playing – seems quite limited.

VIII

We have seen that ever since he published his first article in 1917 at the age of 25, Viner had produced, for a third of a century, only a single, rather untypical comment on methodological questions, in a discussion of 'quantitative economics' in 1928. From 1950 until 1962, on the other hand, though – with one possible exception – not having written a single essay or review explicitly and solely devoted to general methodological issues, he published a series of criticisms of both classical and contemporary methodological practices, which at some points followed quite closely his first youthful essay of three or four decades previously.

Two very different developments are noteworthy in this period of the 1950s and early 1960s, which served as the background to Viner's comments and criticisms.

First, the 1950s and early 1960s, when Viner was publishing his repeated methodological complaints, was a period of great prestige and influence for economists and their subject. In most of the economically more 'advanced' countries economic performance was highly, even surprisingly, successful in terms of levels of employment, and, in some countries, in terms of growth as well, while inflation was not regarded as serious. The contrast with the last previous peace-time decade of the 1930s was striking. As regards the apparent success and prestige of the subject, the 1950s and early 1960s resembled the middle decades of the nineteenth century, when English classical political economy achieved a peak of prestige and influence against the background of English economic success as 'the workshop of the world'. When the fashionable patter of economists seems to mesh broadly with outstanding, contemporary real-world, economic success, something of a boom in prestige and confidence may be expected. Sir John Hicks wrote of 'a besetting vice of economists to overplay their hands, to claim more for their subject than they should' (1983, p. 364). This 'besetting vice' is especially liable to flourish in such 'boom' periods as the 1850s, 1950s and early 1960s. At these junctures attempts such as Viner's to call attention to fundamental, methodological questions or vulnerabilities are hardly likely to get much of a hearing.

Anyhow, by way of contrast with Viner's critical and sceptical questioning, quoted above, in his Ely lecture to the AEA in 1962, two years later the President of the AEA declared in the following confident terms:

> The age of quantification is now full upon us. We are now armed with a bulging arsenal of techniques of quantitative analysis and of a power – as compared to untrained common sense – comparable to the displacement of archers by cannon. . . . I am convinced that economics is finally at the threshold of its golden age – nay, we already have one foot through the door. . . . Our expanding theoretical and empirical studies will inevitably and irresistibly enter into the subject of public policy. . . . And then, quite frankly, I hope that we become the ornaments of democratic society whose opinions on economic policy shall prevail.
>
> (Stigler, 1965, pp. 16–17)[11]

There was, however, a second, very different kind of development which can be dated from around 1950: that is the ever more intense abstraction in economic theorizing, facilitated and encouraged by the ever more widespread application of mathematical analyis, combined with the rise of the doctrine, or fashion, that 'anything goes' with regard to the realism, or unrealism, of assumptions. Viner, quite explicitly, referred very critically to increasing abstraction and the total disregard of realism in assumptions. Unfortunately, however, he did not name names or cite particular examples, just as, even more unfortunately, he did not publish more full-length, specifically methodological essays or reviews. Viner's repeated criticisms and comments preceded the considerable outburst of methodological criticism which occurred around 1970, by when, as the result of institutional-historical changes, the two decades or so of policy success had ended, and profoundly serious, new, real-world policy-problems had arisen, which the prevailing orthodoxy, even when equipped with the proliferation of magnificent, new mathematical techniques, seemed quite incapable of solving. Viner died in 1970, his persistent and profound methodological hints and warnings of his last two decades, pretty completely disregarded. Moreover, his great prestige was not available to support the searching and authoritiative criticisms of Leontief, Phelps Brown, Ward and others which began to be forthcoming at that time.[12]

IX

On the dust-jacket of the 1991 collection of Viner's *Essays on the Intellectual History of Economics*, two very distinguished Nobel prize-winners are quoted as emphasizing his 'wisdom'. Two points should immediately be agreed. First, that 'wisdom' is an almost priceless quality for a 'real-world' economist to possess; and second that Viner commanded this almost priceless quality to a degree and depth probably unsurpassed by the economists of his day. On a third important point, agreement is probably much more doubtful and difficult to achieve: just *what* does this priceless 'wisdom', which Viner so unquestionably and richly possessed, *consist of*? Just how does it show itself and how can one test its possession? These questions must surely be answered if the attribution of 'wisdom' is not to remain simply a vague, cosy eulogism suitable for inserting into a blurb about a distinguished elder statesman, recently deceased.

It is a fair and interesting question to ask what quotations or actual passages from Viner's writings, one would cite or quote as examples and proofs of the outstanding wisdom which he is so authoritatively agreed to have commanded. It would probably be accepted that Viner's 'wisdom' can hardly have been rooted in any mathematical proficiency on his part (to judge, at any rate, from his widely noticed geometrical peccadillo regarding the tangency of short-run and long-run cost curves). I fear, indeed, that the examples which I would first want to cite, or quote, of Viner's wisdom might rather be passed by in silence by many authorities, and *perhaps* even by both of the Nobel laureates quoted on the dust-cover of his posthumous collection of essays (1991). For, as I see it, Viner's genuine wisdom was profoundly at odds with the conventional methodological 'wisdom' during much of his life, and increasingly, sharply, and fundamentally so in his last decade or two.[13]

A few months before he died Viner remarked to a student that 'care in avoiding over-statement and over-certitude is not exactly a fashionable virtue these days, but it is still a true one in my judgement' (introduction to Viner, 1991, p. 14). In fact, intellectual modesty, or unpretentiousness, should be regarded as not only a moral quality, but as an essential practical virtue in policy argument. In practice, many economists seem to lurch between serious over-confidence and excessive nihilism. I would, in any case, certainly suggest that Viner's great wisdom was, in one direction, exemplified by the value he attached to intellectual restraint.

I would add what seem to me to be two further examples of Viner's wisdom: the first example is contained in his 'Modest Proposal' of 1950 'to harmonize training in professional skills with training in scholarship' in the graduate curriculum and reverse the trend towards more and more intensive, 'aggravated specialism'. Needless to say, in the following decades, 'conventional wisdom', and practice, regarding graduate curricula, for the most part ran rapidly, confidently, and diametrically in the opposite direction to that recommended by Vinerian wisdom.

Secondly, there was Viner's conclusion, very challenging to much of the 'conventional wisdom' of economic methodology over the past half-century, that in the *Methodenstreit*, Carl Menger failed to face 'the real challenge' regarding abstraction in economics. Did not this unorthodox methodological judgement demonstrate Viner's discerning methodological insight and wisdom?

In any case, it can surely be agreed that this wisest of leading economists, and great 'all-rounder', in the last two decades of his career, was persistently and profoundly critical about the prevailing methodological trends in his subject, and that his warnings and proposals were totally disregarded. Moreover, we can go decisively further. For Jacob Viner, a, or the, major twentieth-century embodiment of wisdom in economics, himself explicitly stated his attachment to 'wisdom and insight' as an overriding value and priority – as contrasted with 'rigor' and pointed to the directions in which it could be cultivated and applied.

In short, in the last two decades of his life (1950–70) Vinerian wisdom was insistently and profoundly at odds with the conventional wisdom, or fashion: with regard to the general importance of fundamental methodological criticism – which was so often complacently dismissed as a waste of time – or with the increasingly dominant methodological ideas of the 1950s and 1960s, both with regard to abstraction, and as to the roles of induction and deduction.

It is quite understandable that after his initial foray, as a 25-year-old in 1917, Viner decided that if he gave to the profound methodological problems, which he had discussed and tackled, the concentration which they demanded and deserved, he might not only need to 'trespass', extensively and 'unprofessionally', across rising departmental barriers between economics and philosophy, but that he would also be unable to concentrate sufficiently on the real-world issues with which he was beginning so successfully to engage. With Viner, however, success did not lead to any complacent illusions, that the subject in which he was achieving success and eminence *must* be free of the serious methodological difficulties which he had discussed so early in his career. He did not abandon the radical critical insights of his twenties, but eventually returned to them, at the peak of his eminence, bringing to bear all his mature learning and wisdom. It may seem a pity that he did not contribute more lengthily, and perhaps in book form, to this kind of profound criticism. But that Viner left a rich legacy of methodological and educational insights must be as plain to those with eyes to see as was his complete failure, with all his prestige, to exercise any significant influence against such a powerfully mounting hostile trend.

NOTES

1 This essay developed out of a review of Viner's *Essays on the Intellectual History of Economics* (1991), which appeared in the first issue of *The European Review of the History of Economic Thought* (Autumn 1993, pp. 216–20). This collection of Viner's essays, edited by Douglas A. Irwin, might be regarded as a *slightly* premature centenary celebration, though such an intention is not indicated by the editor.

2 See above for the contrasting views of Schumpeter and Viner on Mercantilism and the English Classicals (pp. 9–11).

3 I was stimulated to turn to Viner's methodological essay of 1917 by reading his various profoundly interesting methodological comments in the papers in the 1991 collection. This took me back to his 1958 collection, *The Long View and the Short*, where, as the first item in the appended bibliography, his 1917 paper was listed. Viner's stress on induction interested me the more because I had moved towards a similar position:

> There is a further methodological lesson which seems to tell against an excessive or exclusivist pro-deductive, and anti-inductive approach. Rather platitudinous observations are constantly repeated about how one cannot collect facts without a prior principle of selection and a terminology in which to describe them; and that heaps of facts do not, of course, of their own accord, arrange themselves significantly. But if forecasting or predicting in economics inevitably depends on the judicious extrapolation of trends, induction seems to be much more centrally involved than the hypothetical-deductivist methodology allows (distilled as it has been mainly from the history of the more 'advanced' natural sciences). Extrapolation of trends by a kind of induction is a method which has obvious weaknesses. But beggars can't be choosers, and if, in some important branches of economic prediction, inductive extrapolation is an inevitable or demonstrably superior method, *because of the nature of the material*, then it must be recognized, and the best must be made of it. . . .
>
> (1977, p. 23)

Viner would certainly have agreed with Marshall's approving comment on Adam Smith that 'he was always inductive, but never *merely* inductive' (1925, p. 379). Smith's account of induction comes in *The Theory of Moral Sentiments* (1976, pp. 319–20) and includes the proposition: 'The general maxims of morality are formed, like all other maxims, from experience and induction . . . induction is always regarded as one of the operations of reason.'

4 It was Professor F. H. Knight, Viner's one-time colleague at Chicago who, – when engaged, incidentally, aged 55, on a somewhat lengthy and apoplectic methodological contribution – remarked that books on methodology (and also, presumably

articles) 'are most likely to be read and taken seriously by the young' (1940, p. 1). Regarding the relationship between Viner and Chicago, see Spiegel (1987), who observes that Viner never regarded himself as a member of the, or a, 'Chicago school'. Spiegel also calls attention to Viner's remarkable article from the early 1920s which anticipated nearly all the major conclusions of the theory of mono-polistic competition – which, of course became anathema in Chicago.

5 I am deeply indebted to Donald Winch for a copy of his article 'Jacob Viner as Intellectual Historian', not only for the valuable light it sheds on its subject, but because it reminded me that I was in danger of overlooking Viner's 'best statement of his methodological position' (though thirty years previously I had quoted from it).

6 Though I do not remember any such influence, it is possible that I was drawing on this paper of Viner's, on the limitations of general international trade theories, when writing 'The Limitations of General Theories in Macroeconomics' (v. Hutchison, 1981, pp. 233ff.). The classical theory of international trade was robustly defended against Viner's criticisms by Gottfried Haberler (1954). It would be presumptuous to comment on this conflict between two such masterly authorities.

7 As its title implies, Viner's article, 'Fashion in Economic Thought' has profoundly sceptical implications. Viner maintained that 'the history of economics as a discipline is to quite a large extent a history of fashion in economic thinking' (1991, p. 189). Fashions are often reactions – often excessively prolonged reactions – to historical and institutional changes and developments, to which, of course, economists *ought* to respond (up to a point). Unfortunately what are, to some extent, observant and justifiable reactions become over-confident, over-prolonged, over-reactions, which fail to pick up the next historical-institutional changes. It is excessive faith and confidence in a pseudo-'rigorous' deductive method which pro-motes the disastrous neglect of the historical dimension in economics.

8 It is in his article on 'Fashion in Economic Thought' that Viner introduced one of those stories which illuminate his essays so delightfully. Examining the fashionable argument that 'lack of realism of assumptions does not, of itself, detract from their relevance, including, I take it, relevance to matters that are of concern to non-economists' (p. 193), Viner continues:

> It may be that the dispute here has some affiliations with respect to the field of poetry, of literature, of ballet, of the legitimacy of 'art for art's sake', as distin-guished from art for some other purpose, such as giving pleasure, or improving morals, or supporting religious faith. Julian Huxley, when he was director of the Regent's Park Zoo, told the story that a nice lady visiting the zoo, fascinated by the hippopotamus, asked the keeper whether it was a male or a female, and received the reply: 'Lady, I should think that that would be a question that would be of interest only to another hippopotamus'. The same thing, I fear, speaking from inside the profession, can be said of a good deal of modern economic theorizing.

(1991, p. 193)

9 Viner certainly indulged in some extremely severe comments on such auxiliary 'Classicals' as James Mill and McCulloch. Mill (senior) he described as 'so extremely rigid, austere, pontifical, narrow, belligerent, as to be almost a caricature of the classical school in its less endearing aspects' (1991, p. 231). (Caricatures, of course, if any good, contain valid observations.) Viner refers also to 'the blundering and reactionary McCulloch' (1958, p. 401).

It is regarding the *major* classical figures, Adam Smith and Ricardo, that Viner refrained excessively from criticism. While rightly prepared to be very bluntly out-spoken in his criticisms of such leading contemporaries as Keynes, Schumpeter and Hayek, Viner never seemed to question seriously, for example, Smith's confused and confusing treatment of utility and value; nor Smith's dogma that saving *is* investing; nor his anti-'mercantilist' version of the 'money-doesn't-matter' doctrine. On Ricardo, also, Viner was mainly uncritical. We have discussed above (Chapter 4, pp. 97ff.) his complaints about the misinterpretation of Ricardo and his unwillingness to envisage that this was, to a serious extent, the fault of Ricardo and James Mill. Highly over-optimistic moreover, forty years later, seems to have been Viner's prediction that the publication of the Sraffa–Dobb edition would make everything clear as to what Ricardo means and meant. An explanation, however, of Viner's uncritical attitude to Ricardo may be that his (Viner's) special interest was that of the theory of international trade and that this was easily Ricardo's strongest suit.

10 I would only differ from Viner in suggesting the award of *some* genuine – not 'tinsel' – laurels to Gustav Schmoller, whose methodological ideas have so often been written off as 'naively Baconian' (by writers whom one suspects have never read much of Schmoller's writings). Viner stated that Schmoller claimed that 'the task for the economist, at least for another twenty years or so, was to accumulate historical data' (1991, p. 238).

In fact, it could and should, be argued that the collection of statistical data about business cycles, probably the most serious, and sometimes catastrophic, real-world economic problem in the half-century after 1880, should have received the highest priority (as it did from the largely unknown French doctor, Clement Juglar, a fore-runner of Wesley Mitchell). If more economists had followed Juglar, methodo-logically and substantively, in accordance with Schmoller's suggestions – and not concentrated so heavily on purely deductive micro-analysis – then the profound instabilities, dismissed by orthodox theorists as 'abnormalities' and 'frictions', and which finally, in the 1930s and 1940s, had almost fatal consequences for Western civilization, though not prevented, might, at least, have been significantly mitigated.

It should, moreover, be observed that Schmoller expressed sensibly tolerant and balanced views regarding induction and deduction, emphasizing the inextricable interconnections between observation and analysis, as in his analogy of how two legs are necessary for walking:

> What has been achieved is just as much the result of deductive as of inductive reasoning. Anyone who is thoroughly clear about the two procedures will never maintain that there are sciences explanatory of the real world which rest simply on one of them.
>
> (1920, vol. I, p. 110; Hutchison, 1953, p. 184)

Moreover, Schmoller perceived, as Menger sometimes failed to do, the vital differ-ences regarding not only experiment, but abstraction, between the more simplified natural sciences and the more complex social subjects:

> All observation isolates a single occurrence from the chaos of phenomena in order to study it by itself. Observation rests always on abstraction; it analyses a part. The smaller and more isolated this is, the easier the observation. . . . The relative simplicity of the elementary phenomena of nature very much facilitates the observations of the natural scientist. The natural scientist even has it in his power to alter at will the surroundings and the causes at work, that is he can experiment and look at the object from all sides. Not only is this seldom possible, or only with difficulty, in respect of economic phenomena, but even in

their simplest form these are much more complicated. . . . The observation of economic facts is always a difficult operation, the more easily upset by mistakes, the larger, the more extensive, and the more complicated, the individual operation.

(1904, p. 299)

The idea that Schmoller was simply a naive empiricist and exclusivist-historical economist is a serious misrepresentation. In fact, Schmoller's answer to Menger was in closely similar terms to those of Viner's criticism of Schumpeter.

11 One should completely agree with George Stigler that the greatest achievement of twentieth-century economics may be described as 'quantification', and in particular the establishment of agreed and important statistical series and other statistical material. These statistical series and materials have been so much more valuable, in terms of the real-world policy-relevance of economics, than the vast proliferation of abstract mathematical analysis and model-building since about the middle of the century. It is, of course, necessary, however, to recognize the serious inaccuracy and, in some cases, undue belatedness, of much of this statistical material. This constitutes a vast and vital contrast with the precision of the material on which the natural sciences are based, which – to adopt Stigler's comparison – led, for example, to the invention of the cannon which displaced archers, but which is unlikely to lead to a correspondingly striking practical or policy advance in economics or the social sciences. It must be recognized that the deficiencies in the basic material – however great the advances in economics in collecting such material in this century – cannot be compensated by all the brilliant mathematical analysis of 'the best minds' in economics.

12 Regarding the wave of caustic and authoritative methodological criticisms, which broke around after 1970, aimed mainly at the vacuity, in terms of real-world policy relevance, of most, recent mathematical model-building, see Hutchison, 1977, chapter 4, pp. 62ff.; and 1992, chapter 4, pp. 15ff.

13 The two Nobel Laureates who expressed such admiration for Jacob Viner's 'wisdom' were Professor Paul Samuelson and the late George Stigler. Samuelson could hardly have discussed Viner's 'wisdom' as residing in his mathematical proficiency; whereas Viner's repeated insistence on the need for fundamental methodological criticism – and repeated practice of such criticism after 1950 – could hardly seem an expression of 'wisdom' for George Stigler, who maintained the view that the marginal product of methodological discussion averaged about zero. Furthermore, there seems to be a contradiction between Viner's emphasis on induction, together with his scepticism and qualifications regarding abstraction and deduction – together with his view that Carl Menger lost his great debate with Schmoller – and George Stigler's dictum that 'it is more important that good logic win over bad than that good insight win over poor' (1965, p. 324). Viner, on the other hand, would more probably have maintained that bad logic will soon get corrected, if of any importance, as was his own peccadillo regarding cost curves. Good insight, on the other hand is a very rare and precious commodity which should be treasured and protected. In fact, Viner's support for induction was a support for true insight, on which it had to be based.

I might conclude that this author has no difficulty in pointing out examples of the great and rare wisdom of Jabob Viner: this essay is packed with quotations expressing that wisdom – and many more could have been supplied.

REFERENCES

Haberler, G. (1954). 'The Relevance of the Classical Theory under Modern Conditions', *American Economic Review*, 44, pp. 543ff.

Hicks, Sir John (1983). *Classics and Moderns.*

Hutchison, T. W. (1953). *A Review of Economic Doctrines, 1870–1929.*

Hutchison, T. W. (1964). *'Positive' Economics and Policy Objectives.*

Hutchison, T. W. (1977). *Knowledge and Ignorance.*

Hutchison, T. W. (1981). *The Politics and Philosophy of Economics.*

Hutchison, T. W. (1992). *Changing Aims in Economics.*

Hutchison, T. W. (1993). Review of Viner, J.: *Essays on the Intellectual History of Economics, European Journal of the History of Economic Thought*, vol. I, 1, p. 216.

Kadish, A. and Tribe, K. (eds) (1993). *The Market for Political Economy.*

Knight, F. H. (1940). 'What is Truth in Economics?', *Journal of Political Economy*, vol. 48, p. 1ff.

Marshall, A. (1925). *Memorials of Alfred Marshall*, ed. A. C. Pigou.

Mises, L. (1933). *Grundprobleme der Nationalökonomie.*

Robbins, L. C. (1932). *The Nature and Significance of Economic Science*, 1st ed.

Robbins, Lord (1970). *Jacob Viner, 1982–1970.*

Schmoller, G. (1904). *Über einige Grundfragen der Sozialpolitik und der Volkswirtschaftslehre*, 2nd ed.

Schmoller, G. (1920). *Grundriss der Volkswirtschaftslehre.*

Schumpeter, J. A. (1954). *History of Economic Analysis.*

Smith, A. (1976). *The Theory of Moral Sentiments*, eds. D. D. Raphael and A. L. Macfie.

Spiegel, H. W. (1987). 'Viner, J.', *The New Palgrave Dictionary of Economics*, vol. 4.

Stigler, G. J. (1965). 'The Economist and the State', *Papers and Proceedings of the American Economic Association*, vol. 55, pp. 1ff.

Viner, J. (1917). 'Some Problems of Logical Method in Political Economy', *Journal of Political Economy*, vol. 25, pp. 236ff.

Viner, J. (1955). 'International Trade Theory and its Present Day Relevance', in *Economics and Public Policy*, Brookings Lectures 1954, pp. 100ff.

Viner, J. (1958). *The Long View and the Short.*

Viner, J. (1991). *Essays on the Intellectual History of Economics*, ed. D. A. Irwin.

Winch, D. N. (1983). 'Jacob Viner as Intellectual Historian', *Research in the History of Economic Research and Methodology*, 1, pp. 1ff.

13

THE USES AND ABUSES OF
ACADEMIC ECONOMICS[1]

As an economist Wicksell lacked one important quality: that of being able to get into contact with what is generally called practical economics. From this point of view I think that his Austrian training was unfortunate. . . . At a dinner for his seventieth birthday it was pathetic to hear him express in his speech his envy of those who now started economic studies with all the advantages of having at their disposal a growing mass of factual material about what was actually happening. Himself an economist who had learned from all schools of economic thought except the German historical school, his advice turned out to be: study history, study the development of economic life.

(Bertil Ohlin, 1926, p. 503; Hutchison, 1953, p. 231)

I

The adjective 'academic' usually seems, these days, to be employed in a vaguely – or sometimes distinctly – pejorative sense. One reads in one's broadsheet, for example, that yesterday's play in the test match was largely 'academic', because two-and-a-half of the first three days' play having been washed out by rain, far too little time was left for either side to achieve a win. The proceedings, therefore, were 'academic' in the sense of being largely 'meaningless', or 'irrelevant' in terms of the main issue, that is the eventual result of the five-match series.

We are not, however, at this point, yet concerned with the merits or demerits implied by this adjective 'academic' when applied to economics, but simply with the *institutional* implication; that is, we are concerned with the subject as taught, studied, researched into or written about by the teachers or students of 'academies', colleges or universities, as contrasted with the research or writings on economics produced in governmental or business organizations (that is, with work or writings produced by those inhabiting what 'academic' economists themselves sometimes describe as 'the real world').

Adam Smith was, of course, for part of his life, an academic, but not an academic economist, because political economy hardly emerged as an independent subject until some time after he had written *The Wealth of Nations*. Chairs of Political Economy were established at Oxford and Cambridge early in the nineteenth century, but the amount of teaching and the numbers of students were very small, and continued to be so even in the 1860s and 1870s when Jevons, and later Marshall, were beginning their careers. Pretty well to the end of the nineteenth century there was a continuing deficiency of demand for systematic instruction in the subject. Sometimes there was a lack of 'effective' monetary demand to pay teachers adequately. But often, when the financial preconditions were met, there was a lack of 'real' demand, due, simply, to a lack of interest. Repeatedly, professors and lecturers were appointed, and courses launched, only fairly soon to run into declining numbers and cancellation (*v.* Kadish and Tribe, 1993, *passim*). As Keith Tribe has observed, the decisive advance in 'academic institutionalization' came between 1890 and 1905, with the foundation of the Royal Economic Society and the *Economic Journal* in 1890 – though there was nothing essentially academic in these first two developments – followed, however, by the founding of the London School of Economics (LSE) in 1895, of Marshall's comparatively specialized Economic Tripos at Cambridge in 1903, and of Faculties of Commerce at the universities of Birmingham and Manchester. Even then numbers, compared with those of half a century later, remained very small. The concern and interest aroused by the great depression of 1929–32 seem to have increased student numbers somewhat in the 1930s. But it was only after World War II that a large, continuing quantitative increase took place in most countries, with a crucial transformation from small-scale to large-scale 'academic institutionalization'.

The first half-century, or two generations, of academic economics, though comparatively minuscule quantitatively, produced a considerable number of really great economists and works: Jevons and Marshall in Britain, and Walras, Pareto, Menger and Wicksell, in Lausanne, Vienna and Lund, followed, for example, by Keynes, Schumpeter, Viner, Myrdal and Hayek, all born before 1900. Perhaps there was more room to grow in those days.

On the whole, however, right down to the middle of this century, little significant change is discernible in the aims and methods of the subject, as contrasted with what had gone before in the preceding, pre-academic centuries. Certainly there was an increased precision in analysis, and the calculus lent itself to the formulation of marginal analysis and concepts. But a heightened detachment did not lead to any significant decline in realism, or to a systematic turning away from the real world. The use of abstraction became more explicit but certainly no more far-fetched than it had been in the case of Ricardo. It should be noted, also, that it was not only in the numbers of *academic* economists that growth had been comparatively small. In the first half of this century, except for large, temporary expansions during the two world wars, the numbers, and the increases, in business and government economists, in Britain at any rate, remained, down to 1939, very small compared with the expansion that was to come subsequently.

For perhaps half a century after the rise of neoclassical academicism began, around the 1870s, there was little noticeable raising of departmental barriers between philosophers and economists. In Britain, the long tradition of a very close relationship between philosophy and political economy, as represented by such great writers as Jevons, Sidgwick and the two Keynes, continued power-fully (though Marshall's establishment of his *Economics Tripos*, in 1903, inde-pendent of the 'Moral Sciences' was a vital turning-point towards twentieth-century departmentalism). Economist–philosopher–methodologists, however, in spite of the subject having changed its name, continued to hold to the tradi-tional overriding aim, for the subject, of real-world policy relevance. Today, however, at the end of the century, with the formidable rise of departmental demarcations, we are told that methodological standards 'borrowed' from 'external' philosophy departments have 'always been a little suspect' (*v.* de Marchi, 1992, pp. 1–2, who, of course, on the very next page, 'borrows' the authority of the 'external' philosopher Rorty). Anyhow, departmental sus-picions have created what might be called the Tobin-Nozick problem: 'There's nothing more dangerous than a philosopher who's learned a little bit of economics, unless it's an economist who hasn't learned any philosophy' (*v.* above, Chapter 11, section V). So profound methodological problems can only receive the kind of explicit clarification they so urgently require if there are people prepared to risk sniper fire from both sides, when venturing out into what is now a dangerous kind of non-departmental No Man's Land.

II

The more significant and serious effects of 'academic institutionalization' on the aims and methods of economics did not come until the second half of this century, with the transformation from small-scale to large-scale. It is surely on this phase in the development of academic economics, that is, the contem-porary *déformation professionelle*, that experts in the sociological and institutional pathology of the subject, should focus. Obviously, developments such as the following are important.

(a) First there were vast and continuing increases, in nearly all leading countries, in the numbers, both of academic and of governmental economists. Statistics are very hard to come by, notably because of problems in defining an 'economist', so estimates are highly speculative. For the leading country, however, the USA, there are figures which at least suggest orders of magni-tude. There can be no doubt also about the vast increase in the number of journals, which had a considerable effect on the nature of the literature. The age had arrived of the article, or paper, a more quantifiable concept. Books, and chapters thereof, tended to lose in importance.

(b) Vastly increasing numbers brought increased departmentalization, and vastly heightened specialization, with a significantly more unbridgeable 'distance' between specialisms. Moreover, in time, a largely arbitrary pecking order in terms of prestige, or 'high status', between different specialisms, began to be asserted (and all too often rather sheepishly accepted). It became widely assumed that 'the best minds' – even when self-styled, as they sometimes were – were concentrated in a particular specialism, that, in fact, of extremely abstract and largely vacuous 'formalism', and mathematical 'model'-building. There was less and less room for great 'all-rounders', like Jacob Viner, on one side of the Atlantic, or Lionel Robbins, on the other. At the same time, advancing an education in economics seemed, quite often, to mean *retreating* from the real world, which is the diametric opposite of Marshall's attitude, according to which: 'when he gave what he termed "advanced lectures" these did not deal with the kind of technical or mathematical problems which such a course today would be likely to deal'. Marshall 'dealt in his "advanced lectures" with the analysis of some real but difficult economic problems' (Coase, 1975, p. 29).

(c) At approximately the same time as this very consequential process of quantitative expansion, there came a change in the leadership of the subject, which moved across the Atlantic from Britain to the United States. Typical and pivotal American academic institutions, such as the Graduate School, and the principle of 'Publish or Perish', acquired a wider and more powerful influence. The Graduate School, in particular, became a key element in the larger-scale, academic-institutional framework, with a vital role in the self-perpetuation of orthodoxies and 'élites'.

III

The dubious, two-edged, or multi-edged, process of 'professionalization' is, or was, not identical with what may be described as 'large-scale academic institutionalization'; but, as regards the development of economics over the last century, the two processes have coincided, or overlapped, to a considerable extent. Since about the middle of this century these two processes have, together, played an important role in changing the aims and methods of the subject.

It does not seem *prima facie* obvious, or, indeed, likely, that a detached scholar, in the groves of academe – though his detachment can, in some respects, be an advantage – is all that well-placed for studying the economic processes of business, finance and government. For the student and teacher of economics, for example, there is, and can be, nothing which approximates, at all closely, to the teaching hospital, so essential for the teachers and students of medicine.

In the pursuit, however, of professional status, the academic economist must have something impressive to say which enables him to lay claim to a kind of knowledge which is out of reach of those immersed in the actual processes of business and government, and also of journalist commentators. This is where mathematics has proved such a boon and a blessing for the professional, or would-be professional, academic economist. 'Objectively', as a Marxist might have put it, an important function of mathematical economics is to mark off intellectual 'turf' from outsiders (which is not, for one moment, to deny that mathematics is not sincerely believed to further the widely accepted aims of the subject, and does not, in some ways and to some extent, quite genuinely further them). There is, of course, no argument – in spite of the oft-repeated banalities of interested parties – about the usefulness of *some* mathematics and *some* abstraction. It is the (comparative) sheer volume of extreme, ultra-'rigorous' mathematical abstraction, at such a high cost in realism and relevance, which can be, educationally, so pernicious, especially when vacuity and unrealism are veiled and fudged.[2] It might be urged that even the excesses of mathematical abstraction are hardly as thought-destroying as the torrents of polysyllabic gobbledygook which have engulfed much of sociology and literary criticism. But mathematical formulation may be even more dangerous, in concealing much more effectively gross unrealism, irrelevance and vacuity, when pure 'rigour' becomes the dominating aim. A decade or more ago, Karl Brunner was expressing his concern about a new trend, especially among young economists which maintained the view that: 'Whatever is not explicitly and rigorously formalized does not count and cannot possibly contribute to any relevant knowledge' (quoted by Klamer, 1984, p. 191; Mayer, 1993b). It certainly seems that such a view has been growing and has been inculcated in some graduate schools (*v.* Klamer and Colander, 1990). (Before virtually all the great works in the history of political economy are consigned to the dustbin, it might be recalled that long, long ago there was a man called Aristotle, who observed that 'our discussion will be adequate if it has as much clearness as the subject-matter admits of' (1915, trans. Ross; see also Hutchison, 1977, pp. 37 and 153–4).

As Thomas Mayer has recently pointed out:

> mathematics can readily be used to silence most non-economists who pontificate on the subject. Economics is not the only field that uses mathematics as a barrier against criticism by the unwashed. . . .
>
> Another way economists strive for status and self-respect is by using complicated theory even when discussing straightforward problems that could be resolved without it. It is something that only those with training in economics can do and, besides, it seems to justify the effort made in acquiring the theoretical tools of economics. Beyond this, it distinguishes economics from the other social sciences.

(1993a, pp. 16–17)

All too often the (self-styled) 'best minds' in the subject have adopted the self-sealing, Catch-22, ploy against critics that their criticism is necessarily based on their failure of understanding.

Thomas Mayer also observes how, as contrasted with academic researchers in such fields as law and medicine, 'who work for a large market of practitioners, academic economists write for each other. Hence their tastes and not the consumers' determine what is produced' (p. 10).[3]

In turn, such producer sovereignty may lead to 'an over-emphasis on sophisticated high-tech methods' (p. 11). Moreover, it may be assumed that enhancing their own feeling of scientific status has been an important element in the utility function of mathematical economists, which is satisfied by the lavish use of mathematics and by the promotion of abstract, vacuous 'rigour' as the – profoundly unsuitable – overriding criterion and aim of the subject.

IV

An aspect of the attitude of 'professionalism' – often highly acclaimed from some points of view – has recently been described as keeping an eye 'cocked at what is considered to be proper, professional behaviour – not rocking the boat, not straying outside the accepted paradigms or limits, making yourself marketable and above all presentable, hence uncontroversial' (Said, 1993, p. 14).

Accepting such an attitude means, of course, keeping clear of fundamental methodological discussion or criticism, including, of course, discussion of the dangers of mathematics and some of its excessive and irrelevant applications. In fact, Professor Frank Hahn, a frequent spokesman over the years for 'the best minds' and their high status activities, in a valedictory message to Cambridge students, as one of his two most important reflections, has urged them 'to avoid discussion of "mathematics in economics" like the plague, and to give no thought at all to "methodology" ' (1993(a), p. 5; see also the very cogent criticism by Roger Backhouse, 1993, p. 4).

Certainly in terms of the prevailing orthodoxies, or conventional wisdoms, 'methodology', however, precisely we interpret the term, has long ranked near the bottom of the accepted pecking-order (in professional careerist terms). Regarded as fundamental criticism, methodology may well be subversive of prevailing fashions and orthodoxies, as obviously may be the kind of discerning comments we have cited above from Thomas Mayer. Criticizing the unrealism of assumptions is obviously anathema for supporters of the influential and widespread doctrine that unrealism of assumptions simply does not matter. But it may be that upholders of prevailing orthodoxies regarding abstraction and the use of mathematics just cannot imagine (as Jacob Viner found) that there are fundamental flaws or errors in some prevailing attitudes, and, in particular, in the change in aims that has taken place in at least one key sector of the profession, in exalting pure abstract 'rigour' as an overriding criterion or aim, the counterpart of which has been a considerable loss of interest, in at least this one pivotal sector (the graduate schools) in practical issues and policy-relevance as the prime aim of the subject.[4]

Certainly a deepening scepticism regarding the application of economic 'theory' to policy may be increasingly justifiable in view of what seem to be mounting difficulties in getting generally beneficent measures through the political process, when these offend powerful lobbies or interests. It might also appear less than fair-minded to exclude *a priori* the cultivation of pure mathematical rigour for its own sake, or for its aesthetic properties.[5] What is criticizable, however, is, first, the claims which have been made of 'great practical importance' for theory, or analysis, the proclaimed 'rigour' of which may, more often, be *at the expense* of just such 'importance', or relevance. Moreover, when claims to 'practical importance' are abandoned or diluted, they are merely transferred to some nebulous kind of alleged but unspecified 'understanding'.

The surely lamentable intellectual conclusion must be emphasized that for decades, in the face of insistent and often highly authoritative criticism the (sometimes self-styled) 'best minds' in the subject have been either unwilling, or, more probably, unable, to provide a clear account of what they are doing and why they are doing it. Moreover, students are now being professorially warned off methodological criticism, in particular concerning the uses and abuses of mathematics in economics, presumably so as to counter any complaints of the overloading of curricula in favour of 'rigorous', but vacuous and irrelevant, mathematical abstractionism.

V

In literary terms the equivalents of mathematical 'rigour' are, or were, the 'apodictic certainties', and 'praxeology', of Ludwig von Mises. Both the mathematical economists, and the, both, anti-mathematical and anti-empirical Mises, have sought to replace the criteria and objectives of an empirical– historical subject (or 'science'), the one by pure, abstract 'rigour', and the other by the 'certainties' of 'praxeology'. Just as, furthermore, the 'modern Austrian' supporters of Mises have concocted a highly imaginative version of the history of economic thought as a persuasive weapon for their cause, so the mathematical abstractionists now seem to be trying to rewrite the history of the subject so as to enhance the prestige of mathematical abstractionism. Professor Frank Hahn has claimed for example:

> It took us almost two hundred years to translate Adam Smith's vision into something sufficiently precise to allow us to argue about it. It will certainly take a long time to accomplish the same task for Keynes. In the meantime perhaps we should be rather modest.

(1984, p. 75)

At least 'we' can all agree with the concluding, rather comical admonition regarding modesty, immediately preceded, as it is, by a far from modest, and totally unjustifiable claim, combined with a fundamental methodological

288

misconception. First, there is the claim that some unspecified 'we' are unable to argue about a theory or conjecture which is not presented in 'precise', rigorous, mathematical terms, as though all the vast, non-mathematical literature, some at least of which, from Adam Smith to Viner, and after, is of the highest intellectual level, might as well be wiped off the historical record, now that the mathematicians have spoken. Secondly, and more important, Adam Smith's 'vision' has *not* been 'translated': it has been fundamentally distorted and eviscerated into a piece of 'rigorous' and vacuous hyper-abstract, static analysis, based on a range of fantastically unrealistic assumptions, and on a highly questionable concept of a 'Pareto-optimum' (which some would say has no strong claim to be considered optimal). Let us counter-claim at once that this hyper-abstract mathematical analysis – if he had bothered to unravel its meaning – would, quite justifiably, have bored the pants off Adam Smith as almost totally irrelevant to what he was interested in. So much for the 'translation' which has taken 'us' almost two hundred years to produce.

For these purely abstract, static mathematical theorems (not theories) have scarcely the faintest bearing on the great real-world issues and arguments about the general beneficence of free markets, or government intervention or regulation. All that is provided by these purely mathematical exercises – as vacuous as they are rigorous – is a questionable definition of some kind of 'optimum' or 'maximum', which is not necessarily connected with any particular institutional framework, either of which could conceivably, be attached to the 'optimum' or 'maximum' only on fantastically unrealistic assumptions: that is, either to a system of 'perfectly' competitive markets, or to a system managed by angelically benevolent and omniscient governmental regulators. In either case omniscience is of the essence of the exercise. (Incidentally, if Pareto himself regarded his mathematical analysis of an optimum as all that interesting and fruitful, why did he, a year or two later, move from mathematical economics to sociology?)

As regards Adam Smith, it may be noticed first, that he was not interested in defining maxima or optima for a real world steeped in ignorance and uncertainty. He accused Quesnay of irrelevantly and misleadingly trying to apply a criterion of optimality in suggesting that an economy and polity,

> would thrive and prosper only under a certain precise régime of *perfect* liberty and *perfect* justice. . . . If a nation could not prosper without the enjoyment of *perfect* liberty and *perfect* justice there is not in the world a nation which could ever have prospered.
> (1976a, p. 674; Hutchison, 1988, p. 361)

In fact, Smith would have been utterly uninterested in mathematical abstractions. He concerned himself rather with the serious real-world details of policy, supporting many particular exceptions to the freedom of markets, with regard to defence, shipping, public works, and building methods and standards. He was prepared to support the government in fixing maximum interest-rates; and, as regards foreign trade, he supported, in some circumstances, an export duty on wool, and moderate import duties for revenue and for retaliatory bargaining purposes – as Jacob Viner (1926) long ago indicated in a masterly essay, 'Adam Smith and Laissez-Faire'; *v.* 1928, pp. 116ff.

Moreover, Adam Smith was a *political* economist – unlike contemporary mathematical abstractionists – in that he was frequently prepared to support economic freedoms as such, even if they might prejudice purely economic objectives – such as a more rapid growth of income per head.[6]

What was of interest to Smith was the building of his massive, general case for free markets, based on wide-ranging empirical, historical, institutional, political and psychological evidence in support of his (of course unproven) conjecture or 'theory' of a largely or mainly beneficent 'hidden hand'. For Adam Smith was an inductivist, though, as Alfred Marshall insisted, 'never merely inductive'; since, as Marshall repeatedly emphasized, for those who are concerned with theories applicable to the real world induction and deduction are ultimately inseparable.

The Marxian version of the history of political economy and economics has probably been the most persistent exercise, in self-glorification of its kind, preceded by the English classical version, and succeeded by quite a number of other such distortions. Now these are apparently to be joined by the Mathematical Abstractionist version of the history of economic thought, which claims to be 'translating' the insufficiently rigorous visions of the great writers of the past into 'something sufficiently precise to allow us' (for the first time in the 1980s) to argue about them. The mathematical-abstractionist translation of Smith's great conjecture apparently represents the first fruits of this remarkable technique. In awaiting – perhaps for hundreds of years – other such historiographical achievements, involving Keynes and others, we are warned to remain 'modest', which is always excellent advice (but, of course, not always practised by those who advocate it to others). Novelty stores in the USA used to offer ludicrously distorted, postcard maps of the great country, as visualized by Texans, Washingtonians, Chicagoans, Bostonians, etc., etc. These amusing cartographical exercises bore a certain resemblance to some recent, 'vested-interest' versions of the history of economic thought.

VI

It is now time to raise some questions about the aims and work of the, in recent decades, rapidly growing numbers of economists in business, finance and government. This is a large area about which very little seems to be known by outsiders, including the academic sector of the profession – if it is one profession – which often appears to be strangely uninterested. In fact, the relationship between academic economists, and, presumably, their pupils practising in business and government, seems to be a peculiar one. Except as regards the United States, in which at least something approximating to orders of magnitude seems to be available, very little, if anything, in the way of basic numbers, seems to be known. According to one recent estimate, which goes back to 1984, of 60,000 'economists', with degrees in the subject, in the USA, 22,000 were academics and 38,000 were employed 'outside university and college teaching', of whom 22,800 were in the private sector, while the other 15,200 were in government of one level or another (v. Bellinger and Bergsten, 1990, p. 1701n; Hutchison, 1992, p. 157). This estimate from the USA seems to leave the academics quite heavily outnumbered.

There can be little doubt, however, as to the main, overriding aim of the vast majority of non-academic, 'real-world', business and government economists: this is and must be prediction, or less inaccurate and unreliable prediction; whatever the views on this aim may be of the academics, which seem to be increasingly of explicit rejection or tacit abandonment.

The rejection of prediction has come from several, very different quarters. Some 'Modern Austrians', for example, have proclaimed the unpredictability of human action as a basic Austrian tenet. Professor Donald McCloskey, apparently assuming some kind of philosophical support proclaimed, in capital letters: 'PREDICTION IS NOT POSSIBLE IN ECONOMICS' (1985, p. 16). While backtracking on this somewhat dogmatic statement some pages later, McCloskey seemed to accuse those economists offering predictions of intellectual dishonesty. Thirdly, some devotees of mathematical abstractionism, like Professor Hahn, apparently discerning that pure rigour, *by itself*, excludes predictive content, claim to aim at, and achieve, some ambiguous kind of 'understanding'. It is difficult to tell whether declining interest in real-world policy-making has led to the abandonment of the aim of prediction, or whether scepticism about the accuracy of economic prediction has led to a decline in interest in real-world policy guidance, accentuated, perhaps, by further scepticism about sound economic advice surviving contemporary political processes. Anyhow, it may well be, in some cases, that economists regard sticking their predictive necks out as jeopardizing their reputation for 'professionalism'.

Lacking any surveys of such attitudes, which would be extremely interesting (though the questions would be very difficult to formulate) it is difficult to generalize very far and confidently regarding the attitudes of economists to prediction as a possible and desirable aim. The conclusion may only be ventured that there has been a considerable retreat from the forthright position of the great, first generation pioneer of academic professionalism in economics, Alfred Marshall, who proclaimed: 'The dominant aim of economics in the present generation is to contribute to a solution of social problems' (1961, vol. I, p. 42).

It should also be pointed out that such a robust attitude regarding the aim of real-world policy-relevance, must, almost inevitably, be based on a correspondingly robust belief in the possibility and desirability of economic prediction.

Anyhow, the traditional prime aim, or end, of the subject – the 'job' it was assumed to be trying to 'get done' – has apparently been increasingly replaced, in recent decades, by games-playing (as Sir John Hicks described 'much of economic theory'); by displays of brilliantly wise 'new conversation', or by technical virtuosity in the form of empirically vacuous mathematical 'rigour' or aesthetics. Such activities are then dignified as promoting some unspecified, non-predictive 'understanding', 'wisdom' or even 'beauty', or as examples of on-and-on-going, ever-changing, intriguing 'discourse'.

VII

One or two points and questions may be added regarding the vital issue of prediction and forecasting in economics, which for decades there seems to have been a widespread reluctance to confront.

(1) The rejection of prediction as an intellectually respectable, or even 'possible' aim has usually been proclaimed by academic spokespersons in hopelessly ambiguous terms – as, for example, by McCloskey in his upper-case announcement quoted above.

To extricate meaning from such statements one must ask what standards of precision and what sort of margins of error are being envisaged. Obviously, prediction in economics is generally impossible with anything approximating to the precision and near-certainty attainable in physics. Prediction in economics is also obviously impossible with the standards of accuracy and margins of error achievable in meteorology and medicine (which, of course, are well below those of physics and, therefore, much less irrelevant in respect of standards of prediction in economics). In fact, the degree of accuracy with which it may be 'possible' for economists to predict may, on the average, be significantly higher than that which would be attained without their efforts; and would certainly be very much less unsuccessful without the various series of economic statistics, built up mostly in the last half to three-quarters of a century.

Many academic economists, bemused by so long envisaging policy-making in the context of abstract, Utopian models of optimization and maximization (based on the assumption of far-reaching omniscience) may fail to realize that the contributions of economists to real-world policy-making inevitably often have to take the form, in a real world of profound ignorance and uncertainty, of damage limitation and attempts to avoid the more fundamentally serious forms of politico-economic catastrophe (such as occurred, for example, in 1929–33). At least it seems to be the 'rational expectation' of the employers of non-academic economists in business and government that whatever techniques, or forms of knowledge, economists may command, are worth investing in for the sake of less inaccurate and less unreliable predictions.[7]

292

(2) Predictions are described as 'scientific' if they are based on laws and reasonably precisely-stated initial conditions. Since the pretensions of the English 'Classicals' regarding 'the Laws of Political Economy', it has been increasingly recognized by economists, especially since about the middle of this century, that there are very few, and arguably no statements in economics and the social sciences which should be dignified with the title 'law' – and certainly not in the sense in which the term is used in physics.

Predictions in economics have therefore, to be based on inductions from trends, tendencies, patterns, parallels and precedents, which it may seem pointless and pedantic to reject as too unreliable as a basis for predictions, if one accepts the seriousness of the needs of business and government for less inaccurate predictions.

(3) It seems to be very difficult for economists to maintain balanced and moderate views on the subject of economic predictions. Over the last two centuries there have been, at one extreme, the excessively pretentious claims for English Classical Political Economy in the middle decades of the nineteenth century, which were echoed roughly a century later by the pretentious over-optimism of some 'Keynesian' academics in the 1950s and early 1960s. At the other extreme we have today a form of outright intellectual nihilism, which not only describes prediction in economics as 'impossible', but denounces attempts as ridiculous and even dishonest.

It is also difficult for *critics* to preserve a balance. The world being the place it is, the most conscientious, disciplined and expert predictors, or forecasters, may put forward seriously erroneous predictions which nevertheless it may be quite unfair to criticize too severely. Unfortunately, however, there are also quite a number of economic predictions, advanced by those whose conscientiousness, discipline and expertise may, and should, be questioned. For there are few, if any, subjects where constant, robust and forthright criticism is socially more desirable than is the case with regard to political economy.

(4) Alex Rosenberg has recently condemned, in severe but justifiable terms, the lack of predictive improvement achieved by both microeconomic and macroeconomic 'theory', or analysis in this century, or even, in the case of consumer behaviour, since Adam Smith.

Though finding it impossible not to agree with a considerable part of Rosenberg's criticisms, I would like to advance one or two countervailing points, first regarding his charge that 'macroeconomic' theory 'has had a relatively poor record of predictive success' (1992, p. 249). Relative to what, it must be asked? Comparisons with other sciences – which are on many occasions very expertly undertaken throughout his book – may be of little or no relevance if the material these sciences deal with is very different in kind from that faced by economists. Anyhow, it might reasonably be maintained that macroeconomic theory was first created as recently as the 1930s, partly as a result of the most catastrophic economic policy failure of this or any other century, which was responsible for the great depression, and its obvious

293

consequences, the coming to power of Hitler and the Second World War.

The vital omission by Rosenberg, however, has been that of the relatively very considerable quantity of empirical–statistical material, including a number of quite fundamental, vital and previously non-existent statistical series, which the creation of macroeconomic theory, in its various forms, has generated in the course of the last fifty to sixty years. National income accounting was largely the offspring of Keynesian macroeconomic theory, while monetarist macroeconomics has generated a large expansion of new monetary and banking statistical series. The creation of such series has made possible the discovery of trends, tendencies, patterns, parallels and precedents, on which often unreliable, but vitally necessary, and certainly not worse-than-useless, tentative predictions can be based.[8]

How far the macroeconomic predictions, regularly indulged in over the last half-century by government and business, have been derived from formal 'theory', going beyond more-or-less sophisticated extrapolation, may be difficult to determine. However that may be, though it could be argued that it is pure historical luck which has prevented the various quite serious depressions since the Second World War from developing into the kind of catastrophic collapse and politico-economic nightmare such as occurred in 1929–33, it can reasonably be maintained that the creation of a considerable data-bank of fundamental statistical series – inaccurate and belated though they often may be – played a useful or even crucial part in damage limitation.

It should also be borne in mind that even if the predictive record has been poor, or perhaps, in a sense, actually has deteriorated, it seems quite possible, or probable, that economic prediction, in particular macroeconomic prediction, may, in the last half-century, have become significantly more difficult, and more liable to error, because of mounting politico-economic instabilities, due to a markedly more rapid rate of technical innovation, and much more extensive world-wide economic interdependence. It is quite possible (or probable) that improvements in techniques, and in the statistical material, may be failing to show up in improved predictive performance, because greater instability in the social–political–economic world is making prediction more difficult, and not because of any inadequacies on the part of predicting economists. This kind of deterioration does not, however, affect any margin of advantage economists may or may not have over non-economists in providing less inaccurate predictions, assuming that prediction, explicit or implicit, remains an inevitable activity in real-world economic life, and that reduction in the inaccuracy of prediction becomes more, rather than less, important, the greater and more dangerous the instabilities of the real world.

VIII

There is ample and impressive evidence that the increasing rate of economic and social change, which has been gathering further momentum throughout this century, has been increasing at a still faster pace during the last decade or two of the twentieth century. There seems no reason to doubt the blunt statement that today, in the early 1990s, 'the world certainly is changing faster than it ever did before' (Davidson and Rees-Mogg, 1993, p. xi).[9] The most important and fundamental element in these economic, social, political, cultural and other forms of change, all interacting on one another, is probably technological change and its faster spread. An, at first, very gradually increasing rate of technological change could be traced back to the latter part of the eighteenth century, or much earlier. But even throughout most of the nineteenth century the effects of economic change were not, compared with today, nearly so seriously obtrusive. Lord Rees-Mogg describes how his great-grandfather

> was born in 1815, the year of the battle of Waterloo, and died in 1908, six years before the outbreak of the First World War. He never experienced a major war, a social revolution or a significant change in the value of the currency. Indeed, the pound had a purchasing power about 10 per cent higher on the day he died than it had the day he was born. As a businessman he saw interest rates drop very gradually for most of his lifetime. He did live through the first forty years or so of the decline of British farm incomes and therefore of land values, and that was a major social and economic change, but a long term one. If anyone was entitled to believe in continuity, he was. But we are not.
>
> (Davidson and Rees-Mogg, 1993, pp. xiv–xv)

The world of Mr Rees-Mogg (senior) was the kind of economic world which confronted the later English classical economists and the English neoclassicals before 1914. I have sometimes expressed criticism of the intellectual over-confidence of English classicals and am by no means prepared to withdraw much of this criticism. But by way of extenuation it should be emphasized that the kind of economic life they sought to explain had a much greater simplicity, continuity and predictability, and changed, usually, much more slowly and gently, than that which confronts us in the final decade of this millennium.

Though it was the most important contribution of Engels and Marx to have emphasized the importance of technical change, the English classical economists took too little notice of it. Adam Smith and his followers even went back (as noticed above, pp. 13ff.) to the extreme simplification of a hunting and gathering economy for the conditions in which a positive and unqualified labour theory of value would have operated. Perhaps, significantly less unjustifiable, however, in view of the then still very gradual, and comparatively gentle rate of technological and other changes, were such simplificatory devices as the stationary state and comparative statics. Moreover, the comparatively much gentler rate of change may also have, to some extent, justified the confidence of the classicals in their predictive ability, based on laws, or near-laws. Even though the classicals lacked, almost entirely, the range of statistical series which is available today, many of which have only been created in the second half of this century, *economic prediction, in the classical period, was probably essentially much simpler than it is today.* What Pigou called the 'stable general culture' of the nineteenth century in Britain (1929, p. 21; Hutchison, 1978, p. 7) though basically the effect of economic stability on social and political stability, also, in part, reacted back on and promoted or assisted economic stability.[10]

The fact that economic prediction has probably, for most of the twentieth century, been becoming gradually, but significantly, more difficult is, of course, no good reason for economists to abandon all attempts. Quite the reverse, in fact. If in the twenty-first century there is going to be considerably less stability and continuity – economic, political, social and cultural – then attempts to reduce the inaccuracy of predictions may be more urgent than ever before, not, of course, in establishing the optimizing and maximizing equilibria of blackboard exercises, but in damage limitation, or the mitigation of the more serious real-world disasters. We are assuming, of course, that feasible efforts by economists remain, on the average, capable of reducing the inaccuracies of predictions below what they would have been *without* the inputs of economists.

Some academic economists may prefer games-playing or mathematical aesthetics as the aim and object of their efforts, or some fascinating 'New Conversation', focused on academically introverted 'ongoing, ever-changing, intriguing research and discourse'. Some may find it prudent to withdraw from the dangers of prediction, so as to protect their 'professionalism', or 'rigour'. Some may see less inaccurate prediction as the ultimate aim, but confine themselves to analysing the main factors shaping economic activities, while leaving the final quantitative, predictive judgements to more entre-preneurial decision-makers. But the quite reasonable demand for less unreliable economic predictions, which has probably been rising significantly (to judge by the increasing numbers of 'real-world' government and business economists) seems more likely to increase than decline. It could be especially dangerous and myopic if dissatisfaction – justifiable or unjustifiable – with the advice or predictions of economists were to lead to a reduction in resources going to the maintenance and improvement of economic statistics, often questionable, belated and inaccurate though these may be. Once, when he was Chancellor of the Exchequer, in the 1950s, Harold Macmillan com-plained that using the economic statistics he was provided with for drawing up his annual Budget – and inevitably budgeting, and *any* planning, involves, of course, prediction – was like looking up the times of trains 'in last-year's Bradshaw'. But the use of last year's Bradshaw, and even of a defective copy, may, probably, turn out preferable to waiting around at the railway station without the slightest idea as to when, or whether the right train is ever going to turn up.

We have seen how Alexander Rosenberg, as a specialist in scientific method, suggests that academic economics now seems to be so dominated by the pursuit of the vacuities of pure, abstract 'rigour' that it should abandon pretensions to the guidance of policy – the traditional overriding aim of the subject. A closely similar suggestion has come from Richard Whitley, a specialist in the study of scientific organization. Whitley has observed how the dominant orthodoxy, consisting of what he calls 'theoreticians', can

> obtain high reputations by producing highly abstract and general models of 'ideal' worlds without considering how they are related to economic phenomena in actual worlds; their work is partitioned from empirical economic studies, and they do not need to demonstrate any systematic connection to them.
>
> (1986, p. 192, quoted by Mäki, 1992, p. 87)[11]

Sixty years ago, in the early 1930s, writers on methodology, notably Robbins, Hayek and Knight, following the pretentious claims of Friedrich Wieser, as further developed by Ludwig Mises, claimed an 'unquestionable' and 'indisputable' quality for the basic axioms of Economics – as they understood the subject – which rendered its foundations more certain and secure than those of the natural sciences. (Robbins and Hayek, it should be added, soon withdrew from this pretentiousness.) Imre Lakatos, lulled into over-optimism, was later to maintain that what he called 'Euclidean A Priorism', as represented by Mises and his followers, was finished in economics, that is the notion that 'there exists a set of trivial first principles from which all truth flows'. Lakatos concludes:

> The fallible sophistication of the empiricist programme has won, the infallible triviality of Euclideans has lost. Euclideans could only survive in those underdeveloped subjects where knowledge is still trivial.
>
> (1978, vol. 2, pp. 6 and 10; quoted by Hutchison, 1981, p. 303)

Just as the Misesian deductivists scornfully rejected mathematics, so the claims of Mises and his colleagues scornfully (and justifiably) came to be rejected by leading mathematical economists (notably by Paul Samuelson).[12] Now, however, the wheel has come round full circle. Mathematical economists are pretentiously putting forward claims, essentially similar to those of Mises, and of those who, in the 1930s, claimed not merely parity with, but superiority over, the natural sciences for the fundamental axioms or assumptions of economics. In fact, a dominant orthodoxy, controlling much of graduate programmes, has largely been built round the vacuous pretensions of pure mathematical rigour. It may be that, at the moment, all that can be done is to maintain constant and contentious criticism. After all, it may be worth recalling that what we are justifiably concerned about is the subject as created and practised by almost all economists from Petty to Keynes. And as Thomas Mayer has concluded: 'Who knows, such resistance may succeed, for the high status of formalism is not written in the stars. It depends on what we ourselves think is good economics' (1993b, p. 9).

IX. A BRIEF BIBLIOGRAPHICAL APPENDIX: FROM MARSHALL TO THE PRESENT DAY

For robust and authoritative criticism of the use of abstraction and mathematics in economics one can, and should, go back to Alfred Marshall. Professor Ronald Coase's 'Marshall on Method' (1975) is an indispensable guide, which indicates Coase's own views as generally corresponding very closely with Marshall's.

Regarding induction and deduction, Marshall insisted that they were inseparably interlocked. As he put it: 'every genuine student of economics sometimes uses the inductive method and sometimes the analytical, and nearly always both of them together' (Pigou, 1925, p. 309; quoted by Coase, 1975, p. 27).

On the role of theory Coase quotes Marshall's words to Edgeworth:

In my view 'Theory' is essential. No one gets any real grip of economic problems unless he will work on it. But I conceive no more calamitous notion than that abstract, or general, or 'theoretical' economics was economics 'proper': It seems to me an essential but a very small part of economics proper: and by itself sometimes even – well not a very good occupation of time. . . . Economic theory is, in my opinion, as mischievous an impostor when it claims to be economics proper as is mere crude unanlysed history.

(v. Coase, 1975, p. 20; Pigou, 1975, p. 437; Hutchison, 1953, p. 71)

Regarding the ambiguous term 'theory', Marshall observed that there was 'scarcely any limit to the developments of theory that are possible; but of those which are possible only a small part is useful in having a direct relation to practical issues' (Pigou, 1925, p. 162). In fact, in a letter to Foxwell, Marshall said that in economics there was 'no "theory" to speak of' (see Coase, 1975, p. 28).

Professor Coase summarizes what it was 'that Marshall found objectionable about the use of mathematics':

He thought we lacked the data to support any but relatively simple constructions. He feared that factors that could not easily be dealt with in mathematical form would be neglected. But above all, he thought that we would be tempted to engage in what he termed 'mathematical diversions' or, as Pigou put it, we would be led to pursue 'intellectual toys, imaginary problems not conforming to the conditions of real life'. Marshall thought it would tend to divert our attention from the real world in which poverty causes degradation and to the study of which we should devote our whole energies.

. . . it would be hard to deny that the extensive use of mathematics has encouraged the tendencies that he thought its probable consequence. Marshall's thought was that the extensive use of mathematics would lead us away from what he considered to be 'constructive work'. I very much doubt that what has happened in recent years would have led him to change his mind.

(1975, p. 31)[13]

For his wise and insistent criticisms of excessive deduction, abstraction, and of graduate education, see the preceding essay on Jacob Viner. The following is a selection of twelve notable critiques since Viner's death in 1970:

1 R. Frisch (1970). 'Econometrics in the World Today'.
2 W. Leontief (1971). 'Theoretical Assumptions and Unobserved Facts'.
3 Sir H. Phelps Brown (1972). 'The Underdevelopment of Economics'.
4 B. Ward (1972). *What's Wrong with Economics?*
5 G. D. N. Worswick (1972). 'Is Progress in Economic Science Possible?'.
6 R. H. Coase (1975). 'Marshall on Method'.
7 H. Simon (1976). 'From Substantive to Procedural Rationality'.
8 P. J. D. Wiles (1984). 'Epilogue' to *Economics in Disarray*, Wiles and Routh, eds.
9 M. Blaug (1988). 'John Hicks and the Methodology of Economics'.
10 M. Friedman (1991). 'Old Wine in New Bottles'.
11 D. McCloskey (1991). 'Economic Science: a Search through the Hyperspace of Assumptions?'.

The culminating and crowning work in this series is

12 Thomas Mayer (1993). *Truth versus Precision in Economics*.

to which I have obviously been much indebted in writing this paper. This is, of course, a personal list to which many additions might be made.

NOTES

1 This paper was written in 1993. Sections VI and VII draw on a contribution to Roger Backhouse (ed.) (1994). *New Directions in Economic Methodology*.
2 Exemplifying a nadir of miseducation and half-baked semi-literacy is surely the attitude of a graduate student reported by Klamer and Colander, 1990, p. 26:

> Policy is sort of for simpletons. If you really know your theory, the policy implications are pretty straightforward. It's not the really challenging meat-and-potato stuff for a really sharp theorist. I think that's another reason why they don't spend much time on applications.

It might be added that this kind of attitude has been by no means unknown in England since the 1950s.
3 For the transformation of much of academic Literary Criticism into an introverted academic game, or 'discourse', from being a serious subject concerned with the interpretation and appreciation (partly by non-academics) of great works of

literature – the existence of which may now be denied – see Lehman, 1991. On the state of academic history and its narrower and narrower specialization, which has led to the disappearance of broader overviews and patterns, 'which are professionally dangerous for academic historians', see Davidson and Rees-Mogg, 1993, pp. 269–71.

As regards economics, the change to one particular, great new aim, away from trying to contribute to the alleviation of real-world policy problems, such as poverty and unemployment, has been exquisitely summed up in the final words of a recent essay entitled 'Deconstruction, Rhetoric and Economics' (Rossetti, 1993, p. 228): 'Since no deconstruction is ever final, it also provides us with the opportunity for on-going, ever-changing, intriguing research and discourse'.

Common to much of the new treatment, or *déformation professionelle* of Literary Criticism, History and Economics, is the intense academic introversion: The academic treatment of a subject is regarded as existing strictly and solely for the purposes and interests of academics. For economics this means the disappearance of an interest in policy problems (which might be academically dangerous) or even in an interest in the methodological problems of how less unreliable knowledge about policy problems may be found. Such real-world interests are to be regarded as suspect and replaced by 'ever-changing, intriguing research and discourse', on – and 'on-going' (from nowhere to nowhere) – churning out endless lists of publications (or rather 'discourse').

4 Nothing like even approximate quantitative estimates are available regarding the changes in the aims and criteria of economists in recent decades. It seems, however, that in the key, pivotal sector of the graduate schools in the USA the changes have been considerable.

5 As regards the pursuit of truth 'for its own sake' the following pointed passage from Edwin Cannan, one of the pioneers among economists at the LSE is notable:

> Laborious students whose investigations have interested scarcely anyone but themselves have been known to seek comfort in the assertion that truth is valuable for its own sake. I do not believe that this is the case. A great deal that is true is not worth knowing. The most inveterate bore is often the most truthful man [and, in economics, it might be added, he is often the most 'rigorous' man].
> (Quoted by Kadish, in Kadish and Tribe, 1993, p. 240)

6 That a profound misconception regarding Adam Smith and 'rigour' may have spread to what might be called the 'Nobelity' of the profession is indicated in James Tobin's paper 'The Hidden Hand in Modern Macroeconomics' (in Fry, 1992, pp. 117ff.). Tobin states indisputably that 'in *The Wealth of Nations* the invisible hand was a conjecture . . . an unproved assertion' (p. 122). He then goes on to add, however, that 'Smith's conjecture was eventually rigorously proved by Arrow and Debreu' (p. 122).

It was *not*, of course, Smith's conjecture which was 'eventually rigorously proved by Arrow and Debreu'. What was 'eventually rigorously proved' was a vacuous mathematical theorem of *very* jejune relevance for anyone seriously interested in real-world policy-making, which has almost no bearing on the case for or against either a free-market, or a government-regulated economy, because of the fantastically unrealistic assumptions on which the theorem depends. Smith's profoundly rich and complex 'conjecture' relied mainly, but not entirely, on induction, and was supported by a very wide range of evidence; but it was not, of course, capable of 'rigorous' proof – as no *theory* of an empirical–historical subject conceivably can be.

Actually, there seem to be important aspects of Smith's monetary and 'macro' economics which call for serious criticism. Exactly how high-powered mathematics can help in this critical task seems doubtful, especially if they are to be applied by mathematicians who do not read Smith's writings with much care. Meanwhile, the prospect is hardly attractive of having the writings of the great economists of the past bowdlerized or eviscerated in the interests of exhibitions of what – from a *practical* point of view – are, quite frankly, pretty boring and irrelevant mathematics.

7   In this section I rehearse, in a revised form, some of the arguments of my 1992, section 10. It has been argued that the great slump of, and after 1929–30 was 'unforecastable'; and that 'the leading explanations of the Depression are . . . based on unforecastable policy and economic disturbances' (Dominguez *et al.*, 1988). It is also, however, pointed out that early in 1929 'the indexes of the Harvard Economic Service indicated that a sharp downturn in economic activity was imminent'; and (on 18 May) that 'the signs pointing to recession continue to pile up' (p. 595). It is also suggested that these gloomy predictions were not published because of their possible damaging effects. Doubtless delicate questions *may* arise as to whether certain predictions are suitable for, or worthy of, publication. But if no predictions of sharp downturns are to be published then, certainly, much or most economic prediction and forecasting becomes questionable. It remains obscure, however, just what is meant by 'unforecastable'.

Obviously it cannot be claimed that predictions could have been made, with sufficient promptness, accuracy and probability, to have made possible the complete smoothing out of most major economic fluctuations, in particular that of 1929–33. It simply seems reasonable to suggest that the tremendous, world-wide damage brought about by that great depression, especially in Germany, might have been *somewhat*, but significantly mitigated if two such conditions as the following had been met by more of the neoclassical economists of the day.

(1) That in the half-century before 1929 more economists had followed the great examples of Jevons and Juglar in seeking to build up empirical knowledge and statistical series regarding what happened in business cycles – even at the expense of a diminished effort regarding 'rigorous', microeconomic analytical refinements – in the way in which many such monetary and other series actually were built up in the half-century after 1929.

(2) That more serious critical examination had been directed at the policies put forward by some theorists who rejected all measures, monetary or fiscal, aimed at countering excessive deflation, however severe: policies which were forcefully advocated down to and including 1932, but which were recognized as mistaken, by one or two of their most prominent spokesmen, a few years later when the depression had lifted.

8   I would like, not altogether irrelevantly, to correct at this point a view indirectly attributed to me by Professor Alexander Rosenberg, when he states that some writers, 'following T. W. Hutchison' (1938) 'have derided it [economics] as a body of tautologies, as a pure system of implicit definitions without any grip on the real world' (1992, pp. 244–5). I must concede that if I have been misinterpreted it may be, to a considerable extent, my own fault, since quite a number of critics seem to have misunderstood that part of my juvenile book.

On re-reading, however, I find that although I did indeed describe what I called – in the terminology of the period – 'pure theory' as consisting of tautologies and implicit definitions, I made it clear that 'pure' theory was not the whole of 'theory', and that 'applied theory' did, indeed, possess empirical content. I certainly did not describe the whole of economics as consisting of tautologies, nor did I say that *all* 'pure theory', though without empirical content, was 'without any grip on the

301

real world'. On the contrary, I pointed out that 'propositions of pure theory', by providing precisely defined concepts, could and sometimes did facilitate the formulation of precise empirical questions. In chapter II, section 3 (pp. 33–6), entitled 'The Use and Significance of Propositions of Pure Theory', I observed that: 'A sharply and clearly defined system of concepts enables sharp and clear answers to be obtained from empirical investigation', adding the Baconian apopthegm '*prudens interrogatio dimidium scientiae*'.

This attempt to defend a very ancient text is not irrelevant to the argument at this point; because it was just such a precise set of concepts, generated by Keynesian, macroeconomic analysis (or 'pure theory') which facilitated the development of national income accounting and national income statistics. Whatever, or how far, in addition, the analysis, or 'pure theory', of consumer behaviour has generated a system of precise concepts, possibly useful to statistical market researchers trying to construct firms' *ex-ante* demand curves, I am not able to answer. But it seems possible that precise concepts, such as the income and substitution effects of price changes, *may* have helped market researchers to get a useful 'grip on the real world' at some points.

Rosenberg apparently maintains that the contemporary 'theory of consumer behaviour does not actually improve(s) on our ability to predict consumer behaviour any better than Adam Smith' (1992, p. 235). This seems to me unduly pessimistic. My own hypothesis would be that although market researchers today are very far from attaining the standards of precision and reliability which their customers hope for, with the aid of trends, tendencies, patterns, parallels and precedents, derived from statistical series – in turn possibly aided by the precise concepts provided by modern 'theory' or analysis – they can and do today, on the average, predict considerably less inaccurately than Adam Smith would have done, in the almost complete absence, in his day, of statistical market research, though in the far less complex conditions of 1776. If any such predictive improvement has indeed occurred, I would award more credit to those who created the statistical series than to the 'pure' theorists, even though the latter may have asisted with the provision of more precise concepts.

On the dust-cover of his book, the blurb states – though Rosenberg himself may not be responsible for this – that: 'Economics [*tout simple*] is no better at predicting the likely outcome of specific events today than it was in the time of Adam Smith'. I would disagree strongly with this statement with regard to quite a wide range of important and interesting economic events. In assessing the improvement, or non-improvement, of the ability of economists, from Adam Smith to the present day, to predict less inaccurately, it is misleading to draw a pessimistic conclusion simply from the development of 'theory' or analysis, without taking into account the vast growth – which has been the most valuable achievement of economists in the twentieth century – in many forms of empirical material, including a number of vitally useful statistical series, whatever their failings in up-to-dateness and reliability.

Alexander Rosenberg has concluded:

> If economics is best viewed as more akin to a branch of mathematics on the intersection between pure axiomatization and applied geometry, then our long-term perspective on the bearing of economic theory on policy must be qualified. And the vacuum that economic theory leaves in the guidance of policy must be filled by something else, something that will provide improvable guidance to policy, both private and public.

> (1992, p. 252)

Rosenberg's insistence on 'the guidance of policy' – *and, therefore, on prediction* – as the aim, or duty, of the economist is to be heartily applauded. Also deserving much sympathy, *but not complete acceptance*, is Rosenberg's judgement that:

> Much of the mystery surrounding the actual development of economic theory – its shifts in formalism, its insulation from empirical assessment, its interest in proving purely formal, abstract possibilities, . . . the controversies about its cognitive status – can be comprehended and properly appreciated if we give up on the notion that economics any longer has the aims or makes the claims of an empirical science of human behaviour.
>
> (*op. cit.*, p. 247)

What Rosenberg seems to overlook is that, according to US statistics, there is a markedly larger number of *non*-academic economists in business and government – almost entirely concerned with prediction – than there is of academics. It is surely in this direction that the 'something else' is to be found, which Rosenberg is looking for 'to fill the vacuum which economic theory leaves'. It is up to the academics to decide, how far or not, positively or negatively, to shape, or reshape, what they call their 'theory', so as to support the predictive efforts of the non-academic economists (or, otherwise to have them banned from 'the profession'?).

9 Regarding the perhaps much greater instabilities of the twenty-first century, see the two profoundly impressive, and profoundly sombre, works of Davidson and Rees-Mogg, *The Great Reckoning*, revised ed., 1993; and Paul Kennedy, *Preparing for the Twenty-First Century*, 1993.

10 The politico-economic principles of the long Victorian period experienced by Lord Rees-Mogg's grandfather were superbly summed up, and their methodological foundations magisterially set out, by J. S. Mill. In a book (1992) in which there is much that is acceptable and valuable, Professor David Hausman's message might be tersely summarized as: 'Get back to J. S. Mill and put Popper in the trash can.' A glance at his index certainly suggests such a dual slogan. Mill and Popper are referred to on many times more pages than anyone else. Hausman lists about six times as many references to J. S. Mill than to Smith, Marshall, Meager and Keynes, *added together*.

At least Mill's methodology is that of a supreme 'insider', in the pre-academic-departmental days when leading economists (or some of them) could be outstanding contributors to philosophy and scientific method, and leading philosophers made distinguished contributions to political economy. But Mill's political economy, and his methodology thereof, however triumphantly successful, and, up to a point, deservedly so, *for his own day*, even then, and very seriously and fundamentally so 150 years later, can be seen to suffer from excessive narrowness and oversimplification, as correspondingly does its methodological foundation. For Mill's politico-economic world, though probably suffering from more instabilities and discontinuities than that of Adam Smith, seems to have suffered from immeasurably less, of a quite massive kind, than does the twentieth century in its closing years. One only needs to review some of Mill's fundamental assumptions, first regarding microeconomics, and secondly macroeconomics:

(a) Mill's *Principles*, and, in his view, *the very possibility of a 'science' of political economy*, depend on the assumption of competition (which necessarily includes full knowledge, or what Carl Menger called 'Allvissenheit') (*v.* 1909, II, IV, 1). At the same time, Mill, remarkably pretentiously, claimed regarding microeconomics, or the theory of value: 'Happily there is nothing in the laws of value which remains for the present or any future writer to clear up; the theory of the subject is complete' (1909, III, 1, 2).

(b) Regarding macroeconomics, aggregate fluctuations and the business cycle were to be regarded as frictions, Anyhow, the economy was approaching the stationary state, which was 'only a hand's breadth away'; while it was 'only in the backward countries of the world (about whom Mill was not concerned) 'that increased production is still an important object' (v. IV, V, 1; and IV, VI, 2). Moreover, only in 'outlying possessions', or where 'it comes into contact with savages' need a country worry about war.

Mill's might well be regarded as an excessively simplified version of political economy, even as a textbook for his own period. But as this century approaches its end it is surely necessary, if very serious oversimplification is to be avoided, that uncertainty, instability and discontinuity – including the effects of much more rapid, and more rapidly disseminated technical change – must be taken much more seriously, with fundamental implications for the methodology of the subject – as Herbert Simon (1976) has observed. Also, surely needing to be taken much more seriously than they were by Mill (or are by Hausman) are the historical dimension together with much more rapid, medium-term institutional change, particularly as concerns macroeconomics.

As regards what seems, at some points, to amount to Hausman's trashing of Popper, I might venture to comment that I may well, overall, disagree with Sir Karl almost as widely as does Professor Hausman (for example, regarding historicism, prediction and a too exclusive emphasis on deductivism). For my part, however, I regard what are rather disdainfully described as Popper's 'slogans' as having, in economics, more than ever, a tremendous amount of essential hard work still to achieve, that is such 'slogans' (in Hausman's words) as: 'Empirical criticism is crucial to science, and scientific theories must, however indirectly be open to empirical criticism. The most important evidence in support of scientific theories comes from hard texts and . . . not from adding up favourable instances. Scientific knowledge is corrigible, and scientists may be forced to surrender even the best established theories' (1992, p. 203). I firmly agree (and admit) that 'a greater measure of philosophical agnosticism among economic methodologists would, I think, be sensible' (p. 203). I also think that more of such agnosticism might be 'sensible' among academic philosophers.

As Whitley discerningly and accurately notes regarding what he calls 'the dominance of the ideals and standards of analytical economics: 'Issues which were recalcitrant to standard techniques tended to be ignored or else regarded as peripheral to the field and hence unlikely to lead to high reputations' (1986, p. 194). Whitley observes also 'the growing tendency of economists to write for each other rather than for other publics' (p. 196), and how 'economists in the United States were able to use the formalism of economic theory as a means of differentiating themselves from noneconomists' (p. 197). As Whitley also explained: 'To substitute a more historically specific and empirically derived theoretical structure would . . . threaten existing prestige structures and intellectual competences within the academic world' (p. 197).

12 In a recent 'critical review' of 'Mises on Mathematical Economics', Professor J. C. Moorhouse concludes that there is 'no major methodological gulf between praxeology and neo-classical mathematical economics' (1993, p. 71). If this conclusion applies solely to many recent formulations of mathematical economic analysis, in which pure, abstract 'rigour' is regarded as the overriding objective and criterion, it may well be a correct and justifiable aperçu. The pure rigour of the mathematicians simply replaces the 'apodictic certainties' of Mises. Moorhouse has discerningly perceived the epistemological similarities between the two kinds of 'discourse', one loosely formulated in German, and the other in more precise

symbols. Although Moorhouse perceives that, 'uncertainty remains a conundrum for both approaches', he seems to be blind to the shared limitations and empirical vacuity of the conclusions of both Mises and the contemporary mathematicians. It seems somewhat ironic that Professor Paul Samuelson who, some three decades ago, very justifiably dismissed with derision the methodological claims of Mises, now finds the method, of which he has become such a leading exponent, so pretentiously and seriously abused as to be, not unjustifiably, recognized as putting forward, closely similar epistemological claims to those of Mises.

13 We have recently discussed the Marshallian Rules for the use of mathematics in economics, as supported by Professor Milton Friedman (see Pigou, 1925, p. 427; Friedman, 1991, pp. 3ff.; and Hutchison, 1992, pp. 90–1). Also worthy of mention is Marshall's answer to C. R. Fay, the economic historian, who confessed:

> I am a fool at mathematics; and on the one occasion when we talked about it, he, the great mathematical economist, declared with impatience that this part of economics was now-a-days much overdone. The tonic has lasted me from that day to this.
>
> (Pigou, 1925, p. 77)

REFERENCES

Aristotle (1915). *Nicomachaean Ethics*, trans. W. D. Ross.

Backhouse, R. (1993). 'Should We Ignore Methodology?', *Royal Economic Society Newsletter*, June, p. 4.

Bellinger, W. K., and Bergsten, G. S. (1990). 'The Market for Economic Thought', *History of Political Economy*, 22, pp. 1697ff.

Blaug, M. (1988). 'John Hicks and the Methodology of Economics', in N. de Marchi, ed., *The Popperian Legacy in Economics*, pp. 183ff.

Coase, R. H. (1975). 'Marshall on Method', *Journal of Law and Economics*, 18, pp. 25ff.

Davidson, J. and Rees-Mogg, Lord (1993). *The Great Reckoning*, revised ed.

Dominguez, K. M., Fair, R. C., and Shapiro, M. D. (1988). 'Forecasting the Depression: Harvard versus Yale', *American Economic Review*, 78, pp. 595ff.

Friedman, M. (1991). 'Old Wine in New Bottles', *Economic Journal*, 101, pp. 33ff.

Frisch, R. (1970). 'Econometrics in the World Today', in W. Eltis and M. Scott, eds, *Induction, Growth and Trade: Essays in Honour of Sir Roy Harrod*, pp. 162–3.

Fry, M. (ed.) (1992). *Adam Smith's Legacy*.

Gordon, R. A. (1976). 'Rigor and Relevance in a Changing Institutional Setting', *American Economic Review*, LXVI, pp. 1ff.

Hahn, F. H. (1984). 'On Keynes and Monetarism, A Comment', in G. D. N. Worswick and J. Trevithick, eds, *Keynes and the Modern World*, pp. 72ff.

Hahn, F. H. (1993a). 'Reflections', *Royal Economic Society Newsletter*, April, p. 5.

Hahn, F. H. (1993b). 'Answer to Backhouse: Yes', *Royal Economic Society Newsletter*, June, p. 4.

Hausman, D. (1992). *The Exact and Separate Science of Economics*.

Hutchison, T. W. (1953). *Review of Economic Doctrines, 1870–1929*.

Hutchison, T. W. (1977). *Knowledge and Ignorance in Economics*.

Hutchison, T. W. (1988). *Before Adam Smith*.

Hutchison, T. W. (1992). *Changing Aims in Economics*.

Kadish, A., and Tribe, K. (eds) (1993). *The Market for Political Economy*.

Kennedy, P. (1993). *Preparing for the Twenty-First Century*.

Klamer, A. (1984). *Conversations with Economists*.

Klamer, A. and Colander, D. (1990). *The Making of an Economist*.

Lehman, D. (1991). *Signs of the Times*.

Leontief, W. (1971). 'Theoretical Assumptions and Unobserved Facts', *American Economic Review*, LXI, pp. 1ff.

Leontief, W. (1982). 'Academic Economics', *Science*, 217, pp. 104ff.

McCloskey, D. (1985). *The Rhetoric of Economics*.

Mäki, U. (1992). 'Social Conditioning of Economics', in N. de Marchi, ed., *Post-Popperian Methodology of Economics*, pp. 65ff.

Marshall, A. (1925). *Memorials of Alfred Marshall*, A. C. Pigou, ed.

Mayer, T. (1993a). *Truth versus Precision in Economics*.

Mayer, T. (1993b). *Why is there so much Disagreement in Economics?* Working Paper 93-20. University of California, Davis.

Mill, J. S. (1909). *Principles of Political Economy*, ed. W. J. Ashley.

Moorhouse, J. C. (1993). 'A Critical Review of Mises on Mathematical Economics', *History of Economics Review*, 20, pp. 61ff.

Ohlin, B. (1926). 'Knut Wicksell, 1851–1926', *Economic Journal*, 36, pp. 509ff.

Phelps Brown, Sir Henry (1972). 'The Under-Development of Economics', *Economic Journal*, 82, pp. 1ff.

Pigou, A. C. (ed.) (1925). *Memorials of Alfred Marshall*.

Pigou, A. (ed.) (1929). *Economics of Welfare*, 3rd ed.

Rosenberg, A. (1992). *Economics – Mathematical Politics or Science of Diminishing Returns?*

Rossetti, J. (1993). 'Deconstruction, Rhetoric and Economics', in N. de Marchi, ed., *Post-Popperian Methodology of Economics*, pp. 211ff.

Said, E. (1993). 'Professionals and Amateurs', *The Independent*, 15 July.

Simon, H. (1976). 'From Substantive to Procedural Rationality', *Method and Appraisal in Economics*, ed. S. J. Latsis, pp. 129ff.

Smith, A. (1976a). *The Wealth of Nations*, R. H. Campbell, A. S. Skinner and W. B. Todd, eds.

Smith, A. (1976b). *The Theory of Moral Sentiments*, D. D. Raphael and A. L. Macfie, eds.

Tobin, J. (1992). 'The Invisible Hand in Modern Macroeconomics', in M. Fry, ed., *Adam Smith's Legacy*, pp. 117ff.

Viner, J. (1928). 'Adam Smith and Laissez-faire', in J. H. Hollander, ed., *Adam Smith, 1776–1926*, pp. 116ff.

Whitley, R. (1984). *The Intellectual and Social Organization of the Sciences*.

Whitley, R. (1986). 'The Structure and Context of Economics as a Scientific Field', *Research in the History of Economic Thought and Methodology*, 4, pp. 179ff.

INDEX